History of British Intelligence

# State Surveillance, Political Policing and Counter-Terrorism in Britain

# History of British Intelligence

ISSN 1756-5685

Series Editor
Peter Martland

With the recent opening of government archives to public scrutiny, it is at last possible to study the vital role that intelligence has played in forming and executing policy in modern history. This new series aims to be the leading forum for work in the area. Proposals are welcomed, and should be sent in the first instance to the publisher at the address below.

Boydell and Brewer Ltd, PO Box 9, Woodbridge, Suffolk IP12 3DF, UK

Previous volumes in this series:

*British Spies and Irish Rebels: British Intelligence and Ireland, 1916–1945*, Paul McMahon, 2008
Available in hardback and paperback editions

*The Spy Who Came In From the Co-op: Melita Norwood and the Ending of Cold War Espionage*, David Burke, 2009
Available in hardback and paperback editions

*The Lawn Road Flats: Spies, Writers and Artists*, David Burke, 2014
Available in hardback and paperback editions

*Britannia and the Bear: The Anglo-Russian Intelligence Wars, 1917–1929*, Victor Madeira, 2014
Available in hardback and paperback editions

*The Secret War Between the Wars: MI5 in the 1920s and 1930s*, Kevin Quinlan, 2014

# State Surveillance, Political Policing and Counter-Terrorism in Britain

1880–1914

Vlad Solomon

THE BOYDELL PRESS

© Vlad Solomon 2021

*All Rights Reserved.* Except as permitted under current legislation no part of this work may be photocopied, stored in a retrieval system, published, performed in public, adapted, broadcast, transmitted, recorded or reproduced in any form or by any means, without the prior permission of the copyright owner

The right of Vlad Solomon to be identified as the author of this work has been asserted in accordance with sections 77 and 78 of the Copyright, Designs and Patents Act 1988

First published 2021
The Boydell Press, Woodbridge

ISBN 978-1-78327-387-4

The Boydell Press is an imprint of Boydell & Brewer Ltd
PO Box 9, Woodbridge, Suffolk IP12 3DF, UK
and of Boydell & Brewer Inc.
668 Mt Hope Avenue, Rochester, NY 14620-2731, USA
website: www.boydellandbrewer.com

A catalogue record for this book is available
from the British Library

The publisher has no responsibility for the continued existence or accuracy of URLs for external or third-party internet websites referred to in this book, and does not guarantee that any content on such websites is, or will remain, accurate or appropriate

This publication is printed on acid-free paper

Printed in the UK by TJ Books Limited, Padstow, Cornwall

*FOR MY MOTHER*

The police is a public and magisterial service which, beyond its ordinary functions, has perforce to employ irregular, yet just and useful measures in order to augment the means and resources available to the government. Such power, the efficacy of which fades the more it is advertised, is frequently employed in matters of great importance; small matters inevitably fade out of sight and escape its reach.

Within the standing social order not everything is externalized and not everything is visible. A secret lies at the heart of this public tumult; one which the ordinary powers of the state cannot unravel.

Joseph Fouché, *Letter to the Duke of Wellington* (1817)

The Special Branch collects information on those who I think cause problems for the State.

Merlyn Rees, Home Secretary 1976–79 (1978)

# Contents

*List of illustrations* ............ ix
*Acknowledgements* ............ x
*List of abbreviations* ............ xi
*Principal characters* ............ xii

Introduction ............ 1
Prologue ............ 18

**Part 1: 1881–91**

1. 'A spider's web of Police Communication' ............ 27
2. 'Panic and indifference' ............ 38
3. Mr Jenkinson goes to London ............ 50
4. 'The new detective army' ............ 63
5. 'Waiting games' ............ 80
6. 'A long and complicated inquiry' ............ 90
7. The battle of Trafalgar Square ............ 99
8. Scandal averted ............ 112

**Part 2: 1892–1903**

9. 'A bomb has burst' ............ 127
10. 'Men of bad character' ............ 145
11. 'Surtout pas trop de zèle' ............ 161
12. 'We do not prosecute opinions' ............ 179

**Part 3: 1904–14**

| | | |
|---|---|---|
| 13 | Dangerous aliens | 195 |
| 14 | 'A doctrine of lawlessness' | 213 |
| 15 | 'Suffrage forces in the field' | 222 |
| 16 | The waning of militancy and the rise of counter-espionage | 238 |
| | Conclusion | 257 |
| | *Notes* | 270 |
| | *Bibliography* | 322 |
| | *Index* | 332 |

# Illustrations

1. Sir William Vernon Harcourt in the 1880s (Wellcome Collection).   26
2. Detail of an American satirical drawing showing Jeremiah O'Donovan-Rossa (left) and Johann Most (right) trying to escape the very violence they are urging others to commit. *Puck*, 1885 (Library of Congress, Prints & Photographs Division).   36
3. Edward G. Jenkinson, ca. 1900 (*Grace's Guide to British Industrial History*)   46
4. Materials confiscated by police during the investigation into the Walsall bomb conspiracy of 1892 (The National Archives of the UK, ref. ASSI6/27/9).   130
5. William Melville in the 1890s, *Windsor Magazine*, 1895 (Internet Archive).   131
6. Raid on the Autonomie Club, © British Library Board, *Daily Graphic*, 1894.   148
7. Police officers standing in the ruins of a house following the Siege of Sidney Street, 1911 (Library of Congress, Prints & Photographs Division).   211
8. Tom Mann. ca. 1913 (Library of Congress, Prints & Photographs Division).   219
9. Christabel Pankhurst, ca. 1910 (Library of Congress, Prints & Photographs Division).   225
10. Arrest of a suffragette in London during a demonstration, October 1913 (Library of Congress, Prints & Photographs Division).   243

The author and publisher are grateful to all the institutions and individuals listed for permission to reproduce the materials in which they hold copyright. Every effort has been made to trace the copyright holders; apologies are offered for any omission, and the publisher will be pleased to add any necessary acknowledgement in subsequent editions.

# Acknowledgements

I am indebted to Brian Lewis, Elizabeth Elbourne and Nancy Ellenberger for their helpful comments and suggestions relating to earlier drafts of this book. Valuable research assistance has also been provided by a number of institutions and I wish to thank here the staff of the McGill University Humanities and Social Sciences Library, the National Archives (Kew), the British Library, and the Library of Congress for their general helpfulness. Finally, I extend my sincere gratitude to the editors and staff at Boydell & Brewer for their continued support and advice.

# Abbreviations

| | |
|---|---|
| AC | Assistant Commissioner |
| CID | Criminal Investigation Department (Scotland Yard, unless otherwise indicated) |
| DC | Detective Constable |
| DCI | Detective Chief Inspector |
| DI | Detective Inspector |
| DS | Detective Sergeant |
| FO | Foreign Office |
| HC | House of Commons |
| HMG | Her/His Majesty's Government |
| HO | Home Office |
| IRB | Irish Republican Brotherhood |
| MEPO | Metropolitan Police (London) |
| PC | Police Constable |
| RIC | Royal Irish Constabulary |
| SDF | Social Democratic Federation |
| SWMF | South Wales Miners' Federation |
| TNA | The National Archives (Kew) |
| WFL | Women's Freedom League |
| WSPU | Women's Social and Political Union |

# Principal characters

**Anderson, Robert (1841–1918)**
Dublin-born barrister recruited by the Home Office in the 1860s to head its intelligence-gathering Secret Service bureau. Thereafter acting as adviser to the Home Secretary on Fenian-related matters, Anderson cultivated a network of private informers and served as Henri Le Caron's official handler between 1867 and 1889. Excluded from the political police apparatus in 1884 because of his rivalry with Edward Jenkinson, Anderson returned to the Home Office Secret Service in 1887 thanks to his friendship with James Monro (then head of Scotland Yard). The author of a series of controversial articles seeking to discredit the Irish Nationalist leader Charles Stewart Parnell, Anderson played a prominent role in the 1888–89 special commission into 'Parnellism and crime'. He became Assistant Commissioner at Scotland Yard in 1888, a position he kept until his retirement in 1901.

**Asquith, Herbert Henry (1852–1928)**
A Yorkshire-born barrister, Asquith served as Liberal Home Secretary between 1892 and 1895 and as Prime Minister between 1908 and 1916. Initially a vocal Radical, he moved closer to the mainstream of the Liberal Party later in his career but remained politically idiosyncratic, embracing the economic interventionism of New Liberalism while drawing the ire of suffragettes for his inveterate opposition to female enfranchisement.

**Bradford, Edward (1836–1911)**
An experienced officer in the Indian Army who also occupied various high-level positions in the Indian Civil Service, Bradford was appointed Commissioner of the Metropolitan Police in 1890 following James Monro's resignation. He retired in 1903.

**Harcourt, William Vernon (1827–1904)**
As Liberal Home Secretary between 1880 and 1885, Harcourt established the Irish Branch of Scotland Yard in order to counteract Fenian conspiracies in Britain, laying the foundations for the country's first institutional political police. A man of conflicting impulses and choleric personality, Harcourt had a tumultuous relationship with police and intelligence chiefs such as Robert

Anderson and Edward Jenkinson. During the late 1890s he became leader of the Liberal Party in the House of Commons.

**Henry, Edward Richard (1850–1931)**
As Assistant Commissioner at Scotland Yard between 1901 and 1903 and Commissioner of the Metropolitan Police from 1903 to 1918, Henry became known as a modernizer thanks to his championing of telecommunications and the use of fingerprinting in police work. His handling of suffragette militancy between 1907 and 1914 was often controversial, leading to spectacular violence between police officers and members and supporters of the Women's Social and Political Union. After 1909 Henry worked with Vernon Kell to help establish the counter-espionage agency that later became MI5.

**Jenkinson, Edward George (1835–1919)**
Appointed Assistant Under-Secretary for Police and Crime in Ireland in 1882, Jenkinson quickly became an adept spymaster, building and cultivating a transatlantic network of informers and double agents with the goal of thwarting the conspiracies of militant Fenian organizations. With the support of Home Secretary William Harcourt, Jenkinson was made unofficial head of all counter-terrorist operations in Britain and Ireland in 1884, but was forced to resign from all government duties by the end of 1886 after coming into conflict with the heads of the Metropolitan Police and members of Lord Salisbury's Conservative cabinet. A pro-Home Rule Liberal, Jenkinson ran unsuccessfully for Parliament in 1892, becoming, later in life, the chairman of the Daimler Motor Company.

**Le Caron, Henri [pseudonym of Thomas Beach] (1841–94)**
A member of the US-based Fenian Brotherhood and Clan na Gael, Le Caron was recruited as a spy by British authorities in the 1860s and subsequently began sending regular intelligence reports to his official handler at the Home Office, Robert Anderson. Called to publicly testify against Charles Stewart Parnell during the 1888–89 special commission into 'Parnellism and crime', Le Caron was afterwards forced to give up his intelligence work and lived the rest of his life in hiding.

**Littlechild, John (1847–1923)**
A senior member of the original Irish Branch of Scotland Yard, Chief Inspector Littlechild became superintendent of Special Branch (Section D) after 1887, retiring in 1893 to pursue a career as a private investigator.

### Lushington, Godfrey (1832–1907)

A London-born barrister of Liberal sympathies and a member of the Positivist Society, Lushington became legal adviser at the Home Office in 1869, eventually rising to the position of Permanent Under-Secretary, which he occupied between 1885 and 1895. In 1898 he served as a member of the British delegation to the Anti-Anarchist Conference in Rome.

### Macnaghten, Melville (1853–1921)

The former manager of an Indian sugar plantation, Macnaghten was named Chief Constable at Scotland Yard in 1890 thanks to his friendship with James Monro (then Commissioner of the Metropolitan Police). He replaced Edward Henry as Assistant Commissioner in 1903, retiring in 1913.

### McIntyre, Patrick (1858–1902)

An Irish-born Scotland Yard detective, McIntyre was recruited to the Irish Branch in 1883 and subsequently was a member of Special Branch (Section D) until his demotion for insubordination in 1893. Leaving the force altogether, McIntyre published a serialized account of his time at Scotland Yard in the left-wing *Reynolds's Newspaper* in 1895, alleging the convictions of several Fenian and anarchist revolutionaries had been obtained by British authorities through the use of agents provocateurs.

### Melville, William (1850–1918)

A member of the original Irish Branch, Melville replaced John Littlechild as head of Special Branch (Section D) in 1893 following the latter's retirement. A resourceful and tireless detective, but also a cynical manipulator, Melville quickly acquired and subsequently cultivated a public reputation as the scourge of anarchists in Britain, making extensive use of mercenary informers in his policing activities. In 1897 he secretly advised Pyotr Rachkovsky, emissary of the Russian political police in Western Europe, on the legal steps required to secure the conviction of a Russian Nihilist exiled in Britain. Transferred to the War Office's counter-intelligence section in 1903, Melville became the chief detective in Vernon Kell's MO5 (later MI5) after 1909, investigating cases of suspected German espionage in Britain. He finally retired in 1917.

### Monro, James (1838–1920)

A former Inspector-General of the Bengal Police, Monro became the first Assistant Commissioner in charge of Scotland Yard in 1884, replacing the outgoing Director, Howard Vincent. Embroiled in a bitter rivalry with Edward Jenkinson, Monro took on the title of 'Secret Agent' following the former's forced resignation in 1886 and forged a close partnership with Robert Anderson. Briefly taking over as Commissioner in 1888, Monro resigned in 1890 after a dispute over police wages with Home Secretary Henry Matthews.

**Quinn, Patrick (1854–1936)**
A member of the Irish Branch, the Irish-born Quinn became superintendent of Special Branch (Section D) following William Melville's transfer to the War Office in 1903. A diligent leader lacking the more forceful qualities of his predecessor, Quinn presided over several increases in Special Branch staff, but proved unable to devise efficient strategies for containing suffragette militancy and Indian nationalist agitation in London. He retired in 1918.

**Sweeney, John (1857–?)**
An Irish-born Metropolitan Police constable, Sweeney was recruited to the Irish Branch in the mid-1880s and later became a member of Special Branch (Section D). In 1894 he was involved in the arrest of the Italian anarchist Francesco Polti in London, subsequently playing a role in the active surveillance of other suspected revolutionaries exiled in Britain. He retired in 1903 and published his memoirs the following year.

**Troup, Charles Edward (1857–1941)**
A Scottish-born civil servant, Troup joined the Home Office in 1880 as a junior clerk, becoming Permanent Under-Secretary in 1908. A man of Liberal sympathies, Troup nevertheless worked closely with the Home Secretary in aggressively taking on the challenges posed by organized domestic radicalism. Urging a hard line on suffragette militants, Troup proved somewhat more conciliatory towards socialist and syndicalist agitators. He retired from the civil service in the early 1920s.

**Vincent, Howard (1849–1909)**
A former military officer and barrister, Vincent was tasked by the Home Office with establishing a new Metropolitan Police detective department. Becoming the first (and only) Director of the Criminal Investigation Department in 1878, Howard retired in 1884 and subsequently became a Conservative MP despite his earlier Liberal leanings. As a vocal right-wing critic of lax immigration and political asylum policies, Vincent was invited by Prime Minister Salisbury to join the British delegation at the 1898 Anti-Anarchist Conference in Rome.

**Warren, Charles (1840–1927)**
A distinguished military officer and amateur archeologist, Warren was selected to replace Edmund Henderson as Commissioner of the Metropolitan Police in 1886. Known for his imperious personality, Warren immediately came into

conflict with both the Home Secretary and the head of Scotland Yard, accusing both of subverting his authority. Criticized by the *Pall Mall Gazette* for his militaristic style of leadership and ruthless suppression of an 1887 riot in Trafalgar Square, Warren nevertheless remained popular with the London middle class. He was forced to resign in 1888 following the unsuccessful police investigation into the Jack the Ripper murders and briefly returned to the army.

**Williamson, Adolphus (1830–89)**
A veteran of the old Detective Branch of the Metropolitan Police, Williamson joined the Criminal Investigation Department at Scotland Yard in 1878 as Chief Superintendent. In 1883 he was made head of the new Irish Branch by Home Secretary William Harcourt, playing an active role in several investigations connected to Fenian militancy in Britain. Thanks to his close relationship with Assistant Commissioner James Monro, Williamson was promoted to the post of Chief Constable at Scotland Yard in 1888 but became seriously ill and died the following year.

# Introduction

## Policing high and low

'POLITICAL policing' can naturally be a somewhat confusing and ideologically charged term and it is perhaps made all the more so in this instance by the fact that this work is not, strictly speaking, a history of the British police. The focus here is rather on policing as a security-enforcing practice, planned at and enacted by several different levels of the British government. In this sense my understanding of political policing is indebted to Jean-Paul Brodeur's notion of 'high policing' which stands in contrast with the 'low' policing of ordinary, non-political crimes and which he took to mean 'not only... a certain number of programs and operations undertaken by specialized units inside a police force [but also] a definite pattern of relations between a set of goals and the means to achieve them'.[1]

More concretely, Brodeur identified four main characteristics to high policing which I take to apply equally to political policing as understood in this work.[2] High policing, Brodeur argued, 'is first of all absorbent policing', in that it is focused on the acquiring and control of intelligence. It is also 'not uniquely bound to enforce the law and regulations as they are made by an independent legislator'. This second feature is of particular import in the present narrative given that extra-legality came to be one of the main features of the early political police in Britain. The third characteristic is that 'protecting the community from law violators is not an end in itself for high policing [as] crime control may also serve as a tool to generate information which can be used to maximize state coercion of any group or individual perceived as threatening the established order'. This in effect means that a political police is not reducible to the policing of (subversive) politics by a legally constituted government; it is also, as the German criminologist Hans von Hentig put it, 'a form of political activity [for that government] through the medium of the police'.[3] As the following pages will reveal, there are several examples in the British context which illustrate the validity of this claim (the most telling, perhaps, being the British government's controversial actions during the 1889–90 Special Commission into the political activities of Irish political leader Charles Stewart Parnell).

The fourth characteristic which Brodeur identifies is that 'high policing not only makes extensive use of undercover agents and paid informers,... it also acknowledges its willingness to do so [striving] in this way both to maintain a low operational visibility and to amplify the fear of denunciation'. Amplifying the 'fear of denunciation' emerges as a particularly important strategy for the British political police during the period considered here given the limitations imposed on it by the political establishment and the concerns of the public at large (with the former having the decidedly more constricting effect). To this list I would add a fifth characteristic which, if not universally valid, applies nonetheless all too well to the British context. It is that political policing, especially in its formative stages, relies to an extraordinary extent on the (often conflicting) directive powers and *Weltanschauungen* of specific high-ranking bureaucrats and officials more so than on any methodological blueprints or foreign models. This feature is important to stress given the recent histories of British policing which have tended to dismiss the emergence of political policing as a mere governmental adjustment to worsening social, economic and international conditions (more on this to follow shortly).

Finally, the timeframe adopted here reflects the period over which the British political police came into being through a series of government-mandated organizational efforts before drastically expanding its scope and mission in the years following 1914. Before 1881 efforts by the British government to monitor and suppress the activities of native as well as foreign radicals active within its jurisdiction were of necessity quite limited given the degree of political and arguably popular bias against the perceived 'un-British' nature of secret policing (and even detective work in general). Conversely, after the start of the First World War, the political police became to a large extent part of the war effort and was reorganized and incorporated into the government's wider strategy for counter-espionage and domestic security. For these reasons the period from 1881 to 1914 represents a unique window into the workings of a classic British model of political policing – one less fettered by the stringencies of domestic politics (although, as we shall see, criticism of the police, in government and public opinion circles remained a constant feature throughout these decades) and completely untouched by those of total war.

## The historiography of Britain's early political police

The body of literature dealing with the earliest British attempts to institutionalize political policing can broadly be divided into three categories: histories of the British police in general; histories of the political police in Britain; and histories of radical political movements (such as Fenianism or anarchism) known for coming into conflict with British authorities.

For much of the 1970s and 1980s the historiography of the British 'new police' (which came into being with the 1829 Metropolitan Police Act) was largely dominated by the debate between proponents of a traditionalist 'whiggish' interpretation, who sought to explain the emergence of policing as a rational societal response to rising crime and social disorder,[4] and proponents of a Marxist (or quasi-Marxist) revisionism, who, on the whole, portrayed the police as a bourgeois mechanism for stabilizing capitalist society by disciplining the industrial working classes.[5]

More recently, a new type of revisionist approach has emerged which seeks to reconcile some of the less naive propositions of the traditionalists (e.g. that the functioning of the 'new police' benefited and was accepted by wide sections of society not just an authoritarian elite) with the less abrasive and doctrinaire suggestions of the left-wing revisionists – recognizing in effect that as well as being 'firmly [implanted] in national mythology', policing is also 'embedded in a social order that is riven by structured bases of conflict, not fundamental integration'.[6]

The intricacies and merits of this debate have already been exhaustively discussed elsewhere, and given the scope of this book, I do not intend to add anything to it here.[7] It is nonetheless important to note that this debate has had an undeniable impact on the historiography of the British political police in two significant ways. The first is that whatever disagreements the traditionalists and the revisionists have had regarding the origins and goals of Britain's 'new police', both camps are implicitly agreed on the notion that the political police was not a separate case requiring special attention. The second is that the polarized language and categories generated by this debate have contaminated even those subsequent accounts which have sought to keep simplistic dichotomies at bay.

To illustrate we only need look at the trajectory of the scholarship dealing specifically with the origins of the political police in Britain. Writing in the mid-1970s, Tony Bunyan first attempted to describe the formation of the British political police with what was then a fairly standard trope of Marxist historiography. The political arm of the Metropolitan Police, Bunyan argued, was merely the set of practices employed by the bourgeois state during the Chartist agitation of the 1830s and 1840s 'formalized and extended' as a response to Irish republican terrorism.[8]

Conversely, Philip Thurmond Smith in his quasi-traditionalist *Policing Victorian London: Political Policing, Public Order, and the London Metropolitan*

*Police* stopped short of discussing the formation of the actual political police in the 1880s and lumped the authorities' early efforts at containing Chartist and Fenian radicalism together with the public order and immigration policies of the 1850s and 1860s – reaffirming the idea that late-Victorian developments were merely a curious excrescence of the mid-Victorian status quo. As Smith explained, the 'enlightened vision of [London Metropolitan Police] Commissioners' before the 1880s 'implanted in the public mind, that it was possible to maintain order by use of an essentially unarmed police, acting without the authoritarian demeanour or paramilitary trappings of police forces in other countries'. The majority of Victorians 'would [therefore] have regarded inefficiency as a small price to pay to maintain what they saw as their liberties'.[9]

The first real history of early British political policing came in 1987 with Bernard Porter's foundational monograph on Special Branch of Scotland Yard in which he argued that the nascent political policing of fin-de-siècle Britain, far from being a monolithic apparatus for counter-revolution, was in fact a tenuous negotiation between the liberal impulses of successive administrations and the requirements imposed by the tactics of various revolutionary groups.

Although not lacking in descriptions of political actors and the ideological and personal conflicts they were often embroiled in, Porter nonetheless chose to localize the formative impulse for the creation of Special Branch in the decline of an idealized, all-pervasive mid-Victorian 'age of liberal innocence'.[10] Thus, in an echo of the earlier Marxist revisionism, political policing is identified by Porter with a usurpation by the late-Victorian capitalist state: 'a revolution… against the distinctive and anti-European liberalism of Britain's mid-Victorian past' effected by men who, though significantly different in their respective outlooks and beliefs, were supposedly estranged 'from that [liberal] ethos' by their 'Irish and colonial backgrounds'.[11]

But if the British political police of the period – as embodied in Special Branch – was a bastion of colonial-style reaction, it was also no match for 'a society which still took great pride in its liberal openness'. In Porter's account there 'were still powerful external restraints on [Special Branch's] development, which should be regarded… as a reflection of contemporary society',[12] and it is for this reason that late-Victorian British socialists, for example, completely escaped the atrophied arm of the political police.[13] That such an arm existed to begin with was due to the fact that certain British statesmen, like Sir William Harcourt – who, as Home Secretary, was instrumental in setting up the precursor to Special Branch – lacked the 'liberal courage' to stick to the 'grand [liberal] theorem' of his mid-Victorian forebears.[14]

While the material presented in this book tends to upset such conclusions, this should not detract from the fact that Porter's *Origins of the Vigilant State* remains on the whole a rare, balanced and impressively researched account of early political policing in Britain. The standard it has set has remained largely unsurpassed and it is partly because of Porter's theoretical consistency, and partly because of the difficulty of researching the nebulous origins of counter-extremism in Britain, that most subsequent histories of late-Victorian and Edwardian policing have marginalized the topic of political policing. Instead, they have chosen to give it only a cursory treatment and to accept (either wholesale or with slight modifications) Porter's thesis. Thus, for example, in his landmark *The English Police: A Political and Social History*, Clive Emsley provides a brief discussion of the trajectory of political policing from the 1880s into the early twentieth century and concludes that its major developments during the period 'coincided not only with the threats from Fenian terrorists and international anarchists, but also with a declining confidence in Britain's international superiority which led to anxieties about the future [and] fears that the British "race" was somehow being undermined'.[15]

The same declinist view has largely been echoed by Richard Thurlow, who described the emergence of a so-called 'secret state' in late nineteenth-century Britain as a consequence of the 'decline of Britain as a great power'.[16] More recently, Haia Shpayer-Makov has argued that the formation of Special Branch 'was impelled by the cumulative effects of events in the early 1880s that shattered the feelings of sanguinity of Victorian Britain',[17] while Constance Bantman, in her study of French anarchists in fin-de-siècle London, suggested that 'the British surveillance system' of the period 'represented a concession to continental countries and a… local manifestation of a global trend towards border closure and controlled circulation'.[18]

Progress beyond this declinist view has been only slowly emerging. Mostly it has come from historians of the political movements being policed in late-Victorian and Edwardian Britain, who have tended to focus on the actions and agendas of individual legislators, bureaucrats and police officials to a much greater degree than historians of the British police (with the obvious exception of Porter).

This is not at all surprising. After all, in order to understand why a certain group of political dissidents is being suppressed by authorities, one has to first understand who is orchestrating the suppression, by what specific means, and to what specific ends. The best represented field as far as this approach is concerned is probably the history of nineteenth-century transatlantic Fenianism –

which has been flourishing ever since the late 1960s. Thanks to pioneering efforts by Tom Corfe, Leon O'Broin and K. R. M. Short we have come to possess a clearer picture not only of the goals and means of Irish republican insurrectionists, but also of the controversial strategies employed by individual British administrators bent on pacifying John Bull's other island.[19] Building on their work (as well as on the wealth of governmental and police records that have since been declassified) more recent authors such as Christy Campbell, Niall Whelehan, Shane Kenna and others have been able to further flesh out the particular (and often conflicting) agendas of Britain's early political police officers.[20]

We now know (better than before) that the men in charge of setting up a counter-Fenian strategy in 1880s Britain were not mere portents of imperial 'anxiety' or colonial (and anti-liberal) chickens come home to roost. They were individuals with personal foibles, fixations and prejudices who purposefully and deliberately undertook to construct and reform, even as they claimed to abhor reform, Britain's political police in their own respective images.

Histories of nineteenth-century anarchism have also occasionally produced valuable insights into the workings of the late-Victorian political police, especially its relationship with continental (particularly French, Italian and Russian) equivalents.[21] As with histories of Irish republicanism however, their usefulness is limited by their chronological focus as well as by a decontextualized preoccupation with the venality and unaccountability of (some) British law enforcers in a way that ignores the heated debates and conflicting visions which shaped the wider hierarchy of the British political police, especially in the 1880s and 1890s.[22] Conversely, despite a recent resurgence of interest (popular and academic) in the Edwardian suffragettes, there has been virtually no scholarly account devoted specifically to the subject of their policing – something which I hope to begin redressing in the third part of this book.

Finally, my understanding of late-Victorian liberalism and of the role and importance of the Home Office bureaucracy also owes something to the work of Patrick Joyce, in particular his *State of Freedom: A Social History of the British State since 1800*. As he convincingly argues in that book:

> Shared outlook, social background and education united [politician and civil servant]. Therefore, in using the term 'governing classes' it is these people that we should have in mind, for contrary to some understandings, and to the doctrine of separation of politics and administration, it was in both figures that the real business of government took place. The high bureaucrat, just as much as the politician, was involved in making state policy... These men conceived of themselves as men of the state who had a

particularly close identification with and knowledge of not only the British state but British society, and this further bolstered their power, as by convincing themselves of this they seem to have been able to convince many others too, then and since.[23]

While wary of notions which seek to artificially inflate the supposed 'mentality' of a group, especially an elite group collectively invested with a significant degree of power, I take this analysis to be (in the main) correct. I also believe it has bearing on two of the issues that are at the heart of the present work, namely the role played by 'high bureaucrats' in planning and implementing the British model of political policing, as well as the impact of liberalism on governmental and popular attitudes to the political police.

## The importance of extra-legality

The phrase 'straining the law' was coined in 1898 by Robert Anderson (at the time Assistant Commissioner of the Metropolitan Police and head of Scotland Yard) in a confidential memorandum to Home Secretary Matthew White Ridley which pointed out that:

> in recent years the [British] Police have succeeded only by straining the law, or, in plain English, by doing utterly unlawful things, at intervals, to check this conspiracy, and my serious fear is that if new legislation affecting it is passed, Police powers may thus be defined and our practical powers seriously impaired. [If] the actual powers of Police in this country [become public knowledge], then the methods which successive secretaries of state have sanctioned, and which have been resorted to with such excellent results will be shown to be without legal sanction, and must be abandoned.[24]

There is more than a hint of exaggeration in this passage, and, as subsequent chapters will demonstrate, Anderson was throughout his career as spymaster and police official a fairly duplicitous and unreliable narrator of the activities of the political police in Britain. Despite such exaggeration, however, 'straining the law' – taken to refer to the judicious use of legal loopholes by the political police in a way that arguably perverts the original meaning of existing legislation without necessarily veering into the egregiously illegal – is nonetheless a highly useful concept when looking at the early history of the political police apparatus.

Extra-legality remained a feature of the British model of political policing throughout the period discussed here and arguably evolved into its central, defining tenet. The reason is that even though several competing methodologies of political policing were at play within the upper echelons of the late-Victorian state, they all accepted 'straining the law' as fundamentally necessary or at least inevitable. During the 1880s Edward Jenkinson – head of Britain's and Ireland's anti-Fenian strategy from 1884 to 1886 – came to embody extra-legality with his extensive (and often completely unaccountable) use of double agents and agents provocateurs even as his superiors in Dublin Castle[25] and Whitehall (especially the Home Secretary) wavered between privately supporting his methods and publicly condemning them. At the same time, Jenkinson's professed rivals within the political police apparatus (principally James Monro and Robert Anderson) likewise chose to make use of extra-legal methods in dealing with political threats to the state even as they claimed (particularly in the case of Monro) to abhor such methods.

With the waning of such personal rivalries extra-legality came to play an even more important role for the British political police during the 1890s. Much like Jenkinson before him, Chief Inspector William Melville (Superintendent of the Special Branch between 1893 and 1904) rapidly rose to be the unofficial – and, this time, virtually unchallenged – steward of the institutional political police, even as the Branch continued to be under the nominal leadership of the Home Secretary. Under Melville's tutelage the political police engaged in problematic practices which ranged from mere shadowing and infiltration of seditious groups (sometimes at the behest of foreign governments, as we shall see) to unwarranted house searches and the possible use of agents provocateurs. Melville himself freely colluded with representatives of continental (especially Russian) political police organizations in order to aid the latter in silencing foreign radicals exiled in Britain. Although such practices gradually became more subdued in the first decade of the twentieth century, they did not disappear altogether and the willingness of police and Home Office officials to continue using them was made especially clear after suffragette militants began their campaign of intimidation and destruction of public and private property.

Whether they believed in traditional Victorian methods of policing or, conversely, they favoured covert intelligence gathering and dissimulation, the men involved in setting up Britain's early political police ultimately regarded extra-legality as inextricable from their work and strove to use it to their best advantage. Given an institutional context fraught with internecine squabbles and pressures from the political establishment, 'straining the law' provided a degree of stability and ensured the challenges posed by subversive movements could be met head-on.

## The significance of individual actors

While I have no wish to wax poetic on controversial concepts like 'historical constructionism' or 'methodological individualism', it is my position that history-writing is always reliant on incomplete and fragmented documents (broadly understood) and thus always in the process of being assembled, rather than revealed, by historians. Individual historical actors are of course often, if not always, nothing but collections of such incomplete and fragmented documents, but the relationships between them as individuals outweigh their separate archival afterlives. To frame this issue in the context of early British political policing, we need only ask why Britain did not evolve a more regimented and centralized – in other words more 'European' – system of policing political subversion over the three decades preceding the First World War.

In the Prussian-dominated German Empire, for example, the surveillance of subversive agitators was deeply embedded into police structures and aimed in particular at undermining the persecuted but politically ascending Social Democratic Party. As an 1879 official report by the Police Chief of Berlin warned, socialists were becoming ever more agile at 'deceiv[ing] the police officials entrusted with the movement's surveillance by lulling their vigilance to sleep' with a carefully staged veneer of 'moderation'.[26] Not only were socialists (including members of the Reichstag) kept under close surveillance, however; thanks in part to an ever-increasing police budget, undercover policemen in Berlin were routinely deployed to infiltrate and violently shut down otherwise uneventful Social Democratic election gatherings, frequently engaging in agent provocateuring by distributing incendiary revolutionary pamphlets in the street.[27] One recent historian of modern Berlin has convincingly suggested that in the early 1880s 'the Berlin police employed an army of informers to ferret out "subversives", which resulted in a wave of denunciations'.[28]

In Imperial Russia, political policing likewise betrayed a ruthless willingness to openly and unapologetically employ the state's entire arsenal of intimidation in order to quash militant dissent. As a recent historian of pre-Soviet Siberian exile has described, following the 1881 assassination of Tsar Alexander II by Nihilist insurrectionists, the highly centralized Russian political police 'equipped with telegraphs, card catalogues and extensive networks of spies and informers, hunted down and destroyed the [Nihilist movement]' until, neutralized by a wave of 'arrests and the infiltration of its networks', it completely collapsed 'for a generation'.[29] More importantly, the Russian political police proved highly adept at exporting its activities beyond its actual jurisdiction, opening *agenturas* (i.e. secret bureaus of undercover agents attached to

Russian embassies) in various European cities known for inadvertently hosting anti-tsarist radicals, including Bucharest, Berlin and Paris. Here these agents were tolerated and sometimes even encouraged by local authorities.[30]

Paris, in fact, was the central node in a French political police apparatus that developed – uncertainly, but steadily – alongside the Third Republic's fragile democratic framework well into the twentieth century. The *Sûreté Générale* – headquartered in Paris, but with an exclusively provincial mandate – built on the centralized counter-subversive intelligence networks of the Second Empire but with reduced staff and resources. The capital's political police, meanwhile, was wholly embedded in the *Préfecture de police de Paris*, which thanks to its substantial annual budgets (far exceeding those of the *Sûreté*), managed to employ 'more police than all the other [French] police forces put together'.[31]

Yet just as in Germany and Russia, the French political police relied to a significant extent on 'paid informants with suspect motives [and] agents provocateurs', as well as on 'open[ing] correspondence, illegally enter[ing] premises, eavesdrop[ping] on ordinary citizens going about their lawful business, and [trying] to manipulate public opinion' by colluding with sections of the press.[32] In the mid-1880s the Prefect of the Paris Police, Louis Andrieux, even went so far as to admit to 'financing the first anarchist paper published in Paris, and writing articles for it which inspired the first anarchist bomb outrage'.[33]

Why then, to return to our question, did Britain not adopt a system of political policing more unreservedly in line with those of European powers? One possible answer (and one which has proved quite popular with historians as we have already seen) is that 'liberal Britain' successfully fended off the challenge of an insidious authoritarian conspiracy thanks to the strength of its constitution and the devotion it inspired in the British public. This is, however, wholly lopsided. Granted that the prevailing political orthodoxies of the age had an overall retarding effect on the development of centralized intelligence-driven policing in Britain, the pre-First World War British political police took the shape it did, when it did, because of the impact specific individuals (and the interactions between them) had on it.

Thus, for example, the Special Irish Branch of the Scotland Yard came into being in March 1883 not as an inevitable uniform response to a terrorist threat or because of some mysterious defect in the British government's liberal armour. It came into being because Sir William Harcourt (then Home Secretary) made it his personal mission to create such an organization as part of a wider strategy for aggressively countering Fenian conspiracies in Britain. If in 1884 Edward Jenkinson (then Assistant Under-Secretary for Police and Crime in Ireland) was put in charge of British anti-Fenian operations and given free hand to employ his 'continental' (as one of his critics put it) counter-subversive strategies, it is again because Harcourt willed it, based on a certain set of assumptions, prejudices and negotiations. If, finally, in 1887 Jenkinson was forced to resign (with highly significant consequences), it is because a different Home Secretary, Sir Henry Matthews, decided to side with Jenkinson's rivals within the police hierarchy for personal and ideological reasons. These and many other similar situations will be further described and dissected throughout this book. Suffice it here to say that individual factors proved of greater significance in the development of the methodology and direction of the early British political police than previously acknowledged by historians of British policing.

## Popular and official perceptions of political policing

One of the biggest, and least scrutinized, misconceptions to be found in the historiography dealing (directly or indirectly) with the early British political police is that political policing not only went against a supposed late-Victorian liberal status quo, but that it was positively un-British to begin with. The current formulation of this hypothesis arguably originates in the work of Bernard Porter but an earlier version can be found in the work of traditionalist police historians like Charles Reith and this in turn can be traced back to mid-Victorian commentators such as Charles Dickens who in 1850 suggested that the British 'Detective Police system' was concerned only with common crime, adding that in Britain 'the most rabid demagogue can say what he chooses [without] the terror of an organised spy system'.[34] Dickens was probably voicing a majority opinion at the time, and it certainly would not be a stretch to conclude that the years between the demise of Chartism in the late 1840s and the beginning of the Fenian dynamite campaign in the early 1880s were, with few exceptions, 'essentially spyless'.[35] By the early 1880s, however, popular (though not necessarily political) prejudices against political policing were already disintegrating at a rapid pace.

As mentioned above, the declinist theory of the origins of Britain's political police is a two-pronged one. On the one hand, it is argued, political policing was foreign and inimical to British liberalism and therefore detested by the British public at large; on the other hand, insofar as it existed, political policing was largely the work of a cabal of reactionary figures with decidedly problematic (i.e. Irish or otherwise colonial) backgrounds whose insidious presence came as a consequence of a declining national sense of imperial self-confidence.

What this book will seek to demonstrate, however, is that the early British system of political policing was in fact mostly a liberal one, and, insofar as awareness of it gradually seeped into public consciousness, that it enjoyed widespread support from most sections of British society. It was not of course liberal by any modern definition of the word, but it was liberal by late-Victorian standards in that it proved distrustful of overt government centralization and strove to use existing bureaucracies rather than create new ones; in that it resisted attempts to make legislation more authoritarian and punitive (which is what the right wing of the Conservative Party overwhelmingly preferred); and lastly, in that far from being the work of reactionary colonials, it was in fact a system designed mostly by men committed, at least to some extent, to the principles of the British Liberal Party.

Although sections of the political establishment remained seemingly attached to the mid-Victorian discourse which frowned upon secret policing as inimical to the spirit of the British constitution, the reasons for such an attitude varied according to political necessity. Conservative critics tended to object to political policing because of a general opposition to 'big government'; Liberal critics mostly out of a declared attachment to freedom of opinion and personal liberty; while Irish Nationalists (as a rule) saw in it merely the tool of colonialist oppression.

Whatever the declared nature of their respective oppositions, it must be noted that political policing was never discontinued as a practice either by Liberal or Conservative administrations, and it is significant that Lord Salisbury, one of the most prominent Conservative critics of a stronger police force, took an otherwise very active and committed interest in the activities of the political police during his premierships. This suggests that the oppositional discourse was, by the late-nineteenth century, largely just that – a discourse to be used as needed in political battles.

A further illustration of this duplicity comes from the way in which British authorities chose to deal with native socialist militancy in the later 1880s. Although Bernard Porter has argued that the British political police judiciously avoided infiltrating and even monitoring British socialist organizations following a series of socialist-inspired disturbances in London during 1886 and 1887, my research shows that this was not the case. Although initially discouraged from interfering with an otherwise anaemic British socialist agitation, the political police was nonetheless given carte blanche by the Home Secretary to shadow and infiltrate groups like the Social Democratic Federation (SDF) after 1887. If using the political police against 'freeborn Englishmen' constituted the ultimate sin against a fuzzily defined liberalism, then it was a sin the British government was only too eager to commit given the strength of public opposition to socialism (manifested especially in the wake of the 'Bloody Sunday' riot of 1887).

Outside of Whitehall, there was in fact little discernible opposition to the idea of a system of secret police tasked with subverting 'unacceptable' forms of political activity. The evidence for this comes mostly from newspapers at the time, which were, with few and specific exceptions, overwhelmingly (and regardless of political line) supportive of what was then termed 'the political department at Scotland Yard' even when the government appeared to be less so. It also comes, however, from the many examples of regular, everyday people providing vital information and assistance to authorities in cases of a political nature. Indeed, it can be argued, without fear of exaggeration, that some of the most notorious cases of political conspiracy during the period discussed here only came about thanks to tip-offs from 'concerned citizens'.

## Britain's relationship with foreign powers

Britain's foreign policy in Europe during the former's so-called age of 'splendid isolation' has been exhaustively documented and debated by historians but the relationship between British and continental powers in matters of political policing over the same period has received comparatively little attention.[36] What my research suggests in this respect is that if Britain's isolation in diplomatic matters before 1914 is to some extent debatable, its commitment to isolation in legal matters, especially matters concerning political crime, is beyond any doubt. Examples of this policy will be discussed throughout the book, but here it must be noted that the reasons for Britain's isolation in matters of political policing had little if anything to do with 'liberal values', as some historians have recently suggested.[37]

Certainly there was a lot of heated debate in Parliament on this issue throughout the late-Victorian period, with Liberal leaders usually favouring a 'pro-European' cooperationist stance, and Conservative leaders trumpeting the virtues of an independent, uncompromisingly British legal system. In practice, however, Liberal and Conservative administrations proved equally opposed to committing Britain to any pan-European project for combating organized sedition.

The main reason for this had to do with extra-legality and the need to protect it as the defining feature of British political policing. As Robert Anderson observed after the 1898 Anti-anarchist Conference in Rome, European proposals for systematically clamping down on insurrectionary movements invariably involved two problematic features: a high degree of centralization (away from London) and an indiscriminate degree of information-sharing – both of which were inimical to 'straining' the (British) law. Indeed, as we shall see, British authorities were quite happy to occasionally supply foreign governments with intelligence on the movements of foreign radicals exiled in Britain so long as Whitehall remained in control of how much was communicated, to whom, and especially to what purpose. When there was nothing to be gained from aiding a foreign government in this manner, British officials routinely ignored requests for cooperation.

If there was any genuine cooperation between Britain and Europe in matters of political policing it was usually at the level of practical police work. British detectives occasionally helped in the investigations of foreign counterparts, with sometimes spectacular results (such as the 1892 and 1894 arrests in London of two notorious French anarchists), but even here the limits imposed by the Whitehall bureaucracy could not be overridden. Because of the need to preserve extra-legality, formal cooperation between British and foreign police forces had to be kept at a minimum.

This does not mean that the British stance towards cooperation with Europe was the product of some monolithic 'official mind'. As we shall see later on, the divergence of opinion within the British political police hierarchy meant that some officials (especially at the Home Office) regarded 'the continental system [of policing politics] as [one] which possesses very great and obvious advantages'.[38] Additionally, some of the more practical counter-terrorist measures in use on the continent (such as specially fitted bomb-defusing laboratories) were eventually at least partially introduced in Britain. All the same, for reasons that will be discussed throughout this book, such exceptions to the rule did not ultimately lead to any concentrated attempts to bring the British model of political policing more in line with its European equivalents. While Britain's diplomatic isolation may have finally come to an end in the first few years of the twentieth century, in policing matters it continued all throughout the pre-war years (and arguably until 1928, when Britain joined, if only nominally, the Interpol organization).

## The efficiency of early British political policing

Although my intention here is mainly to examine the workings and structure of the early British model of political policing, a few things need to be said on the issue of its efficiency (or lack thereof). It is, of course, an undeniable fact that the transatlantic Irish republican militancy of the late nineteenth century did not collapse solely because of the pressure put on it by British counter-terrorist strategies. It is also an undeniable fact that after the collapse of Fenian terrorism in the late 1880s the British government was not confronted with any believable insurrectionary threat until the Easter Rising of 1916 (and then only in Ireland). Political threats to national security continued to exist – anarchism in the 1890s; revolutionary socialism, anti-colonial nationalism and militant suffragism in the 1900s – but none proved to be existential threats.

The issue then arises of how to measure the efficiency of the British political police given that after 1890 the forms of subversion it was tasked with monitoring and combating lacked genuine revolutionary potential. Arguably, if there had been no political police whatsoever (as the government sometimes unconvincingly claimed), Britain's national security would not have been much affected for the worse. This may be, but we can only argue this point with the benefit of hindsight and by ignoring the weight of contemporary public opinion. As this book will show, for most Britons the political threats of the 1890s and the 1900s were in fact highly significant ones.

Although anarchist terrorists in Britain never succeeded in orchestrating the kind of bloody outrages that became routine in *Belle Époque* France, events like the 1892 trial of six Walsall anarchists for conspiracy to manufacture explosives, the 1894 Greenwich Park explosion, as well as a string of other, less egregious, incidents convinced many Britons that anarchism was a genuine domestic threat. Similarly, while the socialist and suffragist militancy of the Edwardian years may seem quaint when compared to the revolutionary movements that emerged after 1917, to Britons who had yet to experience the ferocity of the First World War it could easily appear to be 'something very like revolution' (in the words of one Special Branch detective at the time).

With this in mind, the British model of political policing emerges as a moderately efficient one if only because (with a few exceptions) it was seen to be so by public opinion and radical opinion alike. In spite of a problematic structure which promoted secrecy, resistance to change, collusion with foreign agents and internal rivalries; despite several spectacular failures of intelligence and a willingness to, in some instances, use violence or the threat of violence in order to defuse perceived dangers to national safety, the political police managed to combat subversive activity in a way that, overall, appeared to most Britons to be unobtrusive and benign. As a *Sunday Times* correspondent observed in 1897 while visiting the haunts of anarchist revolutionaries in London, 'the very significance of... police espionage [in Britain] is that it is not assertive – is, in fact, subterranean in its character'.[39]

## Sources and structure

Historical facts are imperfect but they nonetheless tend to have fairly long shelf lives; historical theories, on the other hand, are very often perfectly constructed but, like the 'bourgeois' relations of Marxist theory, become antiquated before they can even ossify. For this reason, I have chosen to keep overt theorizing and thematic analysis down to a minimum throughout the book and have focused instead on creating the sort of narrative that might allow the reader to understand not only the evolution of political policing in late-Victorian Britain but the internal ambitions and drives which forged the engine of this evolution.

The narrative proceeds in more or less chronological order and often pinpoints exact dates and locations. To some extent this is an attempt to amplify its historicity; to convey, in other words, the sense of uncertainty and confusion that historical actors would have experienced and to avoid the trap of teleological thinking. More importantly, it is an attempt to present as much of the historical evidence as possible outside of the confines of inherited academic discourses. This is not out of a naïve belief that facts can speak for themselves, but because given the limitations of the current scholarship, the early British political police needs a new chronicle as much as it needs a new history.

The primary sources I have relied on can broadly be divided into official and unofficial. The former overwhelmingly come from the archives currently held at the British National Archives at Kew and include Home Office and Foreign Office memoranda, police reports and orders, official and private correspondence, short notes, witness depositions, telegrams, trial proceedings and annotated newspaper clippings. For relevant official correspondence which I have not been able to consult first-hand, I have relied on the research of other historians (particularly Porter and Campbell) and, where available, on published anthologies.

Unofficial sources are those which are not of governmental provenance and they consist of newspaper accounts, memoirs, works of fiction and of independent journalism, and even the odd archival video recording (in the form of a 1911 Pathé newsreel). Newspaper accounts in particular have proved essential in researching Britain's relationship with continental powers in matters of policing and the British public's perception of the national political police, and it is for this reason that I have tried to cast as wide a geographical net as possible.

When discussing continental (particularly French) attitudes to British politics and policing, I have tended to rely on non-English rather than English-language accounts, not because the former are less biased, but because they reveal attitudes and prejudices which are absent from the latter. Similarly, when discussing the reactions of the British press to the government's practices of political policing, I have tried to avoid reproducing the London-centric, and often *Times*-centric, approach of previous scholarship (although London is for historical reasons still very much the undisputed centre of this narrative) by sampling a wide array of titles from across the United Kingdom of Great Britain and Ireland. To a significant extent this has only been possible thanks to my access to technologies that even two decades ago were still not widely available to scholars, namely the many online databases of digitized historical media.

A majority of official sources deployed here have to some extent been touched on or referenced in previous scholarly works, but I have nonetheless managed to uncover several previously overlooked documents, some of which I believe shine new light on important aspects of early British political policing. Official correspondence on the previously overlooked case of Alfred Oldland (a socialist sympathizer arrested in 1887 for resisting arrest and attacking police officers) reveals that London police were in fact actively monitoring and even striving to infiltrate native socialist organizations like the SDF during the late 1880s. Equally, while the official archive dealing with the South Wales labour disturbances of 1910 has been known to historians for some time, it has never been (so far as I have been able to gather) exhaustively explored. As Chapter 14 will show, documents from this archive go beyond revealing the extent to which British authorities (in London and Wales) thought of the disturbances in the Rhondda Valley – epitomized by the Tonypandy riot of November 1910 – as the product of socialist sedition. They also demonstrate the extent to which, even at this late date, extra-legality was still the dominating feature of British political policing, a fact illustrated by the way in which General Nevil Macready handled the Home Office-engineered mission of pacifying the region.

In the case of previously used archives, my approach has been to explore the available content more deeply, following the guiding principle that individual voices, differences of opinion and unsteady compromises can all bring to light new and interesting aspects to the topic at hand. Several short and nearly illegible (yet often meaningful) notes by Home Office bureaucrats have been uncovered this way. I have also tried to avoid paraphrasing important documents (such as personal and official correspondence) whenever possible, preferring instead to render the original phrasing and authorial voice by means of (occasionally lengthy) direct quotes. Above all, I have endeavoured to write a lively and enjoyable account that might allow the reader to – in the words of Robert Darnton – 'taste the flavor of the distant past'.[40] Whether I have succeeded, even partially, in this last objective will be for the reader to decide.

# Prologue

THE rapid development of political policing and government surveillance in late-Victorian Britain is not easily explained given its apparent contradiction of a centuries-old belief which many Britons arguably subscribed to – namely that, 'under God, they were peculiarly free [and] richer in every sense than other peoples, particularly Catholic peoples, and particularly the French'.[1] This national myth of an uncomplicated Protestant liberty, stretching back to Tudor times and infused with a disdain for the 'Jesuitical' methods of continental governments, permeated public life throughout the nineteenth century, from the halls of Westminster to alehouses and working men's clubs. Yet much about 'British liberty' was always mere political opportunism or sentimental cant and in a time of grave national danger it could hardly be expected to form the bedrock of government policy.

The onset of hostilities with revolutionary France in 1793 swiftly brought home the notion that political radicals across Great Britain and Ireland formed, despite their seemingly diverging goals, a dangerous fifth column, undermining the war effort and possibly the very existence of the monarchy. The Home Office – established in 1782 as a discrete department with a national remit – joined in the effort of securing the domestic front by obtaining detailed intelligence on the extent of indigenous disaffection with the government. A network of spies and informers sprang up across the British mainland, rapidly becoming wide and effective enough to drive the bulk of English radicalism underground and in ever more ideologically extreme directions.

Prominent reformist organizations like the London Corresponding Society were assiduously infiltrated by mercenary agents after 1794, their premises raided, their leaders arrested and tried for treason. While credible evidence of an organized conspiracy for the 'annihilation of Parliament and the destruction of the King'[2] remained scarce, covert support for radical ideas in the Army and Navy, continued Jacobin militancy as far north as Scotland and especially the fear of a Trojan horse of English and Irish insurrectionists working to prepare the way for invading French forces – all made the government more willing than ever to drastically curtail freedom of expression and of assembly.

Following the 1800 Act of Union with Ireland and the several parliamentary acts introduced throughout the later 1790s, which suspended both habeas corpus and trade union activity, the threat of an imminent Jacobin-inspired revolution appeared to finally be contained. Yet the continuing war with an aggressively imperial France taxed Britain's economic resources to breaking point, ensuring the survival of an embryonic revolutionary underground in urban and industrializing areas as well as the emergence of a broader 'plebeian radicalism' – poignantly embodied by the Luddite movement – that was to 'give a new breadth to the demand for reform' in the years to come.[3]

Perhaps the most emblematic and notorious example of the resilience of post-war insurrectionary feeling is the Cato Street Conspiracy of 1820. Briefly, the conspiracy, which involved anywhere between a dozen and nineteen men, was centred on the ill-fated figure of Arthur Thistlewood (a former military officer and unrepentant Jacobin) and aimed at sparking a popular revolt in England through the assassination of Prime Minister Liverpool's entire cabinet during a formal dinner. Though the course of the conspiracy and the events leading up to it have been thoroughly established elsewhere,[4] it will be useful to briefly identify here the ways in which the authorities' response to the scheming of Thistlewood and his acolytes suggested, even at this early stage, the beginnings of a systematic approach to policing and containing organized subversion in Britain.

The most striking, and for our purposes, significant, aspect of this case is the central role played by government-paid informants in the eventual unravelling of the conspiracy. Already a key feature in the authorities' foiling of previous abortive insurrections, most notably the Despard Plot of 1802, the use of spies had also proved instrumental in the quelling of the Pentrich Rising of 1817 – the leaders of which had been goaded into action and subsequently betrayed by a certain Oliver the Spy – as well as the Spa Fields riots of the previous year.

A disorganized and ill-conceived attempt at turning a popular London rally in favour of parliamentary reform into a spontaneous revolution, the Spa Fields riots were largely the handiwork of local Spenceans (revolutionary proto-socialists and followers of the land reformer Thomas Spence), including Thistlewood and several of his friends. For John Stafford, Chief Clerk at the Bow Street Public Office – the second most senior rank in the most powerful police force in the capital – the violence was clear evidence of another Jacobin plot, but for charges of high treason to be successfully brought against the ringleaders, incontrovertible evidence of a political conspiracy was needed.

As the foremost spymaster in Regency London, Stafford enjoyed both a remarkable degree of operational independence as well as the backing of the

Home Secretary (Lord Sidmouth until 1822) and the latter's permanent under-secretaries, all of whom appreciated the need for a vigorous and unrelenting campaign against militant republicanism. That the backbone of this campaign was the systematic use of informants and infiltrators had already been established in practice; unremarkably, the charge of levying war against the king brought against the Spa Fields ringleaders in June 1817 rested exclusively on the testimony of a paid spy who had been groomed, vetted and given assurances of safety by the Home Office.[5]

What *is* somewhat remarkable is that in their efforts at making the charges stick, authorities allowed the same spy, a young man by the name of John Castle, to give his testimony in court. A dissolute petty swindler who had been involved with the Spenceans for less than a year, Castle seemed to embody the very worst of the 'spy system', particularly at a time when Bow Street detectives were popularly known as 'traps' (on account of their reputation for using entrapment schemes) and when it was widely believed that the Bank of England ran its own network of agents provocateurs in order to catch would-be counterfeiters in the act.[6]

The prosecution's case thus collapsed under the weight of an emergent popular spy-phobia[7] and the accused, including Thistlewood, were allowed to walk free. For the government the lesson was clear: excepting the most extraordinary of circumstances, informers were not to be paraded before the public in a court of law – a lesson that nearly a hundred years after, as we shall later see, retained much of its value for police and Home Office officials alike.

After the 1817 fiasco, Stafford's spies continued to keep the Spenceans under close surveillance, with one agent in particular, George Edwards, rising to become Thistlewood's closest friend and 'aide-de-camp' in an otherwise theoretical revolutionary army. Edwards, who came from an impoverished artisan background typical of London radicals, was entirely self-seeking, but relished playing the role of the firebreathing ultra-Jacobin, writing to Stafford in 1818 to offer his services in the knowledge that a well-timed betrayal would likely result in a comfortable and long retirement. One of nine informants reporting on the Spa Fields gang,[8] Edwards was by far the most ruthless and willing to engage in provocation, constantly urging the dangerously delusional Thistlewood to continue planning the 'West End job' – as a proposed massacre of ministers had been codenamed – while threatening those with cold feet into submission.

That Stafford and Sidmouth knew of such provocation and approved of it is borne out by Edwards' written reports. There is also every indication that following the brief suspension of habeas corpus in 1817–18 and the Peterloo massacre of 1819 (both of which galvanized radical opinion nationwide) authorities in London were adamant about being widely seen to deliver a mortal blow to a fully fledged conspiracy against the state. In the absence of a clear post-war mandate for curtailing all subversive activity and given the increasing unpopularity of an overwhelmingly unrepresentative Parliament,[9] John Bull could no longer simply be told that 'Laws suited to the Danger'[10] were necessary; he had to be sold on the idea. This too turned out to be a lesson for the long run.

Thistlewood and his co-conspirators were summarily rounded up at their hideout in Cato Street in late February 1820 (just as they were about to go through with the 'West End job') and put in the dock at the Old Bailey on charges of high treason. Although eleven of the men were found guilty (five, including Thistlewood, being executed for their role), with very few in Parliament asking any questions about Edwards' conspicuous absence from the trial or his all-but-confirmed ties to the Home Office,[11] Lord Sidmouth's 'delight and ... pride in the functions of a political police-officer [sic]'[12] were not to last.

Taking over as Home Secretary in 1821, Sir Robert Peel quickly proved a decidedly more 'liberal' Tory for a markedly less reactionary and economically stable decade, introducing several bills to reduce the number of capital offences while working to reform the prison system. Although spikes in recorded crime (particularly in the capital) and continued social unrest in industrializing areas remained a feature of the 1820s, the government's reaction gradually became 'more measured and less alarmist'.[13] The incipient whiggish zeitgeist that dominated later decades had it that rebellion was 'much more likely to be killed by kindness than by the headsman and his provider, the spy'.[14] Political policing was, after all, the hallmark of 'Boney's' France; the arbitrary tool of Fouché and his *mouchards*.

When it was set up by Act of Parliament in 1829, the London Metropolitan Police was meant, in the wording of the act, to introduce 'a new and more efficient system of police in lieu of [the] ineffective... establishments of nightly watch and nightly police'. Its intended target was the widely decried wave of 'offences against property [which] have of late increased in and near the metropolis'.[15] Nowhere was political crime or subversion of any kind mentioned despite very recent memories of Peterloo, the Cato Street conspiracy and the various gagging acts of the 1810s.

As some historians have suggested, this was likely a calculated move on Peel's part, one meant to convince the respectable classes that in contrast to the dreaded French police, 'the London police did not threaten their liberty'.[16] It did not, however, take long for political developments to begin changing the course of institutionalized policing in Britain. The Chartist disturbances of the 1830s 'provided the government with the opportunity for legislation'[17] and the new London system of policing was extended to the rest of the country, at first on a voluntary basis, through the Rural Constabulary Act of 1839 and then compulsorily after the passing of the County and Borough Police Act in 1856.

The limits of this cautious embrace of increased policing were highlighted in 1833 when Sergeant William Popay of the Metropolitan Police was revealed to have infiltrated a chapter of the Chartist National Political Union and to have incited the commission of violent outrages against established authorities. Two select committees were set up to investigate into the legality of Popay's actions, but the fact that the sergeant's mission had been secretly planned and sanctioned by the Home Secretary himself allowed the two Commissioners of the Metropolitan Police, Charles Rowan and Richard Mayne, to plausibly deny 'the imputation that we could have sanctioned or allowed any such practices'.[18] Popay was dismissed, the Commissioners were exonerated and the select committees concluded that the use of plain-clothes police was perfectly constitutional so long as it steered clear of 'the Employment of Spies… as a practice most abhorrent to the feelings of the People, and most alien to the spirit of the Constitution'.[19]

In 1842 the first unit of the Metropolitan Police dedicated specifically to the detection of crime came into being and with it the groundwork for what later became the Criminal Investigation Department (CID) at Scotland Yard. Although initially numbering only two inspectors and six sergeants, the fledgling detective branch represented the British government's first real effort in setting up an apparatus for systematically investigating criminal activity, acquiring valuable intelligence and infiltrating political demonstrations that threatened public order.

By the mid-1840s, however, Chartism no longer posed a significant threat to national security – a decline that seemed to coincide with the birth of a new, invigorated, imperial Britain which could afford to flaunt its self-assertiveness in the face of a Europe torn between nationalist fervour and unbending reaction. As Bernard Porter has suggested, nothing epitomized this new image of Britannia triumphant better than the tradition of unconditional asylum for the 'hundreds of fugitives from failed revolutions on the Continent', the more genteel of whom could always find a 'warm welcome in whiggish circles'.[20] Even firebrands not entirely fit for polite society, such as Karl Marx, could at least count on toleration.

If British middle-class opinion had found covert policing distasteful before (given its association with revolutionary France) by the 1850s it was adamant that the values of 'liberal England' were wholly at odds with the backhanded ways of spies and infiltrators. Charles Dickens' weekly *Household Words* described the 'Detective Police system of London' as one 'solely [concerned with] bringing crime to justice', not with 'the terror of an organised spy system'.[21] Twenty-five years later, *The Times* proved equally certain that Britain was 'happily free from the baleful institution of a Secret Police employed in the service of Order'.[22]

This discourse had the effect of putting government officials in a defensive and self-censorious stance and although the Metropolitan Police Detective Branch was kept in place and even expanded, its plain-clothes operations came increasingly under strict regulation. In 1845, for example, Commissioner Rowan ordered that 'no man shall disguise himself [except in] very strong case[s] of necessity [and not] without particular orders' from his superiors.[23] The mid-Victorian period thus arguably ushered in a 'vast… chasm of spylessness',[24] even as underneath this apparent calm an uneasy equilibrium between the demands of opinion makers and those of the British state persisted.

Cracks began appearing as early as 1867 when a group of Irish-American members of the revolutionary-nationalist Fenian Brotherhood blew up Clerkenwell Prison in central London, in an attempt to liberate one of their incarcerated comrades. Seven people died, several dozens were injured and more than two hundred properties were damaged as a result.[25] At the time the Home Office still relied exclusively on its informal, sub-institutional Secret Service bureau (set up at the time of the French Revolution) for secret intelligence on matters of national security. The intelligence, however, was based solely on reports from a few scattered spies, not on the accountable operations of police detectives.

The London CID, assembled in 1878 out of the ashes of the old and terminally corrupt Detective Branch, did not yet have any means of assessing the strength of Fenian activity abroad or in Britain and there were no plans to expand its functions in that direction. The Clerkenwell bombing, however, proved to be merely the prelude to a far more destructive terroristic campaign, one that targeted government buildings (including the Scotland Yard headquarters itself) as well as railway stations and public monuments. At last, the government could no longer afford to be seen doing nothing.

# Part 1
1881–91

1. Sir William Vernon Harcourt in the 1880s (Wellcome Collection).

CHAPTER 1

# 'A spider's web of Police Communication'[1]

On the afternoon of 14 January 1881, a seven-year-old boy named Richard Clark and his nanny, Mary Ann Nadin, were walking along Tatton Street in Salford, heading towards Oldfield Road to meet the boy's father at his place of business. Passing by the Infantry Barracks, Richard and his companion were suddenly propelled violently by the force of a sharp blaze that pierced through the sullen fog, sending off bits of debris in every direction. After the dirt and snow had settled, an elderly man who had also been walking in the vicinity of the Barracks prior to the explosion, but had luckily escaped unscathed, could see the injured Mrs Nadin wailing over the motionless body of her young ward; Richard had suffered a major head wound and despite the forthcoming medical efforts to revive him, was bleeding to death. A woman later recalled before an inquest that shortly before the explosion she had seen 'two men [stopping] on the footpath next the barrack wall, and one of them struck a match. They then stood for a few minutes with their faces to the wall, and afterwards walked off… after [which] she saw a light against the wall, and sparks falling from it.'[2]

The two men were never found or even properly identified (a local publican had told police he had encountered two suspicious 'Yankee-Irishmen' carrying equally suspicious packages only hours before the explosion),[3] but in Salford and Westminster alike little doubt remained as to who was responsible for the outrage. Only ten days prior, the War Office had issued orders to volunteer regiments in Liverpool and Manchester to deposit their armaments in 'a place of safety' as information deemed credible suggested 'an organised attempt would be made by some disaffected portion of the population to seize the arms stored… in the district.'[4] That 'disaffected portion' was a euphemism for the sympathizers and agents of the umbrella organization known as the Fenians, which at the time comprised the Irish-based Irish Republican Brotherhood, its American offshoots, viz. the Fenian Brotherhood and the Clan na Gael, as well as satellite groupuscules like the United Irishmen of America.

As the recently installed Home Secretary, William Vernon Harcourt, explained on 22 February in the House of Commons in response to an allegation by the Nationalist MP Timothy Healy that 'a groundless panic' had been created by the government around the 'recent alleged' outrage at Salford:

> I desire entirely to contradict that, and to say there is ground... for believing that a Fenian conspiracy exists... A paper was sent to me a few days ago, belonging to a man who is perfectly well known – a man who was a Fenian convict, but who received the mercy of the Crown by being released before the expiry of his sentence... I refer to [Jeremiah] O'Donovan Rossa.[5] [His] paper... The United Irishman, a copy of which was sent to me the other day... stated that the objects which were pursued by the Party to which the editor belonged were to overthrow the English Government by the sword, and... there was a speech reported in that paper by a man well known in this country, a man who certainly received the grace of the Crown[6] – John Devoy, who... says he will assassinate a single Minister, and then he will assassinate the whole Cabinet. That is what they desire, and... it is the duty of [the] Government... to protect itself against men whose principles are the principles of the Nihilists, and whose practices are the practices of the Petroleurs.[7]

A decade earlier, one of Harcourt's predecessors, Henry Austin Bruce, had been assured by Robert Anderson, the Home Office's resident expert on Fenian matters, that Anderson's 'American correspondent', the later notorious double agent known as Henri Le Caron, was reporting 'Fenian affairs [to be] dead at present'.[8] This fortunate inactivity persisted throughout the 1870s thanks to the internecine squabbles plaguing the Irish republican camp on the one hand, and the rise of the quasi-constitutionalist pro-Home Rule New Departure (embodied by the charismatic and resolute Nationalist MP Charles Stewart Parnell) on the other. Harcourt, however, was quick to understand that things were about to change and it was not by accident that he chose to single out O'Donovan Rossa and Devoy for particular excoriation. The former, who demanded nothing short of 'terror in England – terror in the hearts of Englishmen',[9] represented the flauntingly terrorist wing of radical republicanism, while the latter, as one of the architects of the New Departure, typified the duplicitous nature of Parnellism and the Land League.[10]

Despite being aware of the imminence of renewed violence – a report received on 2 January 1881 had warned that 'ample subsidies have been received from America, arms [and] ammunition have been imported [to Britain] [and] leaders are only awaiting the signal'[11] – Harcourt knew very little about the specifics and certainly did not suspect that O'Donovan Rossa was actively organizing a campaign of terror on British shores of which the Salford explosion was to be only the debut. Writing to the Director of Criminal Investigations at

Scotland Yard, Sir Howard Vincent, on 23 January, Harcourt declared himself 'much disturbed at the absolute want of information in which we seem to be with regard to Fenian organisation in London,'[12] adding that same day in a subsequent letter to Sir Edmund Henderson (Commissioner of the Metropolitan Police) that Vincent was to 'devote his exclusive attention to police supervision of suspected Fenian and Irish plots' and that 'an Irish Inspector [was to] be sent on to England to act in cooperation with Mr. Vincent… in order that the Police of both countries may be brought into direct communication and harmonious action.'[13]

Harcourt was not the only one in the newly formed Liberal government favouring a more proactive approach to the Irish question. Despite Gladstone's belief in 'not abolishing the right to be tried before being imprisoned,'[14] a new Coercion policy for Ireland was now all but inevitable following the intensification of the Land League's anti-rent agitation and the failure to silence Parnell with a charge of conspiracy,[15] and Fenian bombs were unlikely to change that. As Hugh Childers, Secretary for War, put it in a letter to Harcourt, 'what idiots these scoundrels are to think that their outrages will make us slacker about Coercion.'[16] A day later, on 24 January, William Forster, Gladstone's Chief Secretary for Ireland, introduced the new Coercion Bill in Parliament, which, despite its liberal-sounding name – the Protection of Person and Property Act – 'practically enabled the viceroy to lock up anybody he pleased, and to detain him as long as he pleased.'[17] Nationalist MPs mounted a vigorous filibuster, but nothing came of it. The stage was set not only for the oncoming Home Rule crisis, but also for a new approach to subduing political extremism, one that was both interventionist and reluctant (depending on the nature of the threat). Over the course of the next couple of decades, this approach became the norm for successive British governments, both Liberal and Conservative.

As Whitehall was busy coming to grips with Coercion and the terms of the nascent Second Land Act (which aimed at reducing the rents and increasing the political rights of impoverished tenant farmers in Ireland), police authorities were working on implementing the Home Secretary's directive to check the growth of Fenianism in London. Thanks to Vincent's role as head of this operation, Scotland Yard was now host to an embryonic Irish bureau (distinct from the later Irish Branch at Scotland Yard) in charge of monitoring 'Fenian movements [and the] proceedings of the Irish population' in the metropolis.[18] What this meant in practice was, however, far removed from any actual system of surveillance and intelligence gathering as several police reports from February and March of that year reveal. One, for example, detailed the patrolling of the area around Finsbury Barracks by four PCs in uniform as well as 'two PCs in plain clothes on the opposite side of the road [in order] to [better] follow any person who might commit any offence'.[19] Another described how 'a PS and a PC… employed in plain clothes… for about 10 days to make enquiries re alleged Fenianism' failed to obtain any 'information whatever on the subject',[20] while yet another concluded disappointedly that 'having made quiet enquiry at Public Houses in the vicinity of St. Dominic's Priory… [no] information [was gained] as to who posted the Placard [advertising a meeting on Ireland and the Land Question]'.[21]

Harcourt may have been bragging to Queen Victoria about his 'spider's web of Police Communication… woven throughout the United Kingdom… the centre of which is in my office',[22] but in early 1881 valuable information on Fenian activities was still only coming in thanks to Robert Anderson's man in America and the news was not good. In a report dated 17 February, Henri Le Caron warned that 'the whole current of opinion is that something is to be done, that the L[and] L[eague] money will not be used for bread but lead' and that O'Donovan Rossa was actively seeking funds for 'his affair of skirmishing', boasting that with five thousand dollars he would 'have England down on her knees'. Le Caron concluded that 'no one but a very few believe in him',[23] but as the Salford explosion had already demonstrated, those who did believe in Rossa's message were fanatically devoted and eager to prove themselves.

On the night of 16 March, a gunpowder bomb targeting the Lord Mayor's house was serendipitously defused by a passing City constable on the beat. The identity of the unknown perpetrators became once again a matter of speculation, but the intent of the outrage was clearly political. Although himself an Irishman of humble origins, the Lord Mayor William McArthur had voted for Coercion, causing an uproar among his mostly Irish constituents in Lambeth. Just as important, perhaps, was the fact that Mansion House – as the symbolic heart of the City of London – stood as an ideal representation of the financial and political power of the government; the fact that an opulent banquet had been scheduled to take place that same night (hastily cancelled only at the last moment) would have only increased its appeal as a target.

The subsequent investigation into the attempted bombing did not last long. Surprisingly, detectives of the City of London police force (established in 1839 and separate from the Metropolitan Police) received an important lead early on indicating that three American Fenians – Thomas Mooney, Edward O'Donnell and Patrick Coleman – were very likely implicated in the plot. By the time the press got wind of the new developments, however, the three men had already bolted for friendlier shores – O'Donnell and Coleman back to America and Mooney to Paris, where a secret rapprochement between IRBers and

Parnellites had just taken place.[24] A group of City detectives was sent after them, but to no avail. The sense of failure was only compounded when it transpired, as *The Standard* pointed out on 28 March, that Coleman had managed to abscond on a steamer bound for New York just in the nick of time, leaving a file of tugboats filled with frustrated City policemen in his wake.[25]

Meanwhile, Metropolitan detectives remained conspicuously absent from the investigation and did not even seem aware of the City Commissioner's (unsuccessful) efforts of having Coleman extradited to Britain on a charge of arson, as a Home Office memo from late March reveals.[26] After being told by Vincent that Mooney (arguably the most important of the three fugitives) had escaped, the choleric Harcourt exploded in an angry tirade, exclaiming that 'The police are no use at all!' and that he would 'dismiss the whole of them to-morrow morning'.[27] The new Irish Bureau was off to a decidedly rocky start.

The Lord Mayor's banquet had been cancelled a day before the Mansion House incident as a mark of respect for the bereaved Imperial House of Russia, which was mourning the death of Czar Alexander II, who had been assassinated on 13 March in St Petersburg by Nihilist bombs. The Czar's death was in fact very much on the minds of all Londoners in the early spring of 1881, especially those with strong views on Russia's autocratic government, and few people at the time had stronger views, on Russia as well as everything else, than the young German socialist Johann Most, who had been exiled in London since 1878, following the introduction of repressive anti-socialist legislation in Germany. Out of his makeshift printing shop at 101 Great Titchfield Street, Most published and edited the weekly *Freiheit*, a publication reminiscent of O'Donovan Rossa's *United Irishman* in its frequent calls to revolutionary violence, but one which remained virtually unknown outside of London's German-speaking left-wing diaspora.

That comfortable anonymity came to a sudden end on 19 March when Most submitted to his readers a personal interpretation of the assassination in St Petersburg stuffed with the most inflammatory bile he was capable of. It ran:

> At last!... Triumph! Triumph!... One of the most abominable tyrants of Europe, to whom downfall has long since been sworn, and who therefore, in wild revenge-breathings caused innumerable heroes and heroines of the Russian people to be destroyed or imprisoned – the Emperor of Russia is no more. On Sunday last, at noon, just as the Monster was returning from one of those diversions... one calls Military Reviews, the Executioner of the people... overtook and with vigorous hand settled the brute. [News of the event] penetrated into princely palaces where dwell those crime-beladen abortions of every profligacy who long since have earned a similar fate a

thousandfold [and who now] tremble… from Constantinople to Washington, for their long since forfeited heads.

Most then went on to praise the recent failed attempts on Kaiser Wilhelm I as well as the Nihilist policy of assassination (termed *propagande par le fait* in France), decrying only the 'rarity of so-called tyrannicide'. If only, he concluded, 'a single crowned wretch were disposed of every month, in a short time it should afford no one gratification henceforward still to play the monarch'.[28]

Although subtlety was arguably the only victim of Most's 'empty shrieking',[29] his hearty encouragement to would-be tyrannicides proved embarrassing and unnerving to the government. Embarrassing because of the criticism routinely levelled at Britain in continental cabinets and journals for its allegedly indiscriminate protection of dangerous revolutionaries[30] and because of Britain's own criticisms of the United States' refusal to clamp down on the activities of American Fenians. Unnerving because in an age of dynamite bombs, which the new decade promised to become, seditious talk praising the assassination of ruling sovereigns was no longer a trivial matter; and because Most, if held to account, could easily become another Simon Bernard,[31] providing an impetus to a new wave of populist outrage and potentially endangering all of Harcourt's plans for a new system of political policing in Britain.

How exactly authorities were made aware of Most's incendiary article is a matter of speculation. Almost as it was coming off the press, British newspapers were announcing that the 'social democratic organ *Freiheit*… appears to-day, with a red border, and contains articles exulting in the Czar's murder'[32] and within a day of its publication Queen Victoria herself was asking Gladstone (through her personal secretary Henry Ponsonby) whether a paper like *Freiheit* 'should be tolerated in the United Kingdom'.[33] This was followed, a couple of days later, by a private meeting between the German ambassador, Count Münster, and the Foreign Secretary Lord Granville in which the former formally registered his government's displeasure and, problematically for Her Majesty's Government, asked that proceedings be taken against Most and his paper.[34]

The Bernard case would certainly have been on Harcourt's mind as he contemplated the least compromising course of action – the Home Secretary had been one of those young Radicals who were most vociferous in upholding Bernard's right of asylum[35] – but all things considered, the incentive for prosecution was proving hard to resist. On 25 March Scotland Yard tasked one Charles Edward Marr, a German-language teacher from South Kensington who by his own admission had 'lived a long time in Russia [and] Germany', with acquiring four copies of the incriminating issue of *Freiheit* from Most's printing shop in west London. Marr did so promptly, felt 'very much disgusted both with the tenor... and the tendency' of Most's 'tyrannicide article' and consequently reported the findings to his local MP, Lord George Hamilton.[36] This somewhat tenuous ploy – Marr admitted he had had no previous knowledge of *Freiheit* and insisted he had acquired the four copies merely to satisfy his own curiosity after discussions with an unnamed friend – served a very important purpose for the government: it concealed both any connection to foreign powers like Germany, as well as the existence of any endemic political police, which, despite the looming Fenian threat, remained a markedly contentious issue in public discourse.

A day after Marr's 'discovery', Harcourt wrote a short letter to his Permanent Secretary, Adolphus Liddell, outlining not only his intentions regarding Most but also his future plans for dealing with the likes of Most:

> Dear Liddell,
>
> The Cabinet has decided that the Article in the *Freiheit* shall be prosecuted.[37] I have written to the A[ttorney] G[eneral] accordingly. Will you give directions that the copies of the *Freiheit* of this week published I believe yesterday should be obtained. H. Ponsonby has written to me on the subject of a Communistic Meeting printed in the Telegraph where most atrocious doctrines were proclaimed. I have said we can do nothing as we have no authentic record but these meetings should be looked after for the future. Tell the Police to look after them. There will probably be advertisements of them in the *Freiheit* and other papers of the kind.
>
> WVH.[38]

Its brevity notwithstanding, this letter marks an important step in Harcourt's consolidation of his counter-subversive strategy. By having Liddell 'tell the Police to look after' the revolutionary socialists – who were incidentally about to become more visible than usual in the metropolis owing to an international conference of revolutionary socialists scheduled to take place there in July – Harcourt was giving official expression to the as yet unexplored possibility that the operations of the inchoate Irish bureau might be expanded to cover seditious activities of all types, not just Fenianism.

The government did not succeed in obscuring the international dimension of the Most case for long. A few days after the cabinet's decision to go ahead with the prosecution, London newspapers were already reporting, based on intelligence from the continent, that 'strong representations have already been made in London to the Queen's Ministers, impressing upon them the necessity of [undertaking] the prosecution of the *Freiheit*, and in Paris at least... it is thought impossible that the demand should be refused.'[39]

As the subsequent trial transcript shows, such accounts made Most increasingly fearful and he may well have suspected something nefarious when on 29 March a strange young man walked into his shop asking for copies of the 'red border' issue of *Freiheit* in heavily accented German. There were none left in stock, but Most, anticipating a swelling in demand, had had a special batch of copies made just of the tyrannicide article, of which his client – a plainclothes Metropolitan constable – received two.[40]

The following afternoon Most's suspicions were confirmed beyond all doubt. A group of uniformed Scotland Yard detectives headed by Inspector Charles Hagan, himself a native German, walked through the door at 101 Great Titchfield Street and promptly announced to Most, in English and German, that he was being placed under arrest on account of his article on the Russian Emperor. Although the warrant issued to Hagan did not authorize him to seize any of Most's property,[41] the inspector was under direct orders from Howard Vincent to do just that.[42] Of particular import were Most's personal pocket books (containing encryption codes, the names, addresses and even photographs of many associates), the 'enormous quantity' of documents and literature present on the shop premises and the printing type – all of which were taken immediately to Scotland Yard and 'sealed up'.[43]

The purpose of the raid was arguably to add to the government's own files on London's budding anarchist scene – which had been rapidly swelling in recent years as a consequence of the French anti-Communard and German Anti-Socialist laws – but as Vincent explained in a letter to Harcourt, the quality of the intelligence gleaned from Most's documents made the collection a highly valuable asset to 'the several countries interested', mainly Germany and Austria.[44]

That the raid was illegal was not in doubt even by the Director of Public Prosecutions, Augustus K. Stephenson, who on 1 April observed in a memo to the Home Office how 'the police often necessarily in the proper discharge of their duties commit acts which are said to be illegal, inasmuch as there may be no statutable authority for such acts'.[45] Despite some frail opposition from unlikely quarters – Lord Randolph Churchill, for example, demanded to know 'under what Law or Statue [Most had been] arrested, deprived of his watch, money, bank book, and letters'[46] – the controversial aspects of the *Freiheit* case, most of which were widely publicized,[47] failed, however, to elicit anything resembling the populist furore that the Bernard trial had inspired a generation before.

The national press was predictably divided over the need for prosecution with most Liberal and Radical newspapers, as well as the Conservative *Times* and *Globe*, being opposed to it, not so much on libertarian as on practical and patriotic grounds. A trial, *The Times* argued, would only afford a life-giving notoriety to the *Freiheit*'s 'miserable trash' and further taint Harcourt's protestations in the House of Commons (that the government was not acting at the behest of foreign powers) with the stink of *qui s'excuse s'accuse*.[48] Such arguments aside, there was virtually no sympathy for the accused himself outside of socialist and anarchist circles and occasionally there was even open hostility, as in the case of the meeting held in Southwark on 10 April by a group of Most's comrades, all of whom had to be rescued by local police from an angry mob threatening to lynch them.[49]

A month and a half later, on 25 May, Most finally stood trial at the Old Bailey on fifteen counts of libel and 'encouraging [and] endeavouring to persuade... persons unknown... to murder the Sovereigns and Rulers of Europe', with special reference to the Russian and German emperors.[50] His defence counsel (and Nationalist MP for County Meath), Alexander M. Sullivan, was eloquent but inexperienced and plagued by ill health. His cross-examination of key witnesses, especially Charles Marr and the detectives involved in Most's arrest, proved timid and did nothing to underline the controversial, never mind illegal, aspects of the case, while his address to the jury, though pithy in its appeal to 'English principles', ultimately fell on deaf ears.

Most was found guilty on all counts and given sixteen months with hard labour. His name had barely impacted British public opinion and was thereafter all but forgotten. His arrest and prosecution, however, did set an important precedent, and, as we shall see later on, provided the government with a template of sorts for dealing with similar cases of politically motivated libel. More importantly perhaps, the aftermath of the Most case arguably marked the first stage in the government's program of surveillance of non-Fenian radicals – a program that within six years evolved into a separate branch of the Metropolitan Police – entrenching Britain's approach to foreign pressure on the issue of subversion.

As official correspondence from the Home Office file on Most reveals, *Freiheit* continued to remain under close observation until 1883 (when Most took it with him to America) even as 'very little allusion... concerning England' appeared in its pages.[51] At the same time, Harcourt was eager to use the intelligence extracted from Most to assuage critics of Britain's lax immigration and free speech laws (in October of that year Viennese authorities, acting on information received from Britain, arrested fifteen people suspected of distributing

## HOW DO THEY LIKE IT THEMSELVES?

APOSTLES OF VIOLENCE. — "Begob, the Flag has gone back on us!"

2. Detail of an American satirical drawing showing Jeremiah O'Donovan-Rossa (left) and Johann Most (right) trying to escape the very violence they are urging others to commit. *Puck*, 1885 (Library of Congress, Prints & Photographs Division).

*Freiheit*) and as a means of eschewing recent continental plans for international cooperation against Russian nihilists and other revolutionaries. As the Home Secretary explained in a letter to the queen, 'The most effective way to avert the pressure of Foreign Govmnts [*sic*] to alter our laws is to demonstrate that those laws are adequate to give the protection which all Govmnts have the right to demand of their friends and neighbours.'[52] In this context, Most's conviction was 'equal to joining the Nihilist Conference.'[53]

CHAPTER 2

# 'Panic and indifference'[1]

Harcourt had good reason to feel jubilant over the outcome of the Most trial and the recent passing of his Irish Arms Bill, which outlawed the possession of firearms and explosives and gave Irish authorities unrestricted powers of search and seizure. For the Scotland Yard detectives working to implement the Home Secretary's anti-Fenian strategy, however, the summer of 1881 proved an exceedingly difficult and frustrating period. In the words of one CID inspector, '[to] state that every possible resource at the disposal of the Criminal Investigation Department was taxed to its very utmost, [would be to put], even then, the matter very mildly indeed',[2] an impression confirmed by Vincent himself, who later recalled the 'almost daily crop of false alarms and more or less circumstantial report of plots, all of which had to be sifted'.[3]

Not all alarms proved false, however. On 10 April Robert Anderson received a missive from the American consul in Philadelphia, Captain Robert Clipperton, warning of intelligence received from 'different secret sources' which strongly suggested that bombings of 'public buildings' on Merseyside would be attempted shortly.[4] Security at the Port of Liverpool was increased as a consequence, but all the same, in early May a gunpowder bomb rocked the Militia Barracks in Chester and in less than a fortnight, a similar device went off in the outer doorway of a police section house in Liverpool's Hatton Garden.[5] Although neither explosion succeeded in inflicting injuries or serious damage to property, they managed to spread fear amongst the general public, cementing the notion that Rossa's skirmishers were out to do as much damage as possible on the British mainland.

On 10 June, less than a month after the Hatton Garden explosion, Liverpool became yet again the target of an attempted bombing, this time aimed at City Hall. It too failed to do any real harm if only because of the audacity of three local constables, one of whom dragged the bag holding the 'infernal machine' – a dynamite-charged, pipe-shaped device – into the middle of an adjacent street, where it exploded; and the incompetence of the bombers themselves, who, though armed, were easily apprehended and taken into custody following a short foot chase.[6] That the assailants were connected with the Fenian conspiracy was made abundantly clear when one of them, James McGrath, was revealed to be 'the direct agent for the sale of an incendiary publication belonging to... O'Donovan Rossa... bundles [of which] had been left at his [i.e. McGrath's] lodgings'.[7] Both McGrath and his accomplice, a young Ulsterman by the name of James McKevitt, were ultimately found guilty and given harsh sentences of penal servitude for life and fifteen years respectively.

Despite the failure of this initial wave of attacks to achieve anything in the way of 'bringing England to her knees', it was becoming increasingly obvious to authorities in London that Rossa's men were not about to let up in their efforts. Days after the failed attack on Liverpool City Hall, Harcourt was informed that Inspector Maurice Moser, the Scotland Yard man on Fenian duty in the port-city,[8] had made a startling discovery: several cement barrels shipped from Boston, Massachusetts were found to each contain 'a fully-charged infernal machine, fitted with the usual clockwork apparatus [and] an eleven ounce cartridge of dynamite'.[9]

They had been consigned to a fictitious establishment in Hackins Hey and were only spotted after Moser noticed 'the word "Boston"... roughly painted on each cask in black' was spelled with a telltale crossed-out 't' on eight of them.[10] Harcourt was dismayed but also intrigued. Moser received instructions to bring the bombs down to London where they were privately shown to the Home Secretary and 'many members of the House of Peers' and subsequently used by 'Government experts' under the direction of Her Majesty's Chief Inspector of Explosives, Colonel Vivian Majendie, in 'several experiments [which] undoubtedly demonstrated that each of the machines was of the latest and most improved construction'.[11]

More intriguing than the bombs themselves, however, was the possibility that they might be used as political leverage against the American government, especially in the context of the recent assassination of President James Garfield, an event which Harcourt believed would 'considerably modify the views of Lowell[12] and Blaine[13] on the subject of political murder... confirm[ing] those who think us right and confound[ing] those who have been disposed to ridicule our alarms'.[14]

Lowell and Blaine did not hesitate to promise that the US Government would investigate the source of the Boston barrels[15] and 'make every possible exertion to... bring to justice' those responsible.[16] In reality, American officials (including Lowell himself) tended to blame the excesses of the Irish agitation on Britain's authoritarian measures in Ireland, while Congress, under the sway of a substantial Irish American electorate, proved openly contemptuous of Britain's Irish policy.[17] Meanwhile, the Home Office was once again receiving news from Captain Clipperton that ten more bomb-carrying barrels had been shipped to Britain and that 'fifteen others [are] to be delivered to conspirators next week'. Clipperton's informer, a double agent working for O'Donovan Rossa as an explosives specialist, was even able to confirm the identity of the man responsible for shipping the bombs[18] and warned that the Fenians were now planning to use 'coal torpedoes' (iron castings filled with dynamite and made to look like common lumps of coal) to sabotage British ships – information which was seemingly confirmed separately by other informers.[19]

Harcourt and his under-secretaries thought the story of dynamite hidden in coal 'nonsense',[20] but the duplicity of the American Government on the issue of Fenian agitation coupled with the Fenians' own zeal for developing what Johann Most termed a 'scientific' arsenal[21] only further inflamed the Home Secretary's characteristic nervousness.[22] For the rest of the summer he remained in 'unceasing correspondence with Vincent and Scotland Yard as to the various outrages and threatened outrages',[23] even as no new incidents were being reported.

Rossa's skirmishing campaign may have suffered a temporary setback with the arrest of the Liverpool bombers and the interception of explosives coming in from America, but on the whole the mainstream of the American Fenian movement, as represented by the Clan na Gael, was only just beginning to seriously entertain the notion of unleashing a concerted campaign of terror in Britain. Frustrated with the stagnancy of the New Departure program (which sought to find middle ground between Home Rulers and insurrectionists) and mindful of Rossa's newfound notoriety, the movement's leading figures came together in early August in Chicago to discuss change. Also in attendance was Major Le Caron, whose vivid reports to Anderson described the proceedings of this 'Great Dynamite Convention' in fascinating detail. The most notable developments were on the one hand the unanimous decision to devote all future efforts to 'the work of revolution' and on the other the initiation of a new 'regime' within the Clan na Gael, one dominated by fiery insurrectionists like Alexander Sullivan (the Clan's new leader) and dynamite enthusiasts like Dr Thomas Gallagher, who 'expressed his willingness to personally undertake the carriage of dynamite to England and to superintend its use there' (a plan which Gallagher saw through to fruition only a couple of years later).[24]

Le Caron was also able to confirm the absolute failure of Coercion in deterring militant nationalists from joining the ranks of the Fenian conspiracy. As he candidly told his handler at the Home Office: 'action of late on your side… has not [stamped] out the movement [but] has increased it one hundred fold. [Timothy] Healy… has confirmed everything I have heard and [seen] as to the ultimate object in view. He says before two years E[ngland] will be down on her knees.'[25] Healy, a pro-Fenian Parnellite, was widely known for his acerbic and bombastic manner even in the House of Commons (where he stood as the member for Wexford), but he was far from an isolated voice in his inexorable opposition to the British government.

Parnell himself was now at daggers drawn with Gladstone after the passage of the Second Land Act, which promised to finally grant Irish tenants the so-called Three Fs: fixity of tenure, fair rents and free sale. Although the reasons for Parnell's hostility had less to do with the Act itself and more with his desire to keep the nationalist agitation aflame and maintain his own revolutionary credentials,[26] the logic of Coercion dictated that his provocations could not go unpunished. On 12 October Gladstone met with his ministers and after five hours of discussions decided that Parnell would be arrested.[27] The following day the Irish leader was apprehended at Morrison's Hotel in Dublin and taken to the nearby Kilmainham gaol. A week afterwards the Land League was declared illegal.

Coercion, however, was beginning to come apart at the seams as agrarian violence in Ireland continued to increase steadily over the winter months[28] and by early spring 1882, Gladstone had turned against the policy with the same sudden zeal he later embraced Home Rule. After negotiating a truce with Parnell in late April that technically secured Nationalist support for the Liberal Party, the premier had his erstwhile nemesis discharged, much to the chagrin of Forster and Earl Cowper (the Lord Lieutenant of Ireland) both of whom promptly resigned. They were replaced by Lord Frederick Cavendish and John Poyntz Spencer, the fifth Earl Spencer, respectively.

Lord Frederick Cavendish had no special knowledge of Irish matters but was supremely well-born – being the Duke of Devonshire's youngest son and Gladstone's own nephew-in-law – and unenthusiastically accepted his uncle's nomination, making his way over to Dublin where, on the morning of 6 May 1882, he was received to some acclaim by local loyalists and sworn in as the new Chief Secretary. Later that day, Cavendish decided to walk from Dublin Castle to the Viceregal Lodge in Phoenix Park in the company of his new permanent secretary, Thomas Burke, a man who had survived a number of Chief Secretaries as well as many assassination plots in his thirteen years of holding that office.

Several accounts later confirmed the two were leisurely walking through the park on what was a pleasant, warm spring evening, conversing on affairs of state (in particular Forster's Coercion policy), when, without notice, they were ambushed by a group of seven men armed with long surgical knives. The easily recognizable Burke fell almost immediately under a series of deadly blows which left him collapsed on the side of the road in a pool of his own blood. The horrified Cavendish, who may or may not have been known to the attackers, made a pitiable attempt at self-defence, but was also soon struck down with a ferocity that nearly amputated his left arm. In a final act of murderous rage one of the killers decided to 'finish off' the likely already dead Burke by slitting his throat before joining his confreres in the getaway coach waiting nearby. Cavendish was still breathing, but died within the hour.[29]

The impact the Phoenix Park assassinations had on Irish politics and Anglo-Irish relations is difficult to exaggerate. Almost overnight the promises of the Kilmainham Treaty were nullified and the stage was set for a new wave of coercive measures. Despite outspoken and unequivocal condemnations of the murders from virtually all quarters of Nationalist opinion (including Fenians on both sides of the Atlantic, with the predictable exception of O'Donovan Rossa), the palpable sense of outrage rapidly gripping British politicians and opinion-makers was not easily dispelled. 'Mr. Gladstone's latest message of peace has met a prompt and terrible response', warned the *Morning Advertiser*; 'the challenge of rebellion should be taken up and there must be no more faltering and paltering' urged the *Post*. Even the staunchly Liberal *Daily News* refused to pull any punches in calling for the extermination of 'the secret assassins, the pests of society, the enemies of the human race'.[30]

Gladstone's opposition to Coercion did not waver, but his grip over the party and the cabinet was significantly loosened by the events in Dublin and even though Forster did not return to his former duties (Cavendish being replaced by Sir George Trevelyan as Chief Secretary), coercive policies for Ireland found an ardent and unrelenting champion in none other than Sir William Harcourt. After his early experiments with policing Fenianism in England, the Home Secretary was more convinced than ever that 'nothing helps so much to break up gangs of conspirators as the terror of being known to meet together to plot.'[31] Thus, on 11 May Harcourt introduced a new Coercion Bill – officially the Prevention of Crime (Ireland) Bill – which, its nominal toleration of habeas corpus notwithstanding, proved in some ways just as draconian as the old legislation, suspending trial by jury for a host of crimes, granting police powers of arrest without warrant or probable cause and outlawing all, liberally defined, 'unlawful associations'. Despite some frail opposition from progressive Liberals and sections of the press, the House carried the bill by 327 votes (of which twenty-seven came from Irish members) to twenty-two.

The day following the bill's introduction Harcourt's resolve was further strengthened by a fresh attempt to blow up the Lord Mayor's House. By all accounts the effort had been an unusually poor one consisting as it did of a canister of gunpowder mixed in with some dynamite and carelessly placed in the most visible, 'the least vulnerable and the most massive part of the building'. No one was ultimately able to deduce whether this had been one of Rossa's skirmishers rushing things through again, an ill-advised anonymous copycat, or merely a tasteless prank, but there is little doubt Harcourt and Vincent took this incident, along with the host of incoming fresh rumours 'of an exceedingly grave and suspicious character',[32] as powerful omens.

Harcourt confessed to Earl Spencer that he believed 'the attempted explosion at the Mansion House [to be] a Fenian scare of the old clumsy kind', noting, however, that real terrorism 'may be imported any day either from America or Ireland'.[33] Two days later, London itself seemed to be getting a taste of Coercion after scores of Scotland Yard detectives were seen 'on the look-out for suspected persons', going so far as to break up a crowd of about three hundred workingmen who had assembled near Charing Cross Underground station to arrange a foot-race.[34]

Meanwhile, in Ireland, the apparent failure of Superintendent Mallon's 'army of informers' to identify the Phoenix Park assassins,[35] coupled with what Spencer regarded as the general incompetence and venality of the Irish police spelled out a case for reform that London could no longer afford to ignore. In late May Colonel Henry Brackenbury, a Flashmanesque figure known to his superiors for his fickle egotism as much as for his administrative talents,[36] was sent over to Dublin to act as the new Assistant Under-Secretary for Police and Crime.

In effect, Brackenbury served as Spencer's 'Irish Vincent' and had free rein to do all the things that Vincent could not afford to do in Liberal England.[37] As *The Standard*'s Dublin correspondent explained, this Irish CID was to fulfill two missions: the first was to assume charge of Ireland's entire police forces, making all magistrates and commissioners report to Brackenbury's Dublin Castle office and giving Dublin detectives the power to follow 'the investigation of cases into any part of Ireland' and arrest people 'outside the metropolitan district without being compelled to get the permission of [local] constabulary authorities'. The second mission was to employ 'men of superior education', unspoiled by the barracks mentality, who would be able to 'disguise the fact that [they were] in any way connected with the police'.[38]

Brackenbury, whose previous assignment had been to reorganize the colonial police in Cyprus, appeared to embrace his new duties with good grace, proposing a massive funding increase of over £20,000. London grumbled, but Spencer was adamant that anything less than £5,000 would be self-defeating, pleading with Gladstone that if the government was to win the war against the forces of disorder it would have to face up to the fact that 'the forces to which we are opposed are very powerful and supplied with large sums of money. If [Brackenbury] succeeds the cost will be nothing compared to the work performed.'[39] Harcourt too was eager to lend material support, going so far as to inquire into the possibility of having 'the Pinkerton detective agency in the United States send over to Ireland one of their best confidential agents to communicate with [Brackenbury] on their methods of proceeding'.[40]

The Pinkertons did not have to wait for any requests from London to make their views known. In early July Gladstone received a letter from the Scottish-born Allan Pinkerton, in which the veteran spymaster described in fascinating detail his own theories on intelligence gathering, outlining at the same time the differences between the British and the American systems. The British detective force, Pinkerton thought, was over all made up of 'first class, intelligent men'; the problem was the network of informers they relied on. As he went on to explain:

> My opinion is that [informers] should be as honest as their employers, and this, I understand, is not generally the case [in Britain]... Great caution should [therefore] be exercised... in selecting the men and women – and women are very necessary... – for this branch of service. In my own Agencies I employ both sexes and of almost every age and it is astonishing [how] undeveloped talents will sometimes rise to the surface when the opportunities occur... As... the criminal may be a political malcontent or a gentlemanly assassin all grades of society must have their representatives. [Once acquired, this] well drilled force [should] scatter... through the larger cities of the United States... [and] gain admittance to [the various American Fenian societies], and by that means the hidden mysteries of these unlawful conclaves will be fully divulged.[41]

Such a bold scheme, which eerily presaged twentieth-century political policing with its wide-reaching scope and emphasis on specialism, received a predictably unenthusiastic response from the Home Office's experienced Fenian hunters. Anderson and E. M. Archibald (Britain's long-serving consul in New York) both agreed it would be a waste of time and, more importantly, money.[42] Harcourt himself, for all his love of well-schooled and obedient informers, was not exactly brimming with enthusiasm either.[43] In any case, the government now had more pressing matters to consider than a new methodology of snooping. A little over a month after assuming his post Brackenbury rashly decided to abandon it (hoping for a return to military glories) much to the outrage of anyone who had placed any degree of trust in him.[44] Dublin Castle's plans for reform were now faltering, police were nowhere nearer to learning the identities of the Phoenix Park gang and to make matters worse, London Fenians appeared to be once again on the move, if the recent seizure of a sizeable arms cache in Clerkenwell – 'a fortunate capture [which] will make a great stir'[45] – was anything to go by.

To avoid getting stuck with another mercurial soldier of fortune, Spencer decided to give Brackenbury's job to one of the most 'loyal, earnest and trustworthy'[46] people he could think of: his own private secretary at Dublin Castle, Edward George Jenkinson. A refined, forward-looking mandarin who had spent twenty-six years in the Indian Civil Service, Jenkinson had only been in Spencer's employ for a couple of months, but his solid administrative experience, keen interest in Irish politics and unblemished pedigree (he was the nephew of Sir George Grey, the Whig Home Secretary in the 1840s and 1850s) recommended him above all other candidates. Furthermore, despite Spencer's initial uneasiness with Jenkinson's low public profile, the latter proved in fact ideally obscure given the more controversial aspects of his new office. Some Irish MPs grumbled that 'an official who had been trained in the despotic school of Indian officialism was no proper person to be employed in a post of responsibility in a country like Ireland',[47] but Irish papers were less certain what to make of him. The Nationalist *Freeman's Journal* thought that 'he is just one more Englishman added to the powers that be [and it] makes little or no matter'.[48] As subsequent events showed, Jenkinson was in fact far from a brutish *sahib* and even further from a typical Dublin Castle stick-in-the-mud.

Although he had accepted his nomination with a sort of docile eagerness – 'he is strongly in favour of working with what we have got', Spencer told Trevelyan[49] – Ireland's new chief law enforcer did not wait long to make his reforming zeal known. Spurred on by the slow progress of Superintendent Mallon's investigations and the evidence that new conspiracies were in the making, Jenkinson prepared a memorandum for Spencer in late autumn 1882 in which he straightforwardly asked his boss, 'Are we to wait for the commission of another murder before we proceed against any of these assassins?… Knowing what is going on', he continued, 'are we to content ourselves with collecting information?… I think we are bound to take some vigorous action and if the present law fails us, we ought to apply to Parliament for powers which will enable us to destroy these assassination societies.'[50]

The law did in fact already provide for 'vigorous action' as Jenkinson realized shortly after writing that memorandum. His suggestion became to prod Dublin Castle into making good use of Section 16 of the new Crimes Bill, which granted Irish magistrates the power to question under oath anyone who might be in possession of evidence pertaining to a criminal investigation.[51] The measure was adopted and its immediate effect was that the conspiracy of the so-called National Invincibles, as the Phoenix Park murderers had styled themselves, began to unravel. On 13 January sixteen of them were arrested in a major police raid and put behind bars in Kilmainham Gaol. In less than a month eight of them were formally charged with having feloniously, willfully and of malice aforethought murdered Lord Frederick Cavendish and Thomas Henry Burke.

3. Edward G. Jenkinson, ca. 1900 (*Grace's Guide to British Industrial History*).

The situation looked less encouraging in Britain where Fenian bombs were about to make a spectacular return to national headlines. The first strike came on the night of 20 January when shortly after 10.00 p.m. one of the gas holders of Glasgow's Tradeston Gasworks exploded like a Roman candle, sending off a vicious fiery cyclone through the streets of the city's Pollokshields neighbourhood, damaging many houses without, however, claiming any fatalities. This was followed, three hours later, by another explosion in the town's northern side. The target proved inexplicably, but happily, innocuous – a disused railway depot that had already been condemned – and material damage amounted to only 'a few pounds' with no injuries being reported.[52] A third and final explosion occurred further up north only a few minutes later when a group of passing young men accidentally set off a 'large travelling tin box' near the Forth and Clyde Canal, escaping only with minor wounds.[53] All three explosions were subsequently identified as the result of dynamite bombs.

The Home Office had likely expected an outrage in the north for some time judging by the report Le Caron had sent Anderson shortly after the Phoenix Park murders, warning of a 'large haul of arms in or near Glasgow',[54] but as in the case of the Liverpool bombings, local authorities had proved unable to predict the dynamitards' intended target. There was also somewhat less interest in the skirmishing campaign in Whitehall, as evidenced by Harcourt's quip that 'Rossa has so long sworn to take my life that I have almost ceased to believe in him.'[55]

This was partly because the government's 'attitude... to political crime' alternated to a large extent, as Anderson later noted, somewhere 'between panic and indifference'[56] and partly because of the engrossing revelations coming out of Dublin which seemed to suggest what the proponents of Coercion had believed all along, namely that the Phoenix Park assassins had more than likely been in communication (if not in collusion) with the Land League, now reconstituted as the Irish National League.[57] Thanks to the wealth of new information supplied by conspirator-turned-Queen's-Evidence James Carey, authorities now possessed the names of two individuals who could reliably be traced to the leadership of the Invincibles. The first was Frank Byrne, Secretary of the Land League's London chapter, who had funded much of the conspiracy and whose wife had smuggled the actual murder weapons into Dublin in her petticoats. The second man was initially described only as an anonymous stranger known to the Invincibles as 'No. 1' but subsequently identified by Carey, thanks to a police photograph, as Patrick J. Tynan, a 'needy and seedy commercial traveller'[58] with ties to London Fenianism.

By mid-February, however, when this knowledge came to light, the two supposed ringleaders had already managed to escape to France from where they proved frustratingly difficult to extract. Given the slight evidence of their complicity in the Phoenix Park murders (which was all contingent on Carey's confession), British pleas to have the two Irishmen extradited were unceremoniously cold-shouldered by French authorities,[59] while an attempted kidnapping in Cannes, headed by Inspector Moser of the Yard (posing as a spendthrift Polish count), failed miserably after one of Byrne's friends saw through the detective's disguise. Having successfully escaped France, the two Invincibles immediately took refuge in America where they evaded British law for the remainder of their lives, though Tynan briefly returned to public attention in Britain in the mid-1890s, as we shall see later.

Despite this embarrassing setback, the Phoenix Park conspiracy was soon overtaken in importance by an attack on the imperial capital itself. On 15 March, shortly after 9.00 p.m., members of Parliament heard a powerful noise, 'followed by a very perceptible shaking of the building', come from the vicinity of the square. As several MPs and peers who went out to investigate realized, the Local Government Board building had just been the target of a bomb attack and was quite visibly scathed with much of the adjoining Charles Street 'literally paved with plate-glass about a quarter of an inch thick'.[60] Only a few minutes after, amid the confusion of gaping crowds, drawn-up fire engines and nervous policemen, the news came in that a similar attempt had just been made on the *Times* building in Printing House Square.

No injuries or structural damage were reported (the *Times* bomb had only partially detonated), but the message was once again resoundingly clear: the terror had come to London in full force. As Colonel Majendie confirmed in his report on the explosions a few days later, the devices used – tin boxes filled with sawdust and nitroglycerine – were mechanically identical to those deployed in Glasgow only a month earlier. Crucially different, however, the London charges contained almost twice the amount of nitroglycerine – a substance 'not licensed for importation into or manufacture or storage in the United Kingdom'.[61]

Londoners were understandably alarmed. The press seized on what it saw as the indiscriminate and genuinely terroristic aspect of the attacks – 'the Clerkenwell conspirators had at least an intelligible object' – and argued that 'for the murder-clubs [only] intelligent police and incessant vigilance' would do,[62] a sentiment which was echoed by ordinary people, if only more forcefully. In a letter to the Home Secretary one London 'Liberal and workingman', for example, wondered if 'home rule (except on matters imperial)' would not be worth giving 'the blackguards... rather than subject ourselves to these continual scares', adding that 'if truth be told there is too much soft soap business with these scoundrels. Hang a few of the pirates... and you will find that is the best kind of education.'[63]

Harcourt himself was furious and though Home Rule could not have been further from his mind, he certainly agreed that drastic measures were needed; measures requiring plenty of time to implement. The cabinet was induced to agree to transfer some of the Home Secretary's duties over to Charles Dilke, the President of the besieged Local Government Board, who, while convinced that Harcourt was developing an unhealthy obsession with police work, eventually relented. With his more menial responsibilities out of the way, Harcourt could now concentrate on the next and most ambitious step yet: assembling a special unit of police officers wholly devoted to monitoring Irish republican activity in the capital.

The Special Irish Branch of the Metropolitan Police (technically Section B of CID) comprised twelve officers, hastily, but not haphazardly, recruited from that portion of the London constabulary and the CID most familiar with Irish issues (usually by virtue of being Irish and Catholic) and would take its orders from Frederick Adolphus 'Dolly' Williamson, Scotland Yard's veteran Chief Superintendent. On 19 March an internal Police Orders circular made everything official by announcing that:

> The following are authorized to be employed in plain clothes at the Central Office with departmental allowance, from 20th. To report themselves to Chief Supt. Williamson, at 10 am on the date named:-
>
> C [Division]. Inspector Pope
> M [Division]. PC 332 Foy
> D [Division]. PC 49 O'Sullivan
> R [Division]. Inspector Ahern
> E [Division]. PC 50 Walsh
> V [Division]. PS 3 Jenkins
> L [Division]. PC 224 McIntyre
> Y [Division]. PC 492 Thorp
>
> The following are also temporarily attached to the Central Office, and are to report themselves to Chief Superintendent at the same time:-
>
> H [Division]. PC CID Enright
> W [Division]. PS CID Melville[64]
> K [Division]. PC CID Enright
> TA [Division]. PS CID Regan.[65]

The 'political department', as its members often referred to it, was now born.

CHAPTER 3

# Mr Jenkinson goes to London

BESIDES the seemingly imminent danger posed to British cities by dynamite bombs, there was another reason for the Irish Branch coming into being when it did. It had to do with the acquiring and sharing of information, provisions for which, under the pre-17 March status quo, were dangerously out of date. Just how out of date is illustrated by the fact that British authorities, despite being well aware since the summer of 1882 that O'Donovan Rossa was running a bona fide 'dynamite college' out of Brooklyn, New York,[1] had in fact no idea that two of the school's 'graduates' (one of whom was Thomas Mooney, the original Mansion House bomber) were behind the recent attacks in Glasgow and London.[2]

In order to finally address the shortcomings of his 'spider's web', which in early 1883 included the CID's experimental counter-Fenian unit, Anderson's network of informers and sixteen RIC detectives stationed throughout Britain,[3] Harcourt decided to convene Anderson, Vincent and Williamson for an emergency meeting a day after unveiling the Irish Branch. Also in attendance was Spencer's rising new assistant, whose reforms had already produced such stellar results in Ireland.

The meeting was likely an awkward one. Anderson jealously guarded 'his' Home Office Secret Service[4] operations and had no intention of sharing his contacts. Vincent, independently wealthy thanks to a well-placed marriage, was growing altogether tired of police work and planned to resign. Williamson, although the most senior and experienced detective in the land, abhorred disguises, informers and anything smacking of secret policing and didn't think the new Fenians were as serious a threat as the old ones.[5] For his part, Jenkinson found the CID shambolic and amateurish, writing to Spencer that 'Anderson… at the Home Office is a poor fellow (a second class detective Sir W. [Harcourt] calls him!) and except Williamson there is not a man in Scotland Yard worth anything.'[6] Far from marking a mere professional disagreement, Jenkinson's comment gives us a preview of the endemic internecine squabbles that plagued the British political police throughout the rest of the 1880s (with often drastic consequences).

More importantly, it gives us an insight into Jenkinson's personality. Well before the 20 March meeting, in fact, Ireland's new chief law enforcer had – with Spencer's support, but without Harcourt's knowledge – already begun reorganizing British counter-terrorist operations in his own image. As early as late 1882, Jenkinson had seized on an opportunity provided by one of his established agents in New York to recruit one James McDermott (known as 'Red Jim' on account of his ginger moustache), an old comrade of Rossa and an occasional 'peddler of secrets' to Edward Archibald.[7]

McDermott's fee of £100 (the first of several payments) went into buying off Rossa's trust and the possibility that the money might actually be used to manufacture dynamite in Britain was very likely on Jenkinson's mind. Nevertheless, the opportunity of securing a line of communication into the very heart of the most committed section of the dynamite camp (which even Le Caron did not claim to provide) was too alluring to be trumped by ethical concerns. Less than a month after, in late January 1883, Red Jim was already going over the details of his next assignment with Jenkinson in a room at the Birkenhead Railway Hotel on Merseyside.[8] Emboldened by this latest success, it is little wonder that the rising spymaster found his counterparts in London rather moth-eaten and bureaucratic, his personal enmity towards Anderson notwithstanding.

For the moment, however, concord in Whitehall was secure thanks to the heightened sense of emergency and as news coming in from Liverpool suggested, the 'force party' were already well on their way to unleashing a new spate of dynamite attacks. It was in that city – which had of late seen its fair share of Fenian conspiracies – that several arrests were made in late March in connection with a dynamite factory set up in Cork by Timothy Featherstone (real name Edmund O'Brien Kennedy), a veteran of the 1860s Fenian campaigns and an associate of Rossa. Featherstone had temporarily set up shop in Glasgow over the summer and autumn of 1882, but after manufacturing the 'tin boxes' used in the Tradeston Gasworks and London outrages, had returned to Ireland. There he recruited a likeminded old-school Fenian and a Rossa man to boot.

Unfortunately for Featherstone, that man turned out to be Red Jim and it was not long after that authorities became aware not only of the dynamite factory, but also of Featherstone's plan to smuggle the end product back into Britain, via Liverpool, through a young accomplice, Denis Deasy – a plan which Red Jim likely suggested.[9] Deasy was summarily apprehended on 28 March shortly after disembarking in Liverpool and was found to be in possession of a box which he claimed contained cattle food. In reality, it contained lignodynamite, acids, chlorate of potash and 'several pieces of mechanism'.[10] Also on his person were papers bearing the name Patrick Flanagan (Deasy's contact in Liverpool), who was subsequently also arrested and searched.

Flanagan possessed a veritable arsenal of terroristic paraphernalia including loaded guns, assorted chemicals and fake beards. More importantly, however, he provided local CID detectives with the missing link that led back to Ireland: a letter addressed directly to Featherstone. News of the find was quickly telegraphed to the Cork RIC and the dynamite factory was raided. Featherstone and his men were then sent to Liverpool to await trial.

The arrest of the Featherstone gang provided Jenkinson with yet another triumph – 'Jenks has done splendidly' Harcourt noted in a letter to Spencer[11] – confirming the indispensability of well-funded, personally loyal informers who were brave, stupid or greedy enough to push things into agent provocateur territory. However, as the case concurrently unfurling in Birmingham (described below) proved, genuine dynamite conspiracies could easily thrive outside the reach of the paid spy.

In mid-March, Dr Thomas Gallagher, the Clan na Gael firebrand, landed in Britain with the intent of implementing the plan he had put forth at the 'Great Dynamite Convention' in Philadelphia two years earlier.[12] Just what the plan entailed was made clear to his associate William Norman (real name William Lynch) when the two visited the scene of the recent Local Government Board explosion. Asked by Norman if that was the sort of thing they were aiming for, Gallagher supposedly replied, 'Yes, but it won't be child's play', observing as they passed the House of Commons that 'this will make a great crash when it comes down', and further along, at Scotland Yard, that 'this will come down too'.[13]

Both Gallagher and Norman were part of a team assembled in America during the closing months of 1882 with the blessing of Alexander Sullivan, the Clan na Gael's leader. It was far from a Clan operation, however, given that several of Gallagher's men had been schooled in Brooklyn and that Rossa was bankrolling much of the expedition through his skirmishing fund.[14] The cell's centre of operations was Birmingham, where one of the conspirators, Albert Whitehead (real name John C. Murphy) was already established in an unobtrusive little shop in Leasham Street. There, under the guise of a painting-and-decoration establishment, Whitehead was patiently and meticulously applying himself to the creation of nitroglycerine.

On 28 March, just as Deasy and Flanagan were being arrested in Liverpool, Gallagher and Whitehead were finalizing their sinister plan in Birmingham. The operation was doomed before it even started, however. Only the previous day, Whitehead's local chemist had casually let slip in a conversation with his friend Richard Price (a sergeant in the Birmingham police force) that the new painter-decorator in Leasham Street seemed more than a tad suspicious. Not only did Whitehead speak with an unmistakable Irish American accent, but he kept demanding large quantities of the purest grade glycerine, something no legitimate painter required, and displayed a raggedness that suggested a constant handling of dangerous acids. Sergeant Price decided to report the lead to his superiors and was given permission to investigate.

By 4 April, the day that two of Gallagher's helpers arrived in Birmingham to fetch the stuff that was to bring down the Houses of Parliament, local police were certain beyond all doubt that dynamite-making was now one of the city's famous thousand trades. The two Fenians, now in possession of substantial batches of nitroglycerine (contained in rubber receptacles), made their way from Whitehead's shop to the Birmingham New Street train station under the close surveillance of Birmingham and RIC detectives. One of the dynamite runners, a twenty-three-year-old native of the Isle of Wight going by the name of Henry Wilson, managed to board a train unobserved, but the other man, William Norman, was surreptitiously followed all the way to London by three of the detectives.

Meanwhile, in London, Irish Branch detectives were tracking down new leads in connection with the 15 March explosions while keeping watch on a certain Henry Dalton (real name John Henry O'Connor), fingered by Dublin Castle as a member of the Featherstone gang.[15] On the afternoon of 4 April PCs McIntyre and Enright together with Sergeants Melville and Regan reported that:

> [Dalton has] left Pond Place and proceeded by Piccadilly to Brewer Street, Soho, but did not call at any house there; then to the American Reading Rooms, 14 Strand, where he left at 4.15 p.m. and then proceeded to the… Albert Embankment by St. Thomas' Hospital [where] he leant on the parapet of the embankment, took out a paper and appeared to be surveying the Houses of Parliament at the same time making notes onto the paper.[16]

The suspicion that Dalton was now involved in some new plot was only strengthened by the telegram received that evening from Birmingham warning of two young Fenians set to arrive at Euston station that night with trunkfuls of nitroglycerine. The officer on duty at the Yard immediately sent word to Irish Branch's two most senior figures, Williamson and the recently promoted Chief Inspector John Littlechild,[17] who joined the three detectives from Birmingham at Euston in tailing Norman. As the Irish American boarded a hansom cab outside the station, one of the detectives jotted down its registration number before watching it take off without Norman who, perhaps made aware to the possible presence of police, decided to make his way over to the De La Motts Hotel in the Strand in a different carriage.

Not wanting to tip off anyone else who might be watching the hotel, Williamson waited a while before finally giving his men the go-ahead in the early hours of the morning. Up in Norman's room they found only Norman, asleep with a 200 lb rubber bag of nitroglycerine under his bed. He refused to cooperate, but the items found in his pockets – a £5 note stamped 'Colgate, New York, March 10, 1883' and correspondence bearing Gallagher's nom de guerre (Fletcher) – spoke against him. He was arrested and taken, together with his lethal luggage, to Scotland Yard where the recent developments, especially the knowledge that at least one of Norman's London comrades remained at large, had thrown everything into 'a state of chaos'.[18]

Thanks to a bit of old-fashioned detective work, Williamson, Littlechild and Chief Constable O'Shea of the RIC managed to track down the passenger of the mysterious hansom cab to a house in Nelson Square, Blackfriars Road. There they found Wilson and Gallagher along with two rubber waders containing nearly 80 lbs of nitroglycerine and an impressive sum of nearly £1,200 and $2,400 (almost £500). Thereafter the rest of the gang was quickly swept up in a wave of arrests and by 7 April eight men stood accused of unlawful possession of explosives and treason-felony.

Realizing a martyr's fate was not for him after all, William Norman decided to turn Queen's evidence and provided the police with an incriminating testimony. Gallagher's brother, Bernard, who had been picked up in Glasgow after his name turned up in confiscated correspondence, also offered to cooperate, but in the end found he did not need to; there was little by way of evidence against him. Bernard Gallagher was subsequently acquitted along with another man whose only ostensible link to the plot had been a calling card found in his possession. Dalton was also released, then immediately rearrested in connection with the Cork dynamite ring and sent to Liverpool to stand trial with the rest of the Featherstone gang. Dr Gallagher, Albert Whitehead, Henry Wilson and one John Curtin were found guilty at their trial and sentenced to penal servitude for life.

The outcome of the Gallagher case was a clear and widely celebrated success for the British police and Irish Branch in particular (although at the time the latter was not known to the public nor did it officially exist) and the special rewards granted to the officers involved were significant, with inspectors receiving £100 each. Nevertheless, the scale of the conspiracy, its serendipitous discovery and the fact that without Norman's confession Gallagher's men would likely have walked away with only minor sentences (such as were given for illicit possession of explosives under the 1875 Explosives Act) did not sit well with Harcourt. 'There can be no doubt', he wrote to Gladstone the day after the arrests, 'that we are in the midst of a large and well-organized and fully equipped band who are prepared to commit outrages all over the country on an immense scale.'[19]

Three days later, on 9 April, the Home Secretary introduced another bold new piece of legislation in the House of Commons which aimed, this time, at strengthening the laws dealing with explosives and the police's ability to pre-emptively stop dynamitards. Thus, under the terms of this new Explosives Act, anyone found responsible for causing an illegal explosion was virtually guaranteed life in prison, while mere ownership of explosives, 'under such circumstances as to give rise to a reasonable suspicion' that an unlawful object was being entertained, now proved sufficient for sentences of up to fourteen years with hard labour.[20] Despite some faint rumblings from the Irish opposition, Harcourt's bill was quickly passed, making its way through both houses in roughly two hours.[21]

With the new Act in effect, most of the Gallagher gang in prison and his stewardship of the Metropolitan Police secure,[22] the Home Secretary now felt confident that 'the neck of the [Fenian] business is broken so far as violence is concerned in Ireland and Great Britain'. But, he also noted, 'the perpetual reserve of crime in America and the sally-port they have there prevent our eradicating the roots of the mischief.'[23] That impression was only confirmed a few days later by Anderson, who reported, based on missives from Le Caron, that the leaders of the Clan na Gael were 'more determined than ever to persevere [with new agents] ... being selected and trained for another mission of outrage against this country.'[24]

The Northern portion of Harcourt's 'spider's web' was still dangerously weak, as both the Featherstone and Gallagher cases had confirmed, and what was needed was 'a second Jenkinson' to whip it into shape. For the time being, Spencer felt his head of intelligence and his budding network of informers were more needed in Dublin than in London. Luckily for Harcourt, however, Jenkinson had a suitable surrogate in mind: Major Nicholas Gosselin, a former Ulster militiaman and Resident Magistrate for Sligo, who 'understands these Irish scoundrels, and can talk to them.'[25] By late May Major Gosselin was already in charge of overseeing all Fenian-related intelligence in the North of England and Glasgow. He did not yet have much to go on, but his ability to ingratiate himself with local Chief Constables (who were mainly former military officers) and the contacts supplied by Jenkinson constituted important first steps.[26]

In early July, an opportunity arose to finally clinch the case of the Cork-Liverpool dynamite ring when Denis Deasy's solicitor wrote to the Home Office to say that he could persuade his client to turn Queen's evidence for the not unreasonable sum of £100 (substantially less than the £300 paid to Norman for his confession).[27] Deasy refused to testify, but his comrade Timothy Carmody proved more pliable. The latter's testimony coupled with that of William Lamie (a paid Dublin Castle informer whose lurid tales of ribbon societies[28] and secret oaths had already proved effective against the Invincibles) soon brought the trial to a predictable conclusion: findings of guilt against the accused and sentences of life in prison. There now remained only the loose threads of the Glasgow and London outrages and while the London bombers appeared to be still at large, in late August the Glasgow end of the conspiracy unexpectedly came crashing down.

As in the Gallagher case, the initial impetus for the authorities came almost by accident and from an unlikely source: a fifty-three-year-old Glasgow fruit merchant by the name of George Hughes who had since July 1882 been a member of a local ribbon society – ribbonism having by this point become a hotchpotch of 'protest, sectarian solidarity and vague aspirations to an eventual war of national liberation' in Ireland.[29] This, however, was no ordinary social club for frustrated radicals; it was in fact the same organization that had hosted Timothy Featherstone and Henry Dalton on their arrival from America and that had planned and carried out the three dynamite attacks in Glasgow on the night of 20 January. Furthermore, it was one of its members, a man by the name of Terence McDermott who had, along with Thomas Mooney, bombed the Local Government Board and *Times* headquarters back in March.

Hughes was not a paid infiltrator in the mould of Red Jim nor a courtroom performer like William Lamie, but he was a man who could hold a grudge. As he later testified in court, a few months after joining the ribbon society, Hughes had had a minor disagreement and then physical altercation with a fellow ribbonman during one of the group's regular meetings on the Glasgow Green. Chancing into an old acquaintance of his, Constable William Porter of Glasgow City Police, shortly after the scuffle, Hughes reported to have remarked that 'If I had seen you a little earlier, I would have charged a man to the office.' Porter replied that 'you are not too late, come away back', but before Hughes could elaborate, an older, bewhiskered gentleman caught up with the two, gently grabbing the constable by the shoulder and observing wryly: 'Never mind them, the one is as bad as the other. Come away, Mr. Hughes, you are as bad as the other.'[30]

The name of the soft-spoken conciliator was Timothy Featherstone, as Constable Porter found out from Hughes shortly thereafter, a name which at the time raised no alarms except to Hughes himself, who was growing increasingly uncomfortable with Featherstone's dynamite talk. Glasgow police nevertheless kept a low-level surveillance of Hughes' group all through late 1882 and early 1883 until sometime in March 1883 Porter became involved in pursuing 'inquiries with reference to these men being concerned with dynamite'.[31] Remarkably, the authorities in London do not appear to have been involved in the case at this stage (assuming they had been made aware of it) and the Glasgow CID, although continuing to keep a watchful eye on the meetings of suspected Fenians, made little progress with the investigation.[32] In early April, however, just after Featherstone's arrest in Cork, Porter (whose idea of detection was to ask possible suspects if they were involved in smuggling dynamite) once again ran into Hughes who immediately offered to tell all he knew about 'the parties… engaged in [the dynamite business]' so long as his name was not '[brought] to the front'.[33]

Added to this was information freshly extracted by Irish Branch from an ex-associate of Featherstone, a certain John Francis Kearney. A key organizer of the 20 January bombings and Rossa's go-to man in Glasgow, Kearney had fled to Hull in early April 1883, perhaps tipped off by Constable Porter's heavy-handed enquiries. After being cornered by London detectives in June and convinced to give up the whereabouts of his erstwhile comrades, Kearney was paid and allowed to leave for America.[34] Was Jenkinson behind this new 'acquisition'? Whatever the case, by late August, Scottish authorities knew enough about the identities and routines of the Glasgow gang to be able to finally tighten the noose around the whole conspiracy.

The arrests began on the last day of the month, when five Irishmen – Terence McDermott, Peter Callaghan, Thomas Derany, Patrick Macabe and Patrick Drum – were apprehended in Glasgow's South Side and arrests continued over the next few weeks until by early October ten men were in police custody for suspected involvement in the dynamite outrages of 20 January. Armed with the testimonies of Hughes and William Lamie (the latter in his role as archetypal Fenian) and the various pieces of incriminating evidence found during the arrests, the prosecution had a virtually airtight case. Before the end of the year, five of the accused – including McDermott, whose involvement in the London bombings was now all but proven – were serving sentences of penal servitude for life, the rest receiving lesser sentences.[35]

All known dynamiters, except for those who had turned Queen's evidence and the ever-elusive Thomas Mooney, were now in prison, but as the Glasgow case demonstrated, the north still lagged far behind in terms of efficient communication and intelligence-gathering even with the new leadership provided by Gosselin who now claimed, somewhat dubiously, to have 'the address of every [Fenian] Centre in Great Britain, and all the higher officers too'.[36] Not that the Home Counties fared much better. Despite the many precautions taken in the capital since the attacks in March, which by now included 'a large number of extra military guards and sentries… to assist the police in guarding public buildings',[37] panic once again gave way to indifference at the Home Office and 'after the conviction of the dynamitards [it] was even proposed to do away altogether with the political department'.[38]

This complacent mood came to an end on the evening of 30 October, when, just as the 8.00 p.m. train was leaving Praed Street station of the London Underground for Edgware Road, an explosion tore through the side of the tunnel, severely damaging the last three carriages and injuring scores of people 'more or less severely by cuts from broken glass'. Then, only a few minutes later, a second explosion damaged the tunnel between Charing Cross and Westminster stations, knocking down a few unsuspecting passengers and sending 'volumes of black dust' into all directions.[39] The worst was yet to come.

The Metropolitan Railway authorities had been warned by police as early as July 1883 that 'information had been received from America that an outrage [on the London Underground] was contemplated' and the company had apparently taken 'special precautions' as a consequence.[40] Just what those precautions were is not clear, but there is no indication that security was meaningfully stepped up around London Underground stations before or immediately after the 30 October explosions. Indeed, only two and a half months later, on 15 January 1884, 'four or five packages of dynamite' were discovered by a platelayer in Primrose Hill tunnel, shortly before the Prince of Wales' special train was set to depart from Euston station. 'Special precautions' were once more put in place 'against any… outrage on the Prince's return on Friday'.[41] A Fenian sword of Damocles continued to hang over London.

Harcourt now professed that 'we are all of the opinion that things were never worse than they are now in respect of the anticipation of outrage and crime'[42] and took every possible precaution to ensure that at least the rumoured plots against the royal family, of which there seemed to be a fresh batch each month, would not come to pass. A letter sent to the queen's private secretary, Sir Henry Ponsonby, shortly after the queen's return from Balmoral illustrates the uncertainty and anxiety pervading the Home Office at the time:

I was very glad to get news this morning of H.M's safe arrival. I had one of the usual scares last night [when] Williamson at 12.30 a.m. came in with a letter from the U.S. describing the machine with which and the manner in which you were to be blown up on your way from Balmoral... [As] you were already supposed to be half-way through your journey it was not easy to know what course to take. However I sent Williamson to Euston and Paddington to direct that an additional pilot engine should be run at a longer interval in front of you as soon as possible, as the intelligence pointed to bombs to be deposited *after the passage* of the ordinary pilot engine.... I had police at Euston and Birmingham to report to me all night how you were getting on and was proportionately relieved when I heard you were safe and sound at Windsor.[43]

The incipient controversy surrounding the Liberal-backed Third Reform Bill (which sought to expand and reform the political franchise) claimed much of the government's attention during the year's first couple of months, but at the end of February the dynamitards managed to recapture the limelight with a series of plots involving different railway stations throughout London. The first and only 'successful' one materialized on the night of 26 February shortly after the arrival of the last night train at Victoria station. At exactly 1.04 a.m., just as the night inspector and his assistants had finished checking the integrity of the station's fire hose, 'a sound similar to that emitted from a small cannon [followed by] a red sort of flash' burst through the cloakroom walls, felling everything in an instant and leaving a baleful silence in its wake.[44] The cloakroom and the adjacent booking office were turned into a topsy-turvy heap of blackened shards and luggage contents, with the ticket office and ladies' lavatory also suffering extensive damage, but no injuries were recorded besides the minor scratches sustained by two station assistants.

When news of the explosion reached Windsor castle a few hours later, the queen cabled the Home Office to say that she was 'shocked to see account of fresh explosion. Trust it was accidental and no lives lost [sic].'[45] The notion that another outrage had been unleashed on London's hapless commuters evidently still seemed somewhat incredible, but by the end of the day Her Majesty's Chief Inspector of Explosives, Colonel Vivian Majendie, felt confident of the 'clear and unmistakable indication that the explosion here was occasioned by some violent explosive agent and was certainly not due to gas'.[46]

The same explosive agent turned up again only a day later at Charing Cross station where the head porter had joined his subordinates in a pre-emptive and 'unusually careful scrutiny of all articles' deposited in the station's cloakroom. No suspicious packages were detected except a portmanteau which had not been claimed since the previous evening and which on closer inspection was found to contain 'several suspicious-looking packets... a square tin case... an old pair of black trousers... [and] an old coat', both of a decidedly 'American pattern'. Police were promptly informed and the portmanteau brought hastily to Woolwich Arsenal to be studied by Majendie and his assistants. When opened, the tin box revealed a gunlock and a modified alarm clock, also of American provenance, which had stopped at exactly three minutes past four. The 'suspicious packets' were found to contain a substantial number of dynamite cakes; the bomb had apparently failed to detonate because of a faulty fuse which had caused the 'striker [to miss] the mark by the merest fraction of space'.[47]

The general sense of alarm was further heightened only a couple of days later by two new discoveries. At Paddington station another small brown portmanteau with 'a very heavy loose article within it' was found to contain a trigger mechanism attached through a thin copper wire to twenty pounds' worth of dynamite charges. This time the clock itself had been responsible for the device's fortuitous failure, although as Majendie explained in his report, 'the slightest shake would have set it going'.[48] The day after, an almost identical package was located in the cloakroom at Ludgate Hill station.[49]

A look at the stations' registry books and a series of interviews with various luggage-handling personnel revealed that the packages had been deposited Monday evening by as many as five different individuals of unknown identities and only vague descriptions. By 4 March a wanted poster could be seen plastered on walls across the capital offering a reward of £2,000 to anyone whose information might lead 'to the discovery and conviction of the person or persons by whom these crimes were caused or attempted'.[50]

It was a desperate grope in the dark but for the first time Harcourt felt completely overwhelmed. Writing to his son Lewis in late February he wistfully quipped that 'I have sunk now into a mere head detective and go nowhere and see nothing',[51] while in a letter to the queen he inveighed against 'the assassination societies' in America whose 'devilish schemes' appeared to be publicly announced and advertised without the smallest hindrance from American authorities. 'No other civilized country in the world', Harcourt railed, 'does or would tolerate the open advocacy of assassination and murder.'[52]

'American indolence' appeared to be the perfect scapegoat after London's protestations had failed to elicit any sympathy in Washington, but what the Home Secretary could not admit before Her Majesty was that despite his arduous efforts the British state's counter-terrorist strategy appeared to be entirely insufficient. Irish Branch had been gradually augmented almost from day one, but most of its constables were temporary transfers who were paid less than their colleagues on permanent patrols.[53] They were also highly dependent on outside intelligence given the transatlantic nature of Fenianism, and quality intelligence was as hard to come by as ever. Only days before the attack on Victoria station, Anderson had assured Harcourt that the Clan na Gael was 'played out' and that 'at this moment Dublin and not London is the centre of dangerous Fenian activity'.[54] Gosselin too, despite his administrative talents and unorthodox tactics, which included recruiting local urchins as part-time spies,[55] had slowly been running out of relevant things to say since late 1883 to the point where by January 1884 he was forced to concede to Harcourt that 'I have nothing but bad news to tell [and] all my plans have failed so far.'[56]

Although a radically new and still underdeveloped intelligence-gathering network was bound to meet some heavy obstacles early on, to Harcourt it seemed as if the time for half-measures was over. On 4 March Spencer received a letter from the Home Secretary outlining the case for a thorough overhaul of British anti-Fenian operations, especially the 'system of search at the ports for dynamite and dynamiters'.[57] The only man up to the job was evidently the talented Mr Jenkinson and to secure his services Harcourt was willing to briefly put his not inconsiderable ego aside. 'Pray don't refuse' he cajoled Spencer, '[as] it is of most vital consequence [sic]'.[58] The Red Earl (as the auburn-bearded Spencer was popularly known) waited a day before finally consenting. Dispensing with Jenkinson's presence would not be a tremendous sacrifice given the relatively pacific state of Ireland at the time[59] and, as Spencer wryly observed in a letter to the new Chief Secretary for Ireland, Sir George Otto Trevelyan, the following day, 'Jenkinson goes over tonight on Harcourt's earnest request… We can manage his work here [and he] will keep the Special or Secret Police work still in hand.'[60]

For his part, Jenkinson was certainly not enthused by the prospect of relocating, even if only temporarily, but given his loyalty to Spencer he had no other option. He realized, however, that he could at least make a few demands of his own and in a memorandum prepared shortly before his departure, the spymaster traced in broad lines his vision for the position he was to occupy at Whitehall.

First of all, it had to be a real, official position in the Home Office sanctioned by and directly under the Home Secretary – 'an extra Assistant Under Secretary… whose duties would… be confined strictly to matters relating to Fenian organizations'. Secondly, Jenkinson's duties in Dublin would have to remain firmly under his control in order to safeguard 'the direction of a system which I have been carefully and laboriously building up during the last two years'. Ireland and Great Britain, in fact, now had to be 'treated as one' as far as counter-subversion went.

Thirdly and most importantly, Jenkinson's powers would have to be of such a nature as to prevent running the 'risk of a change in the system or... the chain of the work which would almost certainly take place on a change of Ministry'. What this meant in practice was complete authority over Irish Branch and the Home Office's Secret Service (the latter still under Anderson's control), as well as the power to 'issue orders in my own name' and only after 'to lay them for information... before the Secretary of State'.[61]

This was all rather more ambitious than Harcourt had bargained for and more than a little problematic from a legal and administrative perspective. As the Home Secretary explained in his own internal memorandum, Jenkinson could now rightly regard himself as the 'single person to whom all information may be brought... and who will have the means of disposing of all the resources both of Ireland and of Great Britain'. He could not, however, hope to duplicate in England the sort of official czardom he enjoyed at Dublin Castle given the 'difficulties which are at present insurmountable'.[62]

On 10 March a meeting at the Home Office between Jenkinson, Harcourt, the latter's under-secretaries and the chiefs of the Metropolitan Police officially sealed the deal. Spencer's spymaster was to operate in a sort of extra-legal fog out of which he would, with Harcourt's accord, instruct police authorities on 'the proper steps' to be taken in grappling 'with [Fenian] conspiracies as a whole'.[63]

It was not a bad deal; better in some sense than what Jenkinson had originally asked for given that his unofficial status exempted him from intense parliamentary scrutiny (though his role as Assistant Under-Secretary for Police and Crime in Ireland left him exposed to Nationalist attacks). The only catch was that the Metropolitan Police bigwigs could not be ordered about and had to be coaxed out of their long-held beliefs and behaviours. Jenkinson realized this was a herculean and likely impossible task – he told Spencer as much shortly after – but for the time being 'Jenks' (as Harcourt nicknamed him) could at least take some small degree of comfort in having one of the best rooms in the Home Office building – Lord Dalhousie's old quarters – and access to a newly installed personal telephone line.

CHAPTER 4

# 'The new detective army'[1]

JENKINSON'S move to the Home Office did not remain a secret for long, soon becoming fodder for editorials on both sides of the Irish Sea. The staunchly Nationalist *Freeman's Journal*, for example, noted gleefully that 'the peaceful serenity [of] Scotland Yard officialdom... has been rudely dispelled by... Mr. Jenkinson [who] is daily expected to promulgate a scheme for the reorganisation of the detective department, and [who]... has been practically allowed a carte blanche in its preparation.'[2] Pulling no punches in ridiculing this apparent ministerial folly, the paper depicted Harcourt as a hysterical weakling and Jenkinson as an insidious errand boy eager to prey on his paymaster's paranoia in the pursuit of personal profit. For British newspapers, however, the picture was somewhat more complicated.

The Liberal *Lloyd's Weekly Newspaper* tacitly approved of Jenkinson's appointment as 'a sort of Minister of Police under the Home Office', but was somewhat wary of the exclusively political nature of his office, asking wryly why 'the ordinary citizen [could not] also claim the benefit of his services' given that Scotland Yard 'has not failed more conspicuously in attacking political than in trying to capture ordinary criminals.'[3] That unease was more forcefully stated by the Conservative *Standard* which, while granting that 'current arrangements [in combating politically motivated crime] are far from satisfactory', depicted the new appointment as a betrayal of the Metropolitan Police. Mr Jenkinson had 'done good service in Ireland', but his presence at the Home Office would only weaken the 'authority of the Chief Commissioner' and further antagonize the provinces where 'already the authority exercised by the Home Office in Police matters is regarded... with considerable jealousy.'[4]

If such comments appeared, to some degree, to echo those of Jenkinson's critics in Whitehall (Anderson especially) it is because they were almost certainly based on controlled leaks, as the new 'Minister of Police' himself believed. Writing to Spencer only a day after the publication of the *Standard* piece, Jenkinson warned that newspaper chatter could go a considerable way towards harming the vital secrecy on which his new duties depended, railing at the same time against the inability of Scotland Yard men to 'hold their tongues'.[5] His views of them grew more critical over the following months, but initially at least workplace politics had to wait.

Given Harcourt's insistence on increased security at ports, Jenkinson's first major endeavour in Britain was to draw up a workable scheme for having 'all personal luggage of persons coming from abroad... strictly searched and examined for... explosives'.[6] As the meticulous memorandum he drafted specified, seventy-eight detectives (forty-nine to be supplied by Scotland Yard, twenty-nine by Dublin Castle) would, with the assistance of provincial police, oversee the careful inspection by customs officers of 'all persons landing from abroad'.[7] Gosselin and his adjutant, Major Blair, would be in charge of northern English and Scottish ports while Williamson and his officers would have control over the south. In cases of 'persons of interest' being detected, telegrams and detailed descriptions were to be sent over to Scotland Yard and then 'immediately and without delay' forwarded to Jenkinson himself along with all reports from the five men (four Irish Branch, one RIC) stationed at major northern European ports like Le Havre, Rotterdam, Antwerp, Bremerhaven and Hamburg.[8]

The ability of foreign port police (styled Section C of Scotland Yard) to track down suspects in hiding on the continent was often hampered both by British and continental bureaucracy as a letter received by Jenkinson in mid-December 1884 from the British consul at Le Havre reveals:

Sir,

Sergeant [William] Melville [of the Irish Branch] called this morning... and showed me a Memorandum he had just received from London, with instructions to call by on me for my intervention in the event of his discovering the presence in this town of a certain individual. I at once telegraphed you as follows – 'In case necessity arising could do nothing without instructions from Foreign Office.' You will remember a conversation I had with you some months ago when I told you that the Foreign Office wished to know what instructions the Home Office desired should be given me. I have heard nothing more on the subject.

Were I to know that an individual who was on his way to commit, or had committed an attempt to blow up some place in England was here, it would be necessary for me to get the Police to arrest him provisionally, and to formally apply to the Procureur de la Republique for his detention (that official would immediately ask for instructions from the Minister of Grace and Justice) but up to the present moment I have no instructions that would justify my incurring this responsibility.[9]

Jenkinson reacted immediately by reaching out to Sir Julian Pauncefote over at the Foreign Office who assured the spymaster that British consuls in Europe would be instructed 'to give every assistance in their power and to obtain when necessary... the co-operation of the Local Police' so long as the Home Secretary demanded it in writing. Pointing out to Harcourt the urgency of securing such an arrangement, Jenkinson was however only weakly assured that a telegram would eventually be sent to the Foreign Office by Harcourt's Permanent Under-Secretary, Sir Adolphus Liddell.[10] It is not clear whether Liddell (who died only six months later) actually did send that telegram.

A number of key difficulties were also immediately discernible on the domestic side of things. 'Many years' had passed since such precautions had last been used[11] and crucially, Jenkinson had yet to persuade the Home Secretary of the need to include all Irish travellers within the remit of the scheme,[12] or reassure apprehensive customs officials, who were certain that policing traffic across the Irish Sea in this manner meant chaos, that passengers would be searched only 'on reasonable suspicion and at the request of the Police'.[13]

The problem with 'reasonable suspicion', then as now, was its vagueness – Commissioner Henderson had ordered Metropolitan detectives to consider anyone with an Irish accent a potential suspect[14] – which made it easy to misuse or ignore. Thus, only a couple of months later, John Small, the Nationalist MP for Wexford County, was pulled aside and searched by an overzealous customs officer at Holyhead after having been spotted holding a hat box on board a Dublin steamer.[15] The minor scandal that ensued led to rules being made to stipulate that searches had to be performed only at the instruction of police, thus burdening the sixty or so detectives on port duty with even more work.[16]

Complicating things further was the fact that searches had to be arbitrarily performed on board ships as passengers were about to disembark[17] and suggestions by Major Blair and certain customs officers for 'a central deposit through which all passengers and luggage must pass', were dismissed by the Board of Customs as 'difficult to carry out'.[18] Despite this inauspicious start, however, Jenkinson soon managed to once again boost his profile with the sort of devious manoeuvring that had first endeared him to Harcourt.

On the morning of 11 April 1884 (Good Friday) a man was arrested at the railway station in Birkenhead by two Birmingham CID and two RIC detectives. Judging by his flashy suit and diamond-encrusted rings, onlookers might have reasonably thought that some procurer or pickpocket had finally got his comeuppance. The man in custody – a tall Irish American in his thirties named John Daly – was no ordinary wheeler-dealer, however, as the three 'infernal machines' and several bottles of acids found in his coat pockets attested.

The arrest of James Francis Egan, a known Fenian militant and Daly's contact in Birmingham, quickly followed after a group of nine detectives led by Chief Constable Joseph Farndale stormed Egan's house in Grafton Road (which had been under heavy police surveillance since September 1883).[19] A thorough search of the premises accompanied by an extensive excavation of the back garden then led police to a sizeable batch of violently worded Fenian literature and correspondence that seemed 'sufficient corroboration of the suspicions already entertained of Egan's complicity in the schemes of his lodger'.[20]

Authorities appeared to have an open-and-shut case on their hands, but as the continued police searches of the Egan residence seemed to indicate, a vital piece of evidence was still missing. It finally turned up on 1 May when one of the navvies helping police with their excavation work happened on a brown flask hidden in some dug-up roots at the back of the house. It contained nitro-glycerine 'of the most dangerous character, and of sufficient quantity to make three or four of such [bombs] as those found on Daly'.[21]

Given the terms of the new Explosives Act, the fate of the accused seemed all but obvious to anyone following the case (though in the end only Daly received a life sentence, of which he served twelve years). Less obvious were the circumstances that had led authorities to the fortuitous and impeccably timed discoveries in Birkenhead and Birmingham. If anyone knew most of the truth, it was certainly Jenkinson, who on 12 April wrote to Spencer to explain the previous day's arrest:

> Yesterday I heard of the arrest of Daly by telegraph 'with the things on him'... These things are three hand bombs which came over about three days ago in the *City of Chester*. They were brought over by a fireman who managed to elude the vigilance of the customs. Our difficulty was to get the things passed to Daly and then to arrest him with the things on him, without throwing suspicion on our informant. Two plans missed fire... but the third plan succeeded... Daly intended to go up to London and throw one of these three bombs... from the gallery of the House of Commons. He was quite prepared to sacrifice his own life. All that... Harcourt knows is that Daly was being closely watched [and that] he was arrested and the things found on him... I hope Your Excellency will not give any of these details [away].[22]

The 'third plan' was in fact Daniel 'Big Dan' O'Neill, an IRB man who had been in Daly's confidence since the summer of 1882 and in Major Gosselin's pay since the winter of 1883.[23] It was O'Neill whom Daly had met in Liverpool that Good Friday before trying to board the train back to Birmingham; O'Neill who had given Daly the bombs; O'Neill who had afterwards 'confessed' to Gosselin that the explosives were meant for the House of Commons. The letter is almost shocking in its casual mentioning of the employment of agents provocateurs and other less-than-legal schemes, but despite its arresting candour, it is also conveniently vague on several key points. Had Jenkinson knowingly taken advantage of his own port security scheme in order to have bombs smuggled into Britain? What were the two plans that had 'missed fire'? Was the Clan na Gael, of which Daly was a member, once again attempting to blow up Parliament? How much did Gosselin know? And why did Harcourt know so little?

Equally puzzling was the mysterious flask of nitroglycerine found in Egan's back garden. It was 'generally believed to be of American make', while the nitroglycerine it contained appeared to be 'not part of that manufactured by Whitehead but... of a superior kind'.[24] In what manner had it been smuggled into the country, to what purpose had it been deposited at Egan's place and by whom? These were not questions anyone appeared to be publicly asking in the wake of Daly and Egan's arrests, but privately some members of the Birmingham police force, most notably Chief Constable Farndale, felt ill-used by the political police in London.

A year later, in a letter to the Home Office, Jenkinson raised concerns on the 'very small' rewards granted to Birmingham policemen in connection with the Daly-Egan case, urging the importance of keeping 'the local Police in good humour and on our side'. His unheeded advice led to Farndale's long-time grudge erupting in late 1887 with declarations to members of the Birmingham Watch Committee (as well as to prominent local politicians) to the effect that the convictions of Daly and Egan had been 'secured by a plant arranged by the Irish Constabulary'. The case went on to reach the ears of then Conservative Home Secretary Henry Matthews, who after briefly making his own inquiries into the truth of the allegations, decided to smother the controversy outright.[25]

For the time being, however, the busting of yet another dynamite ring was something to be celebrated as a triumph. The Whiggish *Glasgow Herald* noted in an unusually forceful editorial that the 'fresh arrests [in Birmingham] have increased the public confidence in the police as the organisation by which the nation can cope with the secret enemies of life'. It also applauded the recent arrest in London of a high-ranking IRB member which:

> is known to be among the first fruits of an experiment in the way of reorganising the Detective Department in connection with the Home Office... in accordance with the instructions of Mr. E. J. [sic] Jenkinson... It is the beginning, in fact of the work of the new detective army, the necessity for which has been made painfully evident by recent crimes perpetrated by men

who have got off scot free, and by the special kinds of outrage against life and property which are bred by civilisation and by science... Reports [are] growing in loudness and assurance to the effect that Mr. Howard Vincent... will shortly retire, and with him the old system and its ideas, and that Mr. Jenkinson will receive a permanent appointment as head of a new... Crimes Detection and Prevention Office. Something of this kind must be done.[26]

Jenkinson would have certainly approved of this glowing evaluation of his budding 'detective army' and prospects for future officialdom, but despite the successes of early April, the remainder of 1884 and the future in general remained uncertain. It was getting increasingly hard to '[find] anyone for our work' in America and of those who were already engaged in it, many were reporting that the Clan na Gael leaders were looking to 'pick out & recommend... men able to be sent off for active work at a moments [sic] notice – a determined effort is to be made before June to leave a mark which will redound to the credit of the present administration'.[27]

As spring drew to a close, authorities in London were still arguing over the exact arrangements of the port protection scheme, with police inspectors and the Board of Customs alike resisting any further attempts at reform while insisting that the current arrangements worked 'very well'.[28] If the Daly case had not conclusively proved that those arrangements worked in fact not at all well, additional evidence came on the evening of 30 May. The first explosion hit the Junior Carlton Club at 9.18 p.m., marring its austere Renaissance façade and shaking up the kitchen and storeroom. This was immediately followed by a second blast which rattled the nearby residence of Sir Watkin Williams-Wynn, sixth Baronet and Conservative MP, to similar results. When shortly after 9.30 p.m. a boy passing through Trafalgar Square discovered a small black satchel near the base of Nelson's Column, it seemed like the worst had been averted. Inside the bag were more than eight pounds of dynamite that had failed to detonate.[29]

The great coup, however, had been delivered roughly ten minutes before the discovery in Trafalgar Square: the target nothing less than the Scotland Yard building itself. This was an impressive feat for the Clan na Gael-ers whose campaign against London railway stations earlier that year had proved mostly abortive, but its success had arguably more to do with luck than skill. As authorities shortly realized, the bomb that had 'burst in the very headquarters of authority' had been casually placed in the gutter of a public (and poorly guarded) lavatory located on the ground floor of the Scotland Yard building.[30]

The shock of this brazen and impressively timed display of Fenian pyrotechnics was lessened somewhat by the absence of fatalities (although at least ten individuals suffered moderate to severe injuries) and the realization that except for the 'considerable damage' done to the Scotland Yard building, material losses proved on the whole negligible.[31] In his official report on the explosions Colonel Majendie revealed that the dynamite used was unmistakably the same American-made 'Atlas Powder A' (ligno-dynamite) found at London railway stations back in February, but reassuringly concluded that:

> if undertaken with the object of producing serious public alarm and panic the series [of explosions] has… conspicuously failed. The net result which seems to have been achieved is that a number of… humble members of the working classes have been more or less cut and bruised and injured… On the other hand, nineteen conspirators have been sentenced to penal servitude for life or for long terms of years.[32]

Not everyone shared this optimistic interpretation, however. For Jenkinson the explosion was simply further proof of Scotland Yard incompetence, a matter made worse, as he explained in a letter to Spencer, by the fact that 'they have no information and if anything happens they all lose their heads'.[33] Ironically, some Irish Branch detectives seemed to inadvertently agree. DS Patrick McIntyre had already noticed the chaotic atmosphere at the Yard during the investigation into the Gallagher gang, an impression echoed now by DS John Sweeney who, in the aftermath of the 30 May bombings, observed how '[this] affair caused confusion at Scotland Yard for some months'.[34]

What did confusion at Scotland Yard mean? Just days before the Westminster explosions Irish Branch's leading inspector, DCI Littlechild, had been busy following up on information provided to police by a Mr Potter of 30 Charing Cross Road relating to one of his more 'suspicious' lodgers. That the tip-off turned out to be bogus – the lodger was merely a small-time swindler coming and going at irregular times – and the investigation into it a waste of police effort is not necessarily surprising. What is surprising is that a month later Irish Branch was still busy investigating Mr Potter's evidently baseless suspicions regarding a spring-heeled-Jack-type character who turned out to be, as DI Smith confirmed in a report, 'a large cat'.[35]

Even when promising leads did emerge, lack of experience on the part of certain detectives meant that an operation could easily be compromised, sometimes to ludicrous effects. This, for example, was the case with the four Irish Branch detectives sent to investigate the circumstances surrounding the theft of some gunpowder and dynamite from a quarry near Dundee in Scotland.

After failing to track down any potential suspects the four ended up being shadowed by a local policeman who 'to his consternation… found [the men] were members of the same profession'.[36]

The status quo did change somewhat, if not as a consequence of the Scotland Yard explosion. Increasingly convinced that his position 'offered no prospect of advancement' and worried that it now offered perhaps too much excitement, Howard Vincent decided in late June to make good on his promise to retire, trading the vagaries of police work for a trip around the world.[37] Harcourt decided to abolish Vincent's position of CID Director, choosing instead to place Scotland Yard under the authority of a newly created Assistant Commissioner for Crime. The title may have borne a superficial similarity to the Irish Under-Secretary for Police and Crime but the man to get the job was not Jenkinson, as the *Glasgow Herald* had predicted.

It went instead to a certain James Monro[38] who at first sight might have seemed curiously very like 'Jenks' – a middle-aged, upper-middle-class man who had spent the better part of his life upholding law and order in the more troubled regions of the Raj. He was in fact fundamentally different in at least two respects: Monro was an actual policeman (having served as Inspector General of Police in Bengal) who, despite a rather high-strung personality, knew how to command the loyalty of his officers. He was also much more typical of his class and education than Jenkinson, i.e. fundamentally conservative, religiously pious and distrustful of anything smacking of 'foreign methods'.[39] Monro's appointment went essentially unnoticed by the press – a rare, perhaps singular, mention appeared in the Saint Peter Port (Guernsey) *Star* on 1 July – but it signalled an important change of course for Britain's political police. More specifically, it reflected Harcourt's diminishing enthusiasm for secret policing and his changing ideas on how best to fight the Fenian conspiracy.

As Jenkinson explained in a letter to his other boss and sole confidant, Harcourt's newest obsession was with something he called 'picketing', which, despite the militancy it implied, was in fact nothing but Victorian preventive policing at its most old-fashioned. The 'pickets' were actually Scotland Yard patrols that were supposed to conspicuously shadow suspects identified by Jenkinson and Irish Branch, thus – so the theory went – scaring them straight in the process. '[Harcourt] says', Jenkinson observed, not without a hint of irony, '[that] it is the easiest thing in the world to do and if the men are driven abroad they should be followed and picketed there also.' Gosselin had already complained to Harcourt of the fact that chief constables in the north 'as a rule, act in these [Fenian-related] matters with a view merely to keep their own Districts free, and let others look out for themselves', but to no effect.

Harcourt was set on a return to 'wholesome' policing even as recent developments continued to point to a desperate need for quality intelligence, the kind provided by 'reliable agents of good class' who could spy, infiltrate and orchestrate whenever needed. To the Home Office's increasingly embattled spymaster it seemed as if 'Sir W.... blames me [for the recent explosions] and thinks that I am doing nothing and know nothing'.[40]

Part of the reason why Harcourt had resolutely come out against secret policing undoubtedly had to do with the 30 May bombings and the fear that Jenkinson was perhaps losing his touch (despite his very recent successes in Liverpool and Birmingham), but just as important was the political pressure the Home Secretary was under at the time. Members of the Irish Nationalist opposition led by Charles Stewart Parnell routinely delighted in excoriating the more dubious and autocratic features of Jenkinson's administration in Ireland and were already beginning to inquire into the nature of his work in Britain.[41] Should word somehow get out that Jenkinson was in fact attempting to replicate an Irish system on British soil – the papers, it seemed, already suspected as much – the government's enemies would find themselves supremely well-munitioned.

Just how uneasy Harcourt was with this issue is attested by a letter to the queen from early June in which the Home Secretary had complained that 'there is such a violent prejudice against that *espionage* which can alone remark these secret plots that the task of detection is very difficult'.[42] It is doubtful, however, that this 'violent prejudice' was merely the product of a 'widespread... positive *pride* in [British] detectives' lack of prowess'.[43] Most newspapers across the political spectrum, including *The Times*, had applauded, or at least not objected to, the manner in which Daly had been shadowed and apprehended, with one aptly concluding that 'it is unpleasant of course to have to do such work as was done by the police at Birmingham in tracking Daly, but when it has to be done it is a satisfaction to be able to say, as in this case, that it is done well'.[44]

If anyone was dead set against 'espionage', it was in fact the Whitehall establishment. The leader of the Conservative Party, Lord Salisbury, for example, had once warned that it was 'worthy of the meridian of Paris and Berlin'[45] to grant police the power of rescuing street children at risk of being trafficked by criminals and his views on the issue had only 'hardened further in the aftermath of the reform act of 1867'.[46] It would not take much imagination to guess what he might make of police rescuing Fenian double agents from the law in order to continue using their services (as had happened with Red Jim, John Kearney and others).

Besides the fear of political scandal, Harcourt had also to think of the need of maintaining a Liberal approach to police expenditure as embodied by Gladstone himself who had recently turned down personal protection on account of being too 'ashamed of the expense he had already been… inflicting on his fellow ratepayers'.[47] The cost of a few policemen posted at Hawarden castle (the Prime Minister's home in north Wales) was of course negligible, but the cost of managing the Metropolitan Police increasingly was not. The planned gradual augmentation of its force by nearly one thousand new officers had by late 1883 led to a 'large increase in… Expenditure [that] renders it absolutely necessary that the cash balance should be raised above its present figure [of] £125,580'.[48] Ironically, it was the port protection scheme that first came under Harcourt's parsimonious knife and in mid-August 1884 fifteen police officers were dismissed from port duty.[49] Jenkinson raised no objections. He knew he was in no position to argue with Harcourt and was willing to give Monro – whom he regarded as a 'good' if uninspiring individual – the benefit of the doubt. In any case, there were far more worrisome developments at play as an emotional letter addressed to Spencer on 14 September reveals:

> The work of watching the movements of [Fenians] and of obtaining information about them occupied me incessantly and is the cause of great anxiety to me. I feel that so much depends on me, and yet that I am able to accomplish so little. It is almost a single handed fight between me and a set of ruffians who now work on such a secret system that it is next to impossible to find out who their agents are and what their plans are. I feel always as if I were a man beating against the air, and as if my work could not have any lasting or beneficial result. For what I am doing does not go to the root of the matter [and] our successes only exasperate them and make them more bitter against England.[50]

In Jenkinson's view, the only measure capable of going to the root of the matter was in fact Home Rule. The Irish would have to be gradually prepared for it, but it would have to be immediately announced as government policy if Britain was to avert a worsening of 'troubles and difficulties in the future' and a total alienation of the Irish population.[51] For Spencer and the Liberal leadership, however, Home Rule was only 'ridiculous cant'.[52] Jenkinson simply had to find ways of staying one step ahead of the Clan na Gael (which was by then in complete control of the 'active work' being done in Britain) even as its leadership was sworn to complete secrecy and silence.[53] On 2 October a letter sent to Robert Anderson asked that in the future Le Caron should 'write either direct to me or to Mr. Hoare [the new Consul General] in New York'.[54] It was a ridiculous request given that at Jenkinson's urging Harcourt had already relieved Anderson of all intelligence-gathering duties unconnected to Le Caron. It was a request that betrayed an increasing degree of anxiety and despair.

In late November the Tralee mansion of Samuel Hussey, one of the most prominent land agents in County Kerry, was blown up by a tin-box-style dynamite bomb placed at the back of the house beneath a small arch. As RIC detectives quickly discovered, the persons responsible for the explosion were almost certainly recent arrivals of American extraction; what they had no way of knowing was that, like Hussey himself, who had already filed an application for £1,500 in damages 'for malicious injury' and left Ireland, the Yankees too were now headed for London.[55]

William Mackey Lomasney, a veteran of both the Fenian Rising and the American Civil War, had never been much of a dynamite fiend. In March 1881 he had written to John Devoy, the IRB and Clan na Gael leader, from Paris to express his total opposition to Rossa's campaign of terror; '[if] we try to force on a crisis unprepared', Lomasney argued, 'we will have not only the enemy to deal with, but the majority of our own people, who would in no way approve of such tactics'.[56] By late 1884, however, his tune had changed significantly. Lomasney, now living in London and posing as a respectable West End bookseller, was planning the most daring feat of his entire military career and it involved a significant amount of dynamite.

On the afternoon of 13 December, exactly seventeen years – almost to the hour – after the failed raid on Clerkenwell prison had reacquainted the British with gunpowder, treason and plot, Lomasney and two other men, one of whom was his brother, rented a small boat from a wharf at Queenhithe in the City and headed down the Thames in the direction of London Bridge. The boat-keeper later recalled seeing a tall bearded man place a sackcloth-wrapped package at the stern of the boat as his two companions rowed into midstream.

At 5.30 p.m. the boat was uneasily floating in the shallow water (the tide was at its lowest in months) around the Southwark end of the bridge, hidden from view by a thick, wet fog. As the three men reached the vicinity of the second arch, something went wrong. At 5.40 p.m. the Thames suddenly erupted in a roar of water, smoke and light, knocking over some of the people and horses crossing the bridge at the time and smashing hundreds of nearby windows. Half a mile away, at Liverpool Street station, the explosion was heard so well that passersby suspected the station itself was under attack.[57]

The botched attack on London Bridge was materially irrelevant; it resulted in only 'a few... panes of glass shattered... and a number of timid folks temporarily frightened'.[58] Psychologically, however, it proved a great success for the 'force party'. Because no one suspected the perpetrators' gruesome end, the explosion seemed to provide 'conclusive proof that the outrage... was planned with an amount of coolness, determination, and foresight for which the dynamite terrorists have not hitherto received credit'.[59] It also, far from eliciting a swift and concentrated response from authorities, appeared to further deepen the cracks in the government camp.

Only a day before the explosion, Jenkinson, still raw from a recent argument with Harcourt, had given Monro and Williamson a vicious dressing-down after finding that he 'could not possibly hold [his] tongue any longer'.[60] Only a few weeks before, the embattled spymaster had passed on reliable intelligence to Scotland Yard indicating a forthcoming attack on a London bridge was inevitable; the only action taken in consequence had been to have 'iron bars... put over the drain holes of London Bridge'.[61] To Jenkinson the explosion thus confirmed a growing suspicion that Monro was just another stolid Yardite with no intention of '[carrying] out [any] reforms... in the system of working'.[62] Even so, a last-ditch attempt at establishing a *modus vivendi* came on Boxing Day with a letter addressed directly to the Assistant Commissioner:

Dear Monro,

From what I have lately heard I think there can be no doubt that both the explosions of the 30th May and at London Bridge were the work of the same society if not of the same man and this morning I have heard from a very reliable source that they intend shortly to make an attempt on the House of Commons. This is from the same sources from which I heard that attack would be made on the Bridges... I think that special precautions should be taken about the House both on land and on the river side, also about Westminster Bridge, but this must be done very quietly and the greatest care must be taken not to give publicity to your proceedings... The thing would be to station the men both in uniform and in plain clothes [so that] the dynamiters could be watched and then captured in the act... My own idea is that [the dynamiters] will wait a little till the excitement about the last explosion has subsided.[63]

No one else at the Home Office seemed to be in possession of any new facts. On 19 December the City of London's Common Council had put up a reward of £5,000 for any information leading to the arrest of the London Bridge bombers and asked the Home Secretary to match it with a comparable sum and the promise of a free pardon for any cooperating accomplices. Harcourt refused on the grounds that such a move would prove completely useless and, in a revealing letter sent to the City's Town Clerk on 20 December, admitted that when similar rewards had been offered 'of late years' it had been solely 'with a view of satisfying a public demand for some conspicuous action'.[64] No such symbolic gesture would assuage the fears of Londoners this time. As for the promise of a free pardon, an offer extending only to accomplices would automatically exclude 'the possibility of extending the same indulgence even to one or more amongst them who actually took part in the outrage [and] whose evidence is often the most conclusive'.[65]

Unlike previous conspiracies, which had been foiled by the timely interventions of an informer or a weak-willed dynamitard, the one currently holding London in its grip appeared all but impregnable to police and only a couple of days into the new year, its ferocity was once again on display with the explosion in the tunnel between the Gower Street and King's Cross stations of the Metropolitan Railway. As with the previous such attacks on the Underground, the damage proved slight and 'of a much less serious nature than [what had] occurred at Praed Street' two years before.[66] It was also merely the prelude to something altogether grander.

Despite the cold and windy weather, Parliament Square was packed with tourists on the afternoon of 25 January 1885, all flocked to admire the still relatively new architecture of Westminster Palace. Among them, a young Irish woman who, shortly after 2.00 p.m., happened to notice an unusual, smelly roll of cloth lying on the steps leading down from Saint Stephen's Hall. Alarmed, she brought it to the attention of PC Cole who picked it up and ran with it in the direction of the main hall before noticing, along with another nearby constable, that the parcel had begun to heat up and emit a strange whirring sound. Cole instinctively dropped it and it exploded with a tremendous force which instantly created a crater in the pavement wide and deep enough that both policemen fell through it.

Shocked into action, the officer on guard in the Commons ran towards the crypt, followed by more than one hundred gasping and shrieking visitors. A second explosion then tore through the Commons chamber itself just as the crowd had reached the entrance lobby, completely wrecking the benches on the government side and tossing about the seats in the above Peers' Gallery. Nearby police stations were immediately alerted; the Home Office and Scotland Yard were telephoned; Parliament was officially, if not effectively, on lockdown.

Harcourt and Williamson were the first high officials to arrive at the scene, followed by Majendie, Henderson and all the other police chiefs. The fire in the Commons had rapidly been extinguished and although the two unfortunate constables who had handled the first bomb had had to be rushed to hospital after being pulled out of the debris, everyone else appeared more or less unharmed. Harcourt could nearly draw a sigh of relief, turning to the Marquess of Hartington and quipping about the 'dust of ages' now covering the floor in a thick brown layer. Within minutes, however, rumours began to spread through the agitated crowd outside that the Tower of London had also been blown up. Harcourt asked Captain Eyre Shaw, Superintendent of the Metropolitan Fire Brigade, if the rumours were true; they were.

The explosion at the White Tower had occurred almost simultaneously with that in Saint Stephen's Hall but had been considerably less powerful despite taking place in a room full of antique rifles and medieval armour. It had resulted in slight injuries to half a dozen persons, a great deal of broken glass and a small fire that was quickly put out. Now, as the smoke started to clear away, Tower officials were busy sealing off all exits and, with the aid of incoming police, rounding up the panicked tourists for questioning. In a matter of hours 'all [had] come through the ordeal successfully' – all except a 'suspicious' Irish American who 'stuttered his answers' and did not appear to have a valid address.[67]

The initial public reaction to the newest spate of outrages was predictably irate. 'If men or women can walk into the Houses of Parliament in broad daylight', declared *The Standard*, 'with policemen on duty all round them, and deposit charges of dynamite at their leisure... as if they were invisible... a panic totally out of proportion [will soon follow].'[68] The same opinion was expressed more vehemently by the queen herself who suggested that precautions should be tightened to the point of barring the public from virtually any prominent building in Westminster.[69]

Harcourt declined to go that far, but ordered the deployment of eighty-eight plain-clothes detectives for 'inside protection' at several London museums and government buildings in addition to the more than one thousand uniformed officers already posted at various public buildings throughout the capital.[70] Privately, however, the Home Secretary had little hope of ever addressing the failings of the political police, noting in a letter to Spencer that 'our enemies are making rapid progress in the arts of attack, we none in those of defence'.[71]

Jenkinson agreed, if for different reasons, asking resignedly in his own missive to the Irish Viceroy: 'What is the good of getting good information if this is all that comes of it?' In light of his Boxing Day memorandum to Monro, the bombings served only to confirm beyond all doubt the venality and incompetence of the Yard elite – 'in the whole of London they have not got a single informant and they do not know in the least what is going on' – and the 'clumsiness or the stupidity of some [of their] so-called detective[s]'.[72] To add insult to injury, Jenkinson had already insisted on 'men in plain clothes [posted] inside the [House of Commons]'[73] only to have Henderson assure him, in a memo dated 10 January, that 'every precaution [had been] taken' in the matter of 'guarding the Houses of Parliament'.[74]

The day after 'dynamite Saturday', as the yellow press took to calling it, the Yard detectives finally began to understand what was going on. The fidgety Irish American detained during the roundup at the Tower of London did not appear to be a confused tourist after all. Chief Superintendent Williamson and Inspector Frederick Abberline (later of Jack the Ripper fame) were in fact certain they had nabbed one of the Fenians responsible for the previous day's explosions; they just needed to prove it. The suspect – 'an under-sized but stiffly-built young man' answering to the name of James Cunningham – had been living for some time at various locations in the East End under assumed names and, according to one former landlady, had recently been seen with a suspicious-looking 'American trunk' and one 'black box'. Cunningham denied ever owning such luggage, but the black box was soon recovered from his residence in Scarborough Street and thanks to a timely 'public placard' the police were soon in possession of the trunk. A cabman named Robert Crosby had transported one very like it from Great Prescott Street (where Cunningham lived) to the house at 90 Turner's Road sometime around mid-January. On 3 February Scotland Yard detectives made a second arrest.[75]

The second man in custody was Harry Burton, a twenty-six-year-old American cabinet-maker who insisted he had never seen his accused accomplice or his black box before.[76] The evidence told a different tale. Guides to the Tower of London and Westminster as well as a brown American trunk exactly like Cunningham's had already been found at Burton's house in Turner Road. In addition, it soon transpired that by a remarkable coincidence Burton's former residence in Mitre Square had been watched by a 'man in plain clothes' since well before the explosions of 25 January. The reason: one of Burton's neighbours, a City of London policeman, had submitted a report about a suspicious Irish American who appeared to be 'doing no work'.

The plain-clothes detective had seen Burton in the company of Cunningham as early as 18 January 'and there was no doubt that the two prisoners were acquainted with each other'.[77] That by itself would not have sealed Burton's fate if not for two unexpected developments. The first: Cunningham's black box turned out to contain a fully functional detonator clumsily hidden in a sock; the second: Cunningham seemed to fit the description of one of three suspicious men spotted near Gower Street station shortly after the explosion of 2 January. Two witnesses were brought forward – a police sergeant and a train guard – and presented with a line-up at the Bow Street Police Court. Although more than a month had elapsed since the Gower Street explosion, both witnesses 'pointed out Cunningham as being one of the suspected men travelling in the guard's brake on the night of the explosion'. Cunningham's 'great uneasiness' at being scrutinized in this way only seemed to confirm his guilt.[78]

On 9 February Cunningham and Burton were both formally charged at Bow Street on remand with being implicated in the explosions at the Tower of London, Westminster Hall as well as 'the outrage on the Metropolitan Railway on the 2nd [of January]'.[79] Over the course of the next three months the case against them thickened considerably thanks to a parade of witnesses whose testimonies appeared to implicate the two in the outrages on the London Underground of February 1884 and even the explosions of 30 May.

The evidence was purely circumstantial; the tattered trousers and coat found at Charing Cross were very like those Burton had been seen wearing, while the black bag of dynamite left at the base of Nelson's Column was the type Cunningham favoured. However, as Justice Henry Hawkins observed while passing sentence, 'the circumstances have sufficiently established on you guilt of which no human being could have any possible doubt'. The jury certainly seemed convinced that at the very least the explosion at the Tower had been their handiwork, even if doubts were expressed regarding the police's extremely providential finding of the charged detonator in Cunningham's black box.

An explosion at the Admiralty building, initially thought to be the work of Fenians, but later revealed as the vengeance of a disgruntled employee, certainly served to reinforce a sense of desperate urgency. Burton and Cunningham both received penal servitude for life and, as if to dispel any lingering doubts, a day after the sentence was passed, the anonymous account of 'an American informant' appeared in the British press purporting to give a detailed account of the two Fenians' activities in America as 'prominent members' of O'Donovan Rossa's party.[80]

The case was a resounding and desperately needed victory for Scotland Yard, one made all the more poignant by the discovery on 10 February 1885 of a great quantity of dynamite in an abandoned bookshop in the West End – Mackey Lomasney's last earthly abode, as it later transpired.[81] Commissioner Henderson noted that 'great credit is due to Mr. Monro and the officers of the Criminal Investigation Department employed in the case for the able and persevering manner in which the evidence was collected and sifted'.[82] Likewise, Harcourt acclaimed, during a ceremony honouring the bravery of the two constables wounded in the Commons explosion, the merits of the British police – 'the friend of the people', adding that 'it ought always to be remembered that in a free country, as England is, the police work under restrictions in the detection of crime which do not apply to the police of other nations'.[83]

There was more than Rule-Britannia triumphalism to this remark. Harcourt's break with 'un-English' policing was now final and Jenkinson, only days before, had written to Spencer to say that 'things look very ugly all round just now'.[84] On 21 May the inevitable happened. Wanting to appear conciliatory, Jenkinson approached the Home Secretary with details about his latest scoop concerning the recent rift between the Clan na Gael and the anti-dynamite IRB majority. Naturally, Monro had been kept out of the loop because 'secrecy is very important and if the Scotland Yard men get on to these men, my sources of information will be endangered'. Harcourt flew off the handle:

> It is monstrous that the London Detectives should not know of these things. For two years you [i.e. Jenkinson] have been flying in my face, spending money on getting information and doing nothing. I shall this evening write a minute ordering you to tell everything to Mr. Monro, & if you like you can take the responsibility of disobeying my orders. It is all jealousy, nothing but jealousy, you like to get information & keep it to yourself. You are like a dog with [a] bone.[85]

A few days later he reiterated the same criticisms in Monro's presence, refusing to listen to anything Jenkinson 'had to say about the necessity of protecting my informants' and insisting that 'I should give all my information at once to Scotland Yard, and… that I should place my informants at Mr. Monro's disposal.'[86] Adding fuel to the fire was Jenkinson's recent admission that he had been duped by a 'hoax and discreditable plant',[87] further confirming Harcourt's fears about secret agents. The Assistant Commissioner was undoubtedly pleased to see his rival being taken down a peg, but as he later recalled in an autobiographical note, his feelings towards Harcourt were equally rancorous:

> Harcourt nearly drove me frantic. As the enquiry [into the Cunningham-Burton case] went on day by day the copies of statements of witnesses were, under Home Office direction, sent to the Secretary of State and he and Mr. Jenkinson then proceeded to construct a case… [They] wanted explanation of this and that circular which did not suit their view of the facts… [They] had no business [attempting] to direct a police enquiry instead of letting the responsible police officers do the duty.[88]

# CHAPTER 5

# 'Waiting games'[1]

After months of infighting over Ireland, electoral reform and an increasingly unstable foreign policy, the Liberal Party was 'like a man afflicted with epilepsy [whose each] fit [is] worse than the last'.[2] On 9 June 1885 the government fell, having been defeated on the floor of the House of Commons on a part of its budget. By 24 June a new, but short-lived, minority Conservative government was in office with Lord Salisbury as Prime Minister[3] and Richard Assheton Cross (who had been Home Secretary under Benjamin Disraeli) as Harcourt's replacement. Despite Salisbury's stated hostility to increased police powers in opposition, Cross asserted in a memo of July 1885 that this was a time of 'national evil' demanding certain 'political necessities'.[4] Some things undoubtedly had to change, however. There would be no more rewards, Cross said, for officers 'merely doing their duty', at least in theory.[5] More importantly, Jenkinson's nebulous role at the Home Office had to be sorted out once and for all along with all 'questions of difference' left over from the previous administration.[6]

As Cross outlined in a lengthy memo, Monro's control over the Metropolitan Police force and 'the detective part of it in particular' was no longer the subject of debate. Jenkinson's 'abnormal and… temporary' office existed 'solely in consequence of… national danger' and for the time being, both he and Monro had to work together 'as members of a Cabinet' and to communicate to one another 'all information… as to… conspiracies'. Jenkinson lost most of his remaining thirteen RIC detectives in London (who, as Henderson had noticed, weren't even Irish[7]) as well as his ability to organize 'secret watching' – now the exclusive preserve of the Metropolitan Police.[8] Nevertheless, he continued to be 'at liberty to communicate or not to communicate to Mr. Monro the names of his informants, similar liberty being allowed to Mr. Monro'. Cross thought he was merely splitting the difference, as he confessed to the new Irish viceroy and fourth earl of Carnarvon, but in truth the relationship between Jenkinson (now weakened considerably) and Monro (still deprived of access to his rival's informants) continued to deteriorate.[9]

The situation in Ireland was also worsening thanks to an incipient agricultural depression and the rising fortunes of the National League, now bolstered by the vital support of the Catholic clergy. The tenuous truce negotiated in the wake of the Phoenix Park murders was no longer sufficient. Carnarvon had a long and vast experience managing colonial affairs (having previously served as Secretary of State for the Colonies), but little knowledge of Irish matters, relying heavily on information supplied by his Permanent Under-Secretary, Sir Robert Hamilton (now in charge of 'ordinary' criminal investigations) and by Jenkinson (still master over 'special work').[10]

The irony of a Conservative viceroy receiving advice on Ireland from two Home-Rule Liberals was not lost on Jenkinson and by late July the spymaster had made up his mind: the increasingly untenable position of Assistant Under-Secretary in Ireland had to be traded for a stable office in Whitehall. As he explained to Carnarvon:

> [All] the work of the Crime Department should be transferred to the office of the Inspector General of the RIC... I should still receive information from the Special Department through the Inspector General [but] I should no longer be Assistant Under-Secretary [for Police and Crime]. My position would be an imperial one. Practically my work would be very much the same as it is now but I should be relieved of some detail work, and should be able to devote my time to collecting information from all parts and weaving it into one whole.[11]

The viceory fully embraced the idea but Cross proved harder to convince. While not objecting to 'proposals entirely [affecting] the Irish Gov[ernment]', the Home Secretary strongly hinted that 'it would not do to leave [Jenkinson] as a secret officer without any permanence or recognized position paid out of [Home Office funds]'. Carnarvon responded by highlighting the 'excellent work... of a very anxious kind' that Jenkinson had done in the past in spite of 'not [being] very popular everywhere'.[12]

Jenkinson then pleaded his own case before Cross, prophesying that 'if before the close of the next session the Parnellites succeed in obtaining some form of Home Rule we should probably hear no more of Dynamite'. Failing that, he argued, it was adamant that 'we must keep on collecting information and watching all National and Fenian organizations'.[13] Yet Jenkinson could no longer pretend this was merely a professional issue; he simply had to obtain some type of assistant under-secretaryship at the Home Office if he was to be able to 'take a house or settle down anywhere' with his wife and children. 'I naturally cannot be free from anxiety', he blurted out in a rare moment of emotional candour hitherto reserved only for his correspondence with Spencer.[14]

Cross could not be assuaged. The spymaster had to look for other routes into officialdom and one in particular appeared to be promising. For all his misgivings about police powers, Prime Minister Salisbury had already begun to develop a keen interest in Fenian informers, signing off on several reports coming in from America via the Foreign Office.[15] If Jenkinson could ingratiate himself with the Conservative elite (nominally in an alliance with Parnell) he might be able to inch things along in the right direction. There were two problems with this plan, however.

The first became apparent when in early November Jenkinson secretly had one of his lengthy memoranda printed for the use of cabinet members. At its core was something that few British politicians at the time, whether in government or opposition, could countenance: an impassioned, point-by-point defence of Home Rule. Ireland, Jenkinson argued, was 'passing through a revolution' and the government could either choose to quash the Irish people's demands for 'legislative independence' – a 'most foolish and short-sighted' course – or it could acknowledge 'frankly and generously' the vast support for Home Rule in Ireland and try 'in consultation with the leaders… to ascertain whether a separate Parliament could not be granted'. Parnell, he pointed out, was a conservative at heart and in a devolved Ireland the status quo would be 'a strong Conservative party, supported by the Roman Catholic Church… the landlords, the newly-created peasant proprietors, the farmers, and the professional classes'.[16]

It was no use; a few days after circulating the text Jenkinson, during a private meeting with Salisbury, realized just how badly he had misjudged the mood of the new government. The Prime Minister, Jenkinson explained in a letter to Carnarvon the day after, 'takes a rather gloomy view of the future, and… thinks… [that] Home Rule [will] not come from the Conservatives'. This the spymaster naturally judged 'so terrible and so lamentable',[17] but his disastrous attempt at propelling Parnellism into the mainstream of the Conservative Party proved to be the least of his worries.

Jenkinson's second and by far most serious problem was that his reputation had finally caught up with him. To his former masters, his 'lack of political instinct or regard for Parliamentary opinion' had been offset by his industriousness and 'excellent Liberal [credentials]'.[18] To his new Conservative employers, however, the spymaster appeared not only presumptuous but positively dangerous. Just a couple of days after sending copies of his Home Rule 'manifesto', Jenkinson had proceeded to do the same for key members of the opposition (viz. Spencer, Lord Northbrook, G. O. Trevelyan and Lord Rosebery), casually informing Carnarvon of it after the fact.

The viceroy was outraged, but Jenkinson persisted, making his views fully known to no less a figure than William Gladstone, this time furtively and 'in a private capacity'.[19] Having just sketched out his own Home Rule scheme,[20] the Grand Old Man was the only one to receive the memorandum with any degree of enthusiasm, noting in his reply to Jenkinson – of whom he was only vaguely aware – that he agreed 'very emphatically [with] the leading propositions of [his] letter' and that he too was 'enraged [by] people talking of waiting games'.[21]

Salisbury called a general election in December 1885 and it too produced a hung parliament, elevating Parnell to the status of kingmaker. The former played his waiting game and resolutely refused Gladstone's plea for an all-party Home Rule project. The Conservative Party cry was now Coercion for Ireland, the Union at all costs. In the end Parnell chose Gladstone who, despite Queen Victoria's displeasure, was returned to power, setting the stage for the oncoming crisis. In the short term none of this made much difference to the workings of the political police, but thanks to yet another regime change the rift between Monro and Jenkinson widened. The new Home Secretary, Hugh Childers, proved indifferent to the conspiracies of 'dangerous people',[22] but was forced to take notice of the individuals tasked with suppressing them.

On 8 February 1886 London experienced some of the worst rioting since the Reform agitation of the 1860s after a demonstration organized by leading English socialists in support of the city's unemployed degenerated into a spree of window-smashing and looting in the West End. As scandalised commentators delighted in pointing out, the socialist leaders – among them Henry Hyndman[23] and John Burns[24] – had abandoned all pretense of civility, brandishing red flags as drunken looters stopped carriages in the street to demand money from terrified passersby.[25]

Although no government buildings were attacked or even picketed, the scale of the destruction (about £50,000 in total), the nature of the targets (establishment clubs as well as ordinary shops) and the ostentatiously 'revolutionary' symbolism – all invited comparisons to the Paris Commune in the British and foreign press.[26] Worse than the threat of insurrection, however, had been the almost comical degree of incompetence displayed by the Metropolitan Police in responding to the emergency. During the brunt of the West End melee hundreds of constables had been dispatched to the wrong places, if at all, and had, on a few occasions, even refused to engage the looters out of fear of disobeying orders.[27] Editorialists argued that the Met's 'military character', a leftover from its Peelite past, was now 'prejudicial to its efficiency', and warned against turning the force's hapless superintendents into 'scapegoats while those responsible for the system are exempted from its consequences'.[28]

Childers, installed just hours before the rioting commenced, thought the discredit hanging over the London police reflected badly on the Home Office and quickly scrambled together a committee to inquire into the riot. Unsurprisingly, the resulting report put the blame for the fiasco on the Metropolitan Police leadership and recommended a thorough overhaul of the entire administration of the force. In the end, however, the only head to roll was that of Commissioner Henderson – 'the Dodo' as W. T. Stead's *Pall Mall Gazette* had irreverently nicknamed him.[29]

The report was a complete whitewash given that Henderson was not the only police chief to prove incapable of closely monitoring the increasingly uncontrollable situation in the West End. Monro, in fact, had been having tea with the Home Secretary during the worst of the street brawling; worse, despite several plain-clothes detectives infiltrating the crowd, Scotland Yard were unable to produce any relevant evidence during the hearings of the Childers Commission, prompting one Irish newspaper to observe sardonically that Monro 'has adopted the stupid course of inviting evidence by public advertisement… [showing] how exceedingly meagre must be the information already in the hands of the Criminal Investigation Department'.[30]

Finding Henderson's replacement proved tricky given the whiff of taint plaguing the Scotland Yard leadership. One name, however, was consistently floated by several newspapers very early on and by late February it seemed the rumours were materializing. '[To]-night… Mr. Childers has decided to invite Mr. Jenkinson to accept the office [of Commissioner]', declared the *Aberdeen Weekly Journal* on 23 February along with several other newspapers.[31] It is unlikely such rumours were more than the fervent speculation of journalists or that Jenkinson was in fact 'very actively intriguing for the succession to the Chief Commissionership'[32] given his recent exchanges with Cross and Carnarvon. To Monro, however, the prospect seemed real enough and entirely frightening. An 'occasional note' published in the *Pall Mall Gazette* a couple of days later warned that:

> Mr. Monroe [sic], the only efficient member of the Police Junta, would find it almost impossible to work with Mr. Jenkinson, for the friction between Scotland-yard and the Irish police authorities has been very severe. 'If Mr. Jenkinson is appointed', says one who knows the force, 'there will be a mutiny in six months'.[33]

The quarrel at the top of the Metropolitan Police hierarchy was now public knowledge. Risking further isolation, Jenkinson attempted to make an ally of Childers by insisting on Monro's amateurism and on his own indispensability.

As the Home Office spymaster explained in a memorandum,[34] Monro believed there was nothing to be learned about Fenians from 'any Irish in London'. By contrast, Jenkinson attached 'great value to local information', giving Daly's arrest a couple of years prior as an illustration of how 'most valuable clues to what is going on outside are obtained from inside'. Monro, in fact, was dangerously encouraging a wider, systemic, failure within the political police apparatus as the 'detectives in Scotland Yard are excellent at working out a case when they have got clues and after an outrage has been committed [but] they fail when anything like secret work is required or when informants have to be approached'.[35] Some reorganization 'of the staff and some change in the system of work', the spymaster conceded, was indeed required, 'but what is urgently wanted, particularly in connection with this secret political work is a staff of secret watchers [and] good informants... selected with care and secretly organized and known only to the Head of the Department'.[36]

The *Pall Mall Gazette* had predicted the contest for the Commissionership would 'lie between the well-advertised Jenkinson' and an up-and-coming military man,[37] and on 13 March Lieutenant-Colonel Charles Warren (recently appointed to the command at Suakin, a port city in north-eastern Sudan) was revealed as the new Commissioner of the Metropolitan Police. After Henderson's unceremonious dismissal, this appointment seemed only to confirm the official cover-up feared by the *Pall Mall Gazette* in the wake of the West End riots, and yet, surprisingly, Warren's arrival was almost universally acclaimed by everyone with an opinion on the future of the London police.[38]

A lieutenant-colonel he may have been, but Warren was no indolent fogey or jackbooted oaf. A celebrated archaeologist with a love of Masonic arcana and the 'saviour' of Bechuanaland (in the face of German and Boer encroachments), Warren had also run for Parliament in 1885 on a Radical platform of Home Rule and free elementary schooling. Most crucially, he was also a capable detective, having recently apprehended the murderers of fellow orientalist Edward Henry Palmer during an archaeological expedition in the Sinai.

For all his remarkable qualities, however, Warren was still a man who favoured sweeping, uncomplicated solutions, and who revered the uniform – continuing to don his military regalia while insisting that his constables receive military-issue boots – along with the proper chain of command. He took for granted the notion that as Commissioner he would have complete control over the force and the unquestioning loyalty of all his subalterns. The separateness of the Criminal Investigation Department he found suspicious from the beginning, though he did not resent it as much as the extra-legal network of secret agents employed by the Home Office.

Ever aware of his own isolation Jenkinson took 'the earliest opportunity' of explaining to Warren the nature of his political work, putting all his 'confidential papers... in his hands' and offering to 'make over to him all my secret agents... [and] to serve under him... [for a] harmonious and successful action against the Fenian Conspirators'.[39] At first Warren showed no signs of opposition, but he undoubtedly found the state of the political police nothing short of abominable (as he would later admit).[40] A few weeks after the encounter, Jenkinson's agents in London were already being aggressively shadowed and 'examined' by plain-clothes detectives and by May Warren had complained to Childers of the spymaster's 'conduct'.[41] Jenkinson had just made another determined enemy.

Over the course of the following month the simmering dispute between Jenkinson and Monro exploded into a wide-ranging controversy, involving a host of new characters (from Home Office under-secretaries to Lord Morley, the new Chief Secretary for Ireland) and a substantial exchange of memoranda.[42] At the centre of it were two issues: first, the supposed insubordination and uncooperativeness which Monro, and now Warren, continued to vocally impute to the Home Office spymaster; and second, the general incongruity of the latter's position in Britain as well as in Ireland (the post of Assistant Under-Secretary for Police and Crime having been abolished). For the most part, the surviving record reads simply like the chronicle of an acrimonious workplace dispute somewhat toned down by a thin veil of late-Victorian officialese. However, it occasionally reveals valuable insights into how high-ranking policemen and bureaucrats understood the role and limitations of the political police in Britain.

Monro, for example, objected to Home Office plans of placing Jenkinson under the authority of the Commissioner not merely on personal, but also on 'constitutional' grounds given that 'for all practical purposes' his rival 'would be as independent of the Police as he is now'.[43] This was in contrast to Warren, who, though convinced the spymaster had a 'tendency... to create unnecessary scare and panic', was 'ready to make the experiment' of overseeing Jenkinson's future work, since firing him 'will lead subsequently to the supposition in the minds of the public that any outrages are due to [his] absence'.[44]

More surprising than either Monro's implacable opposition to his rival or Warren's fear of a new public backlash, however, was the Home Office's ambivalence, embodied by the new Permanent Under-Secretary, Godfrey Lushington.[45] Lushington sided with Monro in the latter's demand that all 'secret watching by... agents of Mr. Jenkinson' cease immediately,[46] while at the same time underlining, with the frankness of an independent liberal, the inherently unstable and contradictory nature of political policing in Britain:

> [There] are good arguments in favour of a Continental system in which the Government Police as represented by Mr. Jenkinson would be supreme and have control over the Local Police – a system which possesses very great and obvious advantages. Mr. Jenkinson would then of course have all the threads in his hand, and would be able himself to follow up the trail of a conspirator wherever he might go... so too there would be no difficulty in Scotland Yard, Dublin and Mr. Jenkinson communicating which is the point made by Mr. Morley, for Mr. Jenkinson would have control over both.[47]

The point was merely theoretical. Convinced that 'the day for controversy has passed', Childers made his final decision on 9 June; Jenkinson had to relinquish all endeavours in the capital and limit himself to passing along information from outside the UK to the Commissioner. The spymaster understood he was being set up to fail – 'it has been a matter of great doubt with me whether under the altered conditions I could be of any real use' – but reluctantly agreed, as did Monro.[48]

On 20 July the cabinet resigned after Gladstone's version of Home Rule was soundly rejected by the electorate in a general election that proved to have drastic consequences for the course of British politics. It brought Salisbury's Conservatives back into power with a comfortable majority and threw the Liberal Party into an even more pronounced existential crisis after seventy-four Liberal Unionist MPs declared their complete opposition to Home Rule (without, however, expressing support for a formal alliance with Salisbury's party). The new Home Secretary, Henry Matthews,[49] received his first briefing on 'this Jenkinson business', as Salisbury had dismissively called it,[50] the day he took office. It was in the form of a timeline, prepared by Lushington, detailing 'the relations of Mr. Jenkinson to the Metropolitan Police' and the 'several phases... his functions [had passed through]'. It pointed out that the spymaster was still without an 'official position but [being] paid £2400 p.a. out of the English [Home Office] Secret Service Fund', concluding with the following admonition:

> It is obvious that the present partnership – based on the principle of territorial division, the Commissioner taking the Metropolis and Mr. Jenkinson all outside the Metropolis – must be totally ineffective against Fenian Schemes unless thorough confidence subsists between the two partners. It is equally obvious that there is no such confidence and no hope of any. If then the State requires to be protected against Fenianism, there must be a change, or dissolution of this partnership. Were the question only between Mr. Monro

and Mr. Jenkinson, I should still be decidedly in favour of keeping Mr. Monro... but [it] is not... The Chief Commissioner equally with Mr. Monro distrusts Mr. Jenkinson. This then points to the advisability of Mr. Jenkinson going as the one escape out of the difficulties.[51]

Matthews, whose fastidiousness had invited comparisons to a 'French dancing master'[52] even from members of his own party, was certainly not going to tolerate any maverick behaviour from a placeless underling, especially one who happened to be an unrepentant Liberal boring from within in the service of Home Rule.

When in early September one of Jenkinson's men – possibly Major Gosselin – made his way over to Stockholm to trace the steps of a Fenian believed to be in town 'plotting some explosion in London',[53] it seemed as if the spymaster was finally content with doing his job or what remained of it. Monro and Warren, however, only found out about the operation after in mid-October a memo from the British legation in Stockholm arrived at Scotland Yard via the Foreign Office.[54] What in different times might have passed for a mere gaffe or a simple misunderstanding now looked like open insubordination. Matthews warned that 'this incident disturbs the hope I had formed that matters would work more satisfactorily between Mr. Jenkinson and the Met. Police'[55] and suspended the former's Secret Service funds pending further investigation.

On 11 December the inevitable transpired. After 'much anxious consideration' Matthews determined to relieve the spymaster of his duties, fixing 10 January of the following year 'as a convenient day' for his effective termination. The Home Secretary agreed to take 'personal charge' of some of Jenkinson's informants as well as of 'all papers containing information'. Judging by the letter he wrote to Spencer that same day, the now former head of British and Irish counter-Fenianism received the news with resigned disappointment, but also with a tinge of relief. The 'true sum' of his offence, he believed, was merely that he had served the Liberals 'well and that [he] was in favour of Home Rule'.[56]

A few days after his dismissal was announced, Jenkinson went to Dublin where he was now ironically welcomed by the Nationalist press as a 'thoroughgoing Home Ruler', who, unlike the recently deposed Robert Hamilton, 'has not been made to do penance for his convictions [which] for all that... are no secret'. Briefly stopping in Paris to '[wind] up some business connected with his Government work',[57] he finally returned to London on 10 January 1887 to hand over the keys to his office, but not his papers, which Matthews mysteriously never recovered.[58]

Just as it had done the previous year, the *Pall Mall Gazette* managed to get an early scoop, revealing Jenkinson's retirement on 8 January in two separate editorials. 'Mr. Jenkinson', the author(s) pointed out, was 'the man who has in his hands all the threads of the secret conspiracy of dynamitards… the soul and centre of what may be called… our Third Section', and the entire Dublin Castle leadership had vouched for his trustworthiness. How then could Mr Matthews – 'not exactly the most amiable and fascinating of mortals' – dispose of this loyal servant merely because of his 'choleric temper'? The stoppage of Fenian outrages would 'not [be] permanent, and at any moment we may be confronted with the same danger' as before. Would the government be 'left to face [future] conspirators against law and order without the assistance of the man who is practically the head of the Intelligence Department'? Did not the secrecy and the efforts to 'deprecate public discussion' of the spymaster's forced resignation suggest that the Home Secretary himself feared 'much public evil' would be occasioned by it?

It is not clear if the Home Office had in fact attempted to suppress the news of Jenkinson's departure (quickly picked up by other newspapers) but the *Gazette*'s rebukes were certainly not taken in jest. A day after breaking the story, the newspaper received an opinion piece from an unnamed 'member of the Civil Service' (almost certainly Lushington) which appeared in print the following day. 'Under the autocratic system on which English Cabinet offices are constituted', the author of the piece explained, 'it is hopeless to expect that outside departments and officials will work… well under the direct control of a subordinate… [who] did not even belong to the Office' and who had made a habit out of posing 'as a Schouvaloff or a Fouché'. The press was entitled to make pedestrian observations on matters of state but it was not, properly speaking, 'within [its] province… to blame the Minister, who rids himself of a superfluous adjunct whose presence necessarily involves friction and mischief'. 'Mr. Jenkinson', simply put, '[had] to go'.[59]

## CHAPTER 6

# 'A long and complicated inquiry'[1]

IN March 1886, at the height of his conflict with Jenkinson, Monro toyed with the idea of making 'secret work' the province of every Metropolitan officer. As he explained in an internal memo:

> I look to all the members of the force in each Division to aid in picking up information which may be useful... [and to report it] to me confidentially. Every man on the beat, and every officer above him can in the performance of his daily duties, acquire much information as to residents, questionable characters – places used for meetings – lodging-houses where Irish Americans, or men likely to be dangerous may go to... There is a tendency to think that information on such points is to be furnished [solely] by the special men employed... This is not so.[2]

By the end of the year, however, the problem with this plan had already become obvious. The entire CID force consisted of a mere 313 officers, working an average of ten to eleven hours a day, at a time when London numbered more than four million.[3] Out of these, fifty-eight constables, twelve sergeants and three inspectors were employed on 'special duties... in connection with Fenianism' in London and at ports, leading to a 'perceptible weakening of the Staff at the Central Office and of the Divisions'.[4]

Despite his ambivalence towards it, Warren had sanctioned an augmentation of the 'political department' in December 1886 and by early 1887 the request was finally approved. One first-class and one second-class inspector, four sergeants and twenty constables now joined the select fold of detectives performing 'services connected with Fenianism within the Metropolitan Police District'.[5] This, however, was not a mere strengthening of Irish Branch and the public building protection corps and as Warren explained, the augmentation was partially 'intended for the formation of a [new] Special Branch'.[6]

To the extent that its purpose was to fill the void left by 'Mr. Jenkinson's Department', especially his network of spies and informers 'other than in London',[7] the new CID Branch had to be very special indeed. Its initial staff consisted of only one DCI (John Littlechild) and three DIs (John Pope, William Melville and Patrick Quinn), all arguably the elite of Section B; all, except Pope, later key figures in the political police hierarchy. Under a 'verbal agreement' between

Home Office Under-Secretary Stuart-Wortley and Permanent Secretary to the Treasury Sir Reginald Welby, the 'Specials' were paid out of Metropolitan and Special Police Vote funds the amount of £640 (a figure arrived at by Lushington and Monro) over the course of the following financial year – 'considerably less than the cost of the one Chief Inspector and three Inspectors'.[8]

The secrecy surrounding this new venture was underlined by the fact that officially Chief Inspector Littlechild was only being transferred from CID special duty to CID 'special clerical duty' and by the fact that detectives of Section B and Section D continued to be listed together as officers 'employed on special duty in connection with Fenian matters', without any regard for their respective branches.[9]

Just how a nominally independent section consisting of four detectives earning less than their usual pay[10] was supposed to replace the 'private anti-Fenian agents employed by Mr Jenkinson'[11] is not clear, but the Assistant Commissioner immediately took a close interest in the new branch – officially called Section D of CID – especially after it became clear that the Home Secretary, not Warren, was officially in charge of it.[12] Just as he had during his battle with Jenkinson, the Scotland Yard chief longed for his own chance at playing the 'secret agent', a title he assumed shortly after without any hint of irony.

Although Special Branch later came to be associated with the fight against political extremism of all stripes, in 1887 it was only the experimental spearhead of Irish Branch, which meant that it required the sort of intelligence that could not be got from attending a 'social gathering of the Irish-speaking people in London for singing, reciting, and so forth'.[13] To this end, Monro made possible Robert Anderson's return to the Home Office, drawing him 'into still closer touch with Scotland Yard'.[14] A man after Monro's own heart (sharing with him the same devout evangelical faith and deep-seated conservatism),[15] Anderson was also, more crucially, the person in charge of Henri Le Caron – now a vital and singular link to the Clan na Gael's inner sanctum. The only thing needed to consolidate the new status quo was a resounding success.

In April Her Majesty's Chief Inspector of Explosives, Colonel Vivian Majendie, decided to pay the Assistant Commissioner a visit and inform him of his latest experiments with 'Fenian [formerly Greek] Fire'.[16] The report he brought with him was essentially a page and a half of instructions on how to put out a chemical fire, but Monro thought it useful to send a copy to every Chief Constable in Britain. More than 360 copies were printed for this purpose and even the Inspector General of the RIC was apparently 'anxious to have 70 copies'.[17] 1887 was the year of Queen Victoria's Golden Jubilee and intercepted cables from America had already revealed the existence of a fund set up by a ragtag of disaffected Rossa-ites and Clan na Gael-ers for 'celebrating the Queen's Jubilee in a manner becoming Irish Nationalists'.[18] In addition, the press was already speculating on the existence of a Fenian conspiracy,[19] with the Central News Agency reporting the existence of an actual Jubilee dynamite plot on 15 June. Despite fears that 'explosives have probably already been shipped',[20] however, in the spring of 1887 the plan to disturb the Jubilee celebrations, insofar as there was one, remained very rudimentary. In fact, it rested on one person, General Francis Frederick Millen, re-establishing a channel of communication between Fenian exiles in France and the Clan na Gael leadership in New York.

The few details of Millen's life that have survived read like the fevered concoctions of a *Boy's Own* story[21] and they are made all the more remarkable by the skill with which the swashbuckling Irishman managed to navigate between his many separate, and all equally fallacious, identities. The General (a title conferred by Benito Juarez of Mexico for services rendered during the war against the French) had become involved with Irish republicanism during the 1860s, taking part in the Fenian Rising of 1867 and rapidly soaring through the ranks of the Clan na Gael to reach a position on the military council in the 1870s. It is not clear to what extent Millen was actually committed to 'the cause', but as early as 1866 he had begun informing Her Majesty's Consul in New York on the doings of American Fenians. He continued doing this into the 1870s and 1880s, all the while posing as a committed revolutionary on the one hand, and as a respectable correspondent for *The New York Herald* on the other.

Millen's Home Office handler, assuming he had one, remains unknown and the full extent of the General's double-dealing is likewise shrouded in mystery. Jenkinson likely knew him, especially after the spymaster began carefully cultivating his American network of informers in 1883, but evidence of a close relationship, while tempting, remains purely conjectural.[22] What is certain, however, is that Henri Le Caron – the only British spy well-placed enough to know that Millen and the Clan were up to something – *did* have a handler in Anderson, who was now back on the Home Office Secret Service payroll. Anderson had also been, prior to his three years in the wilderness, as well positioned as Jenkinson to receive offers from potential double agents, something which he boasted about in his 1910 memoir *The Lighter Side of My Official Life*:

> I was in daily communication with Dublin Castle, and I kept up a private correspondence with our consuls in … American cities, as well as with Le Caron and my other American informants. And never a week passed without my having to meet London informants, sometimes at my residence, and sometimes at out-of-the-way places – for of course they never came to Whitehall.[23]

For Anderson a typical work day in the early 1880s might have easily involved meeting after hours with one of his 'satellites', who on one occasion, 'had arrived to tell me that another of the [Land] League women had come from Dublin, with money from the League Treasurer to enable the fugitive criminals [Frank Byrne and Patrick Tynan], who were then in France, to escape to America.'[24] That Millen was one of those 'satellites' – one who had now apparently decided to go rogue – is certainly not far-fetched, although, as in the case of theories which seek to implicate Jenkinson, there is no hard evidence one way or the other.[25]

The lack of evidence did not, however, prevent Anderson from resolutely charging his former rival and arch-nemesis with engineering the Fenian plot which now appeared to be hatching in France. While assuring Monro that Millen's every movement in Paris was fully known to him, Anderson was nevertheless careful to add in an official memorandum that Millen's 'schemes of outrage... had been communicated to the gentleman who preceded [Monro] in charge of the Secret Service Department & that in the event of [Millen's] arrest & conviction [Millen] might have made statements on the subject of... a most embarrassing kind.'[26]

Anderson never substantiated his claim that Jenkinson had colluded with the Jubilee plotters, but he happily repeated it in his tell-all memoirs, noting that the conspiracy had been hatched 'during a disastrous interval before [Monro's] appointment; and he [i.e. Monro] had no knowledge of it until a prominent Fenian – I will here call him Jinks – arrived at Boulogne to carry out his twofold mission on behalf of the American Clan na Gael and the British Government.'[27]

That Millen (or 'Jinks' – an obvious allusion to 'Jenks'[28]) should have been on a mission from the British government seems like an extraordinary claim to casually let slip at the end of a minor paragraph, but then that was not the first time that Anderson had manifested a penchant for outrageous claims. In early March 1887 the Secret Service director had begun penning a series of pseudonymous articles for *The Times* under the heading 'Parnellism and Crime' in which he strove to draw as explicit a link as possible between Parnell and the dynamite party by, among other things, quoting a series of forged letters which suggested Parnell had been in collusion with the Phoenix Park conspirators. These articles had quite momentous consequences for the Conservative government, but in April 1887 Whitehall was focused on ensuring the Jubilee celebrations would be a triumph.[29]

The few surviving official records describing Millen's activities in 1887 (there are none for previous years) do not reveal the extent to which Home

Secretary Matthews was familiar with the Fenian double agent. For example, while Monro fully shared Anderson's theory regarding Jenkinson's involvement in the Jubilee Plot, there is no mention of it in the otherwise lengthy report on Millen's activities submitted to Matthews on 14 June. Instead, the Scotland Yard chief specified only that Millen had been 'deputed for active work' by the Fenian Brotherhood and the Clan na Gael and that there was 'no doubt that this man is an agent of the extremists of the dynamite factions'.[30] Monro's omission shows the extent to which he and Anderson were already a law unto themselves, attempting to control the amount of intelligence being circulated in Whitehall in the hopes of using 'Jenkinson's mistake' to their advantage. Anderson later recalled how 'to have carried out the original [Jubilee] scheme, and to have seized these men and brought them to justice, letting [Millen] return to New York – this would have been ostensibly a brilliant police coup, but it would have been achieved by discreditable means'.[31]

The problem was not, however, the discreditable means – which, as we shall see, Anderson later described as vital to the British political police – but the fact that the handling of the Jubilee conspiracy was now significantly in the hands of Prime Minister Salisbury. Once made aware of Millen's presence in Paris, the Prime Minister insisted the Fenian agent should be placed under surveillance by the French (much to Monro's dismay).[32] In spite of previous tensions between the French and British police over the surveillance of Irish radicals on French soil, the seriousness of this new conspiracy and the political weight behind the request from London made the *Préfecture de police de Paris* remarkably cooperative.

In a coded despatch received at the Foreign Office on 15 June and forwarded to Matthews the next day, the British ambassador in Paris explained that following communications with the Minister of the Interior he had been assured that Millen and one of his Paris associates would be 'watched in the manner desired… both at Paris & Boulogne'.[33] A day later Her Majesty's consul at Boulogne received a brief *renseignement* on Millen's movements in that city, although there was little that *Inspecteur* Catart of the railway police could say except that the middle-aged Irishman was very good at keeping himself to himself.[34] Inspector William Melville of Section D, who was also in Boulogne keeping an eye on Millen for Monro, was equally laconic in his despatches.[35]

If Monro and Anderson had ever planned on using Millen to score a 'brilliant police coup', that plan now had to be reconsidered for several reasons. First, the Jubilee was only days away and the possibility that a Fenian double agent might actually be involved in a real plot against the queen loomed increasingly large, especially in an atmosphere of press-circulated alarm. Second, although he had clearly revealed Millen's connection to the Clan na Gael, Le Caron could never be summoned in court without blowing his cover and sparking a public controversy; yet if Millen were to be captured red-handed, the government's case would obviously have to rest to a significant extent on the evidence supplied by Anderson's spy.[36] Third, even if the embarrassing intelligence in Millen's possession implicated only Jenkinson, it also had the potential of tarnishing the entire political police. Monro therefore had to act fast before the conspirators either got out of reach or decided to follow through with the 'display of fireworks'.[37] Millen had to be confronted in the hopes that he would give up either the plan or, as he had done so often before, his brothers in arms.

Adolphus Williamson, who had been promoted to Monro's right-hand man in July 1886 in order to help with the 'secret work' at Scotland Yard,[38] was now in Paris with his wife meeting General and Mrs Millen in the lobby of the Poilly Hotel. Also in attendance – Williamson's 'former chief and colleague at the Yard', James Thomson, who, along with Mrs Thomson, had already managed to strike up a friendship with the Millens.[39] This somewhat surreal couples' retreat was anything but convivial, however. Although Anderson glosses over the incident in his memoir, mentioning only that Millen eventually 'went back to America in ignorance' of the clever ruse that had been played on him,[40] in the report written on behalf of Monro, Williamson is described as having been tasked with 'interviewing [and] warning [Millen] that we were well aware of his character and projects... that we would make no terms with him [and] that [we demanded] an absolute disclosure and abandonment of his mission'.[41]

Millen refused to cooperate and on 21 June, the day of the Jubilee celebrations, he simply wrote to the Paris emissaries of the Fenian Brotherhood and the Clan na Gael that the mission was now compromised, 'attributing his failure to the close vigilance of the Police'.[42] A report submitted by a commissaire L. Tournon on 23 June seems to confirm much of that perception. While noting that the French police had obtained the addresses of Millen's correspondents in Britain with the help of a certain 'agent anglais' (Inspector Melville), the report also describes the General as panicked and despondent: 'He never goes out and sends his wife to the post office on his behalf... He informed the hotel yesterday that he would undoubtedly be leaving the following day... and that he wants to return to America. I will observe his departure and will advise the English agent in due time'.[43]

The 'entire scheme was now rendered abortive',[44] but the farcical 'plot' was far from over. Millen's two daughters, Kitty and Florence, who had come over with their mother, soon left Paris for London where, on 13 July, they received a package from their father. It contained 'three letters addressed respectively to William O'Brien M.P., Matt Harris M.P., & Joseph Nolan, M.P., all serving to 'introduce [Millen's] friend "Joseph Melville", the name adopted by... [John] Moroney for the purpose of his mission'. As Anderson already knew, John James Moroney was one of the men the Clan had sent over from New York to investigate the progress of Millen's work 'and if necessary to supersede him'.[45] Here was 'evidence' not only of leading members of Parnell's party being on friendly terms with a known Fenian (not that Anderson needed it) but, even more disconcertingly, of an ongoing dynamite conspiracy.

Moroney 'appeared on the scene' on 4 August, the day he was first observed by Special Branch detectives meeting at the House of Commons with Joseph Nolan, Nationalist MP for North Louth. Monro had obviously had access to the Millen girls' mail, although he never took the trouble of explaining by what means. A second meeting took place the next day and Nolan 'brought [Moroney] and [Michael] Harkins', one of Moroney's associates, 'into the House... [leaving] at a later hour by the Members' Staircase'.[46] At this point Monro decided to put an end to all this apparent scheming by using the strategy he had already deployed against Millen: instead of 'waiting to seize [Moroney] in the execution of his designs', the Scotland Yard chief placed the Fenian 'openly under strict Police observation'. This was a confirmation of Harcourt's 'picketing' model as much as it was an attempt to prevent the public airing of abhorrent details.

Questioned by Special Branch detectives on the purpose of his stay in London, Moroney gave a painfully weak alibi and absconded to Paris, where he was shortly reported by Inspector Melville to be in Millen's company.[47] He returned to London a couple of weeks later flush with new funds and took up lodgings, along with his mistress, at the glitzy Hotel Metropole. More trips followed, including one to Ireland, but Moroney continued to be 'picketed' and occasionally questioned by Monro's detectives and by 9 September the spendthrift Fenian had finally decided he had enough.

A surreptitious return to Paris followed, where he again met with Millen and another New York comrade, and then a final journey back home to America. Monro had had to let him go, but could not resist having the last laugh, ensuring that shortly after their landing in New York, Moroney and his mistress were stopped at customs for 'attempting to pass dutiable goods'.[48] Within a matter of days Millen also crossed the Atlantic – for the last time as it turned out – having put his revolutionary career permanently on hold. The farcical Jubilee Plot was appropriately over.

Back in London, however, Moroney's 'subordinate emissaries' were now marooned in Islington, powerlessly waiting to be picked up by police. Michael Harkins was the first to be arrested and found to be in possession of a gun, a note with Moroney's (fictitious) business address and 'a newspaper cutting relating to Mr. [Arthur] Balfour's movements'.[49] Arthur J. Balfour – the new Conservative Chief Secretary for Ireland, nephew of the Prime Minister and future Prime Minister himself – had recently introduced a new draconian Irish Crimes Bill and was known as 'Bloody Balfour' in Nationalist circles thanks to his unflinching support for Coercion.[50] He was in a sense the perfect Fenian target, but even so, the evidence against Harkins was, at that point, unconvincing.

Interestingly, that is not how Monro justified his decision not to charge him before a magistrate. Instead, the Scotland Yard chief once again invoked the need to avoid prosecuting 'the agents of a plot where there was even the semblance of justification for asserting that in its inception the govt. was privy to it'. A mere pawn like Harkins (who was illiterate) likely knew very little about the controversial origins of the conspiracy he was involved in, but the Assistant Commissioner was eager to consolidate his leadership over Scotland Yard while openly repudiating Jenkinsonian tactics. As the final paragraph of the Anderson-penned report explained:

> To have permitted the plot to ripen, taking measure only to ensure the apprehension & punishment of the criminals, w[oul]d have involved comparatively little cost of thought or effort or money, while the result w[oul]d doubtless have impressed the public with a belief in the zeal & efficiency of the Police. But the policy I have adopted & steadily pursued, tho' of course a thankless one so far as the public is concerned, will, I venture to hope, receive the approval of the government.[51]

Monro's thankless prevention did not end there, however. One of Harkins's known associates, an Irish American who went by the name of Joseph Cohen, had been found dead at his lodgings in Lambeth Road a day before Harkins' arrest. The death had been the result of tuberculosis, but given the company Cohen kept and the fact that his place had been under surveillance for a while, an inquest had to be called. It took place on 26 October at the Southwark Coroner's Court before a crowd of journalists. Cohen's former landlady (a certain Mrs King) and Harkins were both publicly questioned by Monro on the nature of their connection to the deceased. In a move not without some tactical brilliance, the Assistant Commissioner decided he would 'impress the public' after all and be seen to be doing nothing but 'put[ting] an end to the plot altogether by publishing the details of it'.[52] Cohen – Monro declared before his audience – had been an agent of the terroristic Clan na Gael, an organization led by none other than 'General Millen, who was in London at the Jubilee' along with his assistant Moroney '[who] was in America now'.[53]

A more detailed account was released to the press the following morning, containing most of the (uncontroversial) facts that went into the Assistant Commissioner's official report to the Home Secretary. The impact was significant. Reminiscing many years later, Monro noted with satisfaction how the day after the inquest all the newspapers had commented 'in a bewildered fashion on the inquest… [while] the Radical organs saw in it some deep political design to injure the Liberal Party. But what I wanted was to entice public attention… and I succeeded in so doing.'[54] Some journalists did warn of a possible cover-up – 'nothing like the whole of the circumstances were disclosed' noted one *Dublin Evening Mail* correspondent – but such criticisms proved rare and even the sceptics were ultimately convinced of the 'indisputable evidence to prove the existence of a conspiracy… for assassinating men at the head of the Government… [and] to destroy… public buildings in London'.[55]

CHAPTER 7

# The battle of Trafalgar Square

WHAT Anderson had described as the 'long and complicated inquiry'[1] into the Jubilee Plot finally ended on 18 November 1887 when Thomas Callan (alias Thomas Scott) was picked up in Goswell Road by a City Police sergeant as the former was coming out of a barbershop. Subsequent enquiries indicated that Callan, the last of Harkins' known associates, had been trying for some time to cut loose from the whole operation, but his failure to dispose of nearly twenty-seven pounds of dynamite ended up sealing his – as well as Harkins's – fate. Within a few days of Callan's arrest both men had been charged with conspiracy 'to endanger life or cause serious injury to property' and, after a lengthy and highly publicized trial, were sentenced to fifteen years each.[2]

Despite this apparent success, the year 1887 saw the Metropolitan Police descend into its worst crisis in more than a generation. The first real cracks appeared during the summer of 1887 when Home Secretary Matthews and Metropolitan Police Commissioner Warren found themselves at the heart of two quite separate scandals, one involving the wrongful arrest of a young seamstress for prostitution,[3] the other the execution for murder of a possibly innocent East End salesman.[4] Neither arguably did any widespread damage to the police's reputation, but in the fallout both the Home Secretary and the Commissioner had become legitimate opposition targets where they had previously been promising agents of change or at least honourable servants of Her Majesty's Government. Even to the moderately Liberal *Lloyd's Weekly Newspaper* it was now 'becoming only too evident that under the new regime of... Mr. Matthews and Sir Charles Warren... the Metropolitan Police force is degenerating'.[5]

Such fears were only dramatically confirmed later in the year thanks to a resurgent militancy among London's socialist and radical organizations, several of which now vied to reclaim Trafalgar Square, the site of several consequential demonstrations during the Reform agitation of the 1860s, as the unofficial headquarters of London radicalism. Besides its symbolic value, the square was also increasingly important as a refuge for many of the capital's unemployed and homeless,[6] who, for militant socialists like John Burns and Henry Hyndman, constituted an ideal reserve army for the upcoming revolution.[7]

October saw a series of demonstrations of the unemployed take place across London, with the largest reserved for Hyde Park and, naturally, Trafalgar Square. On 14 October socialist orators led a demonstration of about two thousand unemployed to the Mansion House in the heart of the City (where they were refused an interview with the Lord Mayor) and then to Trafalgar Square, where such luminaries as William Morris, George Bernard Shaw, Annie Besant and Pyotr Kropotkin gave speeches on the labour question and declaimed against the recent sentencing of the Haymarket anarchists in Chicago.[8] These demonstrations continued almost on a daily basis and by late October, after a series of clashes between police and demonstrators at Westminster Abbey, the Mansion House, Hyde Park and Piccadilly, it became clear that a final and likely extremely violent showdown was all but inevitable.

Things had not always been this tense. As recently as 17 February 1886 the Social Democratic Federation could still courteously inform the police 'of a demonstration to be held in Hyde Park' and ask at the same time 'that such steps may be taken as may be necessary to secure the orderly conduct of the meeting to avoid a repetition of the [West End riots].'[9] For its part, the police could do little but take notice given that – as Monro had explained to then Commissioner Henderson – it had 'no informants amongst English socialists, as having such informants… has always been discouraged by [the] Govt.'[10]

Foreign socialists were of course another matter, as a July 1886 incident seems to suggest. It centred on a two-sentence telegram sent from London by someone using the pseudonym 'Nemesis' to the controversial Dutch socialist Ferdinand Domela Nieuwenhuis – then on trial for lese-majesty at The Hague – which forcefully warned of the 'vengeance' that would follow should Nieuwenhuis be found guilty. Having easily intercepted the telegram, Dutch authorities were eager to obtain the sender's true identity and, ideally, the original telegram stub itself (to be produced as evidence in court).

Despite his isolationism in police matters, Monro had helpfully suggested that 'I may be able to find out through an informant who the writer is, as it is in Dutch [and] the number of Dutch-writing people in London must be limited.'[11] The original telegram was located and forwarded by the Postmaster General to the Home Office, but after some half-hearted deliberation, Childers decided that there was nothing to be gained from aiding the Dutch in this manner. The request was therefore summarily refused under the fail-safe excuse that accepting it would prove unconstitutional.[12]

Harder to ignore was the fact that the old spectre of revolution seemed to be once again on the prowl in Europe. The Dutch authorities' interest in the threatening telegram had come on the heels of a massive riot in Amsterdam, inspired in part by popular hatred for the politically motivated actions of local police, while in neighbouring Belgium, martial law had been declared after widespread rioting and extensive looting.[13] In Germany Bismarck's draconian Anti-Socialist Laws had been extended in April 1886 and in the United States the ongoing trial of the Haymarket anarchists, universally believed to be innocent by those on the socialist left, stood out as an international symbol of capitalist injustice.

Although liberal Britain appeared far removed from this type of populist indignation, the overseas popular protest increasingly put the danger posed by 'the mob' (especially in London) in a decidedly new light. *Times* editorialists declared that 'the recent riots in Chicago... Belgium, and Holland... cannot fail to make thoughtful people reflect seriously on the subject of popular disturbances' and proposed strategies for containing riots with a minimum of violence.[14]

The Home Office too appeared less attached to the notion of non-interference with home-grown revolutionaries, sanctioning the active surveillance of some militant socialists, especially certain members of the SDF. One example was Harry Quelch, editor of the SDF official party organ *Justice*, who had rhetorically asked his readers 'whether, being condemned to die, it would not be better to die fighting like men than to be choked to death like rats in a sewer'.[15] Quelch was placed under surveillance in the autumn of 1886 after information had reached Monro that 'some of the men connected with the Socialist agitation and meetings were being instructed in military exercises... at the house of a man... well known as [a] Socialist orator'.[16]

Plainclothes detectives were installed in a neighbouring house and confirmed Quelch's home served merely as a meeting spot for ten eager idealists who seemed more interested in arguing over drill rules than in storming palaces.[17] To Monro and Warren, however, this was no laughing matter. Articles in *Justice* now openly advertised drilling classes in Clerkenwell and Battersea and for the Assistant Commissioner this was enough to cement the notion that 'however contemptible the movement may be in its inception, it may give us trouble if it is allowed to extend... and the police may justly be held responsible for not checking it'.[18]

The Home Office professed a somewhat less pessimistic view, with Matthews dismissing the 'marching' as 'hardly... a "military" movement when it is performed by unarmed men'[19] and Lushington quipping that 'the drilling of these men... is as little likely to be dangerous as Kalisthenics [*sic*]'. Yet even they agreed the ultimate purpose to all of it could not be anything other than 'a violent uprising of the people... [and] however far off this day may be... this drilling [and] even the announcement of drilling keeps alive the feeling – the unwholesome feeling – of the possibility of violence.'[20] By the end of the year the fad for drilling fizzled out, arguably not because of 'picketing' by Yard detectives, although Monro acknowledged the socialists 'may have got wind that they were being looked after.'[21] The surveillance, however, continued in accordance with Matthews' wishes that 'observation... be kept to ascertain whether the drilling is resumed [and] if so to obtain the names of those who conduct it.'[22]

As DS John Sweeney of Section B later recalled in his memoirs, for authorities the 1887 Jubilee marked not only a time of worrying about Fenian 'fireworks', but also a 'time of great anxiety' in connection with an apparent resurgence in left-wing radicalism. While taking a 'very active & discreet part in enquiries' connected to the case of the Islington dynamitards,[23] Sweeney had also had the occasion to observe the activities of London's 'restless' revolutionaries:

> They held frequent meetings; there was quite a small boom in the circulation of revolutionary publications... All this meant that numerous alarming reports reached the Yard [and] extra vigilance was exercised everywhere. All known Anarchists, Nihilists, and other revolutionaries... were kept under the closest observation... We knew the addresses of most of them, and the places where they worked, when they did any honest work, and we kept watch on those places... But when the Jubilee rejoicings were over we breathed more freely.[24]

The claim that all known revolutionaries had been kept 'under the closest observation' may contain more than a grain of retrospective self-justification, but in the wake of the demonstrations of October 1887 the 'political department' at Scotland Yard was increasingly being used to watch and even infiltrate socialist organizations as the overlooked but telling case of Alfred Oldland suggests. Oldland, a casually employed handyman, petty thief and active member of the Peckham branch of the SDF, was arrested on 18 October for 'riotous conduct' and assaulting two police constables 'in the execution of their duty' during a demonstration held in Hyde Park earlier that day.[25]

There was nothing remarkable about this, but Oldland quickly became something of a cause célèbre in socialist circles and a bail fund in his name was soon set up by the Reverend Stewart Headlam and Annie Besant (both prominent SDF sympathizers) which, in turn, raised eyebrows at the Home Office. Hamilton Cuffe, assistant to the Director of Public Prosecutions, demanded to know exactly who the troublemaker was and how 'came Mrs Annie Besant and the Revd gentleman to bail such a man', the implication being that even by socialist standards, the arrestee was a thoroughly disreputable fellow.[26]

Luckily for Cuffe, Scotland Yard knew all about Oldland, as a revealing report submitted by Inspector Pope of Section B, and countersigned by Section D's Chief Inspector Littlechild, shows. The 'Socialist Oldland' was in the habit of changing addresses quite often and was 'a painter by trade but his occupation is home fitting and handyman... and is an indifferent workman'. More crucially, Sergeant Walsh, also of Section B:

> has known Oldland for past 10 months and has had conversation with him in which he [Oldland] has made certain admissions respecting his being a member and one of the principals of the Peckham branch of the Social Democratic Federation, and the [Sergeant] was present on Sunday 23rd inst. at a meeting of this branch at Western Road, Peckham at which Oldland took the credit of originating the meetings of the unemployed and the manner in which he assaulted the Police for which he was arrested.[27]

Although this report tells us two important things – that Sections B and D worked closely together and that far from not being involved in 'any very active surveillance of left-wing groups',[28] the political department at Scotland Yard was becoming integral to the authorities' strategy for dealing with such groups – it does not tell us the exact extent to which the political police was deployed against non-Fenian radicals at this stage. Certainly, the active policing of the unemployed demonstrations was overwhelmingly left up to the uniformed branch of the Metropolitan Police – often to highly controversial results.

By mid-October 1887 Warren, who despite his Radical past was growing increasingly impatient with democratic politics, had decided that the strain put by demonstrators on the Metropolitan Police's resources had reached a critical point. On 17 October the Commissioner's Office released a proclamation, subsequently posted throughout London, banning all meetings in Trafalgar Square. It was, strictly speaking, an illegal manoeuvre and it immediately prompted Matthews to end the ban, pending a final verdict by the Law Office. This decision aggravated Warren considerably and on 25 October the Commissioner wrote Matthews a long, angry memorandum against what he regarded as an untenable situation. While the inhabitants and business-owners of the area were 'rapidly becoming terrorised', the 'mob' was taking encouragement from the authorities' recent volte-face:

> Up till Saturday the mob were all turned off and met in Hyde Park, but both today and yesterday they have proceeded in organized crowds headed by a red flag through the wealthy shop-keeping parts of London, and, though no overt act of violence was committed, spread terror among the inhabitants who in many instances closed their shutters... [The demonstrators],

in a very great part, consist of the veriest scum of the population, and... although these gatherings may fluctuate... we are approaching the 9th November when the Lord Mayor's Show takes place about which there is a strong view often expressed among some of these people.[29]

Warren was now preparing for war and he did not intend to be burdened by any more Whitehall hand-wringing. He ordered Metropolitan constables – two thousand of whom were daily needed to control the crowds in Trafalgar Square – to focus their entire energies on containing the 'reign of terror', even at the expense of enforcing moral order.[30] Magistrates were likewise instructed by the Commissioner to 'abstain from expressing an opinion upon the conduct of constables',[31] while the Office of Works was curtly informed that Trafalgar Square was once again to be made 'unavailable for [all] public meetings'.[32]

Matthews was furious, but the Commissioner redoubled his efforts, pointing out that the Home Secretary had verbally given his consent to the reclosure of the square, and insisting at the same time that 'I am in no way whatever under the direction of the Home Office; in some matters I am directly under the authority of the Secretary of State; in other matters I have my duties and responsibilities defined by Act of Parliament'.[33]

Incorrect in fact and law, Warren was as much a subordinate as 'the Head of any other Home Office department', Matthews retorted,[34] but by now the shutdown of the square was a fait accompli. On 7 November, two days before the Lord Mayor's Day, Warren received a begrudging admission from the Home Office that 'a public notice may be issued warning the public that... until further intimation no public meeting... will... be permitted... in [the] Square'.[35]

Thanks in part to the grim autumnal weather, 9 November saw little unrest, but the new ban on meetings in the square, which was not lifted until as late as 1892, predictably enraged socialist and anarchist militants as well as sections of Liberal opinion. The *Pall Mall Gazette*, as always, led the charge with a series of combative editorials, with titles such as 'Sir Charles Warren: Usurper',[36] in which W. T. Stead declared that 'we have reached a crisis in the political history of the metropolis when something must be done and that, at once, to defend the legal liberties of the Londoner from the insolent usurpations of Scotland-yard'.[37]

In addition to the outrage occasioned by Warren's heavy-handed tactics in London, there was the furore surrounding the arrest of Irish Nationalist MP William O'Brien (incidentally the same O'Brien named in the General Millen controversy) for inciting resistance to Irish Secretary A. J. Balfour's newly enacted Crime Act – an arrest which had previously sparked violent protests at

Mitchelstown in County Cork during the course of which police had opened fire on protesters. Balfour was quick to offer an 'implacable and unapologetic defense of police action',[38] but on opposition benches the indignation was palpable. Despite a long record of support for Coercion in Ireland, all Liberal Party Home Rule converts were up in arms about what they described as the 'Mitchelstown Peterloo' – the first in what seemed like a possible series of 'occurrences resembling those of our anti-reform days'.[39]

With its permanent state of legal exception and judicial procedures which no longer required yearly renewal in Westminster, the new Irish Crimes Act was certainly a far cry from any notion of English due process. The Irish executive could '"proclaim" districts at will, supress organizations it deemed dangerous, remove trials to different venues and give magistrates summary jurisdiction over offences such as conspiracies against the payment of rent or encouraging boycotting'.[40] Rights of free speech, publication and assembly were entirely subordinate to Dublin Castle's vision of law and order in a way that simply bore no comparison with how militant radicalism was being policed in England.

However tenuous the link between agrarian unrest in Ireland and reform agitation may have been, it helped cement the notion that the police constables firing on civilians in Cork were no different from those holding Trafalgar Square against all comers. On 11 November the Metropolitan Radical Association called for a massive demonstration in Hyde Park, fully aware that several contingents of demonstrators would have to pass through Trafalgar Square. The event was immediately endorsed by virtually all left-wing papers, from the Radical-Republican *Reynolds's Weekly Newspaper* to the anarchist *Freedom*, especially after 12 November, when Matthews turned away a deputation of the demonstrators led by prominent Liberals.[41]

As expected, Warren spared no effort preparing for the confrontation and by 13 November thousands of Metropolitan constables and several hundred troops could be seen spread out through Trafalgar Square and the surrounding areas. A *Pall Mall Gazette* journalist described the scene in terms that seemed to conjure up some distant colonial unrest:

> [In all] there were 100 men in single file along the parapet on each side of the Square, outside and inside 120 in double file; at the head of each of the steps leading into the Square stood 100 constables in fours, while 50 more covered the corners at each end, standing two deep. In front[,] the face of the Square was held by fully 750 men standing four deep. [Pairs of]... mounted police patrolled all sides of the Square in couples. Altogether there were 1,500 policemen in the Square; [a further] 2,500 were employed in breaking

up processions and in reserve; 300 of the Grenadiers were behind the National Gallery until four, when they were brought out with fixed bayonets to line the parapet in front of the National Gallery. The First Life Guards were called out at four. Altogether Sir Charles Warren kept the Square clear for the Queen by employing... 5,000 men... from twelve to six, for no other purpose than... trampling roughshod through the crowds.[42]

The trampling commenced at around 3.20 p.m. and lasted for nearly two hours, during which time successive baton charges by mounted and on-foot officers met with one concerted effort to force the square, several attempts to resist the clearing effort and a great deal of hooting and hissing. By 6:30 p.m., as the Life Guards began to move – 'like a machine' – one final time through the square, making sure all roadways were clear, the conclusion that Warren had triumphed over the more than forty thousand demonstrators became undeniable.[43]

This archetypal 'Bloody Sunday' (as the *Pall Mall Gazette* took to calling it) had produced more than two hundred wounded on the protesters' side (two of whom subsequently died of their injuries) and nearly eighty on the police side.[44] The following day W. T. Stead wrote to Gladstone complaining about police brutality – 'a brutality which I have never before seen in the whole of my life'[45] – but Gladstone was now at pains to distance 'the Irish question... [from] this question of Trafalgar Square meetings in all its phases'. Home Rule, he argued, would 'suffer disastrous prejudice were it to be associated in any manner with those who make appeals with Metropolitan disorder'.[46] As a consequence, the majority of Liberal newspapers, with the obvious exception of the *Pall Mall Gazette*, did not go out of their way in condemning police actions. Warren, the *Daily News* pointed out, had indeed exceeded his jurisdiction and while the protesters in the square had only tried to assert 'what they thought their rights... we cannot agree either with their principle or their method of action'.[47]

Deprived of mainstream political legitimacy – the Conservative press was unreservedly for law and order[48] – the protesters' cause rapidly lost momentum as Warren's popularity with the middle-class public only increased. In fact, less than a week after Bloody Sunday, the Commissioner's office was complaining that 'Sir Charles Warren has received so many letters conveying sympathy with the Police Force... that he is quite unable to reply to them individually.'[49] Yet, as the *Pall Mall Gazette* later noted, not without reason, '[it] may be only a minority that distrusts the police and remembers Trafalgar-square, but it is a very blatant minority, which makes its existence felt on every beat throughout London'.[50]

For members of the Special Branches, the tense months following the 'battle' of Trafalgar Square saw their work in the case of the Islington dynamitards finally recognized. As Monro explained in a memo to Warren, who was only minimally familiar with the case, the operation of the previous summer had 'entailed upon myself and all the officers under me, constant watching for many months, and the way in which all the officers employed have worked and assisted me in carrying out orders... especially... Chief Inspector Littlechild, Insp[ecto]rs Melville & Quinn & Serg[ean]t McIntyre... is beyond all praise'.[51]

The financial rewards distributed to the police, totaling £250, were modest compared to those dispensed in the similar Gallagher case of five years before, but they were nonetheless material and liberally dispersed. Some Home Office mandarins complained that when police officers were being rewarded 'for extra clerical work... the system of rewards is being carried too far',[52] while others wryly noted that Callan and Harkins had been 'traced down by a department of the Metr[opolitan] Police especially constituted to watch would be dynamiters and... all the officers whom it is proposed to reward specially were appointed for this very purpose'.[53]

Warren wholeheartedly endorsed the reward scheme, but despite this apparent vote of confidence in Monro, the Commissioner's relationship with his Assistant was beginning to break down completely. The previous year Monro had begun making an impassioned case 'for having an Assistant Chief Constable to aid in performing the work of the CID and Head Quarters [since] neither Mr. Williamson nor I ever had a moments [sic] leisure'.[54] At the time the request had been politely ignored, but after Williamson was diagnosed with 'debility and fainting attacks' in early 1888, Monro began reiterating his pleas more forcefully.[55]

The Commissioner begrudgingly consented, making it clear that he would do his utmost to prevent Monro getting exactly what he wanted. Ostensibly this was because Warren did not think the addition fully necessary. The real reason, as he himself came close to admitting, was pure spite: 'it [is] quite out of place', the Commissioner declared in a letter to Matthews, 'to make the Police Force suffer for the sake of the Irish Branch wh[ich] is really not part of the Police Force [and]... if [anyone is] to leave 22 Whitehall Place [i.e. the Met headquarters] it should be those who [are] in the basement viz. the Irish Branch'.[56]

Warren attempted to push for a 'very highly spoken of' Mr Fitzgerald to get the job of Assistant Constable, but Monro was already set on his own candidate: Melville Macnaghten – an Anglo-Indian Old Etonian ex-planter whom he had known since his days as Inspector General of Police in Bengal. Macnaghten was in many ways the ideal Victorian placeman; supremely well-bred – his father had been chairman of the East India Company while his cousin, Baron

Macnaghten, was a prominent Conservative and Law Lord – 'well-educated' but not university-trained and above all a gentleman 'of the highest character' who knew how to deal with 'a most turbulent set of natives'.[57] Warren objected to Macnaghten's lack of 'official, military or Police experience', but agreed that he 'may be appointed on probation for a period of 6 months' as long as he did not interfere with 'the Criminal Investigation work in [Metropolitan] Divisions' or draw a stipend from police funds for the use of a horse.[58]

Matthews agreed and by late March Macnaghten had already been informed by Monro that he had got the job. That might have been the end of it if not for a colourful little story doing the rounds on the London club scene. Macnaghten, it seemed, was not quite the iron-fisted sahib his friends had made him out to be. As Warren explained to the Home Secretary, 'I have just ascertained that Mr. Macnaghten was the subject of considerable excitement in India some years ago and it caused a good deal of feeling between Liberals and Conservatives not only in Calcutta but also in England.' The incident, which had occurred in 1881 when Macnaghten was still manager of his father's sugar plantation, had seen the former attacked and beaten by some of his workers for reasons never made clear. All the same, Warren argued:

> [regardless of] whether Mr. Macnaghten did anything or not to irritate the natives into beating him, I have merely to point out that such action on the part of Hindoos in Lower Bengal is said to be most exceptional... I have to state that... it is going very far to select a man who has no qualifications of any kind at the present time [and who] is the one man in India who has been beaten by Hindoos.[59]

Monro pleaded for his friend's innocence, adding that he had simply been 'the victim of an agrarian outrage... [by] an incipient "Land League" in the [area]',[60] but to no effect. Warren had already withdrawn his recommendation and it was up to the Assistant Commissioner to communicate the embarrassing about-face – now public knowledge – to Macnaghten. No other candidates would be considered; Monro had to make do with his ailing Chief Constable if he did not wish to give up 'his duties as Secret Agent'.[61]

Tensions only worsened after Matthews called Monro to testify before a select committee into the admittance of strangers to the House of Commons (occasioned by the previous year's revelation that John Moroney and other Fenians had been given a tour of the House by an Irish MP). Although the Assistant Commissioner had been summoned in his capacity as 'the only man [with] personal knowledge of the facts' in the case of the Islington dynamitards,[62] an article in *The Times* mistakenly reported that Monro had been in charge of security at the Palace of Westminster. Convinced that the Assistant Commissioner and the Home Office were now actively conspiring to subvert his authority, Warren took this as a pretext to lash out with another impetuous denunciation:

> I have to point out that Mr Monro is not in charge of the Police at the Palace of Westminster... [and] that although the Secretary of State may over-rule the Commissioner's opinion upon matters connected with the efficiency and discipline of the Police Force it does not appear that... he can take away from the Commissioner the responsibility which rests upon him by statute... I conceive that... [the] Secret Agent [i.e. Monro] as a matter of his existence must be an alarmist, his very being depends upon that... [and] moreover it is eating into the heart of the discipline of the Police Force having a system under which the Assistant Commissioner can go to the Secretary of State direct without reference to the Commissioner.[63]

Matthews defended Monro's performance as 'A[ssistant] C[ommissioner] C.I.D., and... Secret Agent',[64] as did the Home Office mandarins who had never, in any case, cared much for Warren's overbearing manner. Lushington, for example, had complained of Warren's refusal to 'recognize his subordination to the H.O.' as early as April 1887, while Evelyn Ruggles-Brise (Private Secretary to Matthews), Charles Murdoch (senior clerk) and Edward Leigh Pemberton (Legal Assistant Under-Secretary) were all convinced that the Commissioner had blown things out of proportion.[65]

Despite this apparent support, Monro was very much on his own in other matters, a case in point being the thorny issue of arrest warrant procedure. On the morning of 10 February 1888, DS McIntyre of the Irish Branch had been despatched to the House of Commons with orders to arrest James Gilhooly, Nationalist MP for West Cork, for incitement to violence under the terms of the new (Irish) Crimes Act. Due to an inaccurate description of the suspect, however, McIntyre had ended up arresting a different Irish MP and, to make matters worse, had proved unable to produce an arrest warrant when asked to do so.[66] Matthews had initially denied any breach of privilege had taken place, insisting the police had simply made an honest error, but the case of mistaken identity soon provoked uproar in the House, with Irish and Liberal members insisting that the incident needed to be referred to a Committee of Privileges. Parnell declared that:

> if it had been an English Member who had been arrested, not only would the question have been treated as one of breach of Privilege, but the Government would have taken care, and the Detective Department would have

taken care, to send a member of the Force who at least knew the hon. Member who was to be arrested.[67]

He was soon joined by leader of the opposition Gladstone himself who decried 'this very grave matter of [the arrest of] a Member of this House... by an officer of police [who] proceeded without being in possession of the warrant'.[68] The controversy was not ultimately referred to a Committee of Privileges – although Matthews was later forced to issue a public apology to the wrongfully arrested MP – but neither was it referred to any other decision-making body or official.

Monro feared this legal uncertainty might be seized upon by high-ranking Radicals critical of Scotland Yard in order to legally oblige police officers (should the Liberals return to power) to be in possession of arrest warrants before effecting any arrest – a situation in which 'police action will be paralysed'.[69] In this instance, however, it seems the Home Office entirely agreed with Warren that nothing needed to change; there was no 'ruling... that the warrant must be in the possession of the officer arresting' and save for 'serious case[s] involving political considerations... Police are to act without warrant if they know [one] has been issued'.[70] As late as March 1890 Monro continued pressing the Home Secretary for legislative steps towards relieving 'police of the responsibility of acting in violation of the law'[71] when effecting an arrest, but to no result. As Jenkinson had once found out for himself, the will to enact systemic change was simply not there.

Owing to this institutional deadlock and Warren's continued attacks on him, Monro began to feel his life had become 'intolerable' by the summer of 1888.[72] As he explained to Matthews, 'a high appointment in Her Majesty's Bengal Civil Service' had been left behind in order to take up 'the specific duties of Head of the [CID]' and 'to perform [them] with more effect than my predecessor'. Monro was no longer going to put up with Warren's 'aspersions' on his 'personal character', or his dangerous ideas which, if left unchallenged, would soon restore the status quo of the 1870s 'the defects of which [had] led to the creation of the [CID] under the separate charge of a responsible officer'. Given the 'extreme urgency' of the matter 'as affecting the public interests', a 'competent Committee' would have to look into the Commissioner's actions 'with the least possible delay'.[73]

Not only was there no committee; Warren's powers only seemed to be increasing and on 17 August the Assistant Commissioner made the ultimate gesture of protest, relinquishing his duties as head of CID. Among the main reasons stated in his official letter of resignation were the 'insanitary' conditions of the CID basement office, his status in relation to the Commissioner, the rule which prevented CID officers from being promoted unless they had served in uniform and the Macnaghten incident.[74] The resignation was immediately accepted, but by some mysterious agreement, details of which do not seem to have survived in the public record, Matthews 'made arrangements to enable [him] to have the benefit of Mr. Munro's [sic] advice as to crime where it may seem desirable'.[75]

Exactly what this entailed is unclear, but a couple of Home Office notes from later in the year briefly refer to Monro doing 'provincial work' as an unofficial Section D inspector without, however, going into any detail.[76] Monro himself later noted in an autobiographical note that following his resignation Matthews had retained him 'as Chief of the Secret Department'[77] without, again, going into specifics. It is, incidentally, telling that Anderson, as the new Assistant Commissioner, was not entrusted with this responsibility.

The exact nature of Monro's new 'secret work' may have been a mystery as far as the public was concerned; the changes at Scotland Yard, however, were anything but. Thus, on 3 September the Press Association announced that Robert Anderson had succeeded Monro at Scotland Yard and that the latter had in turn 'been appointed to an important post at the Home Office [where]... [his] work will be of a character similar to that formerly performed by Mr. Jenkinson'.[78] A month later, the *Pall Mall Gazette* took it a step further by publishing a lengthy and insightful editorial on the conflict between Monro and Warren and the state of the Metropolitan Police which, in its intimate knowledge of the facts (likely the result of another inside track into Scotland Yard), soon attracted the attention of the Home Office.[79] By that point, however, Warren had bigger problems to worry about than his image in the Liberal press.

# CHAPTER 8

# Scandal averted

Despite his dismissal of Monro's concerns about the legal limits of police action, the Commissioner was himself in a legal conundrum in late 1888. As he explained to Ruggles-Brise on 4 October:

> I am quite prepared to take the responsibility of adopting the most drastic or arbitrary measures that the S[ecretary] of S[tate] can name wh[ich] w[oul]d further the securing of the murderer however illegal they may be, provided Hm. Govt will support me... All I want to ensure is that the Govt will indemnify us for our action wh[ich] must necessarily be adopted to the circ[umstance]s of the case.
>
> Three weeks ago I do not think the public would have acquiesced in any illegal action but now I think they would welcome anything which shows activity [and] enterprise. Of course the danger... is that if we did not find the murderer our action would be condemned & there is the danger that an illegal act... might bond the Social Democrats together to resist the Police & it might be then be said to have caused a serious riot... [Houses] could not be searched illegally without violent resistance & bloodshed & the certainty of one or more Police officers being killed... We have in times past done something on a very small scale but then we had certain information that a person was concealed in a house. In this matter I have not only myself to think of but the lives & position of 12,000 men, any one of whom might be hanged if a death occurred in entering a house illegally.[1]

What specific past case(s) Warren was referring to we do not know, but all the same this letter tells us several important things: firstly, that illegal house searches had been undertaken by Metropolitan Police officers in the past; secondly, that Warren still feared 'the mob' and its socialist instigators; thirdly, that Warren's relationship with the Home Secretary had not necessarily improved following Monro's departure; and fourthly, that 'the murderer' – known to the public only by a macabre letter received by the Central News Agency on 27 September signed 'Jack the Ripper' – was increasingly making a mockery of the police's ability to combat violent crime in London.

The Whitechapel murders were universally regarded as the bane of the Metropolitan Police leadership and when Warren finally resigned on 8 November 1888, hours before 'the Ripper' claimed a fifth and final victim, the public sigh of relief stood in sharp contrast to the flow of support received by the Commissioner in the aftermath of Bloody Sunday. One provincial newspaper declared that:

> military organisation is a good thing for the police when they are called upon to guard Trafalgar-square or charge a mob; but the wisdom... of the serpent is the chief requisite in those who have to detect crime. The Whitechapel assassin perpetrates his atrocities on a pavement still echoing to the heavy tramp of the iron-shod constable.[2]

More so than the Ripper murders, however, it was Warren's irreconcilable conflict with the Home Office that ultimately brought about his downfall. Not content with airing his grievances in internal memoranda, the Commissioner had taken the bold step of publishing them in an article written for the November issue of *Murray's Magazine*. It was highly polemical and, given the time of publication, unduly critical of crime detection and fixated on the dangers posed by 'the mob'. The following excerpts embody the spirit of the entire piece:

> The genius of the English race does not lend itself to elaborate detective operations similar to those said to be practised on the Continent. The free institutions of this country are happily quite against any natural training of the youthful mind towards real detective work... The system in vogue on the Continent... [is] a general system of Government espionage which stamps the mind of the people with mutual distrust, and which is reflected in the schools and institutions... Here the constable in cases of felony has scarcely more power than any other citizen – across the Channel the police are masters of the situation [and] the public give way before them... It is to be deplored that successive Governments have... given way before tumultuous proceedings which have exercised a terrorism over peaceful and law-abiding citizens, and it is still more to be regretted that ex-Ministers, while in opposition, have not hesitated to... [encourage] the insurgent mob.[3]

The inappropriateness of these lines caused a sensation in Whitehall. Lushington reiterated his claim that 'the Commissioner is and has long been... in a state of insubordination.'[4] Matthews agreed and under the pretext of an 1879 rule which prevented Metropolitan Police officers from publishing 'embarrassing' material without the explicit consent of the Home Secretary, he publicly chided the Commissioner in the House of Commons. Warren declined to accept any blame and resigned the same day.[5]

Fully vindicated, Monro was able to return into the Whitehall fold, as Commissioner no less. He also got to keep his duties as Secret Agent despite asking 'to be relieved of [them]' and refusing 'to take any salary for performing them'.[6] Whatever his true feelings on political policing at the time, Monro certainly still regarded Irish republicanism as a threat to national security, noting shortly after his return that 'there is certainly always more or less danger from Fenians'.[7] 'Infernal machines' may still have been relatively easy to find in Ireland,[8] but the rise of Home-Rule Gladstonianism and its alliance with Parnellism, as well as the ever increasing fractionalization of American Fenianism meant that the 'dynamite campaign' was becoming a thing of the past in Britain. Political debates on the Irish Question, however, were becoming more heated.

On 18 April 1887 Robert Anderson's muckraking series of articles for *The Times* on 'Parnellism and crime' (whose authorship he acknowledged only in 1910) had reached its infamous apogee with the facsimile reproduction of a letter, purportedly from Parnell, appearing to excuse the Phoenix Park murders of five years before. It read:

> Dear Sir,
>
> I am not surprised at your friend's anger but he and you should know that to denounce the murders was the only course open to us. To do that promptly was plainly the only cours [sic] our best policy. But you can tell him and all others that though I regret the accident of Lord F Cavendish's death I cannot refuse to admit that Burke got no more than his deserts. You are at liberty to show him this, and others whom you can trust also, but let not my address be known. He can write to House of Commons.
>
> Yours very truly,
>
> Chas S Parnell

Although the Irish leader had initially expressed amusement at the news of the publication, the fact that the letter was a blatant forgery had forced him to denounce *The Times*' accusations in the House of Commons as 'an audacious and unblushing fabrication'.[9] Opposition members accepted this as true (with Gladstone playing a particularly prominent role in defending Parnell's innocence), but on government benches there was wilful disbelief. If genuine, the letter promised to completely bury Home Rule for the foreseeable future.

Parnell had chosen not to sue, but a libel action brought against *The Times* by another (former) Nationalist MP, which finally came to court in July 1888, gave the newspaper's representatives a chance to repeat and enrich – by means of yet another discrediting letter – the allegations against Parnell. The Irish leader demanded the matter be put before a select committee of the Commons. For Prime Minister Salisbury, however, this was an opportunity to go on the attack.

Instead of a select parliamentary committee, the government opted for a special commission of three judges to investigate not the authenticity of the *Times* letters, but the links between Parnellism and (Fenian) crime. The highlight of the commission's dramatic proceedings[10] came shortly after, in February 1889, when the true author of the 'Parnell letters' was finally revealed. His name was Richard Pigott, a disgruntled ex-Fenian and hack journalist who had forged and sold the letters as genuine to *The Times* for more than £1,700. Although insisting on his innocence during his initial questioning, Pigott soon lost his nerve and admitted his guilt in a private meeting with Henry Labouchere, the Radical MP and ally of Parnell. After this, the *Times*' case rapidly began disintegrating and Parnell was able to emerge with his reputation unscathed, albeit temporarily.[11]

The Parnell Commission remains a relatively minor episode in British political history, but its importance in the history of the British political police can hardly be overstated. This is because it demonstrates more than any other event of the 1880s the extent to which the British government used, or at the very least colluded with, Scotland Yard's 'political department' in order to advance its own strategic goals. It has already been noted that the author of the articles on 'Parnellism and crime' was none other than Robert Anderson, at the time head of the Secret Service bureau at the Home Office. What must equally be established is that Anderson, by his own admission, had all along acted with the support of his friend James Monro:

> [As] Mr. Monro was then responsible for the conduct of secret service work, I conferred with him before taking action, and we decided to use 'The Times' in the public interest. 'Spread the light' was a favourite aphorism of the conspirators, and with excellent effect I enabled 'The Times' to 'spread the light' at that important juncture.[12]

Although Anderson went on to state that the government 'refused to render any assistance to "The Times" in its chivalrous crusade',[13] the facts of the case suggest the Conservative cabinet did in fact attempt throwing everything in its arsenal at the embattled leader of the Irish Party. A parade of aggrieved landlords, members of the Irish constabulary and obscure informers was summoned before the Commission in the hopes of conjuring up a tangible link between Parnellism and Fenian outrage.

Equally important, the manner in which authorities wasted neither effort nor funds in trying to secure former Fenians as witnesses for *The Times* suggests the forces behind the prosecution extended beyond Scotland Yard and Printing House Square. P. J. Sheridan, one of the Invincibles involved in the Phoenix Park conspiracy who had taken refuge in America, was supposedly offered the staggering amount of £20,000 to testify against Parnell,[14] although he eventually refused to cooperate. Thomas Clarke (aka Henry Wilson), a member of the Gallagher gang then languishing in Chatham Prison, was similarly approached by DCI Littlechild of Special Branch. As Clarke, who, like Sheridan, decided to turn down the deal, later recalled in his memoirs:

> I was marched away and ushered into a cosy little room, where I found Mr. Littlechild sitting at a table in front of the fire… [He said] that there has been a Special Commission appointed by the Government to investigate certain allegations that have been made against the Irish Parliamentary Party. These allegations are to the effect that there is a connection between that party and the Irish Revolutionary Party in America… Most of the Irishmen prominent in public life are to appear and give evidence before the Commission. In fact, everyone is anxious to go forward as a witness. Certain persons in London, knowing that you came from America in connection with the skirmishing movement, believe that you [Wilson] were in a position there to enable you to speak authoritatively on the subject. These persons have sent me down here to see you so as to give you an opportunity of also going forward as a witness…[15]

Chatham Prison was also where John Daly, arrested with James Egan in 1884, was visited by none other than Richard Pigott, who, quite unlike Littlechild, had no formal authority to do so, especially as Daly had not asked to see him.[16] More surprising than all this, however, proved the decision to call in Henri Le Caron to the witness stand – a decision which, given Le Caron's unique value as an informant, could almost certainly not have been made singlehandedly by Anderson (who later claimed that Le Caron volunteered to testify).[17]

Le Caron had of course nothing to do with the infamous forged letters, but he was supremely well-positioned to attest to Parnell's habit – especially before the latter's 1881 stint in Kilmainham gaol – of privately indulging in revolutionary talk. This Le Caron did very well, but even so, it did not take much effort for Parnell's counsel to successfully blemish the veteran spy with the mark of the agent provocateur. It was only a few days after Le Caron's somewhat lacklustre revelations that Pigott took the stand, much to the chagrin of his former paymasters. What the letter forger might have said had he not fled to Spain immediately after his appearance in court in order to commit suicide can only be guessed at.

Exactly how Pigott was so easily able to get out of the country with two plain-clothes RIC detectives tracking his every move,[18] or how he had been granted access to Chatham Prison and to what end, no one in the government seemed able to clarify. Opposition MPs naturally jumped at the opportunity of grilling the Home Secretary over these apparently nefarious irregularities. Tim Healy, the fiery Nationalist MP for North Longford, demanded to know how 'Pigott, by means perhaps of false keys, or having a pass key, enters Her Majesty's prisons with as much freedom as an official there.'[19] Sir William Harcourt led the charge, declaring on the topic of Pigott's likely collusion with Conservative ministers that:

> It is not enough to say that Pigott went to see Daly. He would not have been admitted until some explanation of the purpose of his visit had been given. We have no need to seek an explanation what he went for. We know – and everybody knows – that Pigott went in to get Daly to swear away the character of the hon. Member for Cork [Parnell]. I want to know who sent him there and who allowed him to go on such an errand?[20]

Somewhat ironically, Harcourt also unleashed a scathing attack on Anderson, who, as head of Scotland Yard, stood accused of unlawfully appropriating, and in some cases misplacing, the sensitive missives sent to the Home Office by Le Caron over the years:

> Who can trust a man who hands about official documents?... I have always done my best to defend the Metropolitan Police, but if transactions of this kind are to take place, I shall be compelled to come to the conclusion that the Metropolitan Police can no longer be entrusted to the Home Office. For the Secretary of State to say that it was a proper proceeding for a man in Mr. Anderson's position to betray official documents is wholly unprecedented. If such a proceeding had occurred during the time of any of the right hon. Gentleman's predecessors, a man in Mr. Anderson's position would not have remained 24 hours in Scotland Yard... [Le Caron] was no doubt a valuable instrument... but having got this valuable instrument, having expended upon him large sums of public money, you hand him over to the Times newspaper, and make him absolutely useless for the public service. You hand over your informer to the Times, and your head of the Criminal Investigation Department hands over confidential documents which – whatever the Secretary of State may say to the contrary – were, in my opinion, the property of the Secretary of State.[21]

Despite such interventions, and the extensive press coverage they received,[22] the Home Secretary's replies remained laconic and evasive and no one at Scotland Yard was taken to task over the shady dealings occasioned by *The Times*' 'chivalrous crusade' against Home Rule. While the Conservative cabinet's role in engineering the special commission and securing the evidence against Parnell is beyond doubt, it is not easy to gauge the extent to which any one of the Irish leader's powerful enemies served as the mastermind behind the 'Parnellism and crime' episode. Prime Minister Salisbury remains the most likely candidate, but as a recent biographer of Arthur Balfour has pointed out, the latter acknowledged in his private correspondence that he had 'been "largely responsible" for the format' of the special commission.[23] For the Irish Chief Secretary – as for Anderson and Monro – the purpose of the 'chivalrous crusade' was not so much to embarrass Parnell as 'to make the public fully aware of the motives and actions of men who hid behind an inflamed rhetoric of national oppression to gain land from the Protestants of Ireland, power for themselves and the destruction of the United Kingdom'.[24]

The only changes to befall the Metropolitan Police in the embarrassing aftermath of the Parnell trial were, predictably enough, at the top. Thanks to Monro's return, Melville Macnaghten was finally given the position of Assistant Chief Constable at CID in June 1889 and, following Williamson's death in December that year, that of Chief Constable. Monro himself did not remain Commissioner for long. He had triumphed over his rivals in the Metropolitan Police hierarchy, but he could still not hope to mount a one-man crusade against the Home Office.

The crisis engendered by the London dockers' strike of August–September 1889 was handled remarkably well, in contrast to the excesses of Bloody Sunday, and even socialists like John Burns were willing to look over past abuses thanks to Monro's explicit refusal to turn his constables into a private army at the behest of dock owners.[25] This, however, was achieved in the face of Home Office indifference – Matthews had gone on holiday as the strike entered its third week – and vacillation over how far to accommodate the employers' demands.[26]

In November 1889 Monro once again attempted to reason with his Whitehall boss by highlighting the overtaxed state of the force in a brief but noticeably angry letter:

> I have repeatedly declared that I could not face the winter with the inadequate force at my disposal & the result of all my representations is that at the end of Nov[ember] with snow on the ground & the labour question as

disquieting as ever I have received no addition to the force at my disposal. I appeal to your sense of justice whether this is now expecting too much of me & whether this is not putting upon me a responsibility which should not be placed upon me... I should wrong both my officers & myself were I not to say very respectfully but very strongly that I cannot for an indefinite period take the responsibility of continuing to overtax the powers of the Police as has lately been necessary.[27]

Matthews, however, waved off such pleas, refusing to budge on the issue of arrest warrant procedure, while continuing to sit on a proposal to increase police pensions. The latter was particularly close to Monro's heart[28] and he was undoubtedly incensed when the Home Secretary appeared at first to agree with the proposal, only to then turn around and insist that the pensions of officers retiring after fifteen or twenty years of service should in fact be reduced. As the *Daily News* explained to its readers, 'feeling that this reduction of existing rights would not be accepted by the men... Mr. Monro came to the conclusion that he should send in his resignation, and he did so', on 12 June 1890.[29] 'Had I not done so', Monro later recalled, 'I should have felt myself to be a coward [and] I could never have looked my recruit in the face, and preached to him the duty of self-sacrifice.'[30]

The new Commissioner, Sir Edward Bradford,[31] was another military man with a vast experience in enforcing *pax Britannica* in the more troubled regions of the Empire, but he had more in common with Henderson than with Warren and he was generally thought to be a remarkably amiable man at the Home Office, although tellingly, Matthews does not seem to have taken to him.[32] Also unlike Warren, Bradford had no strong views on the mandate of Scotland Yard.

Sections D and B – the latter classed as a 'clerical section'[33] – did not, at any rate, have much to do following the debacle of the Parnell Commission, the collapse of Fenian skirmishing and the waning of native socialist 'insurrections' in London. As a request from the Italian government received at the Foreign Office in August 1890 seemed to indicate, however, there were still plenty of foreign revolutionaries in Britain who needed active watching. One such individual was Errico Malatesta, a veteran Italian anarchist exiled in London who was preparing a surreptitious return to his homeland. Although Italian police had their own spies among Malatesta's confidantes in the British capital,[34] key information still eluded them. British authorities proved relatively obliging and on 27 April 1891, Inspector William Melville of Section D submitted the following report to his superintendent, Chief Inspector Littlechild:

I beg to report that the Italian Anarchist E. Malatesta has recently been residing at 112 High St. Islington. ~~I have received i~~ Information has been rec[eive]d that about a week or ten days ago Malatesta and a most intimate friend of his named Consorti (another desperado) left this country en route for Italy, and supposed for Rome, for the purpose of fomenting disturbances on 1st May.

The few Italians in London who are aware of Malatesta's departure, are very silent respecting it, and with a view to deceiving any person who would give information to the Italian Government about it, handbills are being printed announcing that Malatesta will speak in London on 1st May. From this circumstance ~~my informant is of opinion~~ it is believed that Malatesta is gone to Italy on very important business.[35]

The report was then forwarded through the Foreign Office to the Italian ambassador in London, Count Giuseppe Tomielli, who, as he went on to explain in a report to the Italian Foreign Minister a couple of days later, was certainly very glad to get it: 'I urge in a special way secrecy about the note from the Metropolitan Police, an exceptional document because it is customary for the English police not to investigate the political conduct of foreigners. And in any case, they do not communicate the information they possess to foreign governments.'[36] Tomielli was right to note the uncooperativeness of the British government in cases of political crime (a feature that remained relatively unchanged throughout the next couple of decades), but as the following pages will show, investigating the political conduct of foreigners, far from being an aberration, was becoming the very raison d'être of the 'political department'.

\* \* \*

Organizationally, the British political police was defined by conflict during the first decade of its institutional existence. In the main this was a conflict between an earlier Victorian system of preventive policing and a more centralized, intelligence-driven system like the one favoured by Edward Jenkinson. This is, however, a highly simplified picture. As we have seen, Harcourt started his policing career as a 'pseudo-Fouché' (in the words of Charles Dilke)[37] in charge of a tentative 'spider's web of police communication' that was meant to compensate for what the Home Secretary regarded as the reduced capabilities of Scotland Yard in combatting Fenian terrorism in Britain. It was during this phase of his career that Harcourt set about building the first real political police institution in Britain, namely Section B of the CID – the so-called Irish Branch. It was also during this time that he sought out the services of Edward Jenkinson, who at the time of his appointment to the Home Office was already the rising star (and in a sense the progenitor) of Irish counter-Fenian operations.[38]

The fact that Harcourt subsequently turned against intelligence gathering and surveillance and openly embraced the older, preventive model of policing is a consequence of several factors including his personal foibles – what Robert Anderson termed his 'dynamite moods'[39]– the continued 'successes' of the Fenian dynamite campaign and the political sensitivities in Westminster to matters of political policing (which, given Jenkinson's unofficial status, threatened to embroil the government in a costly and untimely controversy).

Harcourt's successor, R. A. Cross, refused, however, to roll back the advances made in intelligence-gathering at a time of 'national evil' and so political policing remained in place albeit in a somewhat stunted and precarious state owing to the growing rivalries between Jenkinson and his detractors. Although such rivalries ostensibly revolved around Scotland Yard's opposition to the extra-legal methods promoted by Jenkinson, the spymaster's forced resignation in late 1886 did not ultimately bring about the end of extra-legality nor the triumph of prevention. James Monro, Robert Anderson and Charles Warren all used extra-legal and borderline illegal manoeuvres in the pursuance of public security as the events of 1887–88 aptly illustrate.

The story of how the political police actually came into being tells us several important things that have a bearing on its later development. First, that once the ball of institutionalized political policing, so to speak, was got rolling by Harcourt – for idiosyncratic reasons and to the unenthusiastic reception of his police chiefs – it proved to have a self-propelling logic of its own. This dictated that since Fenian bombings continued to happen in spite of the political police, the powers of the latter needed to be increased. Given the Scotland Yard leadership's lack of vision (exemplified by Howard Vincent's decision to retire in a moment of crisis), this logic allowed Jenkinson – a man who did have a more or less definite idea of what 'defending the realm' should entail – to fill up the ensuing void. There was, therefore, no straightforward and wholesale adoption of 'Irish methods' by an intimidated British administration.

What, then, did the policing regime introduced in Ireland by Liberal and then Conservative administrations bequeath to the British political police during the later 1880s? Beyond the tenuous experiments occasioned by Jenkinson's tenancy at the Home Office – which occasionally included the use of agents provocateurs – not very much. The Irish Crimes Act of 1887 almost immediately created a highly charged and punitive social atmosphere in Ireland in which the vaguest expression of dissent sufficed as grounds for arrest. As one modern estimate has it, by 1889 'twenty-three sitting members of parliament, twelve priests, the lord mayor of Dublin, mayors of Sligo, Clonmel and Cork, barristers and doctors, newspaper men, poor law guardians, town commissioners and numerous [other] "respectable" country shopkeepers and farmers – almost 2000 people in all – had been jailed' for subversive activities as defined by the new Crimes Act.[40]

In contrast, the anti-Fenian operations orchestrated in London and the provinces following the 1881 Salford bombing were, even at their most problematic, strictly hedged in by precisely the sort of free speech, habeas corpus and due process legislation which the Crimes Act had nullified in Ireland. An illustration is afforded by the Glasgow 'ribbon society' which played host to Timothy Featherstone and other Fenian dynamitards in the early 1880s. Although a hotbed of seditious talk, the society was virtually ignored by Scottish police and the Scotland Yard even after evidence of Featherstone's criminal intentions began emerging.

A second important trend emerging from the political police's trajectory in the first decade of its existence is one of institutional endurance. Despite the intense and acrimonious rivalries engendered by Jenkinson's rise, as well as by his failure to stamp out Fenian skirmishing by 1885, the British political police did not crumble into dust, nor did it revert to the sub-institutional high politics still embodied in that quaint pre-Victorian vestige – the Home Office Secret Service. Rather it moved forward on the path already set with the creation of Irish Branch.

Thirdly, the political police of the 1880s appears not as the product of a reactionary-colonial clique but as the creature of a liberal, and certainly Liberal, mindset. Harcourt, Spencer, Vincent (before 1884), Jenkinson, Lushington, Childers and even Warren – all were prominent Liberals at one time or another. Their liberalism is of course not always easy to spot, especially if measured against modern standards, but it is there nonetheless.

It is evident in Harcourt's modernizing impulses, but also in his traditionalist resistance to the creation of new bureaucracies and institutions, as well as in his misgivings about European interference. It is evident in Jenkinson's reforming zeal and his pragmatic approach to Ireland (exemplified by his early support for Home Rule). It is evident in Lushington's qualified admiration for 'continental systems' of political policing and his circumspection about the threat posed by British socialism (which, his contempt for the SDF notwithstanding, he would not have been in complete disagreement with given his own left-leaning views). Finally, it is evident in how the mainstream liberal press chose to cover the topic of an emerging British political police: not with outrage, not even with worried contempt, but with a sort of detached, rarely enthusiastic, approval. Even the *Pall Mall Gazette*, otherwise the staunchest critic of the Metropolitan Police's 'Tory' leadership, could not but observe matter-of-factly and forlornly in the wake of Jenkinson's forced resignation that the spymaster had been 'the soul and centre' of a necessary 'British Third Section'.

# Part 2
## 1892–1903

CHAPTER 9

# 'A bomb has burst'[1]

THE intense personal rivalries that had put the political police in permanent crisis mode throughout the 1880s did not continue unabated into the following decade. Robert Anderson and Edward Bradford remained comfortably secure and unchallenged as head of CID and Commissioner respectively. Lushington went on as Permanent Under-Secretary (retiring in 1895), while Henry Matthews briefly stayed on as Home Secretary until 1892 when he was replaced by the Liberal H. H. Asquith[2] – a man who, much like the previous Liberal Home Secretary, Hugh Childers, had no great interest in matters of policing subversion.

Subversion meant something altogether different during the 1890s. Although dynamite outrages continued to occasionally disturb the peace of Irish cities (Dublin in particular), in Britain insurgent Fenianism was more of a theoretical concern – a reality illustrated by the fact that Irish Branch, reduced to a clerical section of the CID, was increasingly threatened with extinction. If its detectives were going to detect they had to act through the all-purpose Section D headed by Chief Inspector John Littlechild. Though still the 'brilliant and distinguished' head of the 'political crime department'[3] as far as everyone was concerned, Littlechild was, unbeknownst to his superiors, thinking of taking his talents into the private sector. The political police apparatus – still grounded in gentlemen's agreements and shrouded in extra-legality – was once again ready for a strong-willed and opinionated administrator to bend it to his will.

The new perceived threat to national security was not a movement which aimed specifically at striking the British state, as Fenianism had professed to, but it was a movement nonetheless and it declared itself inveterately opposed to all states everywhere. In Britain it was overwhelmingly made up of exiled revolutionary socialists – or anarchists as some preferred to style themselves – who were opposed, on libertarian grounds, to the state-driven political revolution of Marx and his followers as well as to the gradualist reformism of non-Marxist socialists. They came from Western European countries like Italy, France or Spain where strikes and workers' demonstrations, insofar as they were allowed at all, often ended in bloodshed thanks to heavy-handed interventions by police and the military.

They also came from parts of the Russian Empire where anything smacking of democratic or non-Russian nationalist agitation invariably brought with it harsh prison sentences and one-way trips to Siberia. Most were exiles of necessity, not of choice, and many dreamt and frequently planned to return to their homelands, ideally in a moment of revolutionary crisis.

Some, such as Pyotr Kropotkin and Élisée Reclus were men of science with a fierce, if naive, love of humanity. Others, like Louise Michel and Errico Malatesta, were indignant grandchildren of the Radical Enlightenment who had failed to see their own revolutions materialize beyond short-lived revolts. Others still, like the young Arthur Rimbaud, were desperate poets taking momentary refuge in a London *cercle d'études sociales*.[4]

The majority, however, were struggling artisans, apprentices, down-and-out day labourers and petty thieves – precisely the *damnés de la terre* who still believed in revolution as a bloody war of attrition between haves and have-nothings. These were men (and occasionally women) who conceived of themselves as political action heroes and who lionized the *propagande par le fait* of Ravachol (pseudonym of François Claudius Koënigstein) – guillotined in 1892 for attempting to assassinate judges and lawyers implicated in the suppression of French anarchists – and Auguste Vaillant, guillotined in 1894 for detonating a bomb in the *Chambre des députés*.[5]

Their residences and clubs were scattered all across metropolitan London (Fitzrovia and Soho in particular) and they could also be found, in far less significant numbers, in some of the larger port cities like Liverpool and Glasgow. Their cultural and linguistic isolation meant they tended to keep to their own kind, while their ideological isolation from British socialism (which, with very few exceptions, overwhelmingly supported parliamentary democracy and the state) ensured their status as permanent outsiders even among those who professed to be sympathetic. There were, to be sure, some British anarchists (as the following few chapters will attest) but they were rare and insofar as they came to the attention of the political police it was usually for the praise, rather than the practice, of armed rebellion.

\* \* \*

In January 1892 three men were arrested in the West Midlands town of Walsall, followed by another three in February. All were charged under the Explosives Substances Act of 1883 for conspiracy to use 'a machine intended to… caus[e] an explosion… for an [un]lawful object'.[6] The accused were described, locally and in the press, as anarchists and the 'machine' in question – pear-shaped moulds and iron castings – had been procured by one of them at the request of a London 'comrade'. To what end, nobody was certain, but at the trial which followed the arrests the defence argued the device's intended recipients were Russian Nihilists. Whatever the truth of that claim, only two of the accused were ultimately acquitted due to lack of evidence, with the rest receiving harsh sentences of up to ten years with hard labour.

The 'Walsall plot' marks an important moment in the evolution of political policing in Britain, mainly for three reasons. The first is that, despite its anti-climactic outcome, this incident effectively brought anarchism into the public eye on an unprecedented scale. Previously the British press had reported on the continental anarchists' violent sprees with a sense of detached condescension,[7] but in the wake of the Walsall trial newspapers were more inclined to regard the threat posed by these 'enemies to society'[8] as a very serious one indeed. One *Times* columnist, for example, warned that if 'the anarchists are… resolved to force the world to take serious notice of their existence… they little know the power of the civilization they defy', concluding reassuringly that 'the fate of our domestic dynamiters… shows what a well-organized police can do, even against criminals who conduct their operations under specially favourable conditions'.[9]

This brings us to the second reason why the Walsall incident is important, namely because it revealed, as *The Times* keenly perceived, the uneasy balance between the methods of a 'well-organized police' capable of combating a supposed international conspiracy of murderous fanatics and Britain's 'specially favourable conditions' – an ironic reference to the official policies of unfettered political asylum and overt policing. As subsequent chapters will show, this controversial theme dominated the government's approach to the issue of politically motivated violence throughout the rest of the *fin de siècle*.

The third reason has to do with the possibility that the Walsall plot was nothing more than a set-up masterminded by one of Section D's leading inspectors, William Melville. No hard evidence exists to connect Melville to the instigator of the conspiracy, but there are certainly a number of warning signs that cast serious doubt on any notion of a legitimate bomb plot. As Joseph Deakin, one of the accused, recalled in his trial statement, in the summer of 1891 he had become acquainted with two French anarchists at the Walsall Socialist Club, the local SDF headquarters and an unofficial home to left-wing radicals of all stripes. The two foreigners, Victor Cails and George Laplace, were on the run from French authorities and in desperate need of reliable English friends. Deakin and his associate, Frederick Charles, were more than happy to keep them company.

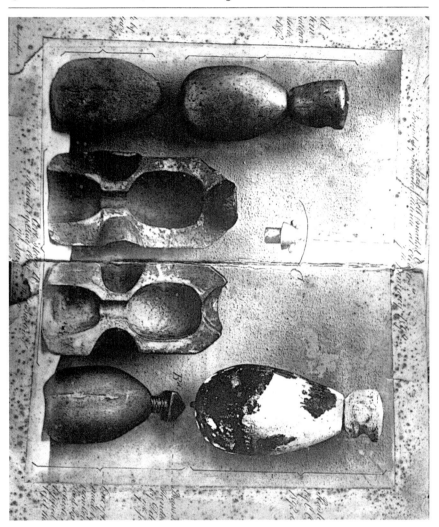

4. Materials confiscated by police during the investigation into the Walsall bomb conspiracy of 1892 (The National Archives of the UK, ref. ASSI6/27/9).

It was only a few months later, in October 1891, that Cails received a letter in French from London, signed by a certain Degiani, asking for a brass casting. Not recognizing the name, Cails contacted the man who had arranged his stay in Walsall – a London part-time schoolteacher and translator by the name of Auguste Coulon – asking for clarification. Coulon assured Cails of the letter's authenticity, specifying that the casting was meant to aid certain Russian comrades in their fight against the Czarist autocracy. This seems to have convinced not only Cails, but Deakin and the rest of their coterie. The men had several moulds made at a local foundry and wrote back to Coulon for further instructions. In December 1891, an Italian calling himself Jean Battola arrived from London to check up on their progress, but finding the moulds 'not suitable', decided to depart empty-handed. As Deakin later found out from friends who had accompanied Battola on the way back to the train station, 'the police were watching them'.[10]

The whole thing might have ended there, but in January 1892 Deakin was arrested in London almost immediately on arrival by Melville and his men; not for bomb-making, but for being in possession of a bottle of chloroform.

5. William Melville in the 1890s, *Windsor Magazine*, 1895 (Internet Archive).

How the police had come to know so quickly of Deakin's presence in the capital or what Deakin was doing with a bottle of chloroform is not at all clear. Robert Anderson claimed he had 'received definite information that [anarchists] were plotting robberies by means of chloroform to be used in drugging the persons they intended to rob' and that Deakin was somehow part of this hatching plot.[11] It is highly suspicious, however, that any real evidence behind such 'definite information', insofar as it existed, should not have later been used against Deakin to secure an even harsher sentence.

In any case, Deakin himself, convinced he had been set up by Charles, refused to explain the origin or the purpose of the chloroform. For their part, the police did not press the issue 'owing to other matters having turned up at Walsall', as Melville later explained at the trial. Having picked up Deakin and Battola in London, the men of Special Branch returned to the Midlands town to blow the lid off the whole dastardly conspiracy. The other four individuals implicated directly in the making of the iron moulds were summarily arrested and the trial was concluded before the winter of 1892 was over. Deakin received five years with hard labour; Cails, Battola and Charles got ten. The other two suspects, John Wesley and William Ditchfield, were released.

Although clearly implicated by the evidence, Auguste Coulon was never brought before the court. When formally questioned on the nature of their relationship, Melville curtly announced that 'I will not swear that I have never given Coulon anything to do for me... [or that] I have not paid him any money', adding knowingly that he had 'paid lots of anarchists money'.[12] How much money and for what purpose, he failed to specify. When the defence counsel asked Judge Henry Hawkins to press Melville on the matter, the Attorney-General intervened to argue that the disclosure of such information was irrelevant to the case and furthermore not 'in the interest of the public service'.[13]

Melville's strange half-admittance that Coulon had likely been in his employ did not go unnoticed, however. In the House of Commons, left-wing Liberal MPs like Cunninghame Graham demanded to know whether unsavoury means had been used against the Walsall plotters, prompting Matthews to declare forcefully that 'the employment of... agents provocateurs was not only not sanctioned, but was forbidden'.[14]

On the anarchist side, there was little, if any, doubt that the Walsall conspiracy had been entirely manufactured by authorities. On 9 April 1892 David Nicoll, the editor of the London-based *Commonweal* – founded in 1885 by William Morris as an organ for the ultra-left Socialist League – published a damning indictment of what he regarded as a travesty of justice:

> The Walsall Anarchists have been condemned... For what? For a police plot concocted by one of those infamous wretches who make a living by getting up these affairs and selling their victims to the vengeance of the law. Surely we ought not to have to warn Anarchists of the danger of conspiracies; these death traps; these gins set by the police and their spies... Surely those who desire to act can [do so]... Are there no tyrants now? What of the Jesuitical monster at the Home Office, who murders men for taking a few head of game? What of the hyena... whose love of the gallows... won him the title of 'Hangman' Hawkins? – this barbarous brute, who... sends our comrades to ten years in the hell of the prisons. What of the spy Melville, who sets his agent on to concoct the plots which he discovers? Are these men fit to live?[15]

The following day, Nicoll reiterated his threats in Hyde Park to an uproarious crowd of socialist and anarchist sympathizers and on 19 April both he and Charles Mowbray, the owner and printer of *Commonweal*, were arrested and charged with incitement to murder. At the trial which followed in May, the Section D detectives who had heard Nicoll's Hyde Park speech were called to testify.

DI John Sweeney (introduced simply as a CID officer) recalled hearing Nicoll declare that the 'Jesuit... Matthews, Inspector Melville, and Coulon are the principal actors [in the Walsall case], and two of them must die'.[16] This account was corroborated by DI Francis Powell (also of Section D) but refuted by every other witness, most of whom agreed that Nicoll had heaped abuse on Melville, Matthews and Hawkins without asking for their heads. This might have worked to Nicoll's advantage if not for the fact that his threats had been published in print a day before the speech.

In a verdict echoing the 1881 trial of Johann Most, Nicoll received eighteen months with hard labour – the same as Most – while Mowbray was acquitted. That same month the police raided the *Commonweal* offices, confiscating type but also 'Nicoll's papers, amongst them the evidence he was collecting as to the shameful proceedings of the police in getting up the Walsall plot', as *Freedom*, another anarchist newspaper, claimed.[17]

It is easy to see in such heavy-handed tactics evidence of a conspiracy to suppress the truth, but as far as we can tell from the historical record, there was not much to suppress. As Melville's barefaced (and widely reported) comment about Coulon had shown, there was little need to cover up the fact that the unlikely dynamite plot had not been unmasked by chance alone; certainly at the Home Office it was well-known and accepted that espionage had been instrumental in bringing the anarchists to justice. Commissioner Bradford even insisted that the informers should collectively enjoy a full half of the £120 set aside for the men involved in the 'exceptionally important' Walsall case.[18]

Who were these individuals whose services were on an equal footing with those rendered by Special Branch detectives? Although Anderson mentioned being kept up to date with the whereabouts of Coulon – at that point a potential suspect – by an unnamed personal source,[19] only two confirmed informants are known to have been involved in the Walsall case. One was John McCormack, a Londoner who in February 1892 was arrested in Walsall for drunk and disorderly behaviour and who claimed 'he had been employed by the Scotland Yard and Walsall Police in getting evidence for the trial of the anarchist prisoners'.[20] As a reporter of the *Birmingham Daily Gazette* was quick to find out, McCormack's claim was, surprisingly, true. Walsall Police representatives admitted to employing McCormack, but noted that 'his statements were absolutely unreliable' and that he was all in all 'a disreputable scoundrel'.[21]

The other known informant was Auguste Coulon himself. In his tell-all memoirs, published serially in the left-wing *Reynolds's Newspaper* in 1895, ex-Special Branch DS Patrick McIntyre tapped into the residual controversy still surrounding the Walsall incident at the time to embarrass his former superiors, particularly Anderson, whom he held responsible for his dismissal from the Branch.[22] According to McIntyre, Coulon had written to the Yard in 1891 to offer his services; whether as a mere informer or as a provocateur, the former detective failed to specify. Melville had accepted the offer and subsequently 'Coulon... became [Melville's] property – that is to say all information that Coulon supplied was taken possession of by Melville, who submitted it to Mr. Anderson... [who] would direct what action was to be taken in the matter... [while] in his turn [being] responsible to... the Home Secretary.'[23]

This was by far the most explicit indictment of Coulon by a (former) police officer, and it forced the Frenchman to respond to the accusations in a column which *Reynolds's* titled 'What Coulon has to say'. What Coulon had to say was not, however, very convincing. He admitted to offering his services to Scotland Yard in a letter to Melville, but attempted to smear McIntyre by implying the latter had opened an envelope meant for a senior officer.[24] McIntyre retorted with a sarcastic barb and was defended in the pages of the same newspaper by none other than David Nicoll, for whom the Walsall case had become an obsession.

Coulon unsuccessfully tried to sue McIntyre for libel, but despite his public exposure as an informer he remained on the Special Branch payroll as a translator and 'expert' on the anarchist movement until 1904, having by that point been paid a total sum of £801 for his services.[25] That year, when the Walsall controversy had all but died off, DI Sweeney also referred to Coulon in his own memoirs as having 'given the Scotland Yard... much assistance in bringing the Walsall Anarchists to book'.[26]

What this assistance actually consisted of remains frustratingly obscure and certainly there is nothing to clearly demonstrate that it went beyond the mere act of informing. When Deakin arrived in London in January 1892, Anderson had been 'led to believe that [the former] was conveying a sample bomb to show to his co-conspirators'.[27] If this was Coulon's work, it was certainly lacking; and yet he was too valuable to shake off, either by virtue of what he knew or what he had done for the Yard. Anderson also noted how in February 1892 he had 'directed a strict search both of Coulon's house and also of the Anarchist Club [in Kingsland Road] and [asked] that Coulon should be detained and brought to... Scotland Yard'.[28]

The duplicitous Frenchman, however, had managed to abscond in advance, rendering the search predictably fruitless. Whoever had tipped him off was certainly in the know to a remarkable extent and it is highly revealing that shortly after the abortive raid, Anderson received a telegram from the Chief Constable of Walsall Police, Inspector Charles Taylor, with the words 'Do not arrest Coulon. Taylor. Walsall.'[29] The Assistant Commissioner cautiously deferred to this advice; it was neither the first nor the last time he found himself out of the loop.

Whether the Walsall anarchists were framed or betrayed is ultimately still a matter of contention. In his biography of Melville, Andrew Cook argues the spymaster was definitely 'at the bottom' of the plot,[30] while Bernard Porter, in his seminal monograph on the early Special Branch, insists 'the actual evidence for provocateuring is circumstantial in the extreme'.[31] Whatever the case may be – Porter's more conservative evaluation seems the more justified – it does not change the fact that Special Branch had only to gain from uncovering and foiling an anarchist plot on British soil. Only a month before, in December 1891, four of its constables had been sacked as a consequence of cuts introduced by Matthews.[32] After Walsall, the Branch's existence was secure – although Section B saw a reduction of four constables in August 1892[33] – Melville's career was on the rise and anarchism became the new bête noire of the British political establishment.

The Club Autonomie, where Joseph Deakin had been headed prior to his arrest, had been set up in 1885 by the German anarchist-in-exile Josef Peukert as an alternative to the group around Johann Most's *Freiheit*. Its initial headquarters were at 32 Charlotte Street in anarchist-friendly Fitzrovia, but were soon changed to 6 Windmill Street in Soho (which also housed an impressive population of foreign radicals) in order to accommodate an expanding membership.

The club house was 'very dingy' and 'badly furnished', with only 'a few rough benches, chairs, and tables', but by anarchist standards it was quite presentable, with 'a section of the house... set aside for singing' and dancing as well as a substantial library.[34] It quickly became the home of a multicultural and multilingual anarchist enclave, serving both as community centre as well as a place for organizing political and educational activities. Melville noted the Club was 'a centre for forwarding anarchistic literature to the continent, but more particularly to Germany' and a means for the anarchists to 'get assistance by means of subscriptions [with] funds [having] frequently been sent from the Autonomie Club to various continental countries'.[35]

Despite the increased police scrutiny in the wake of the Walsall case, the Autonomie remained the main hub for recent émigrés with nowhere else to turn to – men like Jean-Pierre François, suspected by French authorities of involvement in the April 1892 bombing of Café Véry, a small Parisian restaurant.[36] The *Sûreté* (the Ministry of the Interior's political police arm) had only managed to establish that François was 'a member of an anarchist group capable of committing such an attack',[37] but had not produced any solid evidence against him, leading to his discharge by a Parisian *juge d'instruction*. Ironically, François' friend and associate in anarchy, Theodule Meunier, the man actually responsible for the bombing, was at the time serving a two-week sentence in the La Santé prison for unlawful use of a firearm. He had supposed, quite rightly, that the police would not look for him in prison.[38]

Sometime in early May 1892, François, whose newfound notoriety prevented him from practising his trade as an ebony polisher in Paris, decided to look for work in London, where he was shortly followed by Meunier. Making the obligatory appearance at the Autonomie, the latter – a short, slightly built and hunchbacked young man with a distrustful disposition – must have passed relatively unnoticed. François, on the other hand, stocky, tall and built like 'a modern Samson', was altogether harder to ignore.[39] He often boasted loudly of his (fictitious) anarchist exploits and was fond of making wild threats against the bourgeoisie. Unsurprisingly, his penchant for self-aggrandizement soon landed him in trouble.

In early June 1892 the *Sûreté* finally got a hold of some promising leads in the Café Véry investigation. As Gaston Fedé, one of the detectives working on the case, later explained in a deposition to British police, 'a person of the name of "Bricout" [sic]... now in custody... gave on or about 4th June some information as to the place where some dynamite was concealed'.[40] Jean-Baptiste Bricou, a Parisian carpenter and anarchist, had led police to the very same dynamite cache that Meunier had used to manufacture the Café Véry bomb. Facing the death penalty for aiding and abetting a terrorist, Bricou proved remarkably amenable to the 'feasible promises' of French police, giving up Meunier as the mastermind behind the outrage and fingering François as an accomplice.[41]

Also implicating François were two witness depositions, both of which detailed how in the days leading up to the bombing the anarchist had been 'boasting, as he already had done before, that he was blowing up all Paris to revenge Ravachol, and that a blow would be struck... [against] all who were concerned with Ravachol's trial'.[42] The testimonies did not invalidate François' alibi, but they certainly suggested he was intimately connected to the crime.

In late June, British authorities received copies of the French arrest warrants issued for both Meunier and François. Consequently, Sir John Bridge (Chief Magistrate at the Bow Street Police Court) was able to inform the Home Office that under the Extradition Act of 1870, which allowed for the arrest of foreign fugitives convicted of non-political crimes, the two anarchists were wanted men in Britain. Inspector Melville faced the opportunity of tracking down a pair of real revolutionary desperadoes.

Meunier and François were certainly in a precarious position, but not entirely hopeless. Both had found lodgings in the anarchist redoubt of Fitzrovia; Meunier lived at 30 Fitzroy Sreet, a building whose residents (and landlord) were all anarchists, while François, working for a local furniture polisher, rented a room in Pitt Street, off Tottenham Court Road.[43] A collection had been started to help the two, especially Meunier, who, as the London comrades believed, needed 'to get away as soon as possible'.[44] Before the end of summer, Meunier managed to flee, most likely for Argentina,[45] leaving François in an increasingly paranoid state of mind. Although Mme François and the children had joined him in London, they lived separately with a family in Soho. François himself frequently changed residence and lived under the assumed name of 'Mr Johnson'. He also literally slept with a gun and dagger under his pillow, though in the end such precautions, far from being unfounded, proved insufficient.

Scotland Yard received the files on Meunier and François sometime in late August 1892, courtesy of the head of the *Sûreté*, Marie-François Goron, who had previously worked with the London CID during an 1889 murder investigation. The French were willing to at least feign deference to the Yard if that meant speeding up the arrest and expulsion of the two anarchists, but actual cooperation between the two police forces was a different matter.

The details and portraits contained in the files forwarded to London were badly out of date and, in addition, the *Préfecture de police de Paris* maintained its own underground, but significant, network of spies and informers in the British capital, most of whom appear to have been enthusiastic incompetents at best.[46] As DS McIntyre later recalled, one French *mouchard*, who had managed to track down François through local contacts, decided to carry out his own investigation 'instead of communicating straight away with the London police [or] waiting for the assistance of anyone acquainted with the locality'.[47]

François caught wind of this and immediately relocated to the working-class east London neighbourhood of Poplar where French spies could not practise their trade as easily. Frustrated in their amateurish efforts, some of these pseudo-detectives even contemplated paying off the Yard to have Meunier and François delivered to Paris on the sly.[48] It is not certain whether this was a harebrained scheme or merely an attempt to embezzle funds, but nothing came of it in the end.

Having lost 'nearly all hope... of catching either [François] or Meunier',[49] the Special Branch detectives fell back on old tactics. A series of impromptu and legally unwarranted raids of several anarchists' houses in Soho produced nothing except the knowledge that Meunier had almost certainly fled the city and the worrying realization that 'when you are entering back-doors and forcing windows, the occupant of the place may shoot you through the head with impunity'.[50]

There was at least a starting point, however. Using a series of disguises such as Medical Officer for Health and 'Irish loafer', bribes (a street urchin could be debriefed for only 'a few pennies'), shadowing and old-fashioned deductive reasoning, Melville and three of his sergeants – McIntyre, Walsh and Hester – eventually managed to trace François' steps from his initial address in Tottenham Court Road to his new one in Hind Street, Poplar.[51]

It was around 4.00 p.m. on 14 October when the anarchist, returning home with a bottle of 'French oils' (it was laundry day), was taken aback by the sight of four respectable-looking men waiting outside his building. Spotting him immediately, Melville announced: 'François! Je suis un inspecteur de police et je vous arrête!' A scuffle ensued in which François, struggling 'very violently', had to be subdued through the collective effort of all four officers, though not before Mme François – armed with her husband's fully loaded revolver – was herself restrained.[52]

A hearing at the Bow Street Police Court followed the arrest and François' counsel submitted that 'the French government sought his extradition for a political and not a criminal offence', which contravened Article 5 of the 1876 Extradition Treaty with France. Chief Magistrate John Bridge was not convinced given that the testimonials obtained in June by the *Sûreté* (which had inexplicably taken several months to reach London) hinted strongly at François' complicity in the Café Very explosion. François denied all charges, but could not repudiate the many empty boasts he had made prior to the bombing. His innocence was of course not on trial in Britain, only the legality of his extradition and as the Chief Magistrate explained, 'the motive of the offence is not political, but... revenge'.[53] He ordered François be extradited; François appealed; the appeal was rejected.

Back in France by late December 1892, François was tried for his supposed involvement in the Café Very outrage but was again acquitted due to lack of evidence. What his arrest and expulsion from Britain had shown was firstly that Special Branch was capable of keeping the foreign anarchists in London under control and secondly that persecution for 'political crime' was no longer an automatic reason for granting asylum. At the same time, secret policing remained far from uncontroversial. Melville and his men were given modest rewards of £15 each for the arrest of François, but the sum was kept secret as 'some additional risk might follow [the officers] from a public expression of... appreciation of their conduct'.[54]

Despite the legacy of Bloody Sunday, London's poor and unemployed had not lost all political will in the new decade. As a police report received by Chief Inspector Littlechild in March 1892 noted, 'the number of passengers which arrived at Tilbury Docks from Hamburg' between 1889 and 1891 amounted to 10,340 persons, of which 'nearly or quite 80 per cent [were] destitute Jews'.[55] The vast majority of these new arrivals were sweated into London's tailoring industry and many of them were becoming increasingly receptive to left-wing ideas.

In late November 1892 British newspapers announced that 'arrangements… have now been made in connection with [a] proposed midnight march of the unemployed through the streets of London'.[56] The participants were each to 'carry a lighted torch [and] at the stroke of midnight… march as quietly as possible to… the heart of London'. Anderson did not find the news particularly alarming, even though, as he noted in a report to Herbert Gladstone[57] at the Home Office, 'police [had] no accurate information on the subject'.[58] With Bloody Sunday only five years in the past, however, the Scotland Yard chief felt a coherent and proportional police response was needed, should the event actually take place. In the same report to Gladstone, Anderson suggested that a 'torchlight procession would… be more or less dangerous [and it] would most certainly alarm a very large number of the inhabitants of the Metropolis'.[59] Citing an 1887 precedent when a similar procession planned by members of the SDF had been declared illegal, the Scotland Yard chief awaited further instructions from the Home Secretary on how to adequately deal with the marchers.

The new Home Secretary, H. H. Asquith – a vocal Liberal backer of the right to demonstrate in Trafalgar Square and former counsel to John Burns – decided the march would be allowed to take place. However, when on the night of 1 December a crowd of nearly five hundred people, many of them Jewish immigrants,[60] gathered on Tower Hill, they were promptly informed by City police that 'no torchlight procession would be allowed'.[61] The marchers went ahead anyway and 'punctually on the stroke of midnight, the procession… set off accompanied by fifty [City] policemen… planted… so adroitly… in twos and threes amongst the people that at any moment… they could have dispersed them'.[62] Singing revolutionary songs, the crowd eventually reached City limits and was summarily intercepted by Metropolitan constables, who 'as soon as [they] got well into their midst [began] driving [the procession] east and west'.[63] The marchers, offering no resistance, simply 'scampered off, followed by the police in every direction'. Any possibility of another riot occurring had been avoided.

Anderson, however, was not at all pleased. In a report to Asquith, he decried the 'violent speeches... and threats' made by some of the organizers of the march, which could not 'altogether be ignored'.[64] The SDF in particular, 'in a state of quiescence for the past two or three years', seemed to have 'suddenly recovered', encouraging a future increase in the 'gathering together of idlers and loafers'. To drive the point home, Anderson mentioned that even the anarchists were 'requesting permission to hold a meeting on the unemployed in Trafalgar Square'. As far as policing was concerned, it was 'above all things necessary that there should be no want of preparedness'. He proposed that 'a small reserve [of constables] must for some time... be regularly located on Saturdays and Sundays in the neighbourhood of Trafalgar Square' and asked the Home Secretary to 'sanction a temporary augmentation of one hundred [men], which is the smallest number that would meet the requirements'.[65] Although the 1890s saw a liberalization in the government's attitude to public meetings (including those held in Trafalgar Square), public order was back on the domestic security agenda – an agenda increasingly defined by the threat of anarchist agitation.

Unlike its seedier relation in Windmill Street, the anarchist club in Grafton Street, central London, was a 'spacious, comfortable... house [and] the finest meeting place [of] the foreign revolutionaries in London'. It had over five hundred dues-paying members and spanned two floors. Like the Autonomie, it had been set up by German exiles but had gradually evolved into a place for the 'meetings... of French, Italian and other foreign comrades'.[66]

It was in the main hall on the first floor that such a meeting was held in the very early hours of 11 January 1893 to discuss the situation in France as well as François' recent extradition. The individualist anarchists, represented by the Italian *Libera Iniziativa* group and its figurehead Luigi Parmeggiani,[67] favoured a campaign of swift retribution against those who had persecuted François and a renewed effort at sparking an insurrection in Paris. It is impossible to know how many informers were present at that meeting – the police were aware that the Club was the most obvious place 'in which to look for any Anarchist who was wanted'[68] – but it is certain there was at least one.

Later that day and again on the following, the Home Office received two letters from a certain S. Reuschel of Messrs H. Hermann, hardwood importers of 11 Dod Street, London. Both purported to describe the meeting that had taken place at Grafton Hall the day before:

> Sir... Being informed that the 'Internationale' intend to overthrow the present state of order here, in Berlin and Paris on the 15th inst., I consider it my duty to draw your attention to it... The anarchists will... blow up in the three

named capitals a number of public buildings to such an extent as the world has never witnessed before... I [also] beg to report the resolution past [sic] at the meeting... which is to the effect that with all power the brethren in Paris should be assisted by the 'Internationale' to bring about the revolutions in France [sic]... I am told a great number of anarchists were against this resolution... Although I could not learn where and who the leaders of this section are... they can be found at Grafton Hall, as that place was accidentally mentioned by my informer, who with a great number of roughs has left for France via [the London] Chatham [and] Dover [railway].[69]

Who this S. Reuschel or his informer were – it is unlikely that one of Melville's spies would simply be giving away his intelligence to the Home Office – or whether the information was credible, it was impossible to ascertain. All Charles Murdoch, Assistant Under-Secretary at the Home Office, could do was verify the sender's address (it checked out) and pass the letters on to Anderson at the Yard along with the question of whether the French should be notified of the alleged plotting. Without mincing his words, Anderson consented to forwarding 'the information to the French government', but did not think it 'fair to give copies of the man's letters [as] his informant is an anarchist, and foreign governments are... very stupid in using information given them'.[70] Deciding to investigate the matter on his own, the Assistant Commissioner debriefed Reuschel in a private tête-à-tête and reported to Under-Secretary Gladstone that:

> [Reuschel's] informant is a Russian Nihilist whose acquaintance he made in London some time ago... I find no reason to doubt the good faith of the person who communicates this information and therefore I would wish that his name should not be disclosed to anyone. But yet I doubt the value of his statements... It seems improbable that his informant if really implicated in a plot of such a serious kind would speak of it this freely... At the same time I am not prepared to say that there is nothing in it and I have directed inquiries to be made.[71]

The French had already been informed by Her Majesty's Government in December 1892 of an anarchist meeting in Geneva where 'intelligence was submitted from [the] London group of "Individual Initiative"[72] respecting organization of explosions to take place in London on the occasion of extradition of François [and in] Paris... on his arrival there'. This new intelligence seemed to give credence to that previous report, but Anderson's scepticism proved well-founded. In the end, the conspiracy to blow up London, Paris and Berlin was either aborted, or, more likely, remained in the realm of wishful thinking. The rest of 1893 proved far from uneventful, however, at least on the continent.[73]

On the night of 7 November 1893 Spain experienced one of the worst terrorist attacks of the entire Restoration period. To avenge the execution of a comrade a few months earlier, an anarchist bootlegger by the name of Santiago Salvador Franch threw two hand grenades into the audience at the Liceo Opera House in Barcelona during the second act of Rossini's *Guillaume Tell*, killing at least twenty-five and injuring scores.[74] An immediate wave of repression followed: martial law was declared, many anarchists were arrested without charge (and some executed) and anarchist publications were declared illegal. In the aftermath of the incident, a Spanish newspaper observed how 'notables of all political stripes lamented that Barcelona [has]… become a refuge for French, Italian and other foreign anarchists'.[75] To Spanish authorities the advice of Great Britain, that other reluctant refuge of European anarchy, was certainly worth having.

On 20 November Sir Henry Drummond-Wolff, the British ambassador to Madrid, received 'a note… enquiring whether [the British] would be disposed to enter into arrangements for common international action against anarchists, [in which case] the Spanish Gov[ernmen]t were prepared to take the initiative and propose measures for carrying out the object in view'.[76] Wolff forwarded the note to London, but gave the Spanish a preliminary reply to the effect that such a bilateral effort would require the introduction of new legislation and 'all legislation of this kind [would be] regarded with the most jealous suspicion in [Britain]'.[77] This line was subsequently echoed by Asquith as well as by Lord Rosebery, the Foreign Secretary, whose official reply to the Spanish stated that:

> our laws are strong enough to deal with anarchism if directed against our own government. But they do not deal with abstract anarchism such as the announcement of general anarchistic principles, nor with anarchism as directed against foreign governments, unless it amounts to incitement to murder. Persons committing acts of violence abroad and fleeing to England would be extradited unless the offence were deemed political, and this I feel sure it would not be if the offence were anything like the bomb throwing… in Barcelona.[78]

This fundamentally conservative and laissez-faire approach which conceived of political crime either as a continental aberration or as a mere miscategorization of ordinary crime was by no means exclusive to the Liberal establishment. It remained in place throughout the Salisbury administration of the late 1890s and was reiterated in full force, as we shall see, at the 1898 Anti-Anarchist Conference in Rome by the British delegation. More reform-minded voices existed – Anderson, Colonel Majendie – but in 1893 even they saw little need to fiddle with existing legislation. The worst an 'English Ravachol' seemed capable of was smashing a jeweller's window in Birmingham without even stealing any of the jewellery, or shouting 'The hell with the law!' in the streets of Manchester.[79] As for the foreign anarchists in London, they remained conspicuously abeyant.

A brief distraction came on 25 November when an anonymous *Commonweal* editorial trumpeted that 'A bomb has burst in... Barcelona, and the English people are trembling even now... Well, I am one of those who welcome [this] great and good act... because of the death of thirty rich people and the injury to eighty others. Yes, I am really pleased.'[80] It did not take long for the offending words to reach Scotland Yard and then Parliament, where on 30 November they became the subject of a heated debate between Charles Darling, Conservative MP for Deptford, and Asquith.

Asked whether the editor of *Commonweal*, Henry Samuels, would be prosecuted for 'incitement to murder', as Most had been back in 1881, Asquith replied evasively that 'the wisdom of taking legal proceedings in matters of this kind depends largely upon the circumstances of the particular case.'[81] Samuels was not ultimately prosecuted, ironically drawing further ire from the Commonwealers, who, in order to protest Asquith's 'suppressing [of] Anarchist opinion', decided to hold an illegal demonstration in Trafalgar Square on 10 December, only to be quietly and uneventfully dispersed by uniformed and plain-clothes police.[82]

Much like the German Anti-Socialist Laws of the 1880s (which outlawed all socialist propaganda) the newly minted *lois scélérates* in France – passed in December 1893 following an attempted bombing of the Chamber of Deputies – were beginning to have a drastic and immediate impact on revolutionary activity. Publishing anything with an insurrectionary bent was a crime, one carrying with it the increasingly outdated punishment of expulsion.

On 2 January 1894 Lushington received a report from Anderson on a Franco-Dutch anarchist named Alexander Cohen, who had just arrived in London from Paris 'having been expelled... by the French Police... in consequence of his writing on the recent outrage in the Chamber of Deputies'.[83] The frequency of such reports only increased in subsequent months and years after similar gag laws were passed by other European governments (although none arguably as draconic as the *lois scélérates*), confirming some British politicians' perception, especially within the Conservative opposition, that London was becoming, in Lord Salisbury's words, an 'Anarchist laboratory'.[84]

Unfazed by such criticism, the Liberal government stood its ground, continuing to argue that current laws were 'sufficient' and that the best line of defense would always be 'co-operat[ion] with other countries in any practical measures... for dealing more effectually with Anarchists' (this only a couple of months after refusing the Spanish government's overtures).[85] It was evident that anarchism and Britain's policy of asylum were quickly becoming the stuff of political battles, but outside of Parliament 1894 was proving to be an annus mirabilis for anarchist terrorism – 'a very black twelvemonth', as Special Branch DI Sweeney later recalled.[86]

## CHAPTER 10

# 'Men of bad character'[1]

On 12 February 1894 an unassuming petit bourgeois named Émile Henry threw a dynamite bomb into the 'upper-class' Café Terminus near the Parisian Saint-Lazare railway station, killing one and severely injuring twenty. Although the reasons behind the act were varied and convoluted, having as much to do with Henry's doctrinaire idealism as with his pathological personality and difficult family history, chief amongst them had been a desire to avenge Auguste Vaillant, the guillotined comrade behind the ill-fated attempt to blow up the Chamber of Deputies.[2]

The anarchist den at 30 Fitzroy Street had been of interest to Scotland Yard ever since Meunier had briefly lodged there in the summer of 1892. A couple of days after the outrage at Café Terminus, such interest must have only increased considerably, especially as Henry had been seen at that address 'only a few weeks [before]' crossing the Channel back to France.[3] Among the building's more recent frequenters was also a twenty-seven-year-old journeyman tailor by the name of Martial Bourdin. In anarchist circles he was not a figure of any consequence – although he was related by marriage to Henry Samuels, the notorious editor of *Commonweal* – but all the same, Bourdin envisioned himself as a man on a mission.

On 15 February, around 3.30 p.m., Bourdin left Soho and headed towards Westminster Bridge where he boarded the 379 tram running to East Greenwich station.[4] In the left pocket of his heavy overcoat was a small paper-wrapped parcel about the size of a brick. As the tram pulled into East Greenwich station, Bourdin got off in a hurry, stopping only to ask the station time-keeper the way to Greenwich Park.[5] By 4.45 p.m., Bourdin reached the base of the zigzag pathway leading up to the Royal Observatory just as two park labourers were coming down. Noticing Bourdin was carrying a small parcel and walking very fast, they passed him by, continuing their conversation. It was the last time anyone saw him in one piece.

Around 4.50 p.m. a loud boom, slightly less powerful than a cannon's report, was heard all throughout the park and as far away as Stockwell Street. Rushing towards the place of the explosion, a park-keeper found Bourdin kneeling in a pool of blood at the first bend in the uphill pathway. He was half-eviscerated and his left hand had been completely blown off; the only words he was still able to mutter were 'Take me home.' Although immediately taken to the nearby Seamen's Hospital, Bourdin bled to death after a few minutes, leaving behind only a broken 'glass bottle... a metal watch... a membership card of the Autonomie Club, two cards of admission to a masquerade ball in aid of the Revolutionary party, some documents relating to explosive ingredients, seven bills for food... £12 in gold and 19s. 6d. in silver'.[6] His lasting legacy, however, besides inspiring one of the twentieth-century's first great spy novels,[7] was the embarrassment caused to authorities by his gruesome demise.

In the wake of the Greenwich Park incident, indignant questions began flooding the pages of British newspapers: how could an armed anarchist roam through London if his hiding place was well known to police? How did a young and impoverished immigrant tailor come to possess the non-trivial sum of £13? Was he merely a cog in a vast anarchist conspiracy that would soon unleash a full-blown wave of terror on British shores? Why were London's anarchist clubs allowed to exist in the first place, when their prime purpose was clearly to foment violent revolution? Why was the government so willing to give refuge to people who would gladly blow up all of Britain given half a chance? Were the anarchists poisoning water supplies and spreading diseases?[8]

Scotland Yard received official notice of the Greenwich explosion only on 16 February 'not by telegram but by letter... for which an [unnamed] inspector was fined £4'.[9] Anderson, however, had been informed the day of the incident that 'a French tailor named Bourdin had left his shop in Soho with a bomb in his pocket', presumably by the Special Branch detectives keeping watch on the premises.[10] Why had Bourdin not been followed? According to Anderson, 'to track him was impracticable. All that could be done was to send out officers in every direction to watch persons and places that he might be likely to attack.'[11] Whether such 'impracticability' meant the Section D detectives had simply lost track of their target, or something altogether more shadowy, the Assistant Commissioner failed to specify.

What is certain is that on 16 February the Greenwich incident was threatening to snowball into a massive public relations disaster for the Yard. *The Times* declared sardonically that the reason 'the police have been occupying all these weeks in mere "surveillance" [after having]... abstained two or three months ago from casting their net over the whole club, is best known to Mr. Asquith'.[12] The club in question – the Autonomie – was precisely where Inspector Melville, de facto head of Special Branch following Littlechild's retirement,[13] was headed.

Around 9.00 p.m. in the evening the occupants of the house at 6 Windmill Street heard the secret knock being tapped against the front door. There was nothing strange about this as it was still early and most members only began arriving later into the night. The door opened to a view of Melville surrounded by Special Branch men, all of whom 'might have [passed for] members of the club', as a tag-along reporter from *The Graphic* later noted.[14]

The officers immediately burst through the door and began 'taking possession' of the club premises, examining all inside 'for arms, and... order[ing] them... into... the basement', where Melville, sat inquisitorially at a desk, proceeded to 'rigidly examinate' them one by one. As the other club members – 'not one English name in the whole gang', as the same *Graphic* correspondent observed – began arriving, they were 'admitted' by Sergeant Walsh and led into the basement which, by 11.00 p.m., held almost eighty people.[15] Although one French anarchist attempted a scuffle with the officers, he was quickly subdued and the other Autonomists remained cooperative. By midnight all had been released.

Two other simultaneous raids were carried out that night, the first at Bourdin's residence in Soho, where 'explosives were found concealed in [a] room' and the second at 30 Fitzroy Street, which produced 'nothing of importance'.[16] Tactically, the operation proved a success, conspicuously demonstrating that the 'political department' retained the upper hand vis-à-vis London revolutionaries, but practically the raids yielded uncertain results. Along with the explosives found at Bourdin's place, the only material to be confiscated that night was the trunkful of documents found at the Autonomie Club, including a 'manifesto couched in most violent language, printed on blood red paper, and headed, in large letters, "Death to Carnot!"'[17]

The pamphlet, written in French and dated 6 February 1894, began with a standard abuse-filled excoriation of the French regime and ended ominously with the words 'You had Vaillant's head chopped off, and we'll have yours, President Carnot! Long live anarchy!'[18] The French became aware of its existence on 20 February when representatives of the *Sûreté* met in London with Anderson and Melville 'concerning measures to be taken for keeping the foreign anarchists... under constant surveillance'.[19] What the other confiscated documents were or pertained to we can only speculate, as official records on the intelligence gained by Scotland Yard in the wake of Bourdin's death are simply absent. Although correspondence inside the Home Office file on the Greenwich Park incident mentions the existence of an extensive report by Colonel Majendie accompanied by photographs of 'metal cylinders' (perhaps the bombs found during the raid on Bourdin's residence), no copies have apparently survived, the file consisting almost entirely of clippings from *The Times*.[20]

6. Raid on the Autonomie Club, © British Library Board, *Daily Graphic*, 1894.

The government had good reason to pay attention to what the press, especially the Conservative press, was saying about the Greenwich Park outrage, as most of it was sharply critical of the London police. *The Times* led the charge, arguing that Scotland Yard 'knew very little about the Anarchical movement in England until the affair of Greenwich Park'[21] and that 'the chief danger to be apprehended from [the Liberal-supported] international police seems to be that the foreigners might laugh at Scotland Yard'.[22]

*St James's Gazette* proved slightly more conciliatory, proposing that 'the police in London know these men, and know their meeting places; but their hands are tied' by a Liberal government which used 'fine phrases and debating-society theories' to justify its irresoluteness.[23] Such conjectures must have only been strengthened by Asquith's maladroit comment that he was not 'at the present moment in a position to give any information on the subject' in reply to an MP's question on why no raids had taken place before the explosion in Greenwich Park.[24] There was also the matter of Bourdin's funeral, which the anarchists threatened to turn into a rallying march. On this point, however, Asquith could not be clearer, as he explained on 22 February to Commissioner Bradford in a handwritten memo:

> The funeral is to proceed by the shortest [and] most direct route. No procession of any kind is to be allowed to follow the hearse. If any attempt is made,

either at the starting place, or on route to form a procession, it must be at once prevented, and broken up by the Police. Only the mourning coach and the officials should be allowed to follow. At the cemetery no one is to be allowed to make a speech of any kind.[25]

On 23 February, around noon, a large crowd assembled at the corner of Chapel Street and Marylebone Road in central London, where Bourdin's mangled body had been lying in state in a mortuary for the entertainment of 'morbid spectators'.[26] Besides the anarchist contingent, the crowd also included 'a large number of detectives' and, surprisingly, a great deal of working-class Londoners. As the *Daily News* observed, however, these proletarians, 'even the groups of the "genuine unemployed"... were utterly and demonstratively out of sympathy with the cause of Anarchy and the political or social use of dynamite'.[27]

This spontaneous popular reaction against the anarchists quickly turned into a low-level melee replete with 'hissing and hooting, as well as attempts to break through the line in order to wreck the mourners' coach, [plus] every kind of insult and menace hurled at those inside it'.[28] Intimidated in part by the police's show of force, but also by the cortege's intentionally circuitous route, most of the crowd, pro and anti-anarchist, soon petered out. Arriving at St Pancras Cemetery, where the body was to be interred in an unconsecrated lot, Henri Bourdin (the deceased's brother) and his wife Kate passed through the heavily guarded gates, finding the graveside itself surrounded by 'a strong force of police' which soon grew even stronger.[29] Although there are no specific figures to argue the case, Bourdin's funeral was perhaps one of the most heavily policed of the entire nineteenth century in Britain.

Meanwhile, robbed of a chance to scuffle with the anarchists, the hostile mob took its revenge on the one place which all British newspapers had identified as the de facto temple of London anarchy: the Autonomie Club. Just as the funeral was being unceremoniously wrapped up in St Pancras, a group of mostly middle-class youths, cheered on by bystanders, descended on the house in Windmill Street and proceeded to tear down its shutters and smash its windows.[30] In the days that followed, the club began receiving its first hate mail, one writer threatening to firebomb the premises '[when] there is a full household of you [so] that your carcasses shall be blown sky high'.[31] In early March, the anarchist *Freedom* finally announced the Autonomie would be ceasing operation, ostensibly because of the 'secret spy system, which has rendered the place useless and dangerous'.[32]

The Greenwich Park incident did not linger long in the pages of the British press, but while it did, it provided a fascinating mystery to the reading public.

The most obvious question was naturally 'Why?' Why had Bourdin done what he had done? At the inquest into his death, held on 26 February in a Greenwich lecture hall, Colonel Majendie suggested the anarchist had been facing the Observatory at the time of the explosion, arguing he could not have accidentally triggered the bomb by falling on it, as 'the wounds would not have been of the penetrating character all over the body which they were'. Therefore, it was 'quite evident that the explosive was not in the man's pocket at the time of the explosion' and that Bourdin's intention had been 'the immediate use of the explosive substance… against the Observatory'.[33]

Despite its farcical nature, a plan to blow up the Royal Observatory would have certainly chimed in with most Britons' perception of anarchists: 'savages [and] enemies of humanity'[34] on the Right; dangerously misguided dreamers on the Left.[35] There is perhaps a grain of plausibility to this theory. In addition to being a government building, in 1894 the Observatory was also the recently designated locus of the Prime Meridian and thus the symbolic guarantor of worldwide capitalist efficiency. It seems, however, far-fetched to consider a philosophical stance against time discipline as the prime reason for an anarchist outrage in the 1890s, when all other anarchist outrages of that decade were either acts of vengeance against figures of authority (judges, politicians, heads of state) or attacks on the perceived opulence of the bourgeoisie (e.g. the Liceo and Café Terminus bombings).

Excluding the possibility of the Observatory as the intended target, we are left with two other arguable scenarios: either the bomb was the result of an agent provocateur-engineered plot, or Bourdin served as a hapless delivery man for foreign terrorists. As far as the former goes, the evidence for provocation is entirely conjectural. Unsurprisingly, 'among the anarchists themselves, rumours of provocation were rife… with the greatest suspicion focused on Henry Samuels', the editor of *Commonweal*.[36] David Nicoll, champion of the Walsall anarchists and himself a former editor of the anarchist publication, was convinced Samuels had engineered the whole thing at Melville's behest, as was the monthly *Liberty*, a 'philosophical' anarchist monthly that set itself above the *Commonweal*'s insurrectionary verbiage.[37]

Unlike Coulon, however, Samuels does not appear to have left any paper trail in the official record, if indeed he served British authorities in any capacity. There is nonetheless something particularly gripping about the melodramatic image of a ruthless and cynical double agent using a gullible younger man to carry out his self-serving evil scheme which explains, in part, why the myth of the Greenwich Park outrage as a tragic put-up job survived in the anarchist oral culture of the 1890s. A decade later, Helen Rossetti, scion of Pre-Raphaelite royalty and former teenage anarchist, defended the theory that Bourdin had been set up by Samuels in a pseudonymous memoir co-written with her sister Olivia – an account which likely inspired Joseph Conrad (a friend of Helen's) to put his own masterful spin on the tale.[38]

The final scenario, according to which Bourdin was acting as a middleman is sadly not much more convincing than the first two, save for a conjecture, advanced by DS McIntyre in his serialized memoirs, that 'Bourdin was to get the bomb [to]... two foreign Anarchists... for them to take back to use in Paris.'[39] In any case, if the popular press was preoccupied with the issue of Bourdin's motivation, the authorities were more concerned with the intelligence failure that had made the outrage possible in the first place. Anderson's excuse that tracking Bourdin had proved 'impracticable' would not have earned him any praise from Asquith, whose constant lack of information on the anarchists' doings left him exposed to Conservative attacks in the House of Commons.

The British government's first move towards a more systematic method of dealing with anarchist 'propaganda by the deed' was by no means revolutionary, but it did mark a surprising departure from the status quo. The Greenwich Park fiasco provided an opportunity for implementing a much-needed upgrade in the Home Office's approach to 'infernal machines', one that Colonel Majendie was eager to seize upon. As he explained to Asquith in early March, 'the recent explosion... and the knowledge that there are... many persons ready and willing to avail themselves of explosives [to] further... their anarchical designs' also pointed to the fact that British authorities were 'trusting... very largely to "luck" to relieve us of any sudden call for the disposal of a dangerous infernal machine'.

Paris, he argued, was many years ahead of London when it came to 'neutralizing the effects of dangerous [explosives]' and a visit to the French capital would certainly prove essential in furnishing 'an opportunity of informing myself as to the precautionary measures adopted... for dealing with emergencies'.[40] Pitching reform to the Home Office by arguing Britain needed to be more in line with France was certainly a counterintuitive approach, even under a Liberal government, but Majendie received the green light the next day. Whatever misgivings they may have had about the 'continental system', Whitehall mandarins nonetheless agreed 'the Bourdin affair has to a large extent brought [the] anxiety [about Britain's vulnerability to anarchist terrorism] to an acute point'.[41]

Despite Majendie's having pioneered the concept of a civilian bomb squad more than a decade earlier, the work performed by the Inspectorate of Explosives was no longer high up on the British government's list of security priorities since the lulling of Fenian activity. By contrast, the explosives unit at the Parisian *Laboratoire Municipal de Chimie* had rapidly risen to prominence thanks to a spate of anarchist attacks and the extent of its resources already reflected its importance to the French Ministry of the Interior. In the report submitted on 12 April to the Home Office, Majendie described admiringly a network of 'four bastions... fitted up for the purpose of examining and opening infernal machines', maintained and operated by a body of specially trained chemists in constant direct communication with the *Préfecture*.[42]

This was a far cry from the situation in Britain where no dedicated bomb disposal facilities existed and where communication between the Inspectorate of Explosives and the Scotland Yard was unduly slow. Majendie did not imagine an exact replica of the French system would ever be set up at home, but urged that 'some points of the French system... call for prompt adoption'. Firstly, communication had to be 'forthwith... in all cases where a package of really suspicious character is discovered', to which end he proposed 'a complete telephonic system with the Home Office and through Scotland Yard'. Secondly, facilities 'for effecting a preliminary examination' of explosives would have to be constructed on premises 'absolutely free from public intrusion [and] even public observance'.[43] There were not many locations in London ideally placed for such arrangements, but Majendie proposed Duck Island – one of three islets in St James's Park Lake – and the Tower of London as sufficiently suitable. Anderson and Bradford approved the plan almost immediately and by November 1894, the facility on Duck Island was already 'practically completed'.[44]

Official views on policing anarchism were further challenged by two other relatively high-profile cases, which occurred in rapid succession during April 1894. The first was the arrest of Theodule Meunier, the Café Véry bomber, who had successfully escaped extradition in 1892. Having recently returned to London, on his way back to the continent, Meunier failed to remain incognito for long and on 13 April, around 8.20 p.m., he was intercepted on a train about to depart from Victoria station by Melville and his men. Keenly aware of his emerging celebrity status and of the impact popular opinion might have on the stability of the 'political department', the Special Branch leader had tipped off journalists about an upcoming arrest well in advance. The anarchist was apprehended after a brief but spectacular scuffle with fifteen policemen and railway officials and taken to the Bow Street police station.[45] As in François' case two years earlier, Meunier's claim to political refugee status failed to carry much weight in court. In June he was extradited to France where, following a lengthy trial, he was found guilty and sentenced to be transported to Devil's Island in January 1895.

It is not clear how Whitehall felt about the press sensationalizing such sensitive operations, but it is fair to assume Melville's swashbuckling was at the very least controversial. Preserved in a Home Office file, a newspaper clipping on the arrest of the Italian anarchist Francis (or Francesco) Polti, complete with a detailed description of his confession, reveals the incomprehension of Assistant Under-Secretary Charles Murdoch at seeing 'so much information... get[ting] out... from what would appear to have been communicated by the Police'.[46]

The second high-profile case of 1894 centred in part around Polti, an 'illiterate and very enthusiastic' youngster[47] with radical sympathies who had left his native Lombardy for London to work as a waiter. Proving easy prey for Special Branch detectives eager to demonstrate their increased vigilance in London's anarchist enclaves, he had inadvertently led the police to a certain Giuseppe Farnara, a middle-aged 'brigand [who had] only adopted Anarchism as a cloak to cover his depredations'.[48] Surprisingly, Farnara appeared to be planning an outrage in London and had co-opted the young Polti as a sidekick.

Wary of avoiding another Greenwich-style fiasco, Anderson and Melville made sure a watch 'by various officers... [was kept] upon Polti and Farnara for a whole fortnight without intermission' and that the anarchists were 'even shadowed to the shops in the City'.[49] In a strange echo of the Bourdin case, on the afternoon of 14 April 1894 Polti, carrying a small parcel, 'mount[ed] an omnibus on the Surrey side of Blackfriars Bridge, going city-wards'.[50] Seated next to him, DI Sweeney and DS Maguire of Special Branch calmly kept the unsuspecting youth in their crosshairs, arresting him only later that evening. The parcel in his possession turned out to contain only an iron casting, but the list of explosives and receipts bearing Farnara's name, as well as the dangerous chemical compounds and anarchist pamphlets later found at Polti's residence in Clerkenwell, painted a different picture.[51]

Making matters worse for Polti, the manager of Mr Cohen's Works in Blackfriars Road, where the iron casting had been poured, had already informed the police 'of the fact that orders had been given for the manufacture of bombs'.[52] This is in fact how Scotland Yard had come to learn of the existence of the 'bomb' in the first place and the original informant (an employee of Mr Cohen's) was subsequently awarded £50 for his services, the same sum as that received by all police officers involved in the case. 'It has been usual in cases of political crime', Bradford explained in a letter to Asquith, 'to grant special rewards, and the case in question was of such importance that I think the same course should again be followed.'[53]

The iron casting was not of course a live shell, but neither had the Walsall casting been, and as Colonel Majendie concluded in his report, Polti's was 'made in a shape well known on the Continent, and designed with a view to a minimum of space and a maximum of destruction'.[54] Polti admitted in a confession – the same which was later leaked to the press – that he had purchased the chemical compounds and casting at Farnara's urging, but denied all sympathy with anarchism.[55] Farnara, in the meantime, had managed to abscond just before Polti's arrest, despite increased police vigilance, and raids in the Italian quarters of Clerkenwell initially produced nothing.

Incidentally, however, one of those whose residences were summarily searched in the raids, a fifty-four-year-old singing teacher named Federico Lauria, happened to be a spy in the service of the Italian embassy. Protesting his innocence to Melville (who had just been promoted to Chief Inspector) Lauria proved his credentials by giving away Farnara's most likely hideout.[56] Melville then debriefed Lauria at length in his usual discrete manner, without disclosing his identity to other Special Branch detectives – a practice which, as Chief Inspector Donald Swanson explained in a report, seems to have been the norm: 'each officer has his own informers, and they are not generally known. The method is for the officers to compare with each other the information they may have received before action is taken.'[57]

On 22 April 1894 Farnara was finally apprehended at an Italian lodging house in Stratford, east London. Wryly conceding defeat with a comment that his captors had been very well informed, Farnara resignedly admitted to the purpose of the 'infernal machine' found on Polti. The two men had gone to Blackfriars Road to order the bomb which Farnara would 'have taken… to France or Italy; but having no money I meant to have it used in London at the Exchange. England is the richest country, and at the Exchange there would be more rich people together than at any other place.'[58] At the trial which followed, both accused were indicted under the third and fourth sections of the 1883 Explosives Act with unlawfully possessing explosive substances for a criminal object. Polti received a sentence of ten years with penal servitude, while Farnara, defiantly unrepentant and pleading guilty to all charges, got twenty years (though he ended up spending the better part of his life in the Broadmoor Criminal Lunatic Asylum).[59]

By and large, London exiles did not appear to share in Farnara's murderous rage against the British state and in an interview with *The Daily Graphic* one anarchist declared candidly that 'we… do not wish to do anything in England, because it is our refuge… [and it] serves us by letting us alone'.[60] The London anarchist press itself seemed equally willing to repudiate propaganda by the deed, with even the usually incendiary *Commonweal* asking rhetorically:

> How many more lessons are required to teach us what not to do? Walsall proved how plots and conspiracies lead to failure; the Greenwich Park explosion proved how foolish and dangerous it is to meddle with compounds that one is not familiar with; Polti, again, has shown how risky it is to trade with shopkeepers.[61]

Yet despite the government's and some anarchists' reassurances, the Polti–Farnara case inevitably suggested that it was perfectly possible for an outrage to be not merely planned in Britain, but directed against British institutions as well. It also spoke, once again, to the dysfunctional channels connecting Special Branch to the Home Office. Anderson, who, with rare exceptions, was subject to Melville's tight control of information,[62] had informed the Home Secretary of Polti's arrest (and existence) only on 23 April, ten days after the event, and then 'only after a request [had been] made to the Commissioner of Police'.[63] As H. W. Primrose, Permanent Secretary at the Office of Works, explained in a note to Charles Murdoch at the Home Office, such a state of affairs could not be allowed to continue: 'whoever is responsible for this oversight [should be informed] that in future the [Home Secretary] desires that he may have immediate official information on all matters relating to the Anarchist movement, and not be left to obtain his news from the papers'.[64]

Asquith continued to obtain most of his news on 'social revolution' from the newspapers, as for the rest of his tenure at the Home Office anarchist outrages remained almost entirely confined to the European continent. Nevertheless, the latter half of 1894 did see a marked increase in police surveillance of London anarchists, as well as a heightened fear of future outrages. On 1 May 1894 detectives searched the premises of one Henry Van Dierk, German anarchist and publisher of *Der Lumpen Proletarier*, carefully 'examining the walls and flooring, removing the stove, and emptying every drawer... trunk [and] bottle' without, however, finding anything incriminating.[65]

The first of May also marked the International Workers' Day and thus an opportunity for a show of force for a variety of left-wing groups. A demonstration was held in Hyde Park, numbering at least three thousand participants and including such luminaries as Keir Hardie, H. M. Hyndman and William Morris. Although the event remained for the most part peaceful, the few violent incidents which occurred tellingly involved attacks on several anarchist speakers by people in the audience. One was 'hurled from his place, and [had his] flag torn to pieces', while James Tochatti, the Italo-Scottish editor of *Liberty*, 'was frequently interrupted with cries of "Shut up!" and finally thrown to the ground'. Both men escaped a potentially worse fate only through the intervention of a 'large body of police in attendance'.[66]

The closest Special Branch detectives came to uncovering a new bomb plot was on 31 May when a 'party consisting of Sergeants Walsh [and] Flood, [DI Sweeney] and three other officers, all under Melville, went to 54 Park Walk' in Chelsea,[67] the home of a certain Fritz Brall. A German anarchist with a passion for dangerous chemicals, Brall had already alarmed his former neighbours in Fitzrovia, who had complained to police about the loud noises and suspicious foreigners coming out of his apartment.

Unaware he had been placed under surveillance, the anarchist had stocked his new place with a number of 'bottles containing powerful acids, glass tubes', implements for manufacturing coin, as well as Johann Most's *Science of Revolutionary Warfare*, an already notorious bomb-making manual first published in America a decade earlier. Detectives also discovered a mysterious hole several feet deep, which Brall had dug into the floor foundation ostensibly for the purpose of keeping rabbits, but which Melville regarded as nothing but a 'private storehouse' for the chemical arsenal.[68]

Under the 1883 Explosives Act the mere possession of dangerous chemicals was sufficient to secure a prison sentence, but Justice Grantham, who presided over Brall's trial at the Old Bailey, proved less willing than Justice Hawkins to send down anarchists for *potential* acts of terror. In his defence, Brall claimed the incriminating materials belonged to friends of his and that some of the chemicals were merely useful in his trade as cabinetmaker. His story about the pit also surprisingly checked out when his landlord's wife confirmed she had seen rabbits in Brall's apartment. Grantham conceded 'the police were thoroughly justified in every step they had taken',[69] but in the end decided to set Brall free, much to the stupefaction of Special Branch officers who had all 'expected... he would be found guilty'.[70]

If Melville saw reason to decry the leniency of some British judges, however, French newspapers had fresh impetus to decry the leniency of British laws in general after the assassination of French President Sadi Carnot on the evening of 24 June 1894. The assassin, a twenty-one-year-old Milanese baker's apprentice named Santo Hieronimo Caserio had only recently arrived in France and despite his unbending devotion to the anarchist cause, he did not claim to represent anyone but himself.

The notion that a 'lone wolf' could so easily murder not merely a judge or a reactionary bourgeois, but the president of the republic himself, was, nonetheless, hard to stomach for French authorities and press alike, especially in the wake of the *lois scélérates* passed a year earlier to subdue the anarchist peril once and for all. A new, even stricter anti-anarchist law was passed in July 1894, outlawing any espousal of anarchism, no matter how trivial, but only a few days after the assassination, the need for a foreign scapegoat was irrepressible. *La Lanterne* alleged that 'an international conspiracy against heads of state and certain political personalities' was to blame. The anti-Carnot pamphlet which Melville had uncovered during the raid on the Autonomie and forwarded to French authorities was proof that Caserio's plot had been hatched in London.[71]

The notion that London was becoming the headquarters of an international murderous conspiracy was not merely the gossip of French newspapers however. It was also what some politicians in Whitehall believed, especially within the Conservative opposition. If under Gladstone the Liberals had done everything to sell the 'war of classes' to the British electorate, as Lord Salisbury believed,[72] under Rosebery (Prime Minister since March 1894) they also appeared to be perfectly willing to harbour foreigners for whom said war meant not speeches and canvassing, but daggers and bombs.

The first proposal for a new Aliens Bill was made on 6 July when Salisbury stood up in the House of Lords and delivered a speech excoriating the government's lax attitude to immigration. Drawing on the report of an 1889 House of Commons Committee on the effects of immigration in London's East End, Salisbury argued that the unbridled influx of 'destitute aliens' (most of them Eastern European Jews) was pauperizing the native working class and that consequently Britain needed to follow the United States' lead in excluding all immigrants who were not financially independent.[73]

At the very least, Salisbury suggested, the Home Secretary had to be reinvested with 'the power to expel any [dangerous] foreigner' (lapsed since the last Chartist scare of 1848) given that the new political exiles were nothing like the old ones. The anarchists' 'conspiracy of assassination' was worlds apart from the respectable struggles of a Garibaldi or a Kossuth and it was therefore vital for Britain's interests abroad that it should not be perceived by its allies as 'the base from which the Anarchist operations are conducted'.[74]

While conceding the merits of Salisbury's stance on 'destitute aliens' and the fact that 'we are hampered too much by traditional watchwords about… being an asylum',[75] Rosebery nonetheless rejected the notion that Britain was naively harbouring dangerous criminals; if anything, the government's policy was preventing more assassination attempts from occurring:

> What happens now is this. Men… of bad character come to these islands… [and] they may when they are here meditate plots… against persons in…

or… outside these islands. But they are under supervision while in this country, and under pretty strict supervision; and it is rare, I think, that we do not know what they have in contemplation. If they are contemplating crimes against people in these islands the law furnishes a sufficient remedy for dealing with them… [and it] is quite obvious that they cannot assassinate persons outside these islands while they remain within them.[76]

This reiteration of the Liberal approach to political policing differed very little from what Asquith had argued in the House of Commons a few days after the Greenwich Park outrage, with the notable exception that it emphasized the 'strict supervision' the anarchists were supposedly under. Salisbury's proposed bill did not ultimately survive its second reading in the Lords, but it did prove a crucial point: as long as a Liberal government was in power, the doctrine of political asylum remained inviolable, though there was, it appeared, ample room for compromise on the issue of non-political asylum. A decade later, as we shall see, this lesson laid the basis for Britain's first comprehensive immigration act.

The policy of 'strict supervision' continued throughout the latter half of 1894. In mid-July, following an incendiary speech by the new editor of *Commonweal* praising the assassination of Carnot and urging the eradication of the British Royal family,[77] police raided the anarchist newspaper's office in Sidmouth Mews, Camden, for the second time in two years. As ex-editor Henry Samuels complained in a letter to *Reynolds's Newspaper*, 'for three weeks the police have held possession of the office of the *Commonweal* [and] uniformed men and plain clothes ones from the Scotland Yard have received from the postman a number of letters addressed to me'.[78] Although the police 'occupation' came to an end before the end of the month, *Commonweal* ceased publication shortly thereafter. Given its already failing fortunes, it is likely the operation was meant to deliver a *coup de grâce* to this once unofficial organ of London anarchism, as much as update the police's already growing records.[79]

Despite this apparent crackdown, the comings and goings of continental exiles appeared to be on the increase. In reply to an inquiry made by Austrian authorities regarding some Bohemian anarchists thought to be en route to London, Special Branch DS Maguire reported that two of the wanted radicals, both ex-members of the Autonomie Club, did not 'mix very much with the other foreign groups partly owing to their not having a knowledge of the language and also owing, it is thought, to the fact of them being very cautious men'.[80] Only three days later, the French government made a similar request concerning the whereabouts of a certain Rosenberg and one of his companions, asking that 'immediate notice be given to the French police' should the former leave

Britain.[81] Much like the Bohemians, the two Frenchmen carefully skirted police attention, so much so that Anderson suggested they were either not anarchists, or that they simply did not exist, 'the French government hav[ing] been misled by some untrustworthy informant'.[82]

Despite his undisguised contempt for French authorities, the Assistant Commissioner may have had a point. The *Préfecture*'s informers did have 'a sorry reputation among the anarchists and across police services',[83] while the *Sûreté*, its many successful investigations notwithstanding, was somewhat prone to wild goose chases. In early August, for example, 'Parisian police, accompanied by a Scotland Yard detective' went looking for a 'dynamite factory' set up by French anarchists in Birmingham, only to find that 'there [was] not the slightest ground for the suspicion'.[84]

From August to December 1894 more continental anarchists continued to join the ranks of the London colony. A precise number is impossible to deduce, but by mid-August, some British newspapers were reporting that as many as four hundred anarchists had arrived in Britain within the span of a few days.[85] Others dismissed that figure as an exaggeration, but warned that 'certain members of [Scotland Yard]' who proved 'a little more communicative' than Commissioner Bradford, had confirmed the mass of new political refugees was a sizeable one indeed.[86]

Rumours aside, the number of press reports on *individual* foreign anarchists arriving in Britain during this period is tellingly insignificant and Home Office files indicate only a handful of arrivals, with most occurring on 24 September when five Italians arrived from Switzerland, and one Belgian from Antwerp.[87] Perhaps the most widely reported case was that of the stately Amilcare Cipriani, who arrived in London on 10 August via Brussels, 'finding that France... has become an impossible place of residence for a conspicuous Italian Anarchist'.[88] A romantic figure who was both a hero of the Risorgimento and a revolutionary anti-capitalist, Cipriani fascinated with his eccentricity and seemed to problematize Salisbury's distinction between 'good' and 'bad' political exiles.

Whether notorious or utterly anonymous, all these men – and they were invariably men – had been expelled from their countries of residence or origin and had chosen to take refuge in Britain, where, despite Melville's fearsome reputation, they knew they would at least be afforded *some* liberties. In certain cases, however, they ended up there even if they did not wish to. This, for example, was the case with François Birdisol and Louis Antoine, two French anarchists who 'had asked to be sent to Germany', only to find that their fares had already been 'paid to Dover, where they [subsequently] landed'.[89]

Despite the bombs, the raids, the parliamentary debates and an increasingly censorious public opinion,[90] 1894 was not looking to be quite the 'black twelvemonth' for British authorities, certainly not on the scale it had proved for the French, Italian and Spanish governments.[91] The two attempted outrages by Bourdin and Farnara had, after all, ended in self-inflicted, unintentional death and miserable failure respectively. Lack of success, however, did not necessarily mean loss of faith.

On the night of 4 November an 'infernal machine' exploded in front of Reginald Brett's house in upscale Mayfair, the only damage being a gaping hole in front of the doorway, a slightly unhinged door and a few shattered windows. Brett – son of Viscount Esher and former Liberal MP – had escaped perfectly unharmed along with Mrs Brett and the servants, but despite this rather undramatic result, the outrage marked the first time in the new decade that a bomb had come this close to claiming the life of an establishment figure.

That Brett should have been the intended target of the attack seemed absurd. His performance as an MP had been unmemorable (though he later went on to have an illustrious career as a civil servant) and he was not known to harbour strong views on political radicals. Brett's neighbour, however, was none other than Sir Henry Hawkins – 'Hangman Hawkins' as the *Commonweal* had once dubbed him – the judge responsible for putting away the Walsall anarchists and, more recently, Polti and Farnara.

Colonel Majendie's report on the incident indicated the bomb's main charge had been picric acid, 'hitherto… used almost invariably by French Anarchists'[92] and in the absence of any forewarnings or direct witnesses, that was just about the only clue police had to go by. In the days that followed, Special Branch detectives tried, to no avail, to locate any possible suspects. For a while, newspapers reported that an arrest seemed likely, based on 'information received at Scotland Yard [stating that] the perpetrator of the outrage [was] without doubt in hiding on the Continent',[93] but such reports proved premature. As DI Sweeney later recalled, 'various anarchists were suspected… but we were never able to fix on any particular individual'.[94]

## CHAPTER 11

# 'Surtout pas trop de zèle'[1]

PRESIDENT Carnot was not the last head of state to fall victim to an anarchist outrage, but by the mid-1890s the tide was beginning to turn against the faction favouring propaganda by the deed. The future, it seemed, belonged to the collectivist vision advocated a generation earlier by the First International anarchists: 'monster unions embracing millions of proletarians'.[2] Although this new syndicalist vision had the advantage of positioning anarchism within the emerging political movement of the industrial working class, it also meant anarchists were forced to compete with the much better organized and better funded parties of reformist socialism.

The anarchist colony in London was increasingly coming under the sway of people like Errico Malatesta, Louise Michel, Rudolf Rocker and other avowed communists, leaving the advocates of 'individual will' in an increasingly uncertain minority. With the exception of Rocker's organizing of East End Jewish sweatshop workers along anarcho-syndicalist lines,[3] however, the communists were themselves shut out of the enfeebled British trade union movement and the reformist late-Victorian socialist revival (embodied by the Independent Labour Party and, to a lesser extent, by the SDF). Consequently, the anarchist movement in Britain had, as a whole, become 'very dull and sluggish' by the end of 1895.[4]

Although there is no indication that British police knew anything about – or were even interested in – the ongoing ontological crisis of émigré anarchism, they must have nonetheless perceived and welcomed the change of pace it gradually brought about. Special Branch had just been strengthened by the addition of four constables to 'meet the emergency'[5] which 1894 had seemed to promise, but a couple of months into the new year, the only cases Melville and his men had to work on involved only the quiet shadowing of recent arrivals, usually on behalf of foreign governments.

Such missions were not, in fact, entirely legitimate, despite being tacitly condoned by the Home Secretary. Just how tacitly is revealed by the reaction of Harry Butler Simpson, a Home Office clerk, to the 1897 request by Spanish authorities for information on the movements of a Cuban revolutionary exiled in Britain. Though closely acquainted with the 'political work' of Lushington and Anderson, Simpson could still naively express disbelief at the notion that 'the English police... [should] shadow a political exile at the request of a foreign government'.[6]

Not that there was much work of this nature to do in early 1895, as evidenced by DI Sweeney's brief report on two London-based anarchists suspected of smuggling seditious literature into Austria-Hungary:

> Alois Kubalck... and J. Petrick... have not hitherto been known to Police as having any connection with the anarchist movements. I find they are members of a Bohemian body who are known to hold extreme views... [but up] to the present I am unable to connect these men with the printing, publishing, distribution, or transmission of any anarchist literature. However I have put a confidential informant in touch with them, and will make further enquiry.[7]

If any arrests were made, it was for mundane infractions to which anarchism was only marginally incidental. This, for example, was the case with Alfred Grandidier, a familiar face on the Fitzrovian scene, who was apprehended on 24 January for a burglary he had previously committed in France,[8] or Edward Leggett who was 'charged with travelling on the Great Eastern Railway without having... paid his fare', something which he could not bring himself to do as 'an anarchist [who] refuse[s] to recognise the right of a section of parasites calling themselves shareholders to make rules... over railways'.[9]

The Walsall case was briefly returned to public attention when on 3 February the Sunday edition of *Reynolds's Newspaper* began publishing weekly instalments of ex-DS Patrick McIntyre's 'Scotland Yard: Its Mysteries and Methods' in which he alleged that '[in the] whole series of dynamite plots... the hand of the spy, or agent-provocateur, [was] clearly visible'.[10] His 'revelation' concerning the Walsall plot, namely that it had all been Auguste Coulon's handiwork, proved especially controversial. It sparked a furore among socialists, many of whom were more receptive than ever to the anarchists' warnings of a 'British Third Section' conspiring to discredit the workers' movement by any means necessary.

Pleading in a letter to Asquith that '[new] facts have come to light which seem to lend confirmation to a suspicion... that the prime mover in the alleged plot was a police agent', Keir Hardie even offered to prepare 'a statement of all the facts of the case' for the cabinet's perusal.[11] It is unlikely that Asquith would have agreed to review the verdict, but at any rate, he did not have to: in July the Liberals lost the general election and Sir Matthew White Ridley became the new Conservative Home Secretary. When the report proposed by Hardie was finally assembled in September 1895 and submitted to the Home Office with the endorsement of left-wing Liberals,[12] Ridley brushed it off with instructions to 'say… that [having] reconsidered the evidence in the case [the Home Secretary] regrets to say… he has been unable to arrive at a conclusion different from that repeatedly expressed by himself and his predecessors in office'.[13]

The controversy surrounding London's 'anarchist laboratory' was also kept alive thanks to a few sensational stories on the near-lynching of a French informer,[14] bogus bomb scares,[15] an 'imminent anarchist invasion'[16] and an attempted outrage on a Parisian financier. The last-named involved the mailing of a letter bomb to Baron Alphonse de Rothschild which failed to hit its intended target when it was opened by Rothschild's secretary, who suffered minor injuries as a result. The incident drew the attention of Scotland Yard detectives after French police put out an official statement claiming 'the plot had been organised in London' – a theory that had to be discarded when the would-be assassin was caught in Paris on his second attempt.[17]

Despite a series of budgetary cuts introduced in 1892, the Home Office Secret Service bureau – headed by Jenkinson's one-time deputy, Major Nicholas Gosselin – still managed to run a small but functional network of 'one secret agent, seven informants and two "sub-agents"' in America.[18] All were under the direction of Harry Gloster Armstrong, a young military officer who reported directly to Gosselin.[19]

In early August 1896 the Home Office received notice that four New York Fenians, all members of the Irish National Brotherhood – an obscure New York-based Clan na Gael splinter group[20] – were on their way to Europe with the intention of unleashing a new dynamite campaign in Britain later in the year. Although the threat of renewed Fenian violence was in itself cause for alarm, the circumstances surrounding this new plot proved especially awkward for the British government.

The news came on the heels of the recent pardoning and release from Portland prison of four high-profile dynamitards – Thomas Devaney, Thomas Gallagher, John Daly and Albert Whitehead – all of whom had received life sentences in the early 1880s. The possibility that the New Yorkers might somehow link up with their recently pardoned comrades and commit a new outrage was, if not entirely plausible,[21] at least conceivable. Added to this was the fact that Ridley was increasingly under pressure from certain ultra-Unionists in his party, such as Sir Henry Howorth, MP for Salford South, for whom 'the explanation given by the Government to justify the release of the dynamitards [was] inadequate, and… calculated to encourage a recrudescence of that form of crime'.[22]

The identities of the new conspirators also gave the Home Office reason to pause for thought. Two of them, Edward Ivory and Thomas Haines, were not previously known to police, but the other two were inveterate Fenians of the old guard. One was John Francis Kearney, who had managed to avoid arrest in Britain by giving up the members of the Featherstone gang in 1883, while the other man was none other than Patrick J. Tynan, the fabled 'No. 1' of the Invicibles and the supposed *éminence grise* behind the Phoenix Park murders. Unsoftened by past failures, both men had apparently remained dyed-in-the-wool dynamitards and, at least in the case of Tynan, staunch insurrectionists opposed to Home Rule and Parnellism.[23]

Finally, there was the Czar's European tour, which was scheduled to include a sojourn at Balmoral Castle towards the end of September. The Emperor and Autocrat of All the Russias was not normally regarded as a traditional enemy in Fenian circles – indeed the Clan na Gael had attempted to liaise with representatives of the Russian government as recently as 1886[24] – but the New York expedition was thought to have the backing of 'Anarchists and Nihilists [who although not] specially interested in freeing Ireland from the British yoke, subscribed funds and dynamite for the leaders'.[25] Naturally, given the circumstances, an attempt on the czar's life could certainly mean an attempt on the queen.

By mid-August the conspirators had all disembarked at various European ports. Staying in London under the assumed name of Edward Bell, Edward Ivory began by inquiring at local chemists about the price of a 'carboy of sulphuric acid',[26] but unable to find the right deal, he moved on to Antwerp in early September. There he reunited with Tynan, Kearney and Haines – the last two of whom had just finished converting a small suburban house into a dynamite-making facility. For reasons that never truly became clear, the four soon parted ways however. On 8 September Ivory returned to London, boarding a train to Glasgow, while Tynan made his way to the French Opal Coast, settling in Boulogne-sur-Mer on 11 September – the same day that Kearney and Haines checked in at the Queen's Hotel in Rotterdam.

In Glasgow, Ivory scouted the local Irish republican scene before realizing the men he was looking for were either long gone or wasting away in hospitals and pubs. As he explained in a cryptic telegram to Tynan in Boulogne: 'I am afraid the stock in Ireland are not good enough... I've got an awful fear that my speculation in London will result badly for me; but if I am able to get a good line in stocks to-night or to-morrow I will be away before the wedding occurs.'[27] Tynan's reply reassuringly asked to 'kindly join me and bring what you can', but a day later Ivory received a telegram from Kearney which boded decidedly bad news: 'We are here. Come right away. Business stopped. Wire Garth [Tynan].'[28] Ivory did manage to wire Tynan, but it was already too late.

On the afternoon of 12 September, having received the go-ahead from London, Glasgow CID despatched a unit of its own detectives along with a few RIC auxiliaries[29] to watch over the Victoria Hotel, where Ivory was staying. By the time Robert Anderson gave the order for his arrest a few hours later, the American was already in custody at the Central Police Office in South Albion Street for 'inquiry as to contravening the Explosives Act, 1883'.[30] Details of the incriminating papers and telegrams found in his possession, which he claimed to have found in a public lavatory, were immediately cabled to London, giving Scotland Yard the pretext to bring down the curtain on the whole conspiracy.

In Antwerp, Special Branch detectives, overseen by Anderson himself and in conjunction with Belgian police, raided Kearney and Haines' suburban 'laboratory'. They had been absent for days, but the materials seized at the house made up an impressive collection: 'utensils of glass and china… clay moulds… a leaden vessel [giving off] a suffocating vapour… phials containing nitro-glycerine… [and] three demijohns filled with acids'.[31] With Tynan already under arrest, it did not take long before the two amateur chemists were traced to a Rotterdam hotel and arrested by Dutch police. The operation looked to be an almost unprecedented triumph for the Yard and thanks to the help lent by Dutch, Belgian and French authorities, a shining example of what could be achieved through actual police cooperation.

Cracks soon began to emerge, however, and the case against Tynan seems to have collapsed almost immediately. Whatever connection he may have had to the Phoenix Park murders, it was legally useless to British authorities. The French government had already recognized Tynan's political refugee status in 1883 and, in any case, the statute of limitations dictated that he could no longer be detained for a crime committed more than a decade earlier.[32] Furthermore, despite Tynan's 'more or less important admissions',[33] including his acquaintance with Ivory, Kearney and Haines, the evidence implicating him in any dynamite plot was deemed insufficient by French police.

The Home Office made a last-ditch request for extradition on 24 September, insisting that while in 1883 Tynan's extradition had been demanded 'merely on suspicion of [his] participation in the Phoenix Park murders', this time it was being requested 'after his condemnation for murder in default'.[34] The French were still not convinced and Tynan lingered on in prison for three more weeks; by late October he was reunited with his family in New York.[35]

Inexplicably, the evidence against Kearney and Haines also proved flimsy in the end. Despite initial reports of 'pockets… simply stuffed with documents…

of a highly incriminatory character', including coded letters which supposedly revealed 'plans [for an] attempt against the Queen of England at Balmoral and the Czar of Russia',[36] by early October Dutch authorities found it impossible to detain the two suspects any longer in the absence of 'any legal grounds upon which they could either [prosecute or] grant extradition', which in this case, the Home Office did not even bother to request.

By mid-October Kearney and Haines were in Amsterdam, boarding the steamer *Wenkerdam* to New York, much to the ire of Anderson who, years later, could still hardly contain his frustration. As he recalled in his memoirs:

> One characteristic of the 'Parisian accent' that is so much cultivated by English people is the vulgarism of accentuating the final syllable of words; and at times I felt tempted to give vent to my feelings of annoyance at the collapse of this dynamite case by repeating [the] names [of Kearney and Haines] aloud in the Parisian fashion.[37]

The reasons for this puzzling outcome only became apparent in November, during the remanding of Edward Ivory's case to the magistrate at Bow Street Police Court, in preparation for trial. Hoping to prevent the complete disintegration of the case, the prosecution decided to call on its star witness at the hearing on 13 November – a certain Mr Jones, whose 'full name was communicated to the Magistrate alone'.[38] Jones, a native of County Armagh in northern Ireland, had since 1890 been employed by Her Majesty's Government to, as he put it, 'make inquiries' in America. What sort of inquiries? This he candidly laid bare before the court:

> Amongst the persons whose acquaintance I made [in New York] was... William Lyman [the leader of the Irish National Brotherhood]. I learned the existence of a secret organisation in America... known amongst its members [as] the 'United Irishmen'... [and in] connection with this organisation there are a number of what are called camps. There are several in the New York district... [and] I received instructions... to join this organisation, and I did so... I was initiated in September 1894. There were present on that occasion William Lyman... John Francis Kearney, and Patrick Joseph Tynan... I saw [Ivory] at [a secret] meeting in Chicago [in 1895]. We were admitted by the secret passport.[39]

Jones followed this up with an impressive number of documents, including the 'constitution and bye-laws' adopted at the Chicago meeting, which appeared to outline a policy of run-of-the-mill insurrectionary Fenianism complete with condemnations of 'constitutional action' and references to 'military companies... to be prepared for action in the hour of England's difficulties'.[40] His testimony seemed to succeed in finally implicating Tynan, Kearney and Ivory in a dynamite conspiracy by showing that all three were members of a secret revolutionary society intent on unleashing terror on British targets. For Magistrate Vaughan this amounted to as good a reason as any to commit Ivory for trial: 'Here is a man who goes to Glasgow. He has letters of introduction to people... They are connected with his organisation... He goes to Brussels. He meets Tynan. They are together at Antwerp, the very seat of the manufacture of the chemicals... intended to produce an explosion.'[41]

The main problem with this line of argument, apart from the inconvenient fact that Ivory's link to the dynamite in Antwerp was purely conjectural, was that it relied exclusively on the testimony of an informer, and a Home Office informer to boot. For the Home Secretary, the risks involved in pursuing the case against Ivory far outweighed the benefits, which, since the release of Kearney and Tynan, were no longer easily discernible. As Anderson explained:

> When I wrote to [Ridley], reporting the arrest of [Ivory], and informing him of the means by which it had been obtained, he formed the opinion that the fact of a confederate having given information to Government was a bar to prosecution. And he remained unmoved by the clear proof I gave him that the informant had done everything in his power to check and thwart the execution of the plot.[42]

Ridley decided to bring the matter before Prime Minister Salisbury, who sided with Anderson. The trial went ahead as planned, but it did not turn out as the Assistant Commissioner might have hoped. After nine days of testimonies from virtually everyone who had come into contact with Ivory during his time in Antwerp and Glasgow, the Solicitor-General suddenly withdrew all charges on 20 January 1897, officially because 'the delivery of the explosives at the house in Antwerp took place after [Ivory] had left Antwerp, and [there was] no legal evidence to show that the prisoner was cognisant of the delivering or of the ordering of the explosives'.[43] Ivory was released and by early February he was back in New York to a hero's welcome. *The New York Times* noted sardonically that 'the British government [had] spent $100,000 on the trial which failed'.[44]

To Anderson the reason for that failure was clear: the unwritten rules behind due process, what he termed the 'prize-ring rules', had prescribed that 'everything must be done openly and above board... [a] legitimate principle in regard to crimes that are committed openly and above board, but utterly inapplicable to [political] crimes'.[45] To the Irish Nationalist members of Parliament, however, the explanation was altogether a different one. As Michael Davitt, MP for Mayo South, explained in the House of Commons on 26 March, the dynamite plot 'had no real existence [and was] in fact the creation of disreputable agents of the secret service [;] the Home Office [had not made] any sincere effort to extradite from Antwerp the alleged prime movers in the plot', because, like Jones, they were in the pay of the government.[46]

There was more to these allegations than righteous indignation and it is plausible that Jones had not in fact been the only 'disreputable agent' involved in the failed conspiracy. Kearney, of course, had cooperated with Irish Branch back in 1883 and it is impossible to know definitively whether he was not still doing so thirteen years later. Testimony given at Ivory's trial by the owner of the Antwerp inn where Kearney and Haines had been lodging before their arrest described how after an impromptu meeting with a mysterious stranger the two Fenians fled the city without even so much as packing their clothes.[47] Only three days later, the police uncovered the dynamite – though not the dynamitards – that proved the only material evidence of a plot to cause criminal explosions.

William Lyman, the leader of the Irish National Brotherhood, was himself likely in the pay of Major Gosselin, who noted in a letter to Arthur Balfour (then First Lord of the Treasury) that '[Lyman]... to whom I am very close... [has] absolute control of the revolutionary fund'.[48] Even Tynan, for all his revolutionary credentials, is ultimately not above suspicion. The publication in Britain of his 1894 incendiary book on the history of the Invincibles by the London house of Chatham and Co had been partially financed by Conservative and Unionist politicians, for whom such a book, given its wildly insurrectionist and anti-Home Rule tone, served as an excellent propaganda piece.[49]

Taking into consideration also the supposed 'nihilist-anarchist' connection, much reported in the press at the time, but which, all things considered, seems to have had no basis in reality,[50] the 1896 dynamite plot emerges as perhaps the most suspicious of the entire decade in Britain and the one most likely to have been the result of outright provocation. Whether such provocation was merely the isolated result of Jenkinsonian tactics, which Gosselin's gang was evidently still steeped in, or part of a wider effort to discredit Home Rule at any price, we can only speculate.[51] What is certain is that after the 1896 fiasco there were no more Fenian dynamite plots in Britain.

The threat of anarcho-terrorism, in the meantime, continued to alarm European powers. On 7 June 1896 a Spanish anarchist, possibly with the aid of several others, threw a bomb into a popular religious procession in Barcelona, killing twelve and injuring scores. The response from Spanish authorities proved likewise savage and indiscriminate, with dozens of anarchists summarily shot and hundreds of radicals of all stripes arrested and locked up in the medieval fortress of Montjuich. Those fortunate enough to be found not guilty by the court-martial were nonetheless forced into exile.

News of the crackdown quickly spread through Western Europe and by early 1897 several progressive and socialist newspapers were already circulating accounts of the flagrant abuses going on at Montjuich, where dozens of political prisoners continued to be held. Most of these accounts were in the form of open letters written by exiled survivors and contained the sort of graphic details that were guaranteed to outrage all but the most reactionary currents of opinion:

> After having torn the flesh from our bodies and the nails from our fingers; after compressing our heads and mutilating our testicles, they want us to disappear, so that we never might bear witness of these infamous proceedings.
>
> Good and right-feeling people, do not let your attention be diverted from this ill-famed Anarchist trial... Rend this, honest men: They want us to sign a document by which we declare that we have not been tortured, and they have resolved to obtain these signatures from us by all means... [Save] us from the power of our executioners! Aid us in our helplessness!

Thus ran the appeal of one Sebastian Sunyer, published initially in a German socialist newspaper and subsequently reprinted in *Reynolds's Newspaper*.[52] The response to these horrific revelations in Britain was almost immediate and by no means relegated to anarchist circles. The matter received an early cursory mention in the House of Commons thanks to the Nationalist MP Patrick O'Brien,[53] but it was only after the formation of the Spanish Atrocities Committee (SAC), which included Edward Carpenter, Walter Crane, Cunninghame Graham and other prominent left-wingers, that it was fully brought to public attention.

Following a series of unsuccessful attempts to elicit a response from the Spanish embassy in London, the SAC nevertheless managed to gather momentum, drawing to its cause leading Liberal MPs like Sir Charles Dilke and Sir Frank Lockwood.[54] By late May it was already preparing to hold a meeting in Trafalgar Square as well as a formal resolution – consisting of a booklet describing the abuses at Montjuich and a sympathetic article from the Liberal *Daily Chronicle* – to be laid before Queen Victoria.

The resolution was delivered to the queen in early June, but given Her Majesty's refusal 'to issue any instructions thereon',[55] it is unlikely that it left a positive impression, with the Home Office proving equally unenthusiastic about appearing to give credence to the SAC's case. As Assistant Under-Secretary Murdoch explained in an official memo, endorsing in any way the views expressed in 'The Revival of the Inquisition', as the SAC resolution was provocatively titled, would amount to 'an insult to the ambassador of a friendly government'.[56]

Besides such diplomatic concerns, the British government was also wary of appearing lenient towards the persecuted Spanish anarchists for the simple reason that many of them, condemned to exile, were likely contemplating making their way over to Britain, and despite an overall slowdown in terrorist activity, anarchism remained a major security concern. In early April, an English anarchist watchmaker had been found guilty of causing a minor explosion at the New Cross post office,[57] while on 26 April a bomb had exploded at the Aldersgate Street (now Barbican) Underground station, killing one and injuring sixteen others. This had marked the first attack on the London Underground in more than a decade and although no suspects were identified by police, Majendie was convinced the bombing bore all the hallmarks of an anarchist outrage.[58]

Fears of renewed violence were all the more acute on the eve of the queen's Diamond Jubilee and as the *Daily Mail* noted on 21 June, 'during the last few days the whole of the route of the [Jubilee] procession has been laboriously examined by officers of the special branch of Scotland-yard, acting under the direction of Chief Detective-inspector Melville'.[59] *Reynolds's Newspaper* likewise observed how 'Mr. Anderson's Political Police Agency' was keeping a close watch on the 'clubs in Soho and Fitzroy-square', emphasizing 'the number of private detectives who will be employed [during the Jubilee, which] will exceed the record in any previous year of English history'.[60] As can be gleaned from the distinct tones of these two reports, in 1897 politics still coloured the British public's perception of the secret police and what for the right-wing *Daily Mail* was merely Special Branch of Scotland Yard, was for the left-wing *Reynolds's Newspaper* 'Mr. Anderson's Political Police agency'. Nevertheless, the very existence of such an organization was no longer an illiberal unmentionable; Special Branch was becoming a recognizable part of the British state, whatever attitude one chose to take towards it.

Compared to the 1887 Jubilee, the celebrations of 1897 were a resounding success from a security point of view. Despite the odd bogus threat,[61] London anarchists did not appear to entertain any 'desire to disturb the few remaining years of life of a fat old woman', as one of their manifestos irreverently declared.[62] The matter of the Spanish anarchists, however, refused to go away:

> They had powerfully cut features, with dark peaked beards, and eyes full of restlessness and fire. There was no hurry, no nervousness, in their gait. It

was a slow self complacent swagger, and as they moved towards the gangway, they flicked their cigarettes in the manner which English people are wont only to associate with the self-confident villain of the drama... The leader of the party... is a woman of about 35, tall, and so full in figure that she would weigh about 14 stone. She had a luxuriant head of black hair and olive complexion,... black bewitching eyes [and] a set of pearly white teeth.[63]

So a Sheffield newspaper colourfully described the twenty-eight anarchists who landed in Liverpool on the evening of 28 July, having been expelled from Spain and refused entry into France. If the press was attracted by the 'exotic' element of this arrival – greatly emphasized by the incongruous presence of a woman and the overall genteel appearance of the Spaniards – the police saw it as nothing more than a dangerous sudden swelling of the dynamitards' ranks. After being 'accompanied' by no fewer than twenty local CID detectives during their brief stay in Liverpool, the anarchists found themselves the centre of even more unwanted attention in London, where they were constantly kept under surveillance for days on end.

Although appearing as a 'hardy, vigorous mob, capable of doing a great deal of mischief'[64] to Melville and his men, the twenty-eight exiles seemed interested only in finding an audience at the German Communist Club, Freedom Club and various other anarchist-friendly locales in the British capital.[65] Chief Constable Macnaghten noted the Spaniards could be easily apprehended 'if necessity arose', but thought excessive surveillance would only 'give "bold advertisement" and undue prominence to the wretched fellows', quipping that 'I think it was Talleyrand who once said "surtout pas trop de zèle"!'[66]

For its part, the Home Office was rather more apprehensive about the unannounced and unwelcome visit, as various internal despatches on the topic reveal. Assistant Under-Secretary Murdoch, for example, thought the arrival of this 'most undesirable crew' was proof that 'this is becoming serious [as] there is no statutory power to stop these persons on arrival',[67] a view shared by both Ridley and Salisbury. An 'immediate and strong protest' was addressed to the Spanish Foreign Minister, who assured Her Majesty's Government that 'there shall be no further shipments of anarchists to England'.[68] There was in fact another 'shipment' of Spanish anarchists to Britain later on, as we shall see, but in early August 1897 any possibility of a serious diplomatic row seemed entirely remote. For the time being, the Home Secretary was willing to give authorities in Madrid the benefit of the doubt.[69]

It was not long, however, before the legacy of Montjuich returned to strike the Spanish government at its very core. On the afternoon of 8 August, while taking time off from the affairs of state in the Basque spa town of Santa Agueda, the Spanish Premier Antonio Cánovas del Castillo was fatally shot in the head and chest by Michele Angiollilo, a twenty-six-year-old Neapolitan printer who, by his own admission, had simply wanted to 'avenge the wounds inflicted on his comrades at Montjuich'.[70]

Naturally, Angiollilo's actual motivations, as with those of most anarchist avengers of the 1890s, were somewhat more convoluted. Tellingly, he had arrived in Santa Agueda from London,[71] where it is possible he had come into contact with the twenty-eight anarchist *perseguidos*. Scotland Yard certainly believed Angiolillo had 'attended... an Anarchist meeting in Trafalgar-square, when a Spaniard spoke of the torture of Spanish prisoners',[72] although the Montjuich survivors were quick to deny all knowledge of his existence when questioned by the British press.[73]

Equally (if not more) important, however, is that Angiollilo had been shunned by his comrades as a likely police spy and so, perhaps, had found that 'in London [his] reputation followed him', making his life 'so unendurable that he was impelled... to the crime he committed'.[74] At any rate, the young Italian saw in the black legend of Montjuich the perfect pretext for – as he put it – striking at 'religious ferocity, military cruelty... and the tyranny of power',[75] while redeeming his damaged reputation in the process.

Angiolillo was not the first European anarchist that year to plan a spectacular assassination. On 22 April, another Italian, Pietro Acciarito, made an unsuccessful attempt on the life of King Umberto I during the Royal Derby (horse race), prompting Italian authorities to round up several prominent anarchists in Rome and sentence them to *domicilio coatto* (house arrest), the government's preferred method for dealing with subversives.[76] Official fears that propaganda by the deed might be making a comeback were proving hard to assuage and whereas in 1894 European governments still believed it possible to legislate anarchist terrorism out of existence, in 1897 they appeared to be at a complete loss on the right course of action for preventing yet another wave of insurrectionist 'martyrs'.

In Britain, the situation on the continent precipitated renewed calls for a stricter control of immigration. Writing in *The Times*, Colonel Howard Vincent described the unhindered movement of continental anarchists in the British capital as an 'international scandal', adding that 'alone among civilized nations have we no power to expel foreigners holding, proclaiming, acting upon, doctrines the entire nation views with abhorrence'.[77] Although this sentiment was widely echoed in the Conservative press, the anarchist threat alone did not prove a strong enough incentive for the government to reintroduce the failed

Aliens Bill of 1894. Officially, surveillance was stepped up and Melville, in a characteristic self-promoting pose, turned up at Dover accompanied by 'the special staff' of the CID to 'watch foreign arrivals',[78] while in London 'foreign clubs, particularly those frequented by Italians', were kept under 'strict and persistent' watch.[79]

There was, however, little need for such measures. Despite the hysteria generated by Angiolillo's coup and his supposed connection to London's anarchist colony, the latter found itself in an increasingly demoralized and inactive state. Many of its newspapers had already folded, while the ubiquity of informers and spies was leading many of 'the... refugees [into] a state of mind closely resembling panic [with] every stranger [being regarded] as a police spy'.[80] It was precisely this panicky state of mind that formed the most potent weapon in the Special Branch arsenal and, as a *Sunday Times* correspondent perceptively observed while visiting the revolutionary haunts of Tottenham Court Road and Soho, 'the very significance of... police espionage [in Britain] is that it is not assertive – is, in fact, subterranean in its character'.[81]

This 'subterranean system' was, of course, not the only obstacle the anarchists faced in London, but it undoubtedly contributed to keeping them quiescent and more importantly, it was 'seen' to be doing so at sensitive moments (such as in the wake of an egregious outrage). So assured were authorities of the anarchists' inertia, in fact, that the only impediment to a second demonstration by the Spanish Atrocities Committee in Trafalgar Square in mid-August proved to be that the day had already been booked by the Spiritualist Society.[82]

The success of the British model, however, continued to remain elusive to continental governments, while the culture of secrecy at the Home Office ensured all matters of state security were jealously shielded from foreign curiosity, notwithstanding the official policy of paying lip service to 'international police cooperation'. Interestingly, this attitude seems to have extended not only to Britain's European and American rivals, but to all international state actors. When, for example, in January 1897 the Uruguayan chargé d'affaires in London made a request to Prime Minister Salisbury for information on Britain's enviable counter-terrorist system 'for the use of [the Uruguayan] government', the Home Office offered the following laconic reply, carefully avoiding any mention of political policing:

> To be an Anarchist is not any offence against English law... If however Anarchists or any other men attempt to enforce their views by crime they are dealt with under the same law that is applied to criminals acting from other motives. The illegal use of explosives is dealt with in various sections of the

Offences against the Person Act, 1861, the Malicious Injuries Act, 1861 and the Explosives Act, 1883. If this crime amounts to treason the criminal can be dealt with under the law relating to that offence.[83]

As several cases of the early 1890s show (most notably the arrest of Giuseppe Farnara in 1894), if genuine cooperation, or 'information sharing' in modern parlance, occurred between Special Branch and the spies of continental police organizations, it was nearly always in a secretive, arguably conspiratorial setting and given the nature of espionage, this trend is not exactly surprising. More controversial, however, is that such shadowy collaboration could very well involve the actual legal representatives of foreign police forces, as the arrest of the Russian Nihilist Vladimir Burtsev in late 1897 demonstrates.

Burtsev, a thirty-three-year-old Nihilist militant familiar with the dungeons of the Peter and Paul Fortress and the harshness of Siberian exile, had managed to flee to London in 1891, thereafter devoting his time to émigré journalism and the study of Russian history and politics. While previously unknown to London police, on the afternoon of 16 December 1897 Burtsev had the dubious pleasure of making Chief Inspector Melville's acquaintance in the Reading Room of the British Museum where he was subsequently arrested on charges of writing and publishing a 'pamphlet encouraging certain persons… to murder His Imperial Majesty Nicholas II [and] endeavouring to persuade certain persons to commit that offence'.[84] As the trial which followed in February 1898 revealed, the incriminating pamphlet, published in April 1897 in Burtsev's *Narodovolets* newspaper, did contain some fairly inflammatory 'calls to action', of which the following passage is typical:

> We are revolutionists not only to the extent of a direct rising of the people, but to the extent of military conspiracies, to the extent of nocturnal invasions of the Palace, to the extent of bombs and dynamite … On the question [of] what is to be done, Alexander III reigned happily for fourteen years and this is already the third year that Nicholas II has reigned not less happily… The fearful mistake which the Terrorist party made was that after their victory of the 1st March [1881], they for a moment, stopped systematic terrorism, for a moment put their sword in its sheath.[85]

The fact that the most violent excerpts were paraphrased from the works of another Nihilist exile, the late Sergey Stepniak, failed to aid the defence's case. Burtsev received a sentence of eighteen months with hard labour, while the printer of *Narodovolets*, Klement Wierzbicki, got two months' hard labour.

Judging solely by appearances, the Burtsev case presents a fairly straightforward narrative of an impassioned – or fanatical, to his detractors – revolutionary paying a hefty price for letting slip a few careless references to palace storming and regicide in an otherwise inconsequential appeal to rebellion. Johann Most had suffered the same back in 1881, while the *Commonweal*'s Henry Samuels had only narrowly avoided a similar fate in 1893. What sets Burtsev apart from Most and Samuels, however, is that his prosecution, while fully conformant with British laws, had been initiated and carried out entirely at the behest and for the interest of a foreign power: Imperial Russia.

Burtsev's article would almost certainly never have landed its author in a British court of law, never mind prison, if not for the ever-watchful eye of the Russian Department for the Protection of Public Security and Order, better known as the Okhrana. It was one of its veteran agents – and Director of the Department of Police in St Petersburg – a man by the name of Sergei Zvoliansky, who had first taken notice of Burtsev's seditious essay. Seeing in it an opportunity to finally silence the pesky émigré,[86] Zvoliansky had sent a copy of the incriminating passages to his personal protégé and head of the Parisian section of the Okhrana, Pyotr Rachkovsky,[87] who had previously tried, without any success, to lure Burtsev out of the safety of his London sanctuary by means of a textbook honey trap. As the Russian spymasters well knew, if a new scheme was going to succeed, it would have to work within the confines of the British legal system.

In late June 1897 Rachkovsky wrote a letter to Melville in London relating the details of Burtsev's recent activities and asking whether it would be possible to bring the young Nihilist to justice. Although the head of Special Branch had only met Rachkovsky in 1896, during the czar's stay in Scotland, it is likely the two had already been steadily corresponding for some time. Certainly, Rachkovsky had been aware of Melville as early as 1891 thanks to an Okhrana spy stationed in London who spoke enthusiastically of having 'made the acquaintance of Inspector Melville... [who] has offered me his services complaining that his superiors at Scotland Yard act too feebly with regard to Nihilists'.[88]

Whatever the literal truth of that claim, Melville had always been willing to circumvent his superiors in the fight against subversion. Replying to Rachkovsky's plea for help in July 1897, the Chief Inspector confessed to already having seen a translation of the *Narodovolets* article without, however, 'discerning anything serious in it'.[89] Still, Rachkovsky was an experienced, like-minded acquaintance and his opinion in a matter of this nature was worth deferring to:

> [Since] you are writing to me about [this issue], I shall naturally not rely on the impression I have formed of it since, as you yourself well know, one cannot trust translators.

Where the question that you put to me is concerned, our laws are very strange... [and] could [not] punish the editor or managing director of a newspaper in which terroristic ideas, murder &c are advocated in a vague form, so to speak. It is a different matter if an article... identifies particular people [since] then we are dealing with a crime that is covered by English laws... If you found it possible to bring a case against Burtsev & Co., you could only go about it in the following way. Send the aforementioned newspaper to the Russian Ambassador in London, having marked in it the most relevant passages, and accompany it with a letter in which you insist on the need to prosecute the editor. Ask the Ambassador to bring this letter to the notice of our Foreign Secretary, who, in his turn, will send it to our Home Secretary. The latter will surely pass it on to me. As you see, one will have to act through the diplomatic channel... I shall be happy to be of service to you and to get at these scoundrels, who essentially are neither more nor less than common murderers. I should very much like you to make the above-mentioned approach, because even if nothing comes of it, I at least will gain the opportunity to worry these fellows and drive them from one end of London to the other. Furthermore [the matter of] Burtsev & Co.... will make our Government turn its attention to them and, whether it comes to a court case or not, the matter will pass through my hands.[90]

Rachkovsky set to work immediately and by early August 1897 the Russian chargé d'affaires in London had already written to the Foreign Office to complain about the offensive nature of Burtsev's article, setting the wheels in motion in precisely the manner Melville had outlined. The only thing the Chief Inspector had failed to fully appreciate, much like Anderson a year earlier, was the controversial nature of the evidence at hand. His copy of Burtsev's newspaper had been acquired by police through underhanded means and could not for this reason be admissible in a court of law, or so argued Sir Hamilton Cuffe, Director of Public Prosecutions.[91] Unlike Anderson, however, Melville saw a way out, instructing one of his DCs to go to Burtsev's bookshop in Tottenham Court Road and legally purchase, albeit under an assumed name, two copies each of numbers 1, 2 and 3 of *Narodovolets*.[92] Satisfied that due process had been upheld, Cuffe relented and on 16 December 1897 a warrant was issued for Burtsev's arrest.

Writing to Melville shortly after the conclusion of the trial in order to express his gratitude, Rachkovsky could not help but notice how the 'success of the case has saved us from any inconvenience at a personal level.'[93] It is not certain what the 'inconvenience' would have been in Rachkovsky's case – certainly he was too valuable to be dismissed for failing to silence a minor nuisance like Burtsev – but for Melville, things might indeed have taken an embarrassing turn were it to become known just how tangled up he was in the Okhrana's affairs at the height of the Great Game. In any case, while 'Burtsev & Co' continued to top the list of persons of interest for Special Branch in the late 1890s, it is not, however, to say that the systematic surveillance of English radicals introduced in the late 1880s had altogether ceased – as a peculiar case from 1898 demonstrates.

Judging by appearances alone, one would have been hard-pressed to detect anything genuinely subversive in the motley assembly of bohemians and progressive literati gathered in the sumptuous Council Chamber at the Holborn Restaurant on the afternoon of 30 April 1898. This was no ordinary society crowd, however; it numbered, among others, a dozen 'dangerous Anarchists, a "woman who did"[94]... miscellaneous... avowed free-lovers, two lady officials of a Rational Dress Society... a novelist of world-wide reputation [G. B. Shaw]... a baby aged eighteen months' and, unbeknownst to anyone but themselves, two Special Branch detectives.[95] The event they were attending was the first and, as it turned out, last annual gala of the Legitimation League, whose minor yet *célèbre* cause was – as Ms Lillian Harman, the League's president explained to a *Daily Mail* correspondent – 'to educate public opinion in the direction of free love, and to create a machinery for acknowledging off-spring born out of wedlock, and to secure for them equal rights with legitimate children'.[96]

That Scotland Yard should deem such an occasion important enough to have two of its elite detectives attend it undercover seems, in retrospect, highly questionable, but given the anarchist connection, not entirely surprising. The Legitimation League had started off innocently enough in 1893 as a group devoted solely to advancing the rights of illegitimates, but had gradually come to attract an assorted host of secularists, social libertarians, feminists and anarchists, openly advocating, by early 1898, its support for eugenics, non-traditional gender roles and free love in the pages of its official organ *The Adult*. Thanks also to the work of its suave chief propagandist, George Bedborough, the League was rapidly making significant advances in membership numbers and as some of these new members were also frequenters of anarchist clubs, there was 'good reason for believing that Anarchistic proselytising took place [at the League's] meetings'.[97]

Assigned to infiltrate the organization, DI Sweeney found it somewhat hard to resist Bedborough – a 'man of fascinating personality... and of the most excellent manners'[98] – but his reports proved incriminating enough to draw the attention of the Public Prosecutor, who, notwithstanding certain reservations about appearing to tamper with free speech, decided to give the green light for criminal proceedings against the League.[99] Despite its risqué subject matter,

*The Adult* had not featured particularly strong language and certainly no death threats against politicians or heads of state. All the same, the Legitimists did have a significant soft spot in Bedborough's connection to a certain Dr de Villiers, owner of the dubiously named Watford University Press.

De Villiers was a petty confidence man and charlatan, but his real crime, as far as authorities were concerned, was having published *Sexual Inversion*, Havelock Ellis' treatise on homosexuality (recently condemned as obscene in a court of law).[100] Given the book's subject matter, Bedborough had offered to buy up a good portion of de Villiers' dead stock in order to distribute it to League members – a fact which might have taken Sweeney some time to uncover if not for the strongly worded complaint sent to police by the concerned parents of a young Legitimist.[101]

Despite Sweeney's assurances that Bedborough was nothing but a harmless dandy, Melville was convinced he was dealing with 'a manufacturer of bombs, or at least an Anarchist plotter',[102] making a point out of personally arresting the accidental 'pornographer' exactly a month after that lavish soiree at the Holborn Restaurant. At the trial which followed in October, Bedborough pleaded guilty to charges of breaking the peace by publishing 'obscene libels' and was entered into recognizances of £100 'to come up for judgment if called upon'.[103] For being cleared with only a slap on the wrist, Bedborough had to end all association with and support for the Legitimation League, which he did (not without some remorse), leaving his erstwhile sympathizers in the Free Press Defence Committee – set up by Grant Allen, G. B. Shaw, Edward Carpenter and other left-wingers – in a daze of anger and resignation.[104]

For them, as for all progressives, the incident marked a serious blow to the advance of the freethinking cause and spoke to the 'scandalous one sidedness with which the laws relating to the sale of erotic literature are administered' – criminalizing works of scientific inquiry while overlooking the genuinely pornographic '*editions de luxe* [available] at huge prices… at almost any respectable shop'.[105] It did not, however, seem to raise any questions on the police's particular role in upholding and administering this moral double standard and it is for this reason, as well as the stunting of the 'growth of a Frankenstein monster [capable of] wrecking the marriage laws of our country',[106] that Special Branch could regard the unobtrusive smothering of the Legitimation League as an unmitigated success.

# CHAPTER 12

# 'We do not prosecute opinions'[1]

THE first real challenge to Britain's system of political policing came later in the year as a result of yet another gruesome, high-profile assassination. On the afternoon of 10 September 1898, shortly after leaving the Hôtel Beau Rivage in Geneva, the sixty-one-year-old Empress Elisabeth of Austria was attacked by a short, burly looking man and stabbed with a triangular needle file. Within the hour, the empress was dead from suffocation (her right lung having been punctured), leaving worldwide public opinion in a state of appalled disbelief. The bereaved Emperor Franz Joseph declared his incomprehension 'that a man could be found to attack such a woman, whose whole life was spent in doing good and who never injured any person',[2] while the socialist *L'Aurore* described the assassination as 'the act of an unthinking idiot [and] a stroke of bloody madness'.[3]

The assassin, a twenty-five-year-old French-born Italian named Luigi Lucheni, had offered no resistance to police when apprehended, appearing simply to bask in his newfound notoriety. Despite boasting of being a 'most dangerous anarchist',[4] Lucheni was also a clearly disturbed individual, as attested by his erratic behaviour, his express wish to be guillotined, as well as the fact that the Empress Elisabeth had been only a last-minute substitute for his actual intended target, the Duke d'Orleans. Following a brief trial in Geneva, where the death penalty had been abolished,[5] Lucheni received a sentence of life in prison, which he served until his suicide in 1910.

Despite this pathetic dénouement, however, in countries where anarchist outrages had been a common feature all throughout the decade, the official mood was decisively vindictive. In the wake of the assassination, Alessandro Guiccioli, the mayor of Rome, dreaded:

> To think the infamous brute was an Italian! What shame this brings once more on our disgraced country! And what a heavy burden for those who with their fanaticism and their ideological sophistry arm these... stupid, perverse animals who call themselves anarchists, and for the governments who have treated this conspiracy of evil forces only with the most benevolent tolerance.[6]

By late September 1898 continental newspapers were already circulating reports of a new high-level conference 'with a view to joint measures against Anarchists… [that would] be held shortly, probably in Rome',[7] and on 29 September the Italian Foreign Minister, Napoleone Canevaro, confirmed the rumours. The conference was indeed held in Rome, starting in November, and included representatives from all major European powers and their allies.

In Britain the news was not greeted with any degree of enthusiasm by the Home Office hierarchy, many of whom had been in office long enough to remember the Spanish proposals of 1893 which the then-Liberal government had successfully fended off. The gravity of the recent situation, however, meant that a similar course of action was no longer an option. Manifestly shocked and saddened by Elisabeth's violent demise, Queen Victoria urged Salisbury – in a rare interventionist stance – to honour the Italian proposal[8] and on 12 October, the premier wrote to the Foreign Office to outline in broad terms the British position in regard to the conference in Rome:

> The Swiss Minister asked me what the policy of Her Majesty's Government would be with respect to the Conference… I replied that of course we sympathized very heartily with the objects the Government of Italy had in view [and that] we could not refuse to take part in [these] deliberations. But we should do so with no very sanguine hope of arriving at any important result. Improved police arrangements hardly require the deliberations of a congress to sanction them; and any proposals for legislative change would be attended with many difficulties. In this country, and possibly in others, great objection would be felt to any attempt to meet the dangers of the anarchist conspiracy by restraining or encroaching upon the liberty of the rest of the community.[9]

The conference opened on 24 November in the majestically baroque Palazzo Corsini and drew together delegates from Austria-Hungary, Belgium, Britain, Bulgaria, Denmark, France, Germany, Greece, Italy, Luxembourg, Monaco, Montenegro, the Netherlands, Portugal, Romania, Russia, Serbia, Spain, the United Kingdoms of Sweden and Norway, Switzerland and Turkey. Representing Britain were Colonel Howard Vincent, well-known by then for his hard-line conservatism and anti-anarchist crusading, the more moderately conservative Sir Phillip Currie (who had recently been appointed ambassador to Italy) and – standing in for the Liberal opposition – the recently retired Sir Godfrey Lushington.

Given the firmness of purpose and sense of urgency expressed by the conference organizers, the first order of business had, surprisingly, nothing to do with combating anarchism, but rather with defining it. What the majority of delegates could agree on, by a margin of fifteen votes, was that anarchism could not be considered a political doctrine; a notion which, as Currie duly noted in a report to Salisbury, betrayed not so much an ignorance of anarchism as the intention to 'exclude anarchical crimes from the exceptions made by Treaties of Extradition in favour of political offences'.[10]

A working definition of what anarchism actually *was* proved much harder to arrive at, however. The French argued that an anarchical act was one which had for its object 'the destruction by violent means of any social organization', while the Russians sought to expand this already broad definition by suggesting that 'anarchists, whatever name they may give themselves… have for their object to destroy any social organization, whatever may be its form, by resorting to violent means or by provoking such means by… their theories'.[11] The French version barely passed by a margin of only two votes, no thanks to the British delegation, which chose to abstain on the grounds that 'so far as existing English law is concerned, a definition of anarchism is not needed and would be useless'.[12]

To drive the point home, Currie read out a statement at the fourth plenary meeting on 3 December, in which he loftily proclaimed that 'We do not prosecute opinions. The only question with us is, is there crime or not? If the act is a criminal one… it is not more so because done out of anarchism. If it is not criminal, it would not become so because it is anarchical.'[13] Here was the official British stance on political crime redux, with no mention of London's 'anarchist laboratory' or the 'scandalous' policy of giving refuge to revolutionaries, decried by Colonel Vincent only a year earlier.

In the three weeks that followed, several other non-binding proposals were tabled, all falling largely into two separate categories, reflecting the conference's own bifurcate structure into administrative and legislative commissions respectively. The first set of proposals highlighted the importance of formalizing and systematizing police cooperation in the struggle against anarchism, urging at the same time the adoption of new methods for keeping track of lawbreakers (political or otherwise). To this end a subcommittee of police chiefs and other law enforcement representatives met to discuss the logistical aspects of expelling anarchists and agreed that their respective governments should begin forwarding each other monthly reports on all expelled subversives.[14] No specific details were set down, but Colonel Vincent believed 'the results of these confidential meetings of heads of police will do good, if only by forming reciprocal friendships leading to greater cooperation'.[15]

More important, however, proved the almost unanimously accepted motion for the establishment of a continent-wide network of central agencies in charge of monitoring anarchist activity and sharing valuable intelligence,[16] as well as the French suggestion for a universal adoption of Alphonse Bertillon's updated system for the anthropometrical identification of criminals.[17] Also called the *portrait parlé*, this system combined meticulous descriptions of an offender's physical appearance with frontal and profile-view mug shots and had already proved immensely successful in France, where it had been widely in use since the early 1880s. Germany and Italy proved especially responsive, with positive reactions also registered from the Portuguese, Romanian, Scandinavian, Swiss and Turkish delegations.

The second round of proposals dealt with the legal side of the argument and generally sought to facilitate the criminalization of anarchism in all its forms along the lines of the French *lois scélérates* and the Italian anti-anarchist laws. Typical of this set were proposals by Austria, Germany and Russia that all anarchist literature and associations be suppressed, that no anarchist acts of a criminal nature be allowed to fall under the 'political crime' clause of any extradition treaties, that press coverage of anarchist exploits be closely regulated (if not censored), that anarchist prisoners be kept in strict isolation and that any anarchist attempt on the life of a head of state or any of their relatives always be an extraditable and capital offence.[18] Despite their controversial character, these motions were ultimately carried, albeit, in some cases, only with slim majorities.

The British delegation's attitude to all this evinced the same reluctance expressed by Salisbury in his letter to the Foreign Office and by Currie in his address to the fourth plenary meeting. As far as the proposals of the legal commission were concerned, it was clear that many, if not all, were incompatible with the spirit of British laws, something which Lushington acknowledged by voting against the most disciplinarian ones, such as those advocating press censorship and solitary confinement for anarchist prisoners, while abstaining on the others.[19]

Even the administrative proposals, for all their focus on practical police cooperation, fared no better. Having professed Britain's sympathy for 'the duty that all nations have to protect each other against criminal attempts',[20] Colonel Vincent was nonetheless forced to admit that the British government would have 'serious difficulty in recognizing, in a formal and official manner, a joint action… with the police forces of foreign nations', adding that 'our laws do not give us any power to expel either indigenous or foreign persons'.[21]

As for the *portrait parlé*, it did not prove enticing enough to supplant Scotland Yard's own much-simplified version of Bertillon's system.[22] For his part, Sir Phillip gave an official endorsement of his fellow delegates' tendency to avoid committing to anything by stating that the British delegation would better fulfill its mission if it abstained from voting altogether and by reiterating the strength and efficacy of existing British laws.[23] Careful not to play into any continental stereotypes of British haughtiness, however, Currie also added that Her Majesty's Government would prepare two legislative proposals to be put before Parliament in the coming year.

The first was meant to expand the Explosives Act to make all explosive-related offences extradable and cover 'as much as possible… cases where a criminal explosion takes place outside, not just within, the United Kingdom'. The second strove to amend extradition law in such a way as to disqualify all murderers 'either of heads of state or any other individual', from claiming political asylum – something which in practice was already the case, as the extraditions of François and Meunier had demonstrated.[24]

When the conference came to a close on 21 December, Britain was the only participating nation not to sign the final protocol and yet ironically also the only nation to draft any actual legislation along the lines suggested in Rome. Back in London there certainly was some support for more punitive measures against political extremists. Colonel Majendie had advocated an 'international agreement… under which [anarchist terrorists] would be debarred from either shelter or sympathy in any part of the civilised world' as early as 1892,[25] while Anderson's hostility to British 'prize-ring rules' had only intensified since the 1896 dynamite campaign fiasco, as he made clear in a memorandum to the Home Secretary:

> Indeed the proposed extension of the Explosives Act and its adoption by Foreign Governments will be of great value to this country. Had it been in place three years ago, it would have led to the conviction of all the agents in the last Fenian Dynamite plot. If the unreasonable objection of some judges to sentences of Police supervision is to influence legislation at all, it would seem to me that it should lead to the abolition of police supervision altogether. But the objection is not only unreasonable but ignorant.[26]

On the subject of expulsion, the Assistant Commissioner also warned that 'if the other European governments agree to expel alien anarchists and no powers for this purpose are obtained here, London will become an "asylum" for these miscreants', stopping short, however, of endorsing the plans for regulated surveillance and systematized cooperation with foreign police forces. In a moment of arresting candour Anderson confessed that:

> in recent years the [British] Police have succeeded only by straining the law, or, in plain English, by doing utterly unlawful things, at intervals, to check this conspiracy, and my serious fear is that if new legislation affecting it is passed, Police powers may thus be defined and our practical powers seriously impaired... [If] the actual powers of Police in this country [become public knowledge], then the methods which successive secretaries of state have sanctioned, and which have been resorted to with such excellent results will be shown to be without legal sanction, and must be abandoned.[27]

Unregulated surveillance (often on behalf of foreign governments), the breaking up of peaceful marches, collusion with foreign agents, unwarranted raids and possibly entrapment, did indeed strain the law, however liberally one chose to interpret it. Despite Anderson's extreme expulsionist stance – dismissed at the Home Office as 'rather beyond the scope' of what Currie et al. had promised in Rome[28] – and penchant for alarmism,[29] the CID chief's main point, namely that Britain's model of political policing could not possibly survive a legal revolution, undoubtedly resonated deeply with his Home Office colleagues.

With that in mind it becomes somewhat easier to explain why the promise to expand, or more accurately, tweak, the Extradition and Explosives Acts remained strictly a promise. In spite of the impressively researched and detailed draft bills,[30] by 1902 the opportune moment to put them before Parliament had still not arrived, as Foreign Secretary Lansdowne put it in a reply to an inquiry made by German officials.[31] The British government was indeed facing more pressing concerns as the nineteenth century was drawing to a close, the South African War being perhaps the most pressing. It is just as likely, however, that the draft bills were quietly allowed to gather dust in a Home Office archive for fear that enacting changes to existing legislation based on 'external' suggestions could serve as a dangerous precedent for the further regulation of the political police.

A little over a year after the Rome Conference, the 'anarchist conspiracy' did not seem to give any signs of weakening. On 4 April 1900, just as their train was set to depart the Gare du Nord in Brussels, the Prince and Princess of Wales were attacked by a Belgian youth who, managing to board their carriage, fired two shots, both of which missed. As Belgian authorities soon realized, Jean-Baptiste Sipido – the sixteen-year-old would-be assassin – had pocketfuls of anarchist literature on him, although his motives were far from straightforward.

While he claimed to be acting on behalf of the Boer cause, testimonies extracted from Sipido's friends suggested the outrage had been 'merely the result of a stupid bet in a public-house, the stake being five francs'.[32] Unfazed by the incident, Prince Edward decided to continue on his journey to Denmark, expressing the hope that Sipido's 'youthful wrongheadedness' would be treated leniently,[33] but to those who subscribed to the notion that anarchism was a dangerously organized terroristic cult, this latest attempt was yet another cause for alarm. Belgian police chiefs were certain the 'plot' had been engineered by a local socialist club of which Sipido and his friends were members – a view which conservative currents of opinion were quick to embrace.[34] The young Belgian was ultimately given a light sentence in a juvenile detention centre and although he remained closely watched by Scotland Yard agents well after his release in 1904,[35] Sipido's ham-fisted attempt at martyrdom was quickly forgotten, being overshadowed by the nineteenth century's last notorious political assassination.

On 29 July 1900, Gaetano Bresci, a thirty-one-year-old, Italian-born weaver from Paterson, New Jersey, fired three shots at King Umberto I of Italy, killing him on the spot. The king, once a relatively popular and forward-looking monarch, had recently awarded General Fiorenzo Bava-Beccaris the Military Order of Savoy, sending ripples of outrage throughout the Italian working class and its overseas communities.

The drastically low wheat harvest of 1897 and the Spanish-American War of 1898 (which had made the importation of American grain more prohibitive) had led to skyrocketing wheat prices in Italy – from 225 lire per tonne in mid-1897 to 330 lire less than a year later.[36] In early May 1898, strikes and demonstrations in Milan had quickly escalated into a full-blown riot, summarily and bloodily suppressed by *il feroce monarchico* – as one popular song dubbed him – Bava-Beccaris, leaving more than a hundred dead and several hundred wounded. Like Sipido, Bresci found himself embroiled not merely in a set of abstract beliefs, but in a chain of events with a decidedly colonial and international dimension which spoke to the rapid and violent emergence of what shortly became the twentieth century.

In Britain, fears of an international assassination campaign continued to linger in the 'official mind' at the Home Office. Despite the continued fragmentation and dissipation of the anarchist colony in London,[37] developments like the sudden arrival in London of a dozen exiled Spanish anarchists in May 1900 and the gravity of 'recent Continental experiences' put the authorities on high alert.[38] The anarchists, however, did not seem in a hurry to strike and over the next couple of years only three assassination 'plots' were uncovered, all of them spurious.[39] The only actual outrage with a British connection occurred once again in Brussels in late 1902, taking everyone by surprise and revealing once again the tenuous relationship between Scotland Yard and its continental counterparts.

This was the so-called Rubino incident in which a forty-three-year-old Italian anarchist named Gennaro Rubino fired three shots at King Leopold II's cortege on the afternoon of 15 November in front of the Cathedral of Saints Michael and Gudula. Luckily for the king, Rubino proved a terrible shot, firing all three bullets at the wrong carriage and completely off-target.[40] For Belgian authorities, however, the story of how the middle-aged Italian had come to be in Brussels that day proved just as worrisome as the failed *attentat* itself. First of all, Rubino had arrived from London, where he had been living for the past five years and where, until recently, he had been 'kept under regular observation' by Special Branch detectives as a dangerous anarchist.[41] Even more disturbing, Rubino had bought the gun and ammunition used in the outrage with money given him by one Hector Prina, a 'subinspector of the Italian Police' and attaché to the Italian Consulate in London.[42]

As Melville explained in an official report,[43] Prina had successfully approached Rubino in the spring of 1901 with an offer of employment. In return for a steady and not unsubstantial income – enough to buy a terraced house in Essex – the Italian Consulate received regular updates on the comings and goings of other Italian anarchists in London. Convinced that Rubino's newfound career represented a 'natural guarantee of his bone fides', Melville had decided to 'relax' the surveillance even as the informer's friends were growing increasingly suspicious. Leaving aside his dubious habit of photographing house guests on every possible occasion, Rubino appeared to be doing unusually well for a failed newsagent who was often out of work.

By April 1902 his reputation was predictably in tatters, leading to a formal accusation of treason during a 'special meeting' convened at the German Communist Club in Charlotte Street. Grudgingly admitting his liaison with Italian police, Rubino attempted to justify himself by claiming he had in fact been feeding Italian police bogus information while trying to unmask the real spies in the movement. The comrades were not convinced; Rubino left the meeting unharmed, but as a broken and essentially friendless man. Having once professed his admiration for Canovas' murderer, Rubino decided to redeem himself in the same manner – by assassinating a 'tyrant'. It is unclear why he chose the king of the Belgians as his target (his testimony to Belgian police gave no specific justification) but as reports of the atrocities in the Congo Free State were just beginning to illustrate, Leopold II arguably did epitomize the absolute corruption of absolute power better than any other European monarch at the time.

Although British authorities bore little responsibility for Rubino's actions, the Home Office feared the information in Melville's report, which the Belgian government was already aware of, would 'furnish effective ammunition for the people who look upon England as the hatching ground for Anarchist outrages and want to have measures taken here for suppressing Anarchist associations'.[44] In reality, the Belgians were all but grateful for Britain's apparent willingness to take in some of the most unsavoury types the continent had to offer. Only a year prior to Rubino's attempt, in October 1901, the anarchist Vittorio Jaffei (believed by Italian authorities to have been an accomplice of Bresci) had been promptly expelled from Antwerp with a one-way ticket to Dover in his pocket, much to the surprise and annoyance of British police.[45]

The Italians seemed equally opportunistic and the man sent to replace Prina in London, a certain Inspector Mandolesi, was proving equally keen on playing the provocateur 'for leaflets are now circulated warning all Anarchists against [him]'.[46] Naturally, proposals made by the Italian ambassador 'that the Metropolitan Police should... work in co-operation with an Agent of his Government' had to be summarily dismissed as posing the 'gravest risk' to Special Branch.[47] British authorities seemed more eager than ever to go it alone in matters of counter-subversion.

Changes were underway at Scotland Yard, however. Like many of his predecessors, the new Commissioner of the Metropolitan Police, Edward Richard Henry, had cut his teeth in the Indian Civil Service, but unlike them he proved supremely qualified to lead a modern police force. Having scored his first triumph in the early 1890s when, as Inspector-General of Bengal, he had pioneered the systematic use of fingerprinting, Henry shot to prominence after being called to London in 1900 to give evidence before the Belper Committee (tasked with investigating the merits of both Bertillonage and fingerprinting).[48] Succeeding Anderson to the Assistant Commissionership in 1901 and then Bradford to the Commissionership two years later, Henry began a sweeping process of modernization (extending far beyond the use of fingerprints) that brought British law enforcement firmly into the twentieth century. Tellingly, it was Henry who inaugurated the now iconic police box by systematizing telephonic communication between police and public (as well as between police divisions themselves) and who finally did away with Scotland Yard's antiquated system of handwritten reports and copies by introducing typewriters and carbon paper.[49]

Priorities were changing as well. Although the defeated Boers had just signed the Treaty of Vereeniging, Britain was far from feeling confident in her imperial supremacy by the end of 1902. Fears of a Franco-Russian alliance and of Russia's own increasingly aggressive policy in the East drove home the importance of a new centralized system for acquiring and managing military intelligence.

As part of the work undertaken by the newly established Committee of Imperial Defense and the Elgin Commission,[50] the War Office was endowed with two new small intelligence-gathering departments: MO2 and MO3 (the MO standing for Military Operations), tasked with handling foreign intelligence and counter-espionage, respectively. Given the hitherto sorry state of British military intelligence,[51] however, the problem of finding the right individual to put in charge of investigative operations was not a small one. Luckily for the government, there was at least one seasoned detective who could easily rise to the challenge.

On 1 January 1904, Walter Emden, the Mayor of Westminster, paid tribute in a *Times* testimonial to the man he regarded as Britain's least well-known hero: after thirty-two years of 'distinguished service [at] the direction of the special or political department of New Scotland Yard', Superintendent William Melville had apparently retired from public service in November of the previous year, leaving behind an impressive legacy of efficacious and evenhanded work 'in the cause of humanity'. As the mayor went on to explain:

> If prevention is better than cure, Superintendent Melville is the greatest of doctors... We know not, but might in gratitude imagine now, what shocks to the civilized world, what public and private grief this one man may have saved us. If we are grateful for what has been done, we should be more grateful for what has not been done.[52]

In the end, *le vil Melville* (as London anarchists had once dubbed him) did have his fair share of admirers, at least forty-five of them, all members of the committee on whose behalf the testimonial was submitted.[53] What even they had failed to grasp, however, was that appearances rarely told the full tale when it came to the Superintendent. His retirement was, for all intents and purposes, entirely fictitious – save for the £240 pension he was entitled to – and in reality Melville had simply been transferred to the War Office's reconstituted counter-intelligence unit (later absorbed by MI5's precursor agencies, as we shall see later on), having been strongly recommended for the job both by the Home Office leadership and by his former boss, Sir Edward Bradford. Henry had also agreed to let his star detective go, sharing in the belief that Melville was 'shrewd and resourceful' albeit somewhat prone to 'adventuring'.[54] As for Melville himself, he was happy to change offices so long as 'a suitable offer' was forthcoming.[55]

In return for a more than comfortable income – his pension was supplemented by a salary of £440 – the Special Branch veteran was expected to 'enquire into... all cases of suspicious Germans which might come to my notice; the same as to Frenchmen and foreigners generally; to obtain suitable men to go abroad to obtain information [and] to be in touch with competent operators to keep observation on suspected persons when necessary'.[56] The days of busting down doors in Fitzrovia and debriefing foreign spies in darkest Clerkenwell seemed to be firmly behind the former head of the 'political department', but while the 'age of Melville' was drawing to a close, the threat of politically motivated violence remained ever-present.

\* \* \*

Although the Home Office continued to play an important role in political policing throughout the 1890s, the decade ultimately saw a temporary consolidation of power in the institutional arm of the political police (namely Section D of CID) and in particular its controversial superintendent, Chief Inspector William Melville. Whereas in 1887 Henry Matthews had been in charge of deciding which socialists were to be kept under surveillance and in what circumstances, in 1894 Asquith (a man of conflicting views on policing subversion[57]) found he had to rely on newspaper accounts in order to learn about the latest arrests of anarchists. Practically this meant that the active policing of anarchism in London and the provinces was often planned and directed by Melville himself, as several investigations reveal, chiefly that into the Walsall dynamite conspiracy.

The Walsall case in fact provides us with a near microcosm of Melville's 'style' of political policing. First, we have the informers, the most important of whom Melville was able to not merely use, but effectively 'own', as both Patrick McIntyre's memoir and classified Special Branch payrolls attest. This suggests that even more so than others before him (Jenkinson, Monro), the Chief Inspector carried out his spymaster duties with an impressive degree of ruthlessness and relish, his only real loyalty being to the British state as an ideal of imperial order. Secondly, we have the extra-legality and secrecy which are aptly illustrated by Coulon's possible, though not wholly provable, role as agent provocateur, but more importantly by the fact that the Home Office and Scotland Yard leadership seemed to have been only marginally aware of what was happening in Walsall (Anderson's embarrassing failure to get a hold of the ever-slippery Coulon being a case in point).

Thirdly, there is the careful manipulation of public opinion embodied by Melville's humble boast that he had 'paid lots of anarchists money'. While we have no way of knowing the extent to which that claim was true, the fact that it was accepted as true by the Attorney-General and the presiding judge in the case, the press and not least by the anarchists themselves, attests to Melville's talents as spin doctor – talents which later proved essential in cementing the public image of an unobtrusive and unassertive political police.

Was such Machiavellian dissimulation the product of an Irish-colonial mentality, as some historians have suggested?[58] Leaving aside psychohistorical suppositions, it must be stated that the notion of Melville's 'Irishness' as a synonym for an inherently reactionary outlook is unconvincing. Melville was indeed a native of Sneem in County Kerry, but as a recent biography by Andrew Cook has revealed, his early upbringing was that of a respectably poor Roman Catholic tenant farmer's son, not one steeped in Unionist politics or Anglo-Irish privilege. Leaving his childhood home sometime in his late teens for unknown reasons, Melville was by 1872, at the age of just twenty-two, already a constable in the London Metropolitan Police – a story which, incidentally, mirrors almost perfectly that of his colleague and successor to the direction of Special Branch, Chief Inspector Patrick Quinn.[59]

The young Melville, it seems, was likely a starry-eyed, teetotal self-improver who supported collective bargaining rights for Metropolitan Police officers, a stance for which he was briefly expelled from the force. He gradually transformed as he came increasingly into contact with the realities of London's most disadvantaged areas, where he was often on the beat. He was also arguably changed by the venality and corruption inherent in the Metropolitan Police hierarchy of the 1870s (Melville's promotion to the newly formed CID in 1879 came on the heels of the previous year's collapse of the Detective Branch under the weight of a notorious corruption scandal).[60] It was London then that ultimately created Melville the arch-manipulator and the *vil Melville* of anarchist demonology, just as it was London that incubated the entire political police apparatus itself.

That aside, it is important to keep in mind that Melville's presence at Scotland Yard was far from revolutionary and that in many ways the political police of the 1890s remained rooted in the post-Harcourt status quo, minus the endemic infighting. The methods employed by Special Branch detectives – viz. shadowing, disguises, raids and house searches (with or without warrants) and especially the use of informers – were certainly nothing new. Neither was

Britain's tenuous relationship with foreign powers in legal and policing matters, as demonstrated by the refusal to participate in the abortive 1893 anti-anarchist conference and the half-hearted participation in the 1898 Rome conference.

Governmental hostility to schemes for international police cooperation was ultimately motivated by the desire to preserve, at home and abroad, the secrecy surrounding the British system of policing subversion and not merely by a nineteenth-century version of Euroscepticism. This is, as we have seen, demonstrated by the internal official correspondence dealing with the anti-anarchist conferences as well as by Britain's refusal to cooperate even with peripheral, non-European states like Uruguay.

There were of course some changes as well. Colonel Majendie got his French-style bomb-disposing compound (though only after the Greenwich Park outrage), and the surveillance of British socialists was gradually wound down – not so much out of fear of irking liberal opinion, but because the native socialist scene seemed endemically fragmented and hopelessly stolid.[61] Conversely, as the curious case of the Legitimation League demonstrates, groups associated – no matter how tenuously – with militant anarchism could easily be interfered with and broken up by legal, or rather legalistic, means.

Although such apparent excesses of zeal were not deplored by the mainstream press, newspapers tended to be somewhat more critical of the 'political department', especially when Scotland Yard appeared pathetically inept, as was the case after the Greenwich Park outrage, without, however, veering into any sustained critiques of political policing per se. What the left-wing *Reynolds's Newspaper*, the independent *Sunday Times* and the right-wing *Daily Mail* could all agree on by 1897, was that the political police formed an irreversible and ultimately legitimate part of the British state.

Whether this was truly the decade of 'utterly unlawful things', as Anderson claimed in his 1898 memo to the Home Office, remains debatable in the absence of more conclusive archival evidence. Certainly, the extra-legality of British political policing never – with the exception of those few cases where provocation by government-employed agents might have been at play – nosedived into outright illegality. Furthermore, even in those cases where the law was very clearly strained, it was strained in a manner that stressed the incongruity of the situation and, paradoxically, the lawfulness of the entire system.

To illustrate we need only think of the 1897 case of Vladimir Burtsev. Although the arrest of the unfortunate revolutionary was procured through extra-legal means by the representative of a foreign power for the exclusive benefit of his political masters, that representative – the infamous Pyotr Rachkovsky – was never able to secure in Britain anything like the vast and lucrative network of patronage he had built up in France.[62] Because, outside the uppermost echelons of the Home Office bureaucracy, British extra-legality was always safely couched in a hollow yet inviolable ur-liberal narrative of strict constitutionalism ('The only question with us is, is there crime or not?'[63]) and legal exceptionalism ('our laws are strong enough to deal with anarchism'[64]), the backdoor into the British political police did not ultimately lead very far even for those clever and unscrupulous enough to find it.

# Part 3
# 1904–14

# CHAPTER 13

# Dangerous aliens

Following the relative stability of the 1890s, the Edwardian decade saw the emergence of new types of political radicalism. Although the peak of anarchist propaganda by the deed seemed to reach a new, truly global dimension after the assassination of both the Italian King Umberto I and the American President William McKinley[1] within the span of just over a year, the anarchist colony in Britain continued to rapidly decline. Instead, the new challenge for British authorities came increasingly from home-grown movements like the militant suffragettes (who after 1906 began advocating violent methods in their struggle for female enfranchisement) and the labour movement, sections of which were increasingly responsive to the advanced socialist doctrines circulating on the continent.

Simultaneously, the problems posed by colonial unrest and the mounting wave of immigration from Eastern Europe were only further highlighted by spectacular and violent episodes involving foreigners active in revolutionary and nationalist politics. At first glance, the British government's response to these new challenges appears to have changed very little when compared to the previous decade. Scotland Yard and the Home Office continued to display the same circumspect conservatism in regard to strategies of containing politically motivated violence, all the while insisting that political crime was not even a category recognized by British law. Change was nonetheless forthcoming and as the following pages will show, the decade preceding the First World War had a profoundly transformative effect on the expansion and development of political policing in Britain.

\* \* \*

On 3 December 1901, in his first annual message to Congress, the twenty-sixth President of the United States, Theodore Roosevelt, decried the assassination of his predecessor William McKinley by a 'criminal whose perverted instincts [led] him to prefer confusion and chaos to the most beneficent form of social order', adding that anarchism was 'a crime against the whole human race; and all mankind should band against the anarchist. His crime should be made an offense against the law of nations, like piracy and... the slave trade... [and it] should be so declared by treaties among all civilized powers.'[2]

A little over a month after Roosevelt's call to action it seemed like an international anti-anarchist crusade might finally become a reality thanks to a new Russo-German attempt to revive the project undertaken in Rome in 1898. By early 1904, however, it was clear that the momentum for concerted action had mostly dissipated. Despite much lobbying by the Russian and German governments, in the end only nine of the twenty-one participants of the 1898 conference – Austria-Hungary, Bulgaria, Denmark, Germany, Romania, Russia, Serbia, Sweden and Norway and Turkey – agreed to reconvene in St Petersburg for a new set of deliberations on the anarchist threat. All of them, except for the Scandinavian states, were either Russian or German allies.

The United States' official response to the Russo-German proposal did not appear to echo the enthusiasm of Roosevelt's speech. In the wake of Leon Czolgosz's trial and execution, outrage over McKinley's assassination quickly subsided and legal solutions devised and managed by the US Federal Government without any interference from the Old World appeared more practical.[3] Britain's response proved equally isolationist, if for somewhat different reasons; whereas Washington preferred grounding its anti-anarchist legislation in the spirit of the Monroe Doctrine, Whitehall continued to remain unconvinced that such legislation was needed in the first place. As in 1898, the government's cautious approach easily outweighed any fears about the confusion and chaos with which anarchists appeared to threaten the established social order.

There was more to Britain's non-participation than a stubborn refusal to alter the sacrosanct 'spirit' of British law. Firstly, there was in fact little need for a harsh disciplinarian response to the continued presence of a 'practically quiescent'[4] and overwhelmingly London-based anarchist colony. Secondly, Britain's diplomatic relations with Germany[5] and Russia appeared increasingly strained. Melville, in fact, later recalled how 'in 1904 there was severe political tension with Russia, and it was considered advisable to get in touch with Poles, Nihilists and other discontented Russian elements in this country'.[6] Ironically, the ex-Special Branch Superintendent was secretly meeting with Polish nationalists at London's Nihilist clubs, encouraging rather than subverting their plans for insurrection, even going so far as donating £10 to one of their propaganda funds.

Lastly and most importantly, the provisions of the anti-anarchist protocol signed in the Russian capital on 1 March (Old Style) 1904 reflected the priorities of the Russian and German governments to an uncomfortable degree. Whereas the Rome Conference had dedicated many of its sessions to debating the definition of anarchism, the St Petersburg Protocol aimed only at dealing with practical administrative measures. Typical of these were proposals to 'pass expelled anarchists across the frontiers by [the] quickest routes to their own country' and for each of the signatories to 'establish a Central Bureau to collect... information as to anarchists in its own area, and their doings'.[7] This latter proposal was nothing especially controversial; a pan-European network of central bureaux forwarding each other valuable intelligence had been a key administrative motion at the 1898 Conference and one which had enjoyed nearly unanimous support. The 1904 version, however, went into considerable detail on the responsibilities and obligations of these central bureaux:

> The Contracting Powers agree that from the Central Bureaux notice shall be sent promptly:-
>
> (a) If an anarchist is expelled or quits the country (notice to be sent to the Bureau of the country he is going).
>
> (b) If an anarchist disappears from under observation (notice to be sent to all Central Bureaux)
>
> (c) If any anarchist plot is discovered
>
> (d) If there are any important events bearing on the anarchist question to record.
>
> Each Central Bureau shall be bound to reply to questions by another Central Bureau.[8]

As the Home Office reply to this outline made clear, such a level of close cooperation with foreign police forces was utterly incompatible with the 'arrangements under which the police in this country is conducted [which] do not provide the means of establishing any central bureau with formal authority over the whole kingdom'.[9]

More importantly, political policing in Britain was premised almost exclusively on 'the private informer', ostensibly due to a lack of continental-style identity documents and domiciliary visits by the police.[10] Should an informer's identity be compromised as a consequence of intelligence sharing across the proposed central bureaux, he and other prospective informers would certainly be less inclined to inform in the future and might even be 'driven to some desperate act – as has happened more than once'.[11] Therefore, Commissioner Edward Henry argued, 'the action of English police in dealing with anarchists should not be fettered by hard and fast agreements with continental police authorities'.[12] There might be informal information sharing on a need-to-know basis, but nothing beyond that. As for the power of expelling anarchists, the Home Office insisted it lacked that as well, although as subsequent developments demonstrated, certain elements within the Conservative Party had far from given up on displacing Europe's 'refuse' from British shores.

On the afternoon of 7 December 1904 Henry forwarded a report to Conservative Home Secretary Aretas Akers-Douglas, illustrating the disastrous situation – 'more acute... this year... than it has ever been' – of newly arrived East End immigrants.[13] The report's author, Superintendent John Mulvany of H Division, described the pockets of extreme penury and misery in his precinct in nearly apocalyptic terms:

> These people have been coming in large numbers for some time past, they are chiefly of Russian nationality, ill fed and ill clothed, mostly without means of any sort. As recently as yesterday some three hundred of them congregated outside a synagogue at Fournier St., Brick Lane and threatened to break the doors open if they were not given bread; many are absolutely starving, they walk the streets by day and night, the shelters being full... Police precautions are taken to keep them in check and prevent damage but the evil is growing daily.[14]

The issue of ever-increasing Eastern European immigration into London was of course not a new one, but if in 1892 it had been relegated to the columns of left-wing papers and the politics of unemployed marches, by 1904 it was becoming the focus of a national debate on economic fairness, moral integrity and racial health.[15] In order to address the concerns of newly formed anti-immigration pressure groups, ranging from the explicitly antisemitic British Brothers League to the moderately right-wing Parliamentary Alien Immigration Committee, a Royal Commission on Alien Immigration had been set up in early 1902 which over the span of forty-nine days heard evidence from no fewer than 175 witnesses.

Its report, published in August 1903, concluded that the flood of Jewish refugees into the British capital was not the cause of any 'serious displacement of skilled English labour' and was unlikely to cease anytime soon given the antisemitic legislation in Eastern European states with significant Jewish minorities – the Russian Empire and the Kingdom of Romania in particular. Nevertheless, new regulations were urgently needed in order to 'prevent so far as possible this country being burdened with the presence of "undesirable aliens" and to provide for their repatriation in certain cases'.[16] This undesirability, however, was framed solely in terms of moral turpitude and/or proclivity towards regular, non-political crime, with special attention given to sex traffickers and 'lunatics'. This interpretation was reiterated in the 1905 Aliens Act, which explicitly barred any 'crime... of a political character' from the expulsion clause.[17]

Such a blatant reaffirmation of the status-quo position on political crime may seem counterintuitive given the previous Conservative attempt at pushing a new Aliens Bill through Parliament had been partly motivated by Lord Salisbury's wish to rid London of the anarchists' 'conspiracy of assassination'. In 1905, however, organized anarchism was no longer what it had been during the *époque des attentats* of the 1890s. In London, the movement was more or less relegated to the fringes of trade union politics, especially in areas associated with sweated immigrant labour, and it was thanks to a group of Jewish activists that the last significant anarchist club in the British capital opened its doors on 3 February 1906 in Jubilee Street.

Named the *Arbeiter Fraint* ('worker's friend') Club and Institute, after an eponymous Yiddish-language anarchist daily, it was a 'big building, with a large hall... a library... [a] reading room [and] educational classes', harkening back to the glory days of the Autonomie Club.[18] According to one of its founding members, the German anarchist Rudolf Rocker, the house on Jubilee Street served not merely as a meeting place for anarchists, but as a community centre for progressive and secular Jewish militants of all stripes who otherwise felt alienated from native left-wing politics. The Social Democratic Federation was coming dangerously close to espousing a British version of Boulangism[19] thanks to its openly antisemitic and nationalistic leader Henry Hyndman, while the anti-alien agitation of British trade unions was arguably at an apex in the years following the Second Boer War. Anarchism was thus slowly turning into a function of a politically radical Jewishness; an expression of 'a hidden Jewish menace of outsiders who could pass as insiders'.[20] Over the next few years the issue of insidious, politically subversive aliens and criminality continued bubbling up in the pages of the conservative press, making a spectacular return to public attention at the end of the decade.

On the morning of 23 January 1909, Albert Keyworth, office clerk at Schnurmann's rubber factory in Tottenham, had just finished picking up the weekly wages from a local bank when he was suddenly seized by two men and violently relieved of the £80 in his possession. Trailed by several incensed locals who had witnessed the assault, the armed attackers were soon overtaken by an automobile carrying a group of police officers from the Tottenham police station. Momentarily repelled by a barrage of bullets that disabled the car's engine and mortally wounded a nearby boy, the constables – armed only with truncheons – nevertheless continued the chase on foot, again coming under fire and losing one man, PC William Tyler, in the process.

The assailants then proceeded to shoot their way through the Tottenham marshes, hijacking a series of vehicles in the heat of the action, including a tram, a milk cart and a horse-driven van. Remarkably, the police succeeded in keeping up with them all the way, the frantic pursuit coming, partially, to an end only as the two outlaws reached the banks of the River Ching. Too exhausted to climb over the tall wooden fence running along the riverbank, Hefeld urged his partner in crime, Jacob, to go on without him, turning the gun on himself immediately after.

Running all the way to Walthamstow, in Essex, Jacob managed to temporarily evade his pursuers by forcing a family at gunpoint out of their small four-room house and barricading himself inside. The plan did not go far; the house was soon encircled by a sizeable contingent of police from across north and east London, who, after a botched attempt to get at Jacob through a first-floor window, decided to storm the building through the front entrance. In a matter of minutes the sound of a shot coming from upstairs announced the assault was already over. Jacob was found splayed out on a bed, his face drenched in blood, his hand still clutching a paper bank bag containing no more than £5.[21] Just who these trigger-happy desperadoes, who had managed to terrorize scores of people in a manner more befitting a Wild West show than the humdrum rhythm of suburban London were remained largely a mystery, but not one without consequences.

What the police came to know for certain was that the man who had committed suicide on the banks of the Ching, Paul Hefeld, had recently been in the employ of Schnurmann 'for a few days' and like his comrade Jacob, whose true identity was never made clear,[22] was a native of Riga. Both men were recent immigrants and, according to a report by Special Branch DI Herbert Fitch, known to be 'connected with various anarchist clubs in the neighbourhood'[23] – something which served to elevate the whole incident from mere botched heist to anarchist outrage.

While Fitch and his colleague DI Harold Brust also believed Hefeld and Jacob had somehow been involved in a failed attempt on the life of French President Armand Fallières in Paris on May Day 1907, this claim remains purely conjectural. An incident had indeed occurred on that day in Paris, involving the Russian anarchist Jacob Law firing five shots at a cordon of cuirassiers charged with policing the masses of demonstrators,[24] but there are no recorded attempts on President Fallières's life and no evidence to connect Law to either of the Tottenham robbers.

Ultimately, the names of the anarchist clubs that had supposedly given shelter to the two Latvians as well as the nature of Jacob and Hefeld's political beliefs (insofar as they had any) were sadly never elaborated on in any official reports and there is every indication that Scotland Yard had been caught completely unawares by this incident. As Assistant Commissioner Macnaghten later recalled in his memoirs, 'such a morning of sensational surprises might have been expected in Russia, but hardly within the generally pacific area of Metropolitan Police'.[25] In a charged post-Aliens Act atmosphere, however, fears of renewed anarchist activity could quickly converge with fears of 'Johnny Foreigner'.

Only a couple of years into his new post at the War Office, Melville had conscientiously submitted an ambitious proposal for a 'scheme of surveillance on all suspected foreigners around the country'[26] and well before the Tottenham incident, British newspapers had already been dutifully sounding the alarm over alien beggars, alien burglars, alien bankrupts, alien lunatics, as well as the presence of 'no fewer than three thousand eight hundred well known-Anarchists in London'.[27]

The Tottenham outrage gave the national press, especially Conservative-aligned newspapers, an opportunity to momentarily shift the focus in the debate on domestic subversion on something other than the increasingly tiresome antics of the suffragettes and '[restore] the question of immigration control to the national political agenda'.[28] The *Daily Mail*, followed to a lesser extent by *The Times*, led the charge with a series of exposés and editorials inveighing against the shortcomings of the Aliens Act, particularly the ease with which some of its provisions could be evaded,[29] as well as the Home Secretary's arbitrary powers over its administration.[30]

The incident also gave some Special Branch veterans a chance to come out of retirement and appear *au courant* with the latest developments. Interviewed by the *Penny Illustrated Paper*, ex-DI John Sweeney reminisced about his days of chasing after Polti and Farnara while keeping watch on the various anarchist clubs in London,[31] while Sir Robert Anderson, writing in *The Times*, decried the 'apathy of our Government toward the anarchist movement... due to a selfish sense of security', warning also that 'if... there should be even one more crime like that on Saturday, the first business of [Parliament] would be to pass a measure to suppress the Anarchists'.[32] Despite Anderson's short-sighted fixation with the largely bygone 'anarchist movement', as he understood it,[33] his claim proved strangely prophetic in a way.

\* \* \*

Two hundred-odd high-ranking officials of the Indian Civil Service and members of the Raj aristocracy mixing together in the sumptuous halls of the Renaissance-style Imperial Institute in London – at first sight, the reception hosted by the National Indian Association (NIA) on the evening of 1 July 1909 appeared to be the perfect picture of the 'integrated, ordered, titular, transracial hierarchy'[34] underscoring the mythology of the British Empire. Founded in 1870 by Keshub Chandra Sen and Mary Carpenter, the NIA represented the confluence of imperialist progressivism and patrician conservatism better perhaps than any other Indian association in London, a fact aptly illustrated by the career of one of its more prominent supporters, Sir William Hutt Curzon Wyllie. As governor-general of central India in the 1890s, Sir William had gained a reputation as a conservative but efficient administrator whose relief measures allowed the people of Rajputana to escape the brunt of the famine of 1899–1900. As political aide-de-camp to the Secretary of State for India from 1901 onwards, he appeared to be nothing if not a genuine Indophile and an indefatigable lobbyist for various Indian causes.[35]

The vision of a 'benevolent' imperial order increasingly had its fair share of detractors, however. Throughout the 1880s and 1890s a series of revolutionary and staunchly anti-British societies had appeared throughout India, especially in the Western Maharashtra region. They gradually came to exert a not inconsiderable influence on groups of young, politically conscious Indian men, many of whom, their aversion to Empire notwithstanding, looked to the British metropolis for opportunities of furthering their careers.[36] Such was the case of Madan Lal Dhingra, the twenty-five-year-old scion of a middle-class Punjabi family who in 1906 was sent by his surgeon father to study civil engineering at University College in London. Like many of his generation, Dhingra quickly lost faith in the prospect of a lifetime spent serving the Raj and gradually began taking part in the political activities of the radical Indian diaspora concentrated around the notorious India House in Highgate.

Founded in 1905, ostensibly as a hostel for London's South Asian community, India House – a small two-storey red-brick mansion – had quickly morphed, under the influence of its founder, into a hotbed of 'seditionist' (i.e. Indian nationalist) activities. The man responsible for this transformation, Shyamji Krishnavarma, published a violently anti-British newspaper entitled *The Indian Sociologist* and enjoyed the support of leading British left-wingers like Henry Hyndman and Charlotte Despard (the latter a prominent suffragette and founding member of the Women's Freedom League). Attracted to Krishnavarma's eclectic philosophy, which borrowed freely from Spencerian individualism, Blanquist insurrectionism and Hindu nationalism, Dhingra became increasingly radical and eager to prove himself. Unlike many other self-styled revolutionaries in London, his target was not some faraway autocrat, but the British establishment itself.

Only days before the soiree at the Imperial Institute Dhingra had received an invitation from the NIA's secretary to attend the event, as well as a personal letter from Curzon Wyllie himself, urging the young student to call on him at the India Office for a private tête-à-tête. As Dhingra well knew, this unwanted attention was the result of his older brother's surreptitious attempts to rescue him from the grip of India House, something which the fledgling revolutionary strongly resented.[37] Instead of ignoring the invitation, however, Dhingra decided to make an appearance later in the evening, around 10.30 p.m. Donning a simple dark lounge suit and blue turban, he was clearly not in his natural element,[38] but soon managed to strike up a couple of conversations and affect an amiable, if somewhat demure manner.[39]

As the reception began drawing to a close around midnight, Dhingra – in a decidedly excited mood – trailed the departing guests into the lobby, waited a moment or two for the crowd to disperse downwards and then brusquely approached Sir William, who had just finished catching up with some of his Indian friends. A 'few words of conversation' were exchanged after which Dhingra pulled out a Colt revolver from his jacket and fired four point-blank shots in rapid succession, taking out Curzon Wyllie's right eye and severely disfiguring his face. As the latter fell in a daze to the ground, Dhingra made a few steps forward and callously delivered the *coup de grace*, only to then turn around and fire another fatal shot at Dr Cowasjee Lalcaca (a leading figure of the Parsi diaspora) as the latter was attempting to rush to Curzon Wyllie's aid. With one bullet remaining in the magazine, Dhingra attempted to turn the gun on himself, but was soon overpowered by two other men and subsequently handed over to PC Nicholls and DS Eadley of B Division, the first police officers to arrive at the scene.[40]

As in the wake of the Tottenham outrage, the authorities were left in the embarrassing position of having to explain how a member of a known extremist organization had been able to brazenly carry out an assassination – made even more egregious by the fact that the two victims were prominent representatives of the Anglo-Indian establishment – in the physical and symbolic heart of the Empire. Although initially there was no evidence to suggest the existence of a conspiracy, public opinion was encouraged by the press to put the blame on 'extremist agitation' rather than 'some imaginary personal grievance'.[41] This view was also echoed by the Prime Minister, who saw in the seditious pro-assassination pamphlet found on Dhingra after his arrest 'a startling and emphatic piece of evidence as to the character and the methods of [this] desperate and determined… conspiracy'.[42] Dhingra himself put all doubt to rest by reading out a prepared statement at the conclusion of his trial, praising the virtues of political assassination in no uncertain terms:

> I maintain that if it is patriotic in an Englishman to fight against the Germans if they were to occupy this country, it is much more justifiable and patriotic in my case to fight against the English. I hold the English people responsible for the murder of 80 millions of Indian people in the last fifty years, and… [just] as the Germans have no right to occupy this country, so the English people have no right to occupy India, and it is perfectly justifiable on our part to kill the Englishman who is polluting our sacred land… I wish that English people should sentence me to death, for in that case the vengeance of my countrymen will be all the more keen.[43]

Special Branch had been aware of India House since its opening four years before and, if the recollections of one inspector are to be believed, knew Dhingra himself as 'a dangerous man, a travelling storm-centre [who had] openly and defiantly… avowed before Sergeant MacLaughlin of the Special Branch… that he hated the British Rule in India and meant to "kill somebody some day!"'[44] Undercover detectives had occasionally attended meetings at the House as early as 1907 as had a special police officer sent over from India, whose intelligence, though pertinent, had been of limited value, failing to mention Dhingra's activities.[45] In addition, the India Office-based Indian Department of Criminal Intelligence (established in 1904) employed its own agent to report on the activities of Krishnavarma's group, although his intelligence (likewise incomplete) had failed to reach Scotland Yard.[46]

Despite 'continued police warnings',[47] no efforts were made to clamp down on the propaganda activities of Indian nationalists or to have Dhingra placed under continued surveillance. To some extent this was due to prevalent racial prejudices, which dictated that 'coloured men' were incapable of organized subversion unless 'stirred up' by 'anarchist leaders',[48] but a more important reason was that despite the reforms introduced at Scotland Yard by Henry, Special Branch remained in many ways the same small extra-legal unit it had been during the 1890s.

The first steps towards restructuring the 'political department' had already been taken in late 1907 with a directive formalizing the de facto structure of the organization for the first time in more than fifteen years. Thus, Section B, no longer explicitly associated with Irish republicanism, along with Section D were officially made responsible for monitoring the Metropolitan Police District, while Section C continued to remain in charge of home and foreign ports. The directive also outlined some of the key duties of special officers, mandating the establishment of so-called 'permanent patrols', formed of constables 'selected on account of their knowledge of foreign languages or other exceptional qualifications' and instructing each officer to 'make himself acquainted with the appearance, names and habits' of suspicious persons as well as 'where they lodge, who they associate with, the public houses they frequent, the places they visit, and from their past history learn their mode of carrying out their criminal operations'. Additionally, detectives were also expected to keep notebooks with precise entries on 'persons known… to give reliable information… persons on whom reliance cannot be placed [and] persons respectable by repute but known to be otherwise', especially as information provided by informers, while 'necessary', had to be 'carefully weighed and used with judgement'.[49]

Despite this change of pace, however, Special Branch continued to remain short-staffed[50] and increasingly unable to cope with the challenges posed by a diverse spectrum of political radicalism. The assassination of Curzon Wyllie finally changed that by providing the impetus for an increase in manpower and on 7 July 1909, six days after the tragic event at the Imperial Institute, Superintendent Patrick Quinn submitted a proposal to Commissioner Henry 'with a view of applying to the Secretary of State for an augmentation of two second class Sergeants, and two Constables in Section B CID'. The point-by-point justification for this request is perhaps the most elucidating description we have of what the British political police regarded as its main challenges in the five years preceding the First World War:

> (1) The increasing demands upon the Special Branch in consequence of the Indian agitation, involving personal protection to Statesmen whose lives are considered to be in danger through the presence in London of Indians of extreme views; the close supervision of Indians and the many enquiries required by the Indian Authorities…
>
> (2) The large number of Russian, Polish, Yiddish and Anarchists of other nationalities, resident in London, involving enquiries regularly, and a measure of close supervision at times…
>
> (3) The careful protection of Their Majesties the King and Queen when the Court is at Buckingham Palace has also to be arranged daily.
>
> (4) Enquiries of a highly important nature made for some of the Governments Departments [sic] demand the services of Officers of the Branch.

(5) The agitation by Suffragettes has necessitated the Prime Minister being specially protected by a Sergeant and Constable of Special Branch.

(6) ...other duties such as enquiries for the Irish Government, and enquiries into applications for Naturalization...[51]

The request was approved by the Home Office on 12 July for a period of six, then twelve, months, at the end of which Quinn had to submit a report explaining whether and why the augmentation was still justified.[52] Although following consultations with Henry[53] the India Office secured the creation of its own intelligence unit (later the Indian Political Intelligence Unit), the first operation of the strengthened Special Branch, in accordance with the priorities set out in Quinn's list, aimed at finally clamping down on the activities of India House.

While Shyamji Krishnavarma had fled to Paris in 1907, the House continued to function and publish the monthly *Indian Sociologist* under the leadership of the young law student and avowed Hindu ultra-nationalist Vinayak Damodar Savarkar. Savarkar, who had publicly proclaimed his admiration for Dhingra, was being closely watched, but in the absence of any evidence connecting him to any criminal conspiracy, the most authorities could do to castigate him was sabotage his plans of practising law in the future.[54] The *Indian Sociologist* was, however, another matter. Undeterred by the public backlash against Dhingra, the paper published the assassin's 'manifesto' in its July issue along with an editorial by Krishnavarma praising his disciple's 'martyrdom' and the virtues of tyrannicide in general.

This was as good a pretext as authorities were ever going to get for shutting down the publication and on 19 July 1909, Arthur Fletcher Horsley, printer and publisher of the *Indian Sociologist*, was put in the dock at the Old Bailey for 'maliciously and seditiously printing and publishing... a certain scandalous printed article... calculated and intended to stir up and raise discontent and unrest among His Majesty's liege subjects'.[55] Horsley, as his solicitor was quick to point out, was a patriotic Englishman who had agreed to publish the paper 'in error' without 'exercising proper care in preparing the proofs which had brought him into his present position'. Choosing to plead guilty, he was given four months as a first-class misdemeanant.[56]

Quinn might have considered this an open-and-shut case, but much to his annoyance it appeared the *Indian Sociologist* refused to die. In mid-August 1909 a new issue came out, this time under the auspices of the erstwhile unknown Bakunin Press, seemingly confirming the notion that anarchists were indeed stoking the fire of Indian seditionism. The owner-operator of this enterprise was a man by the name of Guy Aldred, a Londoner known to Special

Branch since 1907 as an occasional contributor to the left-wing *Justice* and frequenter of the Jubilee Street anarchist club.[57] It was not difficult to apprehend him, but as the Burtsev affair of 1897 had demonstrated, the manner in which evidence was procured by police in a case of seditious libel could be vital to securing a guilty verdict. Taking a page out of his predecessor's book, Quinn decided to have one of his detectives write Aldred 'in an assumed name… for four copies of the incriminating number, enclosing stamps for same'.[58]

Once legally obtained, the evidence proved damning; the August issue was in many ways even more inflammatory than the July one, containing not only the usual call to arms by Krishnavarma, but also an article by Aldred himself excoriating the 'despotism' of British rule in India and accusing the government of 'high treason' for allowing Special Branch to trample on 'the principles of a free Constitution'.[59] Arrested on 25 August for seditious libel against the king and the 'administration of the laws in force in the… Indian Empire', Aldred was in no position to invoke Horsley's defence. At his trial, the following week, no fewer than five Special Branch detectives gave evidence against him, revealing that 1,500 copies of the August issue had been printed in total, out of which one thousand had already been sent to Krishnavarma in Paris. Refusing to contest the charges, Aldred furthermore insisted on explaining that he had taken on the task of publishing the paper 'because he claimed the right of an enlightened race to have a free Press'.[60] The jury was not impressed; he was found guilty and received twelve months as a first-class misdemeanant.

A month later, on 24 October, the embattled Savarkar invited the still relatively unknown Mohandas Gandhi, who had arrived in London days after Curzon Wyllie's assassination, to give the opening speech at one of his India House dinners. The future founder of the Indian nation later described the event as 'practically [controlled] by the extremist Committee', noting that 'I accepted the proposal unhesitatingly so that I might speak to those who might assemble there on the uselessness of violence for securing reform.'[61] A few months later, Savarkar was extradited to India for complicity in an assassination carried out by his brother Ganesh and summarily imprisoned, being released only in 1937. Under increasingly intense scrutiny from the police and with its publishers and charismatic leader gone, India House slowly collapsed into irrelevance by the end of 1910. The issue of 'anarchist' violence, however, was not quite buried yet.

Nearly two years after the Tottenham outrage had brought anarchism back into the limelight, London's remaining anarchist scene did not appear capable of posing any credible threat to the safety of the British public. As the *Penny Illustrated Paper* explained in one of its popular lurid investigations into London's 'creatures of the night', Soho's old horrible crew of French and Italian bomb-throwers had largely been replaced by a medley of Eastern European refugees, who, despite a penchant for using knives to settle their scores, seemed, for the most part, political innocents – Tolstoyans and sentimental Nihilists who became teary-eyed at 'the thought of the torture of a human being'.[62] And yet there was still real danger lurking in the streets of London's underworld.

Although the Tottenham shooters' connections to anarchism remained uncertain in light of their mysterious identities, a small but active colony of radical socialists from the western territories of the Russian Empire called the streets of Tower Hamlets and Whitechapel home. These men and women whose insurrectionary fervour estranged them not only from the law but also from the social-democratic parties of their homelands[63] had chosen to settle in Britain, where, despite the occasional intrusions of Okhrana spies and Special Branch agents, they could lead, or pretend to lead, ordinary lives. Their scorn for political means and preference for 'expropriation' placed them in the lineage of the anarcho-individualist groups of the 1890s, but their ideology was a confusing mix of revolutionary socialism, ethnic populism and gangsterism.[64] To British authorities it was anarchism by virtue of its extremeness.

On 30 November 1910 a group of recently arrived Russian and Latvian anarchists rented several adjacent apartments in a complex near Houndsditch Street in central London (then an impoverished and largely immigrant area) with the intention of planning a jewellery heist. The jewellery shop, owned by a certain Henry Samuel Harris, was just on the other side of the complex and its premises were easily accessible through an outhouse which abutted it. For the cash-strapped revolutionaries it was an opportunity too good to pass up. They set to work on the evening of 16 December, but the task of drilling through the back wall of the shop soon proved noisy enough to arouse the suspicions of Mr Harris' neighbour, who then promptly alerted the police. Confronted with the presence of five City of London policemen demanding to inspect the premises, the robbers panicked and proceeded to shoot their way out of the building, fatally wounding three of the officers in the process. 'In its savagery the outrage vied with the anarchical outbreak at Tottenham two years ago', noted *The Times*, not yet knowing the whole truth about the perpetrators' identities.[65]

The first clue on the whereabouts of the gang came early next day, after police received notice that a dead body had been located at 59 Grove Street in east London. It turned out to be that of one of the robbers, George Gardstein, who, as an investigation shortly established, had been fatally hit by friendly fire during the escape, dying during the night after refusing to be taken to hospital. In the back room of the same house police also found one of Gardstein's friends, a certain Ms Trassjonsky, alive and busily disposing of a quantity of Gardstein's, presumably incriminating, documents and photographs.[66]

She was detained along with several others acolytes of Gardstein, but to the disappointment of City and Metropolitan officers (the case was nominally under City control) no palpable evidence could link any of the suspects to the events of 16 December. Questioning did, however, produce one major breakthrough: the room in which the body had been found had been 'occupied by [three men] with whom [Gardstein] was associated, and who were evidently concerned with him in the Crime, and had taken him to their rooms after he was wounded'.[67] The three men, all ethnic Latvians, were Fricis 'Fritz' Svaars, William Sokolov aka Jakov Vogel aka Joseph and one Jānis Žāklis, known only as Peter the Painter.[68] As the owner of the Grove Street building was quick to reveal, Sokolov had been known to frequent the home of one Betsey Gershon, a Russian-speaking immigrant dressmaker who lived at 100 Sidney Street in the East End.

By 2 January 1911 Svaars and Sokolov had been reliably traced to the location in Sidney Street where they appeared to have barricaded themselves in the hopes of evading their pursuers. That night, Metropolitan and City superintendents met at the Arbour Square police station in order to figure out how best to apprehend these 'desperate men... who would not be taken alive'.[69] Rushing the building was out of the question given its steep and narrow staircase and a blockade was decided on as the least risky option. By 4.00 a.m. the next day, 100 Sidney Street had been quietly evacuated (save for the two outlaws) and sealed off from the rest of the neighbourhood by a cordon of over two hundred constables.

The first shots were fired around 7.30 a.m. after police made a last-ditch attempt to get the two men to surrender by throwing some gravel up at the window of their room. A police officer was almost instantly injured and it soon became painfully obvious that the Latvians' guns 'were far superior to our revolvers, of which at this time we only had a few'.[70] Around 11.00 a.m. Home Secretary Churchill received a phone call asking whether military aid might be deployed to help the embattled police officers; the troops, however – one lieutenant, two NCOs and seventeen privates of the Scots Guards – were already on site returning fire.

In light of the extraordinary circumstances, Churchill felt it was his 'duty to go and see for myself what was happening'.[71] While later claiming that he 'did not in any way direct or override the arrangements that the police had made',[72] surviving footage of the operation in Sidney Street – Pathé's first reel of British police in action[73] – shows the Home Secretary in his usual self-sure pose, conferring with superintendents and pointing at various things in a manner that certainly suggested active leadership to police officers and journalists alike.[74]

At about 1.00 p.m. plumes of smoke began to emerge from the roof of the besieged house (likely as a result of stray bullets hitting a gas pipe) and within the span of a few minutes, the building's upper floors were almost entirely engulfed in flames. Firefighters from nearby stations arrived shortly after, but were immediately 'stopped by the police from going nearer'.[75] Objecting to this course of action, a fireman later recalled how 'an official informed me that the Home Secretary was in attendance and had charge of the operations... and [when I] spoke to the Home Secretary... I was told to keep my engines there [as] nothing could be done at present'.[76]

The two desperadoes defiantly refused to be smoked out, however, and shooting continued for at least another hour. By 2:45 p.m. Churchill had already left the scene and much of the fire had subsided. Svaars' body was found shortly after 3.00 p.m. 'burnt beyond all recognition', followed by Sokolov's a few moments later.[77] The coroner's verdicts were 'suffocation by smoke during the conflagration' and 'justifiable homicide' respectively.

Although the mysterious Peter the Painter remained at large (never to be heard from again), the deaths of Svaars and Sokolov – whom the authorities could plausibly connect to Gardstein thanks to artefacts found in the wreckage of the building in Sidney Street – effectively marked the conclusion of the Houndsditch affair. Despite its ultra-violent and spectacular nature, the aftermath proved surprisingly anticlimactic; there was no raid on the Jubilee Street Club (supposedly a familiar haunt of Gardstein and his associates), no increased surveillance on other immigrant clubs and no real attempt to understand what had motivated the two young Latvians to commit suicide in such a public and dramatic way. Unsurprisingly, an offer by Riga's Director of Criminal Investigations to come to London and convey 'valuable information respecting the [Latvian] Anarchist band in London' was bluntly waved off by Henry as useless and likely to cause embarrassment to British authorities.[78]

Public outrage, however, erupted almost immediately after the events of 3 January, most of it directed at the already much-maligned Aliens Act and to some extent at Churchill himself – criticized on the left for being an irresponsible adventurer with no 'knowledge of how to handle masses of men in... critical times'[79] and on the right for being a xenophile Liberal hypocrite.[80] More worryingly, the siege of Sidney Street, as the event became memorialized, also added fuel to the fire of antisemitic agitation (no longer the preserve of far-right populists and ideological racists).[81]

7. Police officers standing in the ruins of a house following the Siege of Sidney Street, 1911 (Library of Congress, Prints & Photographs Division).

After Sidney Street the anarchist momentarily regained his status as folk devil and thanks to the new medium of cinema, the British public could revel in Lieutenant Rose's valiant foiling of a dastardly anarchist plot to assassinate King George V or shudder at the thought that 'aerial anarchists' might one day drop bombs over London out of improvised zeppelins.[82] For a short while, in early 1911, rumours that a real plot to assassinate the king was being hatched in Chicago by Italian anarchists were deemed credible enough by the Home Office to require the services of local Pinkertons, but investigations ultimately ended in a wild goose chase.[83] Anarchism as a credible political threat no longer existed, yet its ethos proved longer-lived.

## CHAPTER 14

# 'A doctrine of lawlessness'[1]

THE redistributive People's Budget (which became law in April 1910) pre-figured an 'implacable warfare against poverty and squalidness'[2] for the reformist wing of the Liberal Party, but in many of Britain's industrial areas the lives of a great deal of 'the people' continued to be marred by falling wages, rising food prices and systematic underemployment.[3] Nowhere, perhaps, was this more noticeable than in the coalfields of South Wales, where in late 1910 approximately thirty thousand miners of various pits in the Mid Glamorgan region (more than a sixth of the entire mining workforce) were engaged in a protracted and hopeless strike against their employers.

The strike had begun back in August 1909 with a petty wage dispute between the workers of the Naval Colliery in the Rhondda Valley and the alliteratively named Cambrian Combine Colliery Company, a conglomerate which owned that colliery and many of the surrounding ones. The miners demanded a rate of 2s 6d per ton of coal while the owners refused to go a penny over 1s 9d. On 1 September the miners struck, setting in motion an unforeseen wave of sympathy strikes which, by early November, had paralyzed all the collieries of the Cambrian Combine. Meanwhile, up north, in the Aberdare Valley, the workers at Powell Duffryn Collieries had also gone on strike in late October because of the management's refusal to recognize their traditional right of using discarded wooden props for firewood.[4]

Despite the scale of the conflict, long-drawn-out strikes were not an uncommon occurrence in South Wales – as the example of an unsuccessful five-month strike in 1898 attested – and initially there was little to indicate tensions between workers and management would flare out of control. Things took a turn for the worse, however, when on 2 November 1910 miners in the village of Cwmllynfell rioted over the importation of strikebreaking labour, sabotaging the local pit and driving the proprietors out of town. As the Chief Constable for Mid Glamorgan, Captain Lionel Lindsay, explained in a report to the Home Office, the 'doctrine of lawlessness which has been preached in this valley for some time... has made the rowdy element... rather more difficult to deal with than heretofore'. Fearing the worst, local magistrates decided 'that it was necessary to call in Military aid'.[5]

The 'doctrine of lawlessness' which Lindsay decried was the radical socialism that had made inroads into the traditionally Liberal and Labour-supporting workforce of the region, chiefly through the influence of the South Wales Miners Federation (SWMF). Significantly, the SWMF's socialist wing was closer in thinking to syndicalism – a term recently coined to describe the radical, anarchist-inspired methods of some continental trade unions – than to the doctrines of the Labour Party.[6] Although strictly a fringe tendency, this uncompromising version of socialism found a receptive audience among union men let down by their leadership[7] – as illustrated by the election of Charles Butt Stanton (a SWMF organizer with a love of 'direct action' and penchant for strong-arming mine owners) as unofficial leader of the Aberdare strikers.

Despite his ingrained anti-socialism and predilection for law and order, Churchill understood the importance of a tactful and commensurate response to the situation developing in South Wales, especially with yet another general election looming large.[8] He agreed to send a contingent of infantry and cavalry troops under the command of General Nevil Macready,[9] along with 802 specially selected Metropolitan Police constables, but insisted the military should only be deployed if 'the police reinforcements [proved] unable to cope with the situation'.[10] Churchill's message to the miners, as transmitted to Captain Lindsay, was that, while 'their best friends here are greatly distressed at the trouble which has broken out, and will do their best to help them to get fair treatment [, all] rioting must cease at once'.[11]

Rioting only got worse, however. On 7 November 1910 strikers at the Glamorgan pit, near the town of Llwynpia, attempted to drive out the officials and stokers keeping the mining equipment functional and were pushed back only after intense fighting which saw several local policemen get injured.[12] The violence erupted once again on the following evening when the battle-hardened strikers decided to march through the nearby town of Tonypandy. As the local butcher later recalled in a testimony to police:

> I was protecting my premises from the violence of a mob of about five or six hundred people, consisting of men, women, and youths... [the] majority... carrying mandril sticks [and] pieces of timber... from the Glamorgan colliery fencing. The rioting commenced about half past six p.m. and continued... until 9:45 p.m. I saw the arrival of the London Police at Pandy Square about 10 o'clock. A shout of "Police are coming" was given and the crowd quickly dispersed... The Police... marched down by my premises in a compact body; [but] after [they] passed, a crowd again assembled and broke the windows of several shops in the Square... The looting of shops continued and a body of London Police came from the Skating Rink and on their appearance [the

crowd] flew in all directions. The Police remained about the vicinity of the Square and... things assumed a normal condition [afterwards].[13]

Similar scenes simultaneously unfolded in Aberaman where between two and three thousand striking workers, many also accompanied by wives and children, engaged in pitch battle with a contingent of Welsh police.[14] Although General Macready's troops remained stationed nearby with orders to 'block the streets on the high ground and work gradually downwards'[15] should the situation require it, the efficiency of police in dispersing the crowds ultimately pre-empted any military intervention. Receiving the news of the worsening violence with alarm, Churchill urged Macready to stay the course and let the reinforced Metropolitan Police contingents subdue any further rioting with 'vigorous baton charges [as this] may be the best means of preventing recourse to fire-arms'.[16]

No fatalities occurred at Aberaman, but at Tonypandy one miner, a man called Samuel Royce, was fatally injured by a blow to the head – likely delivered by a police truncheon, although conflicting evidence suggested a 'stone thrown from behind'[17] – further deepening the strikers' profound antipathy to the Liberal government. Over the following days, however, Macready's tactical shrewdness and political talents managed to secure a fragile yet sustainable peace between miners and authorities, albeit without putting an end to the strike.

The first change of pace came once Macready became fully aware of the extent to which opportunistic mine owners took advantage of the venality of local police in order to arrange for 'the importation of "blacklegs" or fresh work in the pits... without consideration as to how it might influence the strikers'.[18] Even Captain Lindsay, for all his seeming professionalism, seemed 'a little nervous in throwing off [the] influence [of] the local magnates'[19] and when a few days after the clashes in Tonypandy and Aberaman rumours began to spread that some miners were planning to set off a bomb, Macready arranged to personally meet with the strikers' leaders, including the syndicalist firebrand C. B. Stanton.

Reassuring them that his forces were not there at the behest of the mining interest, Macready also warned forcefully that 'if [bomb explosions] should occur, the affected area will pass practically into... Martial Law',[20] even as no orders had been received from Whitehall authorizing such a drastic move. Macready then proceeded to set up a working intelligence-gathering network with the help of two War Office detectives. This allowed him to remain one step ahead of the strikers' plans while avoiding taking excessive precautions against potential violence (fresh reports of a bomb outrage against a colliery manager turned out to be 'totally unfounded [and] concocted by the mine owners').[21]

With the exception of a scuffle in Pennygraig on 21 November, which Macready regarded as merely 'an ebullition against "blacklegs" and imported police',[22] there were no other major episodes of organised violence for the remainder of the strike, which nevertheless continued for another eight grueling months, concluding with the victory of the Cambrian Combine.[23] The riots in early November, however, especially the one in Tonypandy, set the tone for what shortly became the great industrial unrest of the antebellum years – in less than a year five hundred Metropolitan Police officers were again sent to keep the peace between strikers and local authorities, this time at Hull – creating a black legend of callous military repression that haunted Churchill for the rest of his life. The violence also suggested, at least to authorities, that revolutionary propaganda, while essentially 'un-British', could easily find a receptive audience with working men and women in a time of crisis. Tellingly, despite their tactical and personal differences, both Macready and Lindsay blamed 'extreme socialism' for the extent and intensity of the rioting.[24]

In addition to the presence of C. B. Stanton and other far-left SWMF organisers, the strikers had also played host to foreign agitators like the French anarchist Antoinette Durand de Gros, better-known as Madame Sorgue, who, as *The Times* of 15 November 1909 noted, 'has been in the Aberdare district for some time [and will no longer] be permitted to address any more meetings in the locality'. Although it is hard to quantify the real support for revolutionary socialism in the southern Welsh valleys at this time, it is worth noting that in 1911 four syndicalists – Noah Ablett, John Hopla, Noah Rees and Tom Smith – were elected to the SWMF executive committee. Equally, syndicalist literature like the 1912 pamphlet 'The Miners' Next Step', which sought to build on the experiences of the 1910 strike, or *The Rhondda Socialist* periodical could claim a readership of several thousand before 1914.[25]

On 13 August 1911 riots by striking transport workers in Liverpool led to the intervention of local police and soldiers from the Warwickshire Regiment, causing two deaths and several injuries. Only several days later, on 19 August, troops from the Worcestershire Regiment intervened in a riot by striking railway workers at Llanelli in South Wales – an incident which likewise saw two workers killed and many more injured. Both tragedies appeared to illustrate that the moderating strategy of General Macready and the Metropolitan Police was still far from easily replicable by provincial authorities, while also pointing to the general gravity of this unprecedented situation.

As a railway strike threatened to paralyse the entire country, affected areas passed into the state of quasi-martial law Macready had once bluffed about, with Churchill instructing all local authorities that armed soldiers were in charge of protecting railroads and strikebreaking labour and that 'the Army regulation which required a requisition for troops from the civil authority was suspended'.[26] There were few signs that the unrest would be receding any time soon and 1912 began with a winter of discontent which saw the Miners' Federation inch ever closer to declaring a strike over the issue of minimum wages.[27]

An indication that home-grown socialist agitation enjoyed a privileged position on the Home Office's list of security threats came on 15 January when Assistant Commissioner Macnaghten forwarded Charles E. Troup, Permanent Under-Secretary at the Home Office, a copy of the latest issue of *The Syndicalist*. This was the monthly organ of the recently formed Industrial Syndicalist Education League,[28] whose chairman – the eloquent and unabashedly radical Tom Mann[29] – had been on the authorities' radar ever since his active involvement in the 1911 Liverpool transport strike.[30] The Permanent Under-Secretary found the publication interesting, going so far as to praise one of the articles, 'a history, from the syndicalist standpoint... of the Italian railway question' as 'probably substantially true'.[31] The only potential for subversion came from a seemingly theoretical discussion on industrial sabotage and an 'open letter to British soldiers' – the latter a heartfelt appeal to non-violence which had first appeared at the height of the 1911 agitation in the Liverpool-based *Irish Worker*. It began:

Men! Comrades! Brothers!

You are in the Army.

So are We. You in the Army of Destruction. We in the Industrial, or Army of Construction.

We work at mine, mill, forge, factory, or dock, &c., producing and transporting all the goods, clothing, stuffs, &c., which make it possible for people to live.

You are Working Men's Sons.

When We go on Strike to better Our lot, which is the lot also of Your Fathers, Mothers, Brothers, and Sisters, YOU are called upon by your officers to MURDER US.

Don't do it!

You know how it happens — always has happened.

We stand out as long as we can. Then one of our (and your) irresponsible Brothers, goaded by the sight and thought of his and his loved ones' misery and hunger, commits a crime on property. Immediately you are ordered to Murder Us, as You did at Mitchelstown, at Featherstone, at Belfast.

Don't You know that when You are out of the colours, and become a "Civy" [sic] again, that You, like Us, may be on Strike, and You, like Us, be liable to be Murdered by other soldiers.

Boys, Don't Do It!

"Thou Shalt Not Kill," says the Book.

Don't Forget That![32]

Despite reading it as a 'direct incitement to mutiny', Troup thought the piece on sabotage was the more insidious given its 'calculated [attempt] to suggest to English workmen the commission of acts of sabotage', but did not ultimately see any 'possibility of taking action on this paper [unless] in [the] future Mr. Mann should go further and say what he means more plainly'.[33]

Mann did not need to go any further after on 25 February 1911 a young railwayman by the name of Frederick Crowsley took the train from Willesden to Aldershot, distributing some three hundred copies of the *Syndicalist*'s open letter among the soldiers there before being seized by military police.[34] Subsequently charged with 'maliciously... [endeavouring] to seduce... persons serving in his Majesty's forces... from his or their duty and allegiance to his Majesty'[35] under the Incitement to Mutiny Act of 1797 – the first time in more than a hundred years the Act had been invoked[36] – Crowsley was released on bail to await trial.

Less than two weeks later, the printers of *The Syndicalist*, the brothers Benjamin and Charles Buck,[37] along with the paper's publisher-editor Guy Bowman[38] were also arrested at their printing shop in Walthamstow and charged with the same felony of incitement to mutiny.[39] The next logical step for authorities was to apprehend Mann himself, who was in Manchester on a speaking tour. Although he could not be held legally responsible for the material published in *The Syndicalist*, being only the chairman of the organization sponsoring the publication, Mann's predilection for frank talk soon gave the Home Office all the ammunition it needed.

Addressing a meeting of the Workers' Union group at Pendleton Town Hall in Salford on 14 March, Mann did not shy away from discussing the recent arrests of his associates and, as a plain-clothes policeman in attendance later testified in court, 'took up a [copy of] the "Syndicalist" and read out the first

8. Tom Mann. ca. 1913 (Library of Congress, Prints & Photographs Division).

three passages of the "Open Letter to Soldiers" [saying that] he was pleased to take responsibility for that'.[40] What seems to have really sealed his fate, however, is the fact that Mann personally helped distribute copies of the incriminating paper in the building's lobby after the talk, something which could easily be construed as active propaganda under the terms of the Mutiny Act. He was arrested six days later and tried in early April on the same charges as Bowman and the Bucks (who had already been found guilty on 22 March and given sentences of nine and six months' hard labour respectively).[41]

Despite some divided opinion at the Home Office over the need to prosecute – one senior secretary thought Mann's words were 'not likely to spread disaffection among the lieges [and] scarcely [demanded] a case for prosecution'[42] – and the presiding judge's own reluctance to find him guilty,[43] Mann's refusal to seek legal counsel, his insistence that 'I did not publish the letter, but I do not differ from the letter,'[44] as well as his general notoriety all worked against him. He was found guilty of felony and given six months in the second division.

The outrage over the government's role in the *Syndicalist* prosecutions in left-wing and labour circles was manifested very early on – with Labourites like George Lansbury and Radicals like Josiah Wedgwood speaking against it in Parliament – and only further exacerbated when on 18 June Frederick Crowsley was given an equally harsh sentence of four months with hard labour for his refusal to recant and promise he would not recidivate.[45] By this time, however, Reginald McKenna, the new Home Secretary (a Liberal Imperialist in the Asquithian mould) had already been forced to concede not only to the undue harshness of the sentences, but also to the weakness of the prosecution's case against the four men.

The first issue which spoke to the unfeasibility of consistently enforcing the Mutiny Act in this way was, in the words of George Lansbury, the double standard involved in taking 'proceedings against [Crowsley et al.] for asking men not to attack their fellow men and no proceedings... against the... Member for Dublin University,'[46] Edward Carson, who at the time was engaged in recruiting and drilling his paramilitary Ulster Volunteers. The second issue was that prominent left-wingers found it exceedingly easy not only to repeat the message of 'An Open Letter' without fear of arrest, but to amplify it as well.

Thus, for example, on 31 March the Labour MP Victor Grayson told an audience of workers in Wigan to not be 'bamboozled' by the recently passed Minimum Wage Bill, which had successfully neutralized the miners' strike, and to 'organize yourselves into one solid phalanx and pull down the wretched prison they put [Tom Mann] in'.[47] Equally, Keir Hardie, at a May Day demonstration in

Hyde Park, declared, 'I say not only don't shoot, but don't enlist... [The] crime of shooting a German workman, who is also your comrade, is just as great as shooting a British workman here.'[48]

Following consultations with Judge Bankes and the Attorney-General, McKenna urged the king on 29 March to use his royal prerogative of mercy in order to reduce the Buck brothers' sentence to a month each in the second division.[49] On 20 May Mann and Bowman also received a mitigation of their sentences 'in view of the fact that this is [their] first breach... of the provisions of a Statute under which it has not been necessary to prosecute for a very considerable period of time.'[50] Crowsley, whose excessive sentence had shocked even the Home Office,[51] was similarly favoured a week after his trial and ended up serving only one month in the third division.

The government's backtracking may have marked a recognition of the fact that it could not hope to simply throw the book at all forms of seditious talk without risking the credibility of its position on home-grown political crime (namely that there wasn't any) or the alienation of its failing but still substantial support within the labour movement. It did not, however, suggest a less suspicious attitude towards high-profile socialist agitators – Mann continued to be kept under surveillance long after his release[52]– or a willingness to repudiate the Mutiny Act, which in the 1920s became 'an important weapon in the response to the rise of communism.'[53] By the end of the Edwardian decade, however, the establishment's new 'enemy within' was no longer relegated to radical socialist circles or the derelict tenements of industrial areas; it could be found in the respectable middle-class neighborhoods of London, Manchester, Birmingham and other British metropolises.

CHAPTER 15

# 'Suffrage forces in the field'[1]

On the afternoon of 23 October 1906 a group of roughly sixty women began making their way towards the Houses of Parliament, where, thanks to a timely wire from a 'plain clothes man' watching their movements, a contingent of uniformed officers from the nearby Cannon Row police station had been posted to 'strengthen the approaches'.[2] Initially the women – all supporters of Emmeline Pankhurst's Women's Social and Political Union[3] – expressed only the wish to petition MPs with the 'usual request to grant women the vote that session',[4] but once the Liberal whip confirmed what everyone in attendance already knew, namely that the newly installed Prime Minister, Henry Campbell-Bannerman, had no intention of considering female enfranchisement 'during this Parliament or at any future time',[5] things took a decidedly more animated turn.

Seizing on the propaganda value of the occasion, Mary Gawthorpe, one of the twenty women allowed inside the Central Lobby, climbed on top of the armchair next to the stern-faced statue of the earl of Iddesleigh and began addressing the crowd 'viz. Votes for Women, Votes for Freedom, We are slaves etc.,' as Chief Inspector Charles Scantlebury, head of police in the House of Commons, dismissively put it in his report.[6]

Gawthorpe was immediately pulled off her makeshift platform and, along with her comrades, discourteously removed to Old Palace Yard, where 'the poorer women who had come up from the East End' had been standing around for hours, waiting for news.[7] The sudden commotion revitalized the combative spirit of the 'suffragettes' – an epithet coined by the *Daily Mail* which the WSPU had been quick to reclaim[8] – and many began forming human chains around the 'ringleaders' in order to protect them from police.

Intense scuffles with reinforced numbers of increasingly brutish constables ensued and by the early hours of the evening ten of the women – Annie Cobden-Sanderson (daughter of Richard Cobden), Annie Kenney,[9] Adela Pankhurst and Dora Montefiore among them – were taken into custody and charged with 'using threatening and abusive words and behaviour with intent to provoke a breach of the peace'.[10] All of them refused to be bound over in the sum of £5, denying the magistrate's 'right to try their case… because they had no vote and consequently no voice in making the laws', opting instead to serve a sentence of two months in Holloway gaol.[11]

This incident did not mark the first example of the tactics militant suffragettes were to become notorious for during the Edwardian years. In October 1905, for example, Annie Kenney and Christabel Pankhurst[12] had launched the WSPU's strategy of hijacking public events by heckling Sir Edward Grey's address at the Free Trade Hall in Manchester and assaulting policemen in order to elicit arrest. This had been followed a few months later, in March 1906, by a sit-in of about thirty women in front of 10 Downing Street, during which Annie Kenney had managed to scale the prime minister's car before being arrested.[13]

Increasingly such tactics appeared – to proponents as well as detractors – able to put women's suffrage in the limelight far better than the usual pacifist methods. In an open letter to *The Times*, the leader of the strictly constitutional National Union of Women's Suffrage Societies (NUWSS), Millicent Garrett Fawcett, conceded that the suffragettes' actions in Westminster 'far from having injured the movement... have done more during the last twelve months to bring it within the region of practical politics than we have been able to accomplish in the same number of years'.[14] Conservative and Liberal newspapers alike continued to rail against 'frantic women' and 'shrieking sisters',[15] but to a public increasingly receptive to some notion of extending the franchise, the embarrassing spectacle of policemen roughing up and arresting a group of mostly 'respectable' ladies (some of advanced years) had gone a step too far.

Asked in the House of Commons by Keir Hardie to 'secure [the] immediate release' of the ten convicted suffragettes, Home Secretary Herbert Gladstone initially insisted he could not 'interfere with the sentences',[16] backtracking only a month later when the women were suddenly discharged from Holloway to the acclaim of sympathizers (who then celebrated their release with a festive dinner at the Savoy Hotel).[17] Within a matter of weeks, a wave of new volunteers and financial contributions emboldened the WSPU even further[18] and in early December a new series of protests erupted in the Central Lobby of Parliament, humiliating the new Liberal cabinet once again and demonstrating the police's continued unpreparedness.[19] The stage was set for an increasingly acrimonious and drawn-out confrontation between militants and authorities.

The WSPU's strategy for 1907 was revealed on 13 February at Caxton Hall in Westminster with the first of a series of 'Women's Parliaments'. Vociferously decrying the inaction of the 'men's Parliament', suffragettes from across the country formally condemned the government's continued shunning of female suffrage and adopted a resolution to be urgently delivered in person to the Prime Minister. A group, this time of three to four hundred suffragettes, then attempted to force an entry into the House of Commons before being confronted by a number of constables as well as mounted police, who, finding the women were 'very determined… were compelled to use corresponding force to prevent an entrance to Parliament being effected'.[20]

The scuffle went on into the evening, leading to grotesque scenes of armed men on horseback charging into a scattering crowd of already disarrayed and bruised women – a spectacle not witnessed in the capital since Bloody Sunday and made all the worse by the police's subsequent insistence that 'no brutality or unnecessary violence' had been used.[21] The significance of the event was certainly not lost on Emmeline Pankhurst, who later observed, somewhat cynically, that 'the [February] raid… gave the [WSPU] an enormous amount of publicity, on the whole, favourable publicity'.[22]

A total of fifty-six women, as well as two men, were arrested on charges of 'disorderly conduct and resisting police'[23] and arraigned before Magistrate Bennett the following day at Westminster Police Court. Following the established pattern of choosing prison time over paying a fine, most of those arrested received sentences of up to three weeks in the first division of Holloway, where prisoners were allowed their own clothes and access to writing materials. As Christabel Pankhurst, arguably the mastermind behind the militant strategy and in many ways the de facto leader of the WSPU,[24] proclaimed from the dock: 'There can be no going back for us… and more will happen if we do not get justice.'[25]

On 8 March, a day after the trial, a new Women's Enfranchisement Bill introduced by W. H. Dickinson, the Liberal MP for St Pancras,[26] reached its second reading in the Commons, with the Prime Minister's nominal support no less. Justice seemed possible at last – indeed likely. As with previous legislative efforts of this kind, however, hostile elements on both sides of the floor proved too powerful to silence. Citing concerns about its undemocratic nature, which supposedly favored 'a small-minority of well-to-do women',[27] the leadership of the Liberal Party, encouraged by a growing anti-suffrage lobby,[28] proceeded to filibuster the Bill out of existence; by mid-March it was obvious the status quo had once again carried the day. With the Ladies' Gallery closed throughout the debates, the suffragettes' reaction to these developments was not immediately made obvious, but this soon changed with the holding of the second Women's Parliament on 20 March.

Once again, a resolution denouncing the government was adopted and entrusted to a deputation of volunteers to be delivered directly to the Prime Minister. Under the direction of Superintendent Wells, who was already convinced of an inevitable 'demonstration… should the Bill [fail]', the police – fifty

9. Christabel Pankhurst, ca. 1910 (Library of Congress, Prints & Photographs Division).

constables, five police sergeants and two inspectors in all – had already been posted outside Caxton Hall on orders from Commissioner Henry himself.[29] The women remained nonetheless defiant in their plan for a march on the House of Commons and refused to disperse, prompting Wells to instruct his men to 'break them up'.[30]

What ensued was largely a repeat of the events of 13 February if only on a more dramatic scale. Those women who managed to evade the cordon in front of Caxton Hall – including a pugnacious contingent of mill workers clad in traditional Lancashire clogs and shawls – eventually found their way to Parliament Square, where they were met by another 'considerable band of suffragettes', as well as by more than five hundred constables.[31] For the next three to four hours the women repeatedly tried to break through police lines only to find themselves 'taken round the waist and put back on the other side of the line again'.[32] By 10.00 p.m. Henry had realized the only way to completely disperse the remaining demonstrators, as well as the thousands of gaping onlookers, was to send in the mounted police, who subsequently proceeded to make short work of '[clearing] the thoroughfares around St. Stephens'.[33]

Despite the seventy-six arrests and the brutality of the confrontation – on the whole 'not so great as on… February 13'[34] – the 20 March demonstration ultimately failed in its intended purpose and suffered somewhat from the law of diminishing returns as far as publicity went; there were no more 'raids' on the House of Commons for the rest of the year. Scotland Yard was only just beginning to take the suffragettes seriously, however, as a report submitted on 11 April by Chief Inspector Walter Dew shows. In it, Dew describes his meeting with a certain Miss Meehan, whose recent letter to police had decried 'the annoyance caused… by the suffragettes' holding their meetings next door to her in Clement's Inn.[35] A remnant of the old Inns of Chancery that had been sold off for residential development in 1903, Clement's Inn was also the place where the WSPU had lately set up shop thanks to the generosity of recent converts to the cause Emmeline and Frederick Pethick-Lawrence.[36]

Although it does not contain any revelations beyond the fact that the suffragettes were not perhaps the quietest of neighbours, Dew's report does offer some valuable insight into how police authorities viewed the movement's potential for political violence during the incipient phase of its militancy. The main concern appeared to be that the WSPU's newfound support among the upper and middle classes enabled it to recruit an army of working-class foot soldiers in the poorer areas of the capital, a theory which, all things considered, proved hard to substantiate despite Dew's own conviction that it was 'quite correct'. Miss Meehan, whose grievances proved entirely domestic in nature, was for one unable to supply any 'information as to any persons hailing from East Ham… who have been paid to join… [and with] regards to the suggestion that regular drilling goes on in those offices [she explained] that what she means by this is that meetings are held and songs practised'.[37]

Despite the lack of evidence, however, Dew's suspicions were certainly convincing enough to land the suffragettes on Special Branch's radar, with DS Curry being tasked to keep 'casual and discreet observation' over Clement's Inn. Unsurprisingly, the intelligence obtainable through such methods proved of very limited value and much like Dew, Curry ultimately found it impossible to 'justify the conclusion that women of the lower order, with or without children, are drilled or receive instruction in connection with any organized procession of the suffragettes'.[38]

The WSPU leadership was, at any rate, far from contemplating class warfare in the spring of 1907 given Christabel's budding courtship of 'high society' ladies and stated hostility to the Labour Party. Over the following months militancy took a decidedly electoral turn. Hoping to humiliate the ruling Liberals, who faced a long string of by-elections, the Pankhursts took their 'suffrage forces in the field' to campaign assiduously for the 'defeat [of] Government candidates'[39] – a strategy which, on the whole, did not ultimately yield many results, as by the end of the year the Liberals had lost only three seats, all of them to Labour candidates.[40]

Occasionally, however, the suffragettes disturbed, or rather were seen to disturb, the expected outcome, as was the case in the Ashburton by-election of 17 January 1908. There the Liberal candidate, Charles Buxton, managed to snatch defeat from the jaws of victory by a difference of only 1,283 votes after a concentrated effort by several WSPU campaigners, including Emmeline Pankhurst herself, to 'beat the Government… as a message that women must have votes next year'.[41] Spotting a group of suffragettes on the night of the election, a band of young miners wearing the red rosettes of Gladstone's party jumped at the opportunity of retaliating against 'those women [who] did it', smashing up the local Conservative Club, but not before assaulting Mrs Pankhurst and her entourage, who subsequently had to be rescued from a near lynching by local police.

Emmeline later recalled how 'throughout all this disorder and probable crime, not a man was arrested, [in contrast] with the treatment given our women in London'[42] and what this incident serves to illustrate, besides the deep bitterness the WSPU – itself a house divided[43] – was capable of stirring up in intensely partisan communities, is precisely the steep difference between what constituted political violence and the traditional, occasionally egregious, violence which merely accompanied political events.

The culmination of the WSPU's 'mild' militancy phase came with the mass demonstration held on 21 June 1908 in Hyde Park which saw approximately thirty thousand suffragettes, including a delegation of French *féministes*, as well as an audience of anywhere between three to five hundred thousand people attend.[44] Despite the general public's ambivalence – 'not sympathetic... not opposed [but] simply indifferent', in the words of one WSPU organizer[45] – the gathering proved an unprecedented show of force for the partisans of woman suffrage, giving the lie to claims by Prime Minster Asquith (Campbell-Bannerman had resigned in April due to ill health) that most British women were simply 'watching with languid and imperturbable indifference the struggle for their own emancipation.'[46]

Taking inspiration from the legendary electoral reform demonstrations of the 1860s, the organizers of the Hyde Park event – the Pethick-Lawrences chief amongst them – were quick to appreciate the impact of public perception, arranging for no fewer than seven separate processions, each featuring for the first time the iconic white frock and purple-white-green sashes, thirty music bands, twenty platforms and nearly a hundred speakers. Except for a few isolated instances of jeering by groups of loutish youths 'who imagine that their cleverness is shown by guying whatever is going on',[47] supporters ultimately proved stronger than the hecklers, prompting even *The Times* to observe that while 'there may be various opinions as to what this demonstration has proved... there can be no differences as to its magnitude, its organization, and its success.'[48]

Asquith, however, remained unmoved, writing to Christabel immediately after the event that he had 'nothing to add' to earlier statements that any future electoral reform bill would not automatically include female enfranchisement, prompting the latter to retort that 'public meetings will have no effect in inducing the Government to grant votes to women, and... militant methods must again be resorted to.'[49] What this new wave of militancy might consist of was not yet clear, but on 30 June authorities received an early warning after one WSPU march on Parliament ended, in contrast to the events in Hyde Park, in a night of brutality, chaos and gridlock.

Angered at yet another unchallenged assault on their comrades by police, two suffragettes, Edith New and Mary Leigh, drove up to 10 Downing Street and proceeded to smash as many windows as possible, letting out a cry of 'Bombs next time!' as they were being dragged away to Cannon Row police station.[50] A pattern of ritualized vandalism was rapidly being established, but there is little indication that at this stage authorities perceived the WSPU as capable of anything more than colourful exploits.

The WSPU's thirteenth session of the Women's Parliament, held at Caxton Hall on the afternoon of 29 June 1909, did not promise to deliver anything out of the ordinary. The usual request for an audience with the Prime Minister received the latter's customary refusal and was followed by the obligatory march on the Houses of Parliament, a fact which must have loomed large even on the mind of Mrs Pankhurst herself, as she approached the line of policemen blocking the entrance to St Stephen's Hall – part of a force of three thousand officers sent to patrol the Houses of Parliament that day.[51] Presented by her 'old acquaintance' Inspector Scantlebury with an official copy of Asquith's refusal, the WSPU doyenne realized 'the old miserable business of refusing to leave, of being forced backward, and returning again and again until arrested, would have to be re-enacted'.[52]

It largely was, albeit without Pankhurst herself, who managed to get arrested right away for slapping Inspector James Jarvis in the face, or Asquith, who had already quietly absconded in a 'small motor car', accompanied by two Special Branch detectives.[53] The difference this time was that the suffragettes' attack on the state was no longer an angry afterthought, but an integral part of the militant process. Employing the 'time-honoured method' of window-breaking,[54] several WSPUers launched projectiles at the 'expensive plate-glass windows' of the Home Office, the Treasury, the Board of Education and the Admiralty before being overwhelmed by mounted police.[55] Whatever its intended purpose, the intensity of this new attack did not make the government more receptive to granting suffragette prisoners political status, which, of course, was technically impossible in a country where, in the words of Home Secretary Gladstone, 'political offences were not in any way recognised by the common law'.[56]

As the window-breakers soon realized, however, when the government could not be intimidated into doing the right thing, it could still be embarrassed into making significant concessions. After refusing to obey the rules imposed on second division prisoners at Holloway, the fourteen women charged with defacing government buildings on 29 June began a hunger strike and were released within a matter of days. The significance of the achievement was not lost on the WSPU leadership, with Christabel noting in a letter to Arthur Balfour that 'they will never in future be able to keep us in prison more than a few days, for we have now learnt our power to starve ourselves out of prison'.[57] By August hunger-striking was already the norm for imprisoned suffragettes, creating a sense of martyrdom of 'far greater magnitude' than that produced by mere imprisonment.[58]

\* \* \*

Surrounded by the tranquillity of the Kentish marshes, the Prime Minister spent the first weekend of September 1909 away from the looming budget crisis in Whitehall, in the company of family and friends. Here, in the imposing rooms of Lympne Castle, sumptuously restored by his brother-in-law Frank in the Arts and Crafts style, Asquith could forget all about the fear-mongering of tariff reformers and look forward to enjoying a round of golf – 'the only of our national games which I have habitually played'.[59] As he soon discovered, however, where the jeers and threats of Conservative grandees could not reach him, the slogans of militant suffragettes could.

Seizing on the rare chance of catching the Liberal leader out on a limb, far from his London praetorian guard, three WSPU 'shock troops' – Jessie Kenney, Elsie Howie and Vera Wentworth – descended on the village of Lympne on the morning of 5 September with the intention of giving 'old Squiff', as the drink-fond Asquith was popularly known, as rough a time as possible. Following him at all times, from morning prayer to golf course, the three women attempted to harass the Prime Minister at every opportunity, occasionally creating scenes of an almost slapstick absurdity. As Jessie Kenney later told the *Daily Mail*:

> Undetected we stood close to the clubhouse... and as the Prime Minister was descending the steps one of us sprang forward and caught hold of his arm... He tried to push her away, but she was too quick for him and caught hold of his collar... Mr. Asquith called Mr. Gladstone, who came rushing out... They... were trying to push us out, and we were endeavouring to get in. Blows were struck and Mr. Gladstone fought like a pugilist. [He] lunged out and we lunged out [until] we all came down the steps somehow... A man held us, and Mr. Asquith and Mr. Gladstone entered their car and drove away.[60]

Gladstone, however, was not amused, asking indignantly in a missive to his Permanent Under-Secretary, Charles Edward Troup,[61] on 9 September, 'Where did the Lympne gang come from?' and requesting that Henry be consulted on arranging a 'special police organization for containing suffragette violence'.[62] Such an organization already existed of course, but as Quinn's July report had made clear, suffragette violence still featured quite low on its list of priorities, ahead only of 'other duties'.

Change had to be initiated with yet another, this time more substantial, augmentation of Special Branch staff, even as finding a long-term strategy for containing the WSPU's insurrectionist tactics continued proving elusive. As Henry explained to Troup a couple of days later, countering the suffragettes' plans would require a 'considerable addition to Special Branch', adding also that '[in] view of the difficult nature of the duty, for tactical mistakes [to be made] by the police employed on it would only foster the agitation [and] we must employ men of experience'.[63] The Commissioner's proposed augmentation tentatively included two inspectors, eight sergeants and six constables, but due to the substantial cost involved (£3,000 per annum) and the uncertainty of where the money would come from,[64] it was not immediately approved. In the meantime, however, WSPU militants were already preparing their next coup.

On the afternoon of 17 September 1909 Asquith was on the Birmingham leg of his nationwide speaking tour in support of a controversial Liberal budget, accompanied by a retinue of seventy supporters and surrounded by 'precautions that might have sufficed to protect a Czar'.[65] Arriving shortly before dark at Bingley Hall, where almost nine thousand people were waiting for his speech, the Prime Minister noticed the huge building appeared to be preparing for a siege. At the request of the Home Secretary, who wished to 'make impossible the roof climbing and stone throwing performances [seen] at Birrell's Manchester meeting',[66] the Hall's glass-panelled roof had been covered in a makeshift tarpaulin armour, while two hundred stewards and six hundred policemen busied about its entrances making sure no gatecrashers or women[67] were allowed in.

At 7.30 p.m. Asquith made his grand entrance to resounding cheers and choruses of 'For he's a jolly good fellow' and began making the case for the so-called People's Budget as a 'landmark of a new age and a more noble and effective Liberalism'.[68] Outside, however, there were already signs of unrest. Two women, one armed with an axe, the other with a hammer, had leaped forward from the crowds, charging at police, while across the street, from the window of an apartment in King Alfred's Place, three other women were shouting anti-government slogans and throwing 'toy bombs' at the crowds below.[69]

This proved only a diversion. Unbeknownst to the policemen struggling with this first batch of agitators, two WSPU guerillas – Mary Leigh and Charlotte Marsh – climbed up the roof of a house in Cumberland Street (opposite Bingley Hall) and began flinging roof slates into the street, hitting the top of Asquith's brougham just as he was about to leave. While escaping completely unscathed, a final symbolic indignity was awaiting the Prime Minister at the train station, where around 10.30 p.m. two suffragettes, having managed to penetrate the heavily policed platform, threw stones at the official train, hitting only the unoccupied rear compartment. By midnight the tally of arrests stood at eight.

The scenes at Bingley Hall predictably outraged the political establishment across ideological lines and served to drive home the notion that suffragette militancy had reached a dangerous new stage of 'open violence [and] stone-throwing'.[70] Responding to the WSPU's critics in a letter to *The Times*, Christabel Pankhurst put the blame for 'the serious crisis which has arisen' squarely on the government and warned that it had 'wantonly provoked a revolution'.[71] Hyperbole notwithstanding, the Home Office was certainly more inclined than ever to regard the suffragette threat as a grave and pressing one. Although the new augmentation of Special Branch was fully implemented by late September,[72] its usefulness for containing the suffragettes was almost immediately thrown into question when approximately a week after the Birmingham fiasco, Margot Asquith received a letter warning her of the imminent danger posed to her husband's safety by a section of ultra-militant suffragettes.

The author of the letter, a certain Mrs Moore of south London, herself a member of the Women's Freedom League, had come to the conclusion that 'the physical force [party was] getting out of hand' and that the only way to avert an outrage against the Prime Minister was to inform authorities of her comrades' suspicious behaviour. As she explained to DI George Riley, 'at least five women' belonging to the WFL and the WSPU, whom she refused to name, had 'given expression to their intentions to commit acts of violence' and two in particular had even confessed to 'practising with a revolver… at… the shooting range at 92 Tottenham Court Road' (incidentally the same shooting range that Madan Lal Dhingra had been known to favour).[73]

Naturally, the knowledge that an assassination plot against the Prime Minister had only been uncovered thanks to a tip-off from a conscientious suffragette did not bode well at the Home Office. Gladstone feared that 'if things go on as they are, something very bad will happen',[74] while Troup cautioned that 'we have in fact prima facie grounds for believing… that there is something nearly amounting to a conspiracy to murder', wondering whether 'all other precautions having been taken', the time had not come to forcibly remove the commonplace 'pickets at the entrance to the House of Commons… [regardless of] whether [it was] legal or illegal'.[75] In the end, the Permanent Secretary advised against the measure, but not out of any concern for its legality:

> But the serious matter is that [if the pickets were removed] we should have to make known the facts leading us to believe that there is a conspiracy to

murder the P.M. The prominence which would be given to this in the Press would probably act on the minds of these half insane women, and might suggest effectively the commission of the very act which we wish to prevent. Moreover, the removal of the pickets... would make them furious and more ready to commit such a crime... On the whole, therefore... the safer course is to leave the pickets alone for the present and redouble the police precautions for the remainder of the Session.[76]

Despite such serious misgivings and the government's own increasingly harsh treatment of imprisoned suffragettes, which by then included forced feeding,[77] the rest of 1909 was marked only by a string of minor incidents of which the most flagrant involved a bottle being chucked into Asquith's empty car and the attempted horse-whipping of Winston Churchill in Bristol by a young female socialite with suffragist sympathies.[78] Things appeared to be slowly heading for another deadlock, when on 30 November the House of Lords soundly rejected the proposed budget 350 votes to seventy-five, finally achieving what the suffragettes had always been hoping for – an end to the Liberal majority.

The Liberals' Pyrrhic victory at the polls in early 1910, which saw them gain a mandate for passing the budget while losing a third of their seats to (mostly) Conservative-Unionist candidates, resulted in a new Irish Nationalist- and Labour-propped minority government with Churchill as the new Home Secretary (Gladstone having been offered the governorship of the newly formed Union of South Africa). Nevertheless, there were encouraging signs for the partisans of female enfranchisement. In early January the Conservative peer Victor Bulwer-Lytton, whose sister Constance had recently made headlines as one of the WSPU's most tireless campaigners, together with the left-wing journalist Henry Noel Brailsford, whose wife Jane was also a committed suffragette, joined forces to form a non-aligned conciliation committee in order to devise a women's suffrage bill acceptable to MPs of all parties.

The bill eventually agreed upon by the committee's fifty-five members (twenty-five Liberals, seventeen Conservatives, six Irish Nationalists, six Labourites and Brailsford) proposed to enfranchise the roughly one million women who owned a household for which they were solely responsible, or 'a ten-pound occupation qualification, within the meaning of the Representation of the People Act 1884'.[79] This was certainly in line with the WSPU's conservative suffragism, which sought to extend the franchise only to women fulfilling the qualifications of male voters, and unlike Dickinson's Bill of 1907, the Conciliation Bill (as it came to be known) seemed to have genuine across-the-board appeal. On 15 February 1910, Asquith received an open letter from WFL and WSPU representatives declaring that both organizations had 'taken the first step towards a truce by deciding to refrain from a militant protest till the Government has had a fair opportunity of stating its intentions'.[80]

The peace did not remain in pristine condition for long and as the year wore on, the Liberal triumvirate of Asquith, Lloyd George and Churchill began making its opposition to the Conciliation Bill increasingly vocal. By autumn 1910 all hope that the Conciliation Bill might become law was extinguished. Rejected both by Lloyd George and Churchill as 'anti-democratic' and pro-Conservative, the Bill had passed its Second Reading in the Commons on 12 July by a vote of 299 to 189 only to then be 'referred to a Committee of the whole House' and thus allowed to quietly expire.[81] On 18 November Asquith confirmed that the new battle with the Lords would be decided at the polls before the end of the year. The government, it was argued, had more pressing business to attend to in its final days than votes for women.

The police had been expecting 'militant action… in connection with the [Conciliation] Bill' for some time, but given the line pursued by Troup and Gladstone (that 'leaving the pickets alone' would pre-empt criticism of the police and deter any would-be terrorists) Henry had decided to instruct his superintendents to follow a policy of quasi-appeasement towards any future demonstrators. As the Commissioner explained in a memorandum, suffragettes positioned to 'cause annoyance' to cabinet ministers were to 'be cautioned… and… requested to depart… [and if] they do not leave they are to be further informed that Police… cannot allow them to remain'. Only if such warnings went unheeded, Henry added, 'they may be arrested… if possible by an Inspector or Sergeant'.[82]

That strategy failed spectacularly on 18 November when WSPU deputations once again departed from Caxton Hall for the Houses of Parliament in order to protest the sinking of the Conciliation Bill. Although the first group of twelve women, which included Mrs Pankhurst, was allowed to pass through police cordons and 'stand just outside the entrance to the House',[83] all subsequent demonstrators were kept strictly at bay and treated with an increasingly egregious amount of violence. The elderly Georgiana Solomon, devoted WSPU militant and widow of the influential Cape politician Saul Solomon, later recalled in a letter to Churchill:

> I saw several of our members flung repeatedly, like myself, into the crowd rendered hostile by well dressed men in plain clothes recognised as policemen. [One] policeman made a rush at me… held and violently shook me while his helpers twirled round my arms as if to drag them from their sockets. Still worse, another caught me by the shoulders and mercilessly pressed

his heavy weight upon my back, crushing me down... I was [also] gripped by the breast... [and] I am medically informed that... women of an age to be my daughters were also assaulted in this and other repellant and equally cruel ways.[84]

As more suffragettes continued arriving with orders not to retreat,[85] the belligerence of the mob and law enforcement alike only intensified, leading to multiple women being attacked and molested, sometimes by uniformed policemen. By 6.00 p.m. 116 women and three men had been arrested. A picture snapped by a *Daily Mirror* photographer, which appeared on the paper's cover page the following day under the headline 'Black Friday', seemed to sum up with ferocious precision the inhumanity of the previous day. It showed the figure of Ada Wright, a leading WSPU member, curled up on the ground while holding a white handkerchief to her face. On her right a uniformed policeman is seen bending over and shouting something at her, while on her left a man with a silk topper is hopelessly trying to shoulder off the intervention of another policeman – all under the gleeful stare of a frolicking cloth-capped youth.

Authorities clandestinely attempted to suppress copies of the *Daily Mirror* issue and ordered all negatives of the photo destroyed,[86] but the truth about the events of 18 November was irrevocably beginning to emerge. The only way to avert a public airing of all the abhorrent details (and consequently a pre-election public embarrassment) was to drop all charges against the arrested women, which Churchill promptly did on 19 November, all the while insisting on his innocence in the matter. The accusation made by suffragettes and their sympathizers that the government had issued orders to needlessly delay arrests was dismissed as inaccurate; the Home Secretary's orders had been to arrest 'as soon as any defiance of the Law had been committed', but Henry had 'misunderstood' this instruction on account of the appeasing policy previously pursued by Gladstone.[87]

The Commissioner admitted to the mistake in internal correspondence, explaining in a memo to the Home Office that he had 'informed [Churchill] that it was too late... to instruct the men [that] arrests [were] to be effected as soon as possible... as they were already out on the streets'.[88] Publicly, however, Henry was adamant that police had acted with 'restraint and moderation', dismissing firsthand testimonies, which women were only reluctantly beginning to come forward with, as 'little more than hysterical complaints of violence'. He conceded that 'there may be grounds for the belief... that many [demonstrators] were indecently handled', but insisted that there was 'no foundation for the suggestion that this was done by members of the Police Force dressed in ordinary clothes'. Plain-clothes men, including Special Branch officers, had indeed been in attendance, but they had been 'below a dozen' and had taken 'no part in arresting or in restraining demonstrators'.[89]

A host of people came to the defence of the suffragettes, from the London surgeon who described in a letter to *The Daily Telegraph* how women had been 'pushed about in every direction by the police [and] tortured in other nameless ways',[90] to H. N. Brailsford, whose memorandum outlined in great detail (drawing on no fewer than 135 witness statements) 'the treatment of the women's deputation by the Police', urging the Home Office to open a public inquiry into the matter.[91] The loudness of the government's protestations and the incessant victim blaming – 'the women', Churchill explained in Parliament, 'work themselves into a high state of hysteria [and] expose themselves to rough horseplay at the hands of an unsympathetic crowd'[92] – eventually drowned out the critics, however. By mid-December the general election superseded all other political issues on the national stage.

The WSPU and WFL leadership were content to see the dropping of charges as a partial victory against 'the policy of persecution'[93] and resume once more the electoral struggle against the Liberal machine. The Bill, they believed, was not quite dead yet.[94] The truce went on for another year, but authorities were by no means preparing for peace and it is telling that the very first decision taken by Henry after the events of Black Friday was to draft a request for an augmentation of the Mounted Branch of the Metropolitan Police, which he felt 'the events of the past year' completely justified. Experience, he noted, 'shows that mounted men suitably employed are as effective as a much larger number of foot Constables in controlling a crowd'.[95]

By late 1911, thanks to the Liberals' sabotage of yet another Conciliation Bill, the return of suffrage militancy 'on a larger scale than on previous occasions'[96] seemed inevitable. The Commissioner had already begun preparing his strategy as early as January when in a letter to Churchill he outlined – '[so] that the Secretary of State should know in advance the lines upon which I propose to act' – what he believed to be the suffragettes' main tactic, namely that of eliciting public sympathy by deliberately provoking the police. 'The least embarrassing course', Henry argued, 'will be for the police not to arrest too soon or defer arresting too long.'[97]

Clarifications were added a month later after the Commissioner requested the advice of Wontner and Sons, solicitors to the Metropolitan Police, who suggested that police would do well to 'abstain from roughness' and make arrests only in 'cases of actual damage to property or serious assault [and always] under the direct instructions of an Inspector'.[98] Henry accepted the gist of the recommendations and submitted the revised set of instructions to the Home Secretary at the end of February. The main course of action had in fact changed very little, the only additions being Churchill's insistence on speedy arrests ('one rush, one arrest') and the fact that Superintendent Wells, the man in charge of protecting Parliament Square, had to officially 'require police under his orders to act with the utmost moderation'.[99] As Troup resentfully noted, 'the women will find something to complain of in any conceivable course that may be adopted'.[100]

The real change came with the increased surveillance of suffragette meetings – though barred from holding membership, men were allowed to attend WSPU at-homes and formal events – which gave authorities the advantage of knowing well in advance about any future demonstrations. In early November alone, as the Conciliation Bill crisis was reaching a breaking point, at least three individual reports were submitted to Superintendent Quinn,[101] including one on the 9 November meeting at Steinway Hall where Christabel Pankhurst announced that in twelve days a deputation would be sent 'to the Prime Minister [and] the Chancellor of the Exchequer'.[102]

The demonstration on 21 November would have been a tedious repeat of previous such events if not for the intransigence of the WSPU's ultra-militant fringe, which, independent of the march on Parliament, but with the consent of Christabel and her mother, met around 7.00 p.m. at 156 Charing Cross to unleash a campaign of vandalism along the Strand and the surrounding area. Among their targets were buildings belonging to the government and other perceived enemies (viz. the Home Office, Somerset House, the National Liberal Club, the headquarters of the *Daily Mail* and *Daily News*), but also buildings with little or no political significance like the Westminster Palace Hotel or an Aerated Bread Company tea shop.

The window-breakers were all 'led off... very quietly... [with] no rough usage... [or] struggling' – as the actress Kate Parry Frye later recalled in her diary[103]– with the same restraint shown at the Houses of Parliament where police were speedily arresting the women attempting to break through security cordons and bringing them to the Cannon Row police station. Much to Troup's surprise the suffragettes had in fact little to complain about and the former might have reasonably believed the Home Office had won this round. For the WSPU, however, the propaganda value of the events in the Strand was even greater than that of Black Friday. With the truce gone the way of the Conciliation Bill, 'the argument of the broken pane of glass' became 'the most valuable argument in modern politics'.[104]

## CHAPTER 16

# The waning of militancy and the rise of counter-espionage

THE wave of industrial protest which arguably peaked in intensity with the short-lived national coal strike in January continued rippling through the rest of 1912, occasionally with violent consequences. At Rotherhithe, for example, tensions occasioned by a dockers' strike led to Metropolitan Police constables charging into a hostile crowd on the night of 11 June, striking 'right and left with their [rolled-up] capes in a brutal way and without discrimination'.[1]

Such sporadic flare-ups notwithstanding, the latter part of the year saw suffragette militancy quickly rise to the status of foremost domestic security threat. March saw a redoubled campaign of window-smashing and occasional arson, a police raid on Clement's Inn, the arrest and imprisonment of Emmeline Pankhurst and the Pethick-Lawrences on charges of conspiracy, the flight of Christabel to Paris in order to avoid the same fate, as well as an ever increasing torrent of public opprobrium.[2] Following this series of dramatic events, the WSPU entered a new phase in its evolution; one marked by pure hostility to anything supportive of the status quo.

The first major sign of this shift came in mid-July with two alarming incidents involving senior government figures. The first occurred on the evening of 13 July when two 'respectably dressed' suffragettes were apprehended in the vicinity of the Oxfordshire residence of Lewis Harcourt, Colonial Secretary and inveterate opponent of female enfranchisement.[3] While one of the women managed to escape police capture, her accomplice, Helen Craggs (the daughter of a well-to-do chartered accountant), was promptly taken into custody along with a suspicious basket containing '[two boxes] of matches, four tapers, twelve fire-lighters… nine pick-locks… an electric torch [and] a glass cutter'.[4] Pleading guilty to attempted arson, Craggs professed to have 'taken part in every peaceful method of propaganda and petition [to] no avail,' before deciding to do 'something drastic'.[5]

That same impulse manifested itself only five days later in Dublin during an official visit by Asquith, when the battle-hardened Mary Leigh, who had 'pioneered' window-breaking over four years before, threw an axe at the ministerial carriage as it passed through Princes Street, failing to do any real damage other than leaving John Redmond with 'a nasty cut on the eye'.[6] Fleeing the scene, Leigh and three other women managed to sneak inside the Theatre Royal later that day, just as Asquith was preparing to give a speech on Ulster and Home Rule, setting fire to a theatre box during the intermission. No one was hurt and the women were all taken into custody, but Leigh (tried shortly after and given five years' penal servitude) managed, much like her comrade Helen Craggs, to secure an early release and pardon by going on a hunger strike.[7]

The government's willingness to release committed hunger-strikers regardless of the severity of their offences did not, however, make militant suffragettes any less likely to resort to violence. This was partly due to the cabinet's sustained opposition to the Conciliation Bill and the continued use of forced feeding – made all the more egregious by Home Secretary McKenna's insistence that 'no prisoners are now being forcibly fed'[8] – but a more important reason was the polarizing effect the new militancy was having on the WSPU leadership.

After meeting with her mother and the Pethick-Lawrences (recently released from prison after a brief hunger strike) in Boulogne-sur-Mer in July, Christabel made it abundantly clear that she was not prepared to negotiate her authority over the WSPU, and that she expected complete and unquestioning support on the policy of violence against property and government figures. Emmeline was prepared to support her brash and charismatic daughter, as she had many times in the past, but for Frederick and his wife it was all too much. As the former recalled in his autobiography:

> I took the view that the window-smashing raid had aroused a new popular opposition… and that therefore before it was repeated… there was need for a sustained educational campaign to make the public understand the reasons for such extreme courses… Christabel took the view that such popular opposition… was not essentially different from that which had over and over again manifested itself when other new forms of militancy had been inaugurated, and that the right method of overcoming it was to repeat and intensify the attack in early autumn.[9]

Unable to accept the new orthodoxy, the Pethick-Lawrences nonetheless refused to publicly harm the movement to which they had devoted so much time, energy and funds, choosing to go out with a whimper instead of a bang. In early October the Pankhursts moved the WSPU to new offices in Lincoln's Inn and began publishing a new official weekly entitled *The Suffragette*. On 17 October the purge of the Pethick-Lawrences was formally announced in a meeting at Albert Hall and while the announcement might have raised a few eyebrows, no actual opposition materialized. There was no time for petty squabbling when suffragettes had 'a great mission – the greatest mission the world has ever known' to attend to.[10] In her most fervent call to arms yet, Emmeline Pankhurst urged her 'forces in the field' to register their opposition to the government by all available means and to relentlessly 'attack the secret idol of property'.[11]

Support among the rank-and-file proved more or less unanimous, but outside Lincoln's Inn there was little enthusiasm for Mrs Pankhurst's bellicose tone. For constitutional suffragists the militants' new campaign of violence was largely to blame for the continued failure of the Conciliation Bill,[12] while for the public at large the anti-political antics of the WSPU registered only as an increasingly intolerable nuisance. When, for example, a group of suffragettes attempted to heckle Lloyd George during a formal event in his native Llanystumdwy on 21 September, the crowd came close to lynching the women, 'their clothing being torn and hair being dragged'.[13] Although the incident revitalized Welsh suffragism,[14] the WSPU took it as an unpardonable affront, using personal testimonies, press extracts and traditional anti-Welsh stereotypes to depict the 'tribe of Llanystumdwy' as a mass of bloodthirsty barbarians under the spell of a 'medicine man' Lloyd George.[15]

The WSPU's exit from mainstream politics was finalized in late November at the Bow and Bromley by-election which saw the suffrage reform candidate, Labour's George Lansbury – who had managed to earn Christabel's trust despite his socialism – run a highly energetic campaign, but lose the race to the Unionist candidate by a significant margin.[16] For Christabel the message was clear: 'By their rejection of [Lansbury] the majority of the electors [have] ordered women to work out their own political salvation.'[17] Just what that work entailed was revealed only a couple of days later, on the evening of 26 November, when WSPU militants in London, Nottingham, Ilkeston, Birmingham, Manchester and Newcastle furtively damaged scores of postboxes by pouring black ink, paraffin and 'various acids' into them and, in some cases, attempting (unsuccessfully) to set them on fire.[18]

Although the nature and scale of the damage made the operation more obnoxious than outrageous, the terms in which *The Suffragette* justified it left no room for doubt as to its intended goal. 'The Suffragists who have been burning and otherwise destroying letters', the paper proclaimed, 'have been doing this… [so as] to make the electors and the Government so uncomfortable that, in order to put an end to the nuisance, they will give women the vote.'[19]

Initially, authorities were inclined to treat this new campaign of coercion as merely another episodic flare-up that would eventually run out of steam. When in early December a Special Branch report on a WSPU meeting held at the London Opera House a day earlier reached Troup's desk at the Home Office, the Permanent Under-Secretary agreed with McKenna that even though 'there is plenty of incitement to break the law in the speeches... it is no use taking any notice of it.'[20] That attitude remained unchanged even a week later when a speech at a meeting in Wimbledon urged militants to attend the 'political meetings [of] Cabinet Ministers [in order to] find out for yourselves what an easy matter is their destruction,'[21] or after Marie Naylor, one of the WSPU's 'best London speakers,'[22] declared at a meeting on 20 December that 'the Irish... blew up Clerkenwell Prison. That is the kind of thing you want to do.'[23]

Police reports on various WSPU meetings, as well as the occasional anonymous tip-off,[24] continued to be dismissed as unimportant at the Home Office all throughout January 1913,[25] but at the end of the month things finally came to a boil with a campaign of wanton destruction that went beyond mere mailbox vandalism. Flammable letters, explosive envelopes addressed to government figures, the defacing of golf greens with acid, a catapult used to launch clay pigeons from the top deck of a London bus, the burning down of an orchid house at Kew and a refreshment kiosk in Regent's Park, the cutting of telephone and telegraph wires, as well as some old-fashioned window-breaking[26] – all were unleashed in a nationwide two-week blitzkrieg at the beginning of February. The validity of threats uttered a month earlier was no longer in question.

The WSPU's most triumphant feat, however, came on the morning of 18 February when several militants set off a bomb inside the house Lloyd George was having built in Walton Heath, Surrey, doing significant material damage to the premises. As an anonymous letter from one of the bombers (none of whom were ever caught) explained, the date and time had been carefully selected so as to avoid any threat to life and limb.[27] To the WSPU leadership this spectacular coup against the hated Welsh Goat (as the promiscuous Lloyd George was widely known) marked the dawn of a genuine uprising. Speaking in Cardiff the next day, Emmeline Pankhurst compared the emerging 'women's civil war' to the ongoing Mexican Revolution: 'In Mexico', she explained, 'all the members of the Ministry... [have] been arrested and imprisoned. We have not yet... got every member of the present Liberal Ministry into prison, but we have blown up the Chancellor of the Exchequer's house.' Amidst uproarious cheers and chaotic interruptions she continued by praising the actions of the previous couple of weeks as 'a very successful piece of guerilla warfare', adding that 'we are firmly convinced... that this is the only way of creating an intolerable situation' before proclaiming defiantly that 'I have advised, I have incited, [and] I have conspired.'[28]

Although the speech rehashed all 'the usual incitements to commit outrages'[29] that Mrs Pankhurst was already notorious for, the image of a high-profile political agitator boasting with impunity of having advised and incited an outrage on a senior member of the cabinet proved too difficult to ignore for the Home Office. On 24 February Emmeline was arrested and charged at the Epsom Police Court under the terms of the Malicious Damages Act of 1861 with incitement to arson. Having refused bail, she was sent to Holloway prison to await trial, but was released almost immediately after going on hunger strike. The wheels of a new crackdown on the WSPU, however, were already in motion.

Writing to the Home Secretary on 2 March, the Postmaster General, Herbert Samuel, pointed out that *The Suffragette*, as the official organ of the Union, was partly responsible for the recent spate of outrages against the Post Office, and asked at the same time whether the right moment had 'not come for the publishers and printers of this paper and for the Union to be prosecuted for illegal conspiracy'. Suffragettes might have been difficult to charge, but 'the same considerations do not apply to the printers'.[30]

Samuel's proposal was forwarded to the Director of Public Prosecutions and the Attorney-General the following day although authorities were in no hurry to invoke the full force of the law just yet. There remained first of all the matter of forced feeding, which tended to make a mockery of the whole penal system while encouraging whatever sympathy remained for the militants in progressive-liberal circles. Secondly, there was also the issue of the suffragettes' public meetings, which, ever since the renewal of militancy, tended to draw the ire of the general public, or rather those sections of the public who made it a sport out of 'surrounding a little band of… women… [to] howl and yell abuse and threats at them'.[31]

The first issue was solved in mid-March with the enacting of the Prisoners (Temporary Discharge for Ill-health) – popularly the Cat and Mouse – Act, which gave the Home Secretary the power to order the temporary release of hunger strikers and their subsequent re-arrest as soon as it was deemed medically safe. Mrs Pankhurst herself (having been found guilty of incitement to commit felony and given three years' penal servitude) became one of the first militants to be officially released under the terms of the Act on 12 April after staging a week-long hunger strike that left her dangerously emaciated. A month later the issue of public disturbance was also addressed with two measures meant to severely curtail the WSPU's ability to organize propaganda events.

The first came on 16 April with instructions from the Home Office that immediate steps be taken to 'cut off the telephone communication of the offices of

10. Arrest of a suffragette in London during a demonstration, October 1913 (Library of Congress, Prints & Photographs Division).

the [WSPU], as that body... now openly [advocates the] commission of crime'.[32] The second was revealed in a communiqué from Henry, which officially informed the Union that in light of the 'grave disorder' likely to be elicited by suffragettes meeting in a public place and 'in view of the... avowed policy of the [WSPU] to advocate the commission of crime, the Secretary of State... has directed me... to take steps as are necessary and within [my] powers to prevent such meetings being held'.[33]

With its telephone wires cut and its freedom of assembly all but suspended, the only thing keeping the WSPU from being raided was the police's apparent difficulty in finding out who 'the persons conducting the affairs of the Union and the printing of The Suffragette [were]'.[34] The militants, in the meantime, showed no signs of backing down, as the brown parcel found in the public lavatory of Piccadilly station on 29 April appeared to demonstrate. Containing approximately one and a half pounds of nitroglycerine, the bomb was promptly taken by a Special Branch detective to the still-operational Duck Island facility – then under the supervision of a new Chief Inspector of Explosives, Major Aston Cooper-Key – and safely disposed of. No one claimed responsibility, but at the Home Office the operating assumption was that this was the work of the WSPU.[35]

Whether this incident (the first attempted outrage on the London Tube in more than fifteen years) helped spur the Home Office into action is not certain, but by the end of April the necessary evidence against the Union had been 'gradually obtained'.[36] On the morning of 30 April a 'large force, some in uniform and others in plain clothes', entered the offices at Lincoln's Inn under the direction of Superintendent Patrick Quinn, arresting six women – including the assistant editors of *The Suffragette* – and seizing 'a great quantity of books and printed matter, including... the Union's cheque-books and counterfoils'.[37] While the raid proved a largely calm 'everyday affair',[38] consisting only in the taking of names and addresses by six or so 'stalwart policemen',[39] the crackdown was far from over. The following day, shortly after her return from France, Annie Kenney was arrested along with one of her associates, a certain Godwin Clayton, owner of a chemist's shop in Richmond, and hours later, the printer of *The Suffragette*, a man named Sidney Granville Drew, was likewise taken into custody.

The material found in Kenney's Mecklenburgh Square apartment proved far more incriminating than anything uncovered at Lincoln's Inn the day before. It included a letter from Clayton, describing his botched attempts at preparing some sort of explosive substance or device which Kenney had requested of him, as well as several pages of suggestions (also by Clayton) for future outrages, including schemes for setting fire to a timber yard and 'simultaneously smashing a considerable number of street fire alarms'.[40] The confiscated papers also contained a list of 'certain smaller Government offices... where something might be done' and a meticulous description of a series of night-time break-ins at the National Health Insurance Commission building. All nine arrestees were charged with conspiracy at Bow Street Police Court on 2 May and all – save for the printer and one of the sub-editors of *The Suffragette*, who had agreed to cease their involvement with the publication – were denied bail and 'driven away to gaol... amid the cheering and booing' of the crowds outside the court.[41]

The authorities' actions were not without political repercussions. Despite the WSPU's continued estrangement from the fold of not only the Labour Party, but – thanks to Christabel – of all male-dominated parties and organizations, the principle of female enfranchisement still enjoyed considerable support on the Left. Reviving the left-wing Free Speech Defence Committee (formed around the time of the *Syndicalist* prosecutions to advocate for the prisoners' release) the Radical backbencher Josiah Wedgwood, together with sympathetic Labour MPs and representatives of socialist and suffragist societies from across London, set to work planning a great demonstration in defence of 'liberty'.

The meeting, held in Trafalgar Square on 4 May, drew together nearly ten thousand participants and an audience of anywhere between ten and twenty thousand. It was an altogether impressive show of force and, save for sporadic scuffles between pugnacious young men and the more than six hundred police officers in attendance, a relatively peaceful event.[42] To McKenna, however, such public backlash made little difference, and for the remainder of 1913 the government continued pursuing its line of zero, or near zero, tolerance for 'incitement', while enforcing – despite its dubious record in dampening the campaign of vandalism – the Cat and Mouse Act.[43]

*The Suffragette* did manage to remain in publication but not because of any leniency on the part of authorities. As official correspondence from early May reveals, the Home Office was prepared to go to considerable lengths to ensure that the militant publication would not be smuggled into the country from abroad. According to Troup, McKenna was anxious to have the Treasury Commissioners 'instruct the Commissioners of Customs, in the event of any consignments of [*The Suffragette*] reaching... any [British] port, to stop the consignment and send two copies to [Scotland Yard]'.[44]

The Customs Commissioners replied they 'had no legal authority to stop a consignment of [the publication] even if they knew it contained incitement to crime'.[45] This prompted the Legal Assistant Under-Secretary Ernley Blackwell to propose the compromise solution that would have allowed Customs to 'telephone at once to [Scotland Yard] that a consignment had arrived [as well as communicate] the [delivery] address [and] send copies of the paper to the Commissioner who would then take what steps he could to prevent circulation'.[46] McKenna agreed provisionally to Blackwell's proposals, but given their doubtful practicability, *The Suffragette* was ultimately allowed to exist legally, albeit in an anodyne and self-censoring incarnation. Christabel – who intended to use the publication as a vehicle for her newfound ideas on sexual abstinence[47]– resentfully accepted the compromise.

Despite the fracases which often accompanied the WSPU's London meetings, public hostility was likely even more pronounced, and less discriminating, in the provinces. This was amply illustrated over the summer of 1913 during a nationwide propaganda tour undertaken by the NUWSS in support of the constitutionalist agenda, which saw several suffragettes subjected to serious violence by hostile crowds. That this hostility was largely a product of the WSPU's ultra-militant campaign was beyond any doubt to local authorities. Reporting on a constitutionalist meeting in Cirencester, during which a crowd of several hundred townspeople turned viciously on the handful of suffragettes in attendance, the local superintendent observed that 'some two years ago Miss [Ada] Flatman of the Militant Section held several meetings [here] and was accorded a decent hearing'.[48]

If the mounting hostility of the general public and the lack of any viable alternative – short of actually granting women the vote – gave the government the impetus to stick to its guns, the fact remained that whatever the pressure put on the WSPU as an organization, militancy itself did not appear to slacken. On 7 May an attempt to blow up the Bishop's throne in St Paul's Cathedral was only undone after the unexpected failure of the 'very ingenious' timer connected to nearly a pound of nitroglycerine.[49]

The tension only worsened after 3 June, the day when Emily Wilding Davison took her fatal, if likely unintentional, leap in front of the king's horse at the Epsom Derby, giving the WSPU its first real martyr. The arson campaign continued unabated and by the end of the month some militants, namely the Men's Federation for Women's Suffrage and Sylvia Pankhurst's East End branch of the WSPU,[50] felt confident enough to openly defy the ban on public meetings through a show of numbers in Trafalgar Square, urging the audience to march on Downing Street to 'at least let Cabinet Ministers hear our voices'.[51]

Judging by the decreasing number of arsons, anti-government hostility began easing off in July and August, when many WSPUers also went on vacation,[52] but despite pronouncements of victory from anti-suffragist quarters – 'the militant Suffragette conspiracy no longer exists… It has been crushed by the Cat and Mouse Act' trumpeted the *Daily Mail* on 7 July – Pankhurst loyalists were far from giving up the fight. An illustration was afforded by the events of 14 July, when Annie Kenney, then a fugitive 'mouse', was ambushed by a group of Special Branch men as she was coming out of a meeting at the London Pavilion. With the help of other suffragettes and her three male bodyguards, Kenney managed to cause a scene – press reports suggested one policeman was 'almost strangled' – before finally being rushed into a cab by two detectives.[53] Ironically, it was precisely Pankhurstism, as defined by the doctrines of Christabel and Emmeline, not the Cat and Mouse Act, that was slowly proving to be the undoing of the WSPU. By late July the toxic publicity elicited by the arson campaign and Christabel's unflinchingly authoritarian and gender-separatist brand of feminism were considerably driving down the rate of new membership.[54]

Despite the difficulties involved in re-arresting temporarily discharged 'mice', the most worrying aspect of the suffragette problem continued to be the ease with which arsonists evaded capture altogether. This was partly due to the authorities' lack of intelligence on upcoming attacks, but also to the fact that for many militants getaways were made a great deal easier by the WSPU's fleet of automobiles. By contrast, the Metropolitan Police was sorely underequipped in this department,[55] as Basil Thomson,[56] the new Assistant Commissioner at Scotland Yard, pointed out to Henry in October 1913.

Complaining that the WSPU had at least two cars for the London area, 'which they use both for committing acts of incendiarism and for escaping arrest', Thomson added that 'it has been useless to keep observation on the cars because as soon as they are out in the country they travel too fast for any conveyance that Police officers can obtain'. He proposed that two motorcycles be acquired for the use of CID detectives 'at a cost of from £50 to £70', or, failing that, that Sergeant Smith from the Public Carriage Office (who owned his own motorcycle) might be allowed to join Special Branch on a trial basis solely for the purpose of aiding in the surveillance of militant suffragettes.[57] Henry consented to the latter suggestion, but as it soon became obvious, Smith's battered old Triumph motorbike was hardly a match for the WSPU's powerful engines.[58]

Besides the arson campaign, which appeared increasingly inefficient at annoying, never mind terrifying, the British public into submission, militancy had reached an impasse by the end of 1913. The only people within the WSPU attempting anything new were Sylvia Pankhurst's band of East End socialist rebels and even they were struggling to come up with a viable battle plan, as attested by a couple of police reports. The first, based on firsthand information supplied by an informer, described a meeting held in East London on the night of 5 November, during which speeches were given by all the usual suspects. They included Sylvia Pankhurst, George Lansbury (recently released from Pentonville prison under the Cat and Mouse Act), Charles Lapworth (editor of Lansbury's *Daily Herald*), the composer Ethel Smyth and the Irish socialist Sir Francis Vane (arguably the only male left-wing suffragist with an aristocratic and military background).

The main topic at hand was the formation, under Vane's tutelage, of a 'scheme for men and women to form themselves into drilling classes with the idea of protecting themselves against an armed force'.[59] The inspiration for this had come from Carson's paramilitary Ulstermen, at the time the only extra-parliamentary organization able to effectively leverage the threat of political violence against the supremacy of the Liberal government.

As the second police report shows, the scheme for a 'People's Training Corps' was approved by the East End WSPU a week later by an assembly of 'between 250 and 300 men and women crowded in [the] small', but aptly named, Ethical Hall in Libra Street. Despite a few contentious moments elicited by the quasi-patriotic language of the Corps' proposed oath of allegiance (which the internationalists objected to on grounds that they '[had] no country to defend'), the idea of a 'people's police' that could withstand the attacks of the state and protect Sylvia Pankhurst (styled 'honorary colonel') from future arrest attempts, enjoyed more or less unanimous support.[60] Not so within the wider WSPU, where Christabel, invested with a pontifical degree of infallibility, was adamant that 'conflicting views and divided counsels inside the WSPU there cannot be'.[61]

The rupture between loyalists and leftists was formalized in mid-January 1914 after which the latter took on the name of the East London Federation of Suffragettes. Although the ELFS had always represented a minority view within the WSPU, the significance of this new split was amplified considerably less than a month later when the Pethick-Lawrences joined forces with Sylvia's socialists as well as the remaining moderates (who had either been expelled from, or were only nominally attached to Christabel's faction) to form the United Suffragettes, an umbrella (albeit left-leaning) group open to militants and constitutionalists of both genders.

The split may have accelerated the isolation and decline that the WSPU seemed destined not to recover from – in mid-January 1914, Beatrice Harraden, a disgruntled old-guarder, wrote to Christabel that 'the WSPU now has no speakers to rouse and educate the country'[62] – but it still did not appear to subdue the eagerness of would-be arsonists. Many of them were in fact committed to upping the ante by continuing to experiment with explosives and by targeting increasingly significant edifices. On 1 March a bomb went off inside St John's Church in Westminster, damaging a portion of the ceiling and some of the stained glass panels; the message, written on a half-charred piece of cardboard found at the scene, urged 'Mr. McKenna in particular and... every man in general [to] stop torturing women and give them their freedom'.[63] Following official WSPU policy, the bomb – a steel canister filled with gunpowder – had been set off a good twenty minutes or so after the end of evening prayer, in order to prevent any injuries. Such 'restraint' did nothing, however, to assuage the public's hostility and the government's growing impatience.

The re-arrest of Emmeline Pankhurst on 9 March was followed by a spree of retaliatory attacks of vandalism (including the notorious slashing of the Rokeby Venus at the National Gallery), the firebombing of two churches[64] and an attempted counter-demonstration to protest the Ulster Unionists' 'British Covenant' rally. Far from being a comment on Unionism itself, the abortive demonstration (held in Hyde Park on 4 April) was meant to punish Carson for his anti-suffragist stance, as well as showcase the double standard involved in allowing paramilitary Ulstermen to hold an open meeting in defiance of the government while denying militant women the same right.

In response, the Home Office decided to once again step up the pressure. The first of a series of repressive measures was taken in late April and aimed at hampering, if not altogether banning, the publication of *The Suffragette*, which, despite its toned-down editorials, continued publishing reports on militant activity in undisguisedly admiring terms. Citing a litany of 'actionable passages' from the publication (compiled by Special Branch at the request of Assistant Commissioner Thomson), McKenna advised the Director of Public Prosecutions to 'take criminal proceedings against the printers and publishers of the paper'.[65] On 13 May Stanley Drew, the printer of the WSPU's official organ, was back in court on charges of 'soliciting, inciting, and endeavouring to persuade divers women... and others to commit malicious damage to property'.[66]

*The Suffragette* managed to go on all the same and only eight days after Drew's trial some of the original militant spirit was recaptured thanks to the two-hundred-strong suffragette deputation sent to Buckingham Palace to 'interview the King'.[67] Though the ensuing demonstration predictably led to 'several fierce scuffles' between militants and police, it also suggested an eventual rapprochement with the body politic.

Just as the protest was unfolding, however, several Special Branch detectives were winding up a raid on an apartment in Maida Vale, on the other side of Hyde Park, known to police as a WSPU safe house. Five women were arrested on charges of conspiracy and taken in along with a substantial body of evidence, including plans for future arsons, 'a large quantity of stones... a type-written sheet of paper referring to an "improved shrapnel grenade" [and] a considerable number of lengths of... fuse'.[68] Two days later, Lincoln's Inn was also raided and occupied, producing a collection of similar artefacts (including a list of subscribers to the Union's funds) while driving up the number of arrests to six.[69] The WSPU headquarters were hastily resettled to an office in Tothill Street, ironically only a couple of blocks away from New Scotland Yard, but on 9 June, with Lincoln's Inn still under police control, that venue too was summarily searched and stripped of any official documents and correspondence (although no arrests were made).[70]

Far from marking a return to (relatively) civil disobedience, the 21 May demonstration had in fact been the swansong of aboveground militancy and despite the unrelenting aggression of the new government crackdown, the possibility of a cohesive strategy for quelling underground militancy once and for all remained elusive. Writing to the Home Office on 10 June to report on the continued police presence at Lincoln's Inn, Henry asked – convinced that there was 'little hope of introducing legislative measures to strengthen our hands or cripple theirs' – that all telephonic communication be once again discontinued for all WSPU offices as a way to 'hamper' the militants and show them that the government 'means to thrash them as far as it can'.[71] Ernley Blackwell, the Legal Under-Secretary, coolly replied that although 'deprivation of telephones would of course inconvenience [the militants]... the actual work of organizing outrage is done from semi-private [phone-equipped] premises' and, seeing the WSPU's incoming correspondence was already being routinely seized, 'it would strengthen [the militants'] hands' if the Home Secretary were to be seen to continue clamping down on basic freedoms 'by means of special warrants'.[72]

Deferring to Blackwell's cautionary advice, McKenna refused to have the phone line at Lincoln's Inn cut off, but there is every indication he shared Henry's vindictive frustration. A day after receiving the Commissioner's memo, the Home Secretary declared in the House of Commons that militancy was 'a phenomenon absolutely without precedent in our history',[73] and threatened to start proceedings against all known WSPU subscribers in order to hold them accountable for the damage done by militants. Proceedings were never begun, but the raids continued all throughout June 1914 alongside a new spate of arson attacks on churches (including Westminster Abbey) and picture slashings.[74] In late July 1914 the Indian Director of Criminal Intelligence complained that 'the information given by Scotland Yard about the doings of Indian agitators in

England' was becoming increasingly meagre, blaming it on the fact that Special Branch 'officers… were so fully occupied with the Suffragette movement'.[75]

Even so, by late July it was clear that the WSPU's intransigent rump was sinking inexorably into obscurity – on 23 June McKenna had warned 'owners… of [public] halls of the [nefarious] consequences to themselves' should they choose to let to suffragettes[76] – while struggling to keep *The Suffragette* – its last lifeline to the wider world – in circulation. The wider world, however, was arguably not much on the minds of WSPU leaders, as the cover of *The Suffragette*'s final issue, dated 7 August 1914, attests. Featuring an impressionistic pencil sketch of a stylized battle scene, it prominently displayed the headline 'Worse than Women's Militancy'. The only way in which traditional Pankhurstites conceived of the looming European cataclysm at this stage was either as a potential competitor for the government's attention, on par with Irish republicans and Carson's militiamen, or as 'God's vengeance' on the men who had 'held women in subjection'.[77]

The government, on the other hand, was all too aware of the gravity of the situation and eager to minimize all distractions on the home front. The same day *The Suffragette*'s 'war issue' came out McKenna announced that imprisoned suffragettes who promised 'not to commit any further crimes or outrages' would have their sentences remitted and three days later that offer was extended unconditionally to all jailed militants.[78] It was a gamble given the fate of the previous truce, but swept up in the general wave of jingoistic-martial fervour, Christabel, her mother and their remaining acolytes dutifully accepted the olive branch and offered to suspend indefinitely what was left of the militant campaign. On 10 August Mrs Pankhurst, not a month out of Holloway prison, declared emphatically, 'What is the use of fighting for a vote if we have no country to vote in? With that patriotism which has nerved women to endure torture in prison for the national good, we ardently desire that our country shall be victorious.'[79]

\* \* \*

The first decade of the twentieth century may not have brought about a dramatic overhaul of the British political police, but it did mark the beginning of a period of rapid and transformative change. The first and perhaps most obvious change was that unlike the two decades preceding it, this period was not defined by one (perceived) cohesive strand of political extremism, but rather by a series of disparate groups, each with its own potential and justification for organized, ideologically motivated violence.

Although British authorities continued to regard it with apprehension, by the mid-1900s anarchism no longer registered as the urgent threat it had been during the 1890s, and by the end of the Edwardian decade it had in fact been subsumed into the wider issues of immigration and racial identity, as demonstrated by the Tottenham and Sidney Street incidents. By contrast, the rise of a new home-grown radicalism in the form of militant suffragism and a re-energized trade union movement, as well as of new forms of anti-colonial agitation (most notably Hindu nationalism) became more pronounced in the final year of King Edward VII's reign. Such movements challenged the established prejudices and practices of Scotland Yard officers and Home Office bureaucrats alike.

To what extent that challenge was successfully met remains debatable. On the surface the political police, namely that opaque and often ad hoc structure stretching out from the Home Office all the way down to the most junior detective constable, changed very little. Strategies for containing politically motivated violence remained a matter for the discretion of the Home Secretary and the Commissioner of the Metropolitan Police. As several incidents from the half-decade preceding the First World War demonstrate, decisions made exclusively at the top proved at best controversial (Tonypandy, Black Friday) and at worst counter-productive (e.g. the much-spectacularized forced feeding of suffragettes). Special Branch also largely continued operating along the lines set out during the early 1890s by Melville and Anderson, relying on information gleaned from shadowing suspects, paid informants (where available) and the occasional tip-off from members of the general public. The fact that its chief superintendent throughout this period was Patrick Quinn, one of the original members of Irish Branch, further cemented that continuity with the past.

Beneath that unchanging facade, however, two distinct transformative trends can be distinguished. The first is the increasing acceptance after 1900, by the political establishment as well as the public at large, of the legitimacy and usefulness of a British political police – embodied in the popular discourse by Special Branch of Scotland Yard. This was in part the result of a developing mythology centered on the figure of the dutiful and patriotic 'secret agent', which the swashbuckling Melville had helped create at the height of his fame. It also reflected, however, the shift from the relative political stability of the Belle Époque to the chronic instability of the twentieth century. In a mental landscape 'very like revolution',[80] where conniving Germans seemed capable of reaching British shores, where Jewish and Indian 'anarchists' could wantonly rob and murder in the heart of London, where socialist trade unionists could bring a whole industry to a standstill and where 'hysterical' women could go about setting fire to private residences and churches with impunity – a detective force devoted to subverting the subverters was more than a tolerable embarrassment; it was an absolute necessity.

The other transformation came with the changing relationship between the Home Office and Scotland Yard. On the Home Office side, it is important to note the increasingly active role played by the Home Secretary as well as some of his under-secretaries in matters of counter-subversion. That Asquith, during his tenure as Home Secretary, had once had to learn of the existence of an anarchist conspiracy from reading the newspapers would have seemed entirely unconscionable in 1914. Starting with Herbert Gladstone and his strong-willed Permanent Under-Secretary C. E. Troup, the Home Office increasingly took the business of political policing in hand, a trend which arguably culminated under Winston Churchill who brought his famous penchant for brashness and derring-do to the job of defending the realm.

Whitehall's new assertiveness did not, however, lead to a completely one-sided relationship thanks to E. R. Henry's progressive zeal (his political conservatism notwithstanding) and strong leadership. Owing to his insistence on necessary reforms – which the Home Office rarely wished to find ways of paying for – and despite continued shortfalls, such as the lack of a motorized police division, the London CID, including of course Special Branch, was significantly restructured and expanded by 1912.

The same cautious reform also characterized the development of military counter-intelligence in Britain before the First World War and while a full account of this process is beyond the scope of the present book,[81] it will be useful, in closing, to briefly discuss the ways in which the early course of MI5 reflected the power dynamics that had characterized the British political police from its inception.

First conceived in 1908 by a subcommittee of the Committee for Imperial Defence tasked with combating foreign (particularly German) espionage in Britain, the domestic section of the Secret Service Bureau[82] – renamed MO5 in 1914; reconstituted as MI5 in 1916 – survived for much of the pre-war period only as an extension of the existing political police apparatus with all of the latter's inherent particularities and shortcomings. Despite representing the military interests of the state and, more specifically, the intelligence priorities of the War Office, MO5 remained umbilically attached to Scotland Yard and the Home Office. Several illustrations of this survive in the official record, with a few especially significant.

Officially established in late August 1909 as a result of a meeting held 'in Sir E. Henry's room at Scotland Yard' between representatives of the War Office and the Admiralty,[83] the Bureau's home-front operations were placed under the leadership of a young retired officer, Captain Vernon Kell, with the foreign intelligence side (later MI6) being entrusted to Commander Mansfield Cumming. Although Kell was by all accounts an 'exceptionally good linguist'[84] with a passion for intelligence gathering, his organization was chronically understaffed and therefore reliant on the cooperation of civil and police authorities.

Prior to his retirement in 1917, MO5's foremost – and until 1911 only – detective remained William Melville (code-named 'M'), who, despite an unequalled breadth of experience, was by the early 1910s increasingly unable to shadow suspects around the clock or 'think out new schemes for getting hold of intelligence'.[85] Consequently, much of the work involved in investigating rumours of German espionage in Britain, which military authorities in London feared was already dangerously advanced,[86] often had to be assigned piecemeal either to highly qualified and tactful private investigators (whose services came at a hefty price) or to Special Branch detectives. Given Commissioner Henry's foundational role, which included providing MO5 with the legal cover of a private detective firm owned by an ex-CID Chief Inspector,[87] Kell might have reasonably expected his agency to benefit from a close cooperation with Special Branch. In reality, relations between the two organizations were often tense and rarely straightforward.

Though seemingly embraced at the War Office, the claim that the Germans were looking to 'secure sympathy for their agents in Great Britain by using anarchists, labour leaders and such like',[88] proved hard to substantiate, and while Scotland Yard was firmly (and conveniently) established in the popular imagination as the nation's guardian against foreign spies[89] – MO5 being strictly 'non-existent' – the exact remit of Special Branch remained a sensitive issue in Westminster. In 1908 Assistant Commissioner Macnaghten had denied a request from the Director of Military Operations to let CID detectives stationed at Dover 'watch for [a suspected German spy]... as the man was not a criminal and if the matter had leaked out there might have been tiresome questions in Parliament'.[90]

Things changed somewhat after 1909 and owing in part to their personal friendship with Kell, both Henry and Troup responded positively to the MO5 director's frequent pleas for 'a detective in readiness to help "M"... should it be necessary',[91] although the final say continued to remain with the head of Scotland Yard. Macnaghten proved amenable enough, allowing Quinn on several occasions to aid Kell in the latter's investigations and sanctioning, by January 1911, the temporary deployment of two Special Branch men in the shadowing of an elusive spy.[92]

Kell acknowledged the support, noting in his diary that he had 'had to depend, to a great extent, on such assistance in detective work as the Metropolitan and County Police have been able to afford' (with the caveat that qualified provincial detectives proved exceedingly rare), while also decrying the 'obviously undesirable... [and] very costly... system of employing odd men for our kind of work'.[93] For his part, Melville strongly preferred enlisting 'the services of... ex-police officers of his acquaintance', in spite of the costs and irregularity of services, warning Kell against requesting the 'permanent engagement' of any active CID detective. As 'M' went on to explain, 'it is not likely that we should get the best men' and, at any rate, detectives talked too much 'among themselves and consequently all our business would become common property at the Yard'.[94]

Despite the bias underscoring the ex-superintendent's advice, the typically astute Kell seems to have deferred to it entirely, revealing once again the inherent fractiousness of the British high police (contrasted in a 1909 War Office report to the French system in which there was 'the most intimate connection between all... services, diplomatic, consular, secret, police and military'[95]). With the appointment in 1913 of Sir Basil Thomson as Assistant Commissioner in charge of Scotland Yard, this fractiousness only worsened.

An ex-colonial adventurer and former governor of Dartmoor prison,[96] Thomson was a brash intriguer with an affinity for conspiracy theories (particularly those involving Jews) and a desire to consolidate the entire political police under his own leadership in a manner unseen since the days of William Harcourt.[97] Although his boundless hubris led to a summary dismissal in 1921 – followed, in 1925, by an arrest for 'misconduct[ing] himself with a young girl in Hyde Park'[98] – during the Great War and immediately after, Thomson's tendency to take credit for his colleagues' work and efforts to undermine Kell's authority earned him 'the collective enmity of MI5'.[99]

Such lingering mistrust and personal rivalry aside, by 1914 counter-espionage benefitted from a remarkable degree of institutional support. Besides Henry and Troup, Kell could also count on the resolute assistance of the Home Secretary; Churchill, at first, whose expansion of the scope of Home Office warrants allowed MO5 to intercept the mail of practically anyone suspected of espionage,[100] and subsequently McKenna, who during the heady days of August 1914 worked closely with Kell to build up the case for wartime alien restriction. Even more importantly, perhaps, is that the MO5 director proved instrumental in securing the close cooperation of provincial chief constables, many of whom had previously looked on the political police in London with a certain degree of bemusement and resentment (as incidents from the 1880s and 1890s demonstrate).

If in 1907 Melville's proposal for a national 'scheme of surveillance on all suspected foreigners' was dismissed by the Home Office on grounds that provincial police 'were not fitted for such duties',[101] Kell's political talents and clout in Whitehall gave the ambitious project a new lease on life. After a relatively rocky start which saw only a few local chief constables lend occasional assistance with counter-espionage while '[giving] us [to] understand that it is not their business',[102] by 1913 Kell could proudly report that MO5 was actively coordinating 'with all the Chief Constables... in England and Wales' and more than a dozen in Scotland, as well as 'with all Ireland through the Inspector General of the [RIC]'. Equally impressive, 'Alien Statistics and Registers of Aliens by name, address, occupation &c. [had] been compiled concerning 47 Counties... in England and Wales and 22 Counties... in Scotland.'[103]

Whereas Melville had simply decried the 'absolute uselessness' of regular police in counter-espionage work,[104] preferring instead to rely on experienced familiar faces, Kell took great care to cultivate provincial chief constables. This he did through formal meetings (held at the Home Office or at opulent London hotels) and by keeping them well-informed through reports 'on the methods employed by foreign Secret Service Agents and on the work of counter-espionage... so that they may have every opportunity of co-operating with the Bureau'.[105]

Even so, MO5 remained, much like Special Branch earlier in the century, an underdeveloped crisis management unit – with a staff of fourteen in April 1914 out of which only two were permanent detectives[106] – relying heavily on informants and intermittent tip-offs, and operating for that reason under the cloak of extra-legality. Writing in 1912 on the recent secret trials of several pro-German spies (all tried under the previous year's stringent Official Secrets Act[107]), Kell noted how it would be impossible 'in this country to hold trials for espionage... in camera... as [in] ... Continental countries' for the sole reason that 'it was considered contrary to the interests of the State to bring these men to trial... [and so entail] a disclosure of the identity of our informants and other confidential matters'.[108]

Things changed only with the declaration of hostilities later in 1914 and by the end of 1915 MO5 could rely on the services of 227 new recruits, a figure that nearly quadrupled by the end of 1918 (though the vast majority of staff remained clerical).[109] The ostentatious spy-phobia of an earlier time was replaced by spy-mania, Edwardian radicalism gave way to jingoistic fervour – made all the more fervent by persistent rumours of collusion between Germans and British anti-war socialists[110] – and, by the end of the war, 'small but permanent' Special Branches were to be found even in the provinces.[111]

# Conclusion

By the time Robert Anderson wrote his 'straining the law' memo in 1898,[1] extra-legality had already been long established as a defining feature of British political policing, as several official documents attest. Thus, as early as 1881, following a police raid on Johann Most's printing shop in the wake of his arrest for incitement to murder, the Director of Public Prosecutions, A. K. Stephenson, candidly observed in a memo to the Home Office how 'the police often necessarily in the proper discharge of their duties commit acts which are said to be illegal, inasmuch as there may be no statutable authority for such acts'.[2]

As we have seen, extra-legal practices continued throughout the 1880s, becoming firmly established during Edward Jenkinson's tenure as (unofficial) chief spymaster at the Home Office. Jenkinson took charge of an intricate network of informers stretching on both sides of the Atlantic, using it to upset the activities of the Clan na Gael and other American Fenian organizations. On several occasions, this more than likely involved the use of agents provocateurs (Red Jim McDermott, Daniel O'Neill), arguably without the full knowledge of the Home Office or Scotland Yard, but with the cooperation of RIC and provincial police chiefs (the help lent by Chief Constable Joseph Farndale in the 1884 arrests of John Daly and James Egan being a case in point). The rivalries generated within the political police hierarchy, partly by Jenkinson's style and personality, led to the latter's downfall and the abandonment of his particular model of intelligence gathering, but not to the abandonment of extra-legality.

As the events surrounding the abortive Jubilee Plot of 1887 and the Bloody Sunday riot of the same year show, the willingness of Jenkinson's former rivals to act in an extra-legal manner – whether by colluding with Fenian conspirators in order to avoid the public airing of 'embarrassing' information or by unilaterally curtailing rights of assembly and free speech – was beyond doubt. Such methods were also at play in less extraordinary cases, as attested by Charles Warren's admission in late 1888 that 'we have in times past done something [i.e. illegal house raids] on a very small scale but then we had certain information that a person was concealed in a house'.[3]

Despite the disappearance of Fenian terrorism as a credible threat in Britain during the 1890s – notwithstanding the incongruous 1896 dynamite conspiracy – the decade saw the continued dominance of extra-legality in political policing thanks to the rising fortunes of Chief Inspector William Melville, head of Special Branch until his 'retirement' in 1904. The network of informers and double agents that had once been the preserve of British counter-Fenianism was at least partially recreated under Melville's leadership, this time with the purpose of combating anarchist terrorism. The circumstances surrounding the 1892 Walsall case suggest that the established method of employing double agents and (possible) agents provocateurs in order to deter future conspirators, while publicly highlighting the effectiveness of the political police, remained in use to some extent, though less so than in the 1880s. This reflects the reduced threat that anarchism posed to national security during these years and, more specifically, the transition of British political policing away from the proactive approach favoured by Jenkinson to a more reactive one based on surveillance and intelligence gathering.

Notwithstanding this change, such extra-legal tactics as unwarranted raids and house searches, the aggressive clamping down on innocuous organizations (e.g. the Legitimation League) merely on suspicion of being connected to anarchism, as well as collusion with agents of foreign governments, were all routinely used by Melville during his superintendentship. Compared to the 1880s, however, the official record is overall scarce for this period and with the exception of a few confidential reports on the movements of anarchists and a very short, deliberately evasive 'memoir', there is no known body of writings attributable to the Chief Inspector.

Ironically, more survives of Jenkinson's archival footprint even though the spymaster is said to have burned the bulk of his official papers shortly before leaving office. This is not surprising given that Jenkinson, who was often accused by his detractors of unaccountability, was nonetheless often in communication with his superiors. Melville, on the other hand, proved highly adept at keeping his bosses out of the loop as much as possible[4] and, as we have seen, actively intrigued with foreign police operatives like Pyotr Rachkovsky. The Burtsev case of 1897 is of course singular only to the extent that evidence of other similar cases has yet to surface in the historical record, but the disarming casualness and chumminess which characterized the correspondence between the head of Special Branch and that of the Parisian Okhrana points to the likelihood of an established working relationship.

We should be wary, however, of deducing from this and other similar developments (such as the occasional shadowing of European exiles by Special

Branch detectives for the benefit of foreign governments) that the British political police was necessarily 'a cell in a Europe-wide counter-subversive [network]'.[5] Extra-legality may have been used at times to aid the counter-subversive efforts of continental police agencies, but only to a very limited and self-interested (from the British perspective) extent.

Equally important is to note that the means of 'straining the law' did not remain unchanged after Melville's retirement. During the Edwardian years extra-legality was affected by an increased, though not total, centralization of power away from Scotland Yard and into the Home Office bureaucracy. Suffragette militancy was largely contained by extra-legal methods initiated, or at least planned, by the Home Secretary and his aides. They included the violent break-up and then subsequent banning of pro-suffrage demonstrations, the confiscation of personal property (mostly during unannounced raids on the WSPU headquarters), censorship of the press (such as the suppression of *The Suffragette* or of the *Daily Mirror*'s 'Black Friday' issue), the threatened prosecution of all militant suffragettes for encouraging terrorism and the general clamping down on basic freedoms by means of special Home Office warrants.[6]

Similar methods were also used against the syndicalist and socialist agitation of 1910–12, in a manner that not only speaks to the changing nature of the threat, which certainly exceeded the anarchism of the 1890s in importance, but also to the increased centrality of the Home Office in the decision-making process. This is aptly illustrated by the interventionist approach which then Home Secretary Winston Churchill took in response to the 1910 labour unrest in the Rhondda valleys. This approach included not only the deployment of armed troops (already a feature in the government's response to the industrial unrest at Featherstone in 1893), but also special constables and the covert use of intelligence-gathering.

The history of the early British political police is one dominated, for the most part, by strong and remarkable personalities often at odds with each other. This point is crucial to understanding precisely why political policing took the shape it did when it did. We can agree with historians of British policing that the birth of political police institutions in Britain was to a certain degree the result of the importation of colonial methods,[7] but not without underlining the idiosyncratic manner in which those methods were understood and applied by successive Home Secretaries and police officials. We have seen, for example, how Sir William Harcourt founded the first political police institution in Britain (Section B of Scotland Yard) before (unofficially) turning over the entire counter-terrorist strategy to Edward Jenkinson, only to finally turn against intelligence-based policing altogether. The result of this change of heart was of course momentous and it is important to note that in part it happened because of Harcourt's unstable, often choleric, personality.[8]

We have seen how Jenkinson's problematic, yet prescient, vision of a national, quasi-centralized, intelligence-gathering force of 'men of tried capacity and judgment, who would deal with all local details'[9] ultimately brought him into conflict with conservative members of the Scotland Yard leadership, even as the latter did not shy away from using Jenkinsonian methods themselves. Jenkinson's defeat in that conflict, which had drastic consequences for the course of political policing in Britain, is partly explained by the fact that he was a pro-Home Rule Liberal with a pragmatic, if 'politically incorrect' view of policing Fenianism. Equally important, however, were Jenkinson's personal insecurities (exacerbated by his unofficial and unstable position in Whitehall) and his often abrasive manner towards his colleagues.

We have also seen how William Melville cultivated a new network of informers and double agents – a network which, as Special Branch DS Patrick McIntyre recalled in his memoirs, the Chief Inspector effectively 'owned'. The key to understanding the manner in which this network functioned and the ends to which it was used is to keep in mind the Machiavellian-conservative worldview which made Melville see all forms of political subversion, violent or not, as something to be silenced by any means justifiable in a court of law (even those which required going behind his superiors' backs).[10] The fact that the Special Branch superintendent was universally detested and feared by all adherents of revolutionary creeds – something reflected in his nickname, *le vil Melville* – may not surprise us, but it attests to his uniquely and ruthlessly crafty personality and it is certain that no other member of the British political police achieved the same level of public fame and notoriety during the period discussed here.

Finally, we have noted how General Nevil Macready chose to deal with striking workers in South Wales in a manner that arguably exceeded his mandate – which certainly did not authorize him to declare martial law in any part of the country – but which ultimately succeeded in defusing an intensely treacherous situation. Macready, as the historical record reveals, was, unlike the Chief Constable of the Mid Glamorgan region, in some sympathy with the strikers and, generally speaking, a man of militaristic credentials but liberal impulses, despite his later controversial actions in civil war-torn Ireland. Conversely, Home Secretary Churchill was a man of Liberal credentials but frequently of militaristic impulses – something reflected not only in his approach to the labour unrest in Wales, Liverpool and other parts of the United Kingdom, but also in his attitude to suffragette militancy and his involvement in the notorious 'battle' of Sidney Street.

Just as important as individual conviction and prejudice, however, are the interactions between specific historical actors. This can be gleaned from the intense personal rivalries of the late 1880s and the failures of intelligence of the 1890s (particularly in the case of the 1894 Greenwich outrage and the 1896 dynamite conspiracy) which revealed the still-dysfunctional channels between the institutional political police and the government. It is also illustrated by the authorities' convoluted and often contradictory strategy for dealing with Edwardian radicalism, particularly militant suffragism and syndicalist-inspired agitation.

Though we may feel tempted to reduce the events presented in this book to a story of either progress or decline, the transformation of early political policing in Britain did not follow a teleological arc from less to more or vice versa. In the 1880s the political police hierarchy saw a significant concentration of power in the hands of a few Home Office officials and police chiefs and, as a consequence, a high degree of endemic infighting. In the 1890s the balance was tipped somewhat in favour of the police and the power was concentrated, to a significant extent, in the head of Special Branch. A reaction then followed in the 1900s which saw the centralization of power back into the office of the Home Secretary and a handful of his under-secretaries. To illustrate this tortuous transition, we only need recall that if in 1894 H. H. Asquith had had to get his intelligence on London anarchism from the newspapers, a decade and a half later the battle plan for dealing with WSPU militants was actively being prepared by Herbert Gladstone and his Permanent Under-Secretary Charles Troup.

This suggests that the strategy for dealing with political challenges to the state was never continuously devised and planned by the same group of people for exactly the same set of reasons. Some of those reasons, as we have seen, were essentially modernizing in nature (e.g. the setting up of Sections B and D and of permanent patrols of special constables), some were politically opportunist (e.g. the use of the political police during the special commission on 'Parnellism and crime'), while some were purely reactive and short-term, as illustrated by the tactics deployed against anarchist and suffragette militancy.

The emphasis on extra-legality naturally begs the question of whether the political police in Britain was an anti-liberal conspiracy at odds with the political class and the public alike. The answer emerging out of this book has to be a decisive but qualified no, and in explaining why that is we must begin by unpacking the question. First, there is the matter of liberalism and the theory that before the First World War 'liberal Britain [had come] to be policed more and more by men coming from outside the main liberal tradition'.[11] If we take 'the main liberal tradition' to mean the doctrines promulgated by the British Liberal Party, then that claim becomes debatable.

Sir William Harcourt was not only a mainstream Liberal; his ideological trajectory – from Radical to advocating Coercion in Ireland to supporting Home Rule – poignantly reflects the dramatic transformation undergone by his party over the course of the 1880s, highlighting the fact that there never was just one liberalism at play in 'liberal Britain'. Howard Vincent, the first and last Director of Scotland Yard and de facto head of Harcourt's early (pre-Irish Branch) political police, also started out as a Liberal despite ending his political career as a hard-line Conservative MP. Jenkinson was of course an unabashed Liberal, whatever criticisms there are to be made of his policing methods, while Charles Warren, despite being caricatured as the embodiment of militaristic excess later in his policing career, remained devoted to Gladstone's party throughout his life (having at one point unsuccessfully run for Parliament on a Radical ticket).

Equally committed to liberal principles were Godfrey Lushington, who played a key role in the workings of the political police throughout the 1880s and early 1890s (serving also as a British delegate at the 1898 anti-anarchist Conference in Rome), Charles Troup (a member of the Liberal Cobden Club[12]) and the succession of Liberal Home Secretaries (Gladstone, Churchill, McKenna) who played an active role in the suppression of organized radicalism during the Edwardian years.

Conservatives were also represented within the political police apparatus with the example of Lord Salisbury, who took an active interest in investigations of a political nature throughout his years as Prime Minister, serving as an apt illustration. On the Scotland Yard side, in particular, the impact of conservative ideas is perhaps most visible; individuals such as James Monro and Robert Anderson stand out as adepts of an uncompromising conservatism, followed, further down the hierarchy, by the likes of William Melville and those Special Branch detectives, such as John Sweeney or Herbert Fitch, whose memoirs attest to their right-wing sympathies. It is equally true, however, that not all Special Branch officers were dyed-in-the-wool conservatives – the striking example of Patrick McIntyre attests to this – and that out of the aforementioned individuals only Anderson and Melville had any lasting influence on the structure and methodology of the political police in Britain during this period. The point, therefore, is that if some of the men tasked with policing the politics of 'liberal Britain' were unattached to the country's liberal tradition, most of the men who gave shape and direction to the political police clearly were.

The next issue that needs clarification is the extent to which political policing met with opposition from the political class in Westminster. Here it must be observed that if the political police was mentioned at all in parliamentary debates or speeches it was usually as the focus of controversy and with the implication that it was being misused by the sitting government. Such criticism, however, seems to have been far from principled. The case of Lord Salisbury – who was both an unsparing critic of expanded police powers and a keen overseer of the political police – has already been mentioned. An even more telling case is provided by the aftermath of the 1889–90 special commission on 'Parnellism and crime' which brought the conduct of the Conservative government, particularly its use of Special Branch in supplying evidence against Parnell, under strong attack from Liberal and Irish Nationalist benches, with the charge being led, somewhat ironically, by Sir William Harcourt.

While acting as 'head detective',[13] the former Home Secretary had tacitly approved of Robert Anderson's role as handler to Henri Le Caron (the government's highest-ranking spy within the Fenian camp at the time) and of the use of paid informers in the course of securing convictions against Fenian agents. In the wake of the special commission, however, the pro-Home Rule Harcourt was keen to criticize Anderson for jealously guarding the information supplied by Le Caron, and for turning the notorious double agent over to *The Times* to serve as an anti-Parnell witness.

Outside such opportunistic criticism there is little evidence of any scrupulous and sustained opposition to political policing within the Whitehall establishment (i.e. the mainstream of the Liberal and Conservative parties) over the period considered here and we can rightfully conclude, as Constance Bantman does, that 'English reluctance towards political policing was by [1900] largely rhetorical'.[14] As we have seen, the Home Secretary could easily instruct the head of Scotland Yard not to interfere with native socialist groups, presumably out of 'liberal' correctness, only to then grant Special Branch permission to monitor and infiltrate such groups when it was deemed necessary, as the 1887 case of the SDF activist Alfred Oldland illustrates.

Equally slight is the evidence for public criticism of the political police. The nature of the historical record does not allow us to establish to what extent the policing of organised radicalism was the stuff of most Britons' daily conversations, correspondence or diary-keeping although, as at least one letter received by the Home Secretary in the 1880s seems to suggest, ordinary workingmen (even those of Liberal sympathies) were in favour of a highly punitive strategy for dealing with Fenian terrorism.[15] If, however, we take the national press as roughly representative of the opinions of the British public, we can form a relatively clear picture of the latter's perceptions of the political police.

One striking feature is that despite the authorities' studious reluctance to generate any public discussion of political policing, the British public as a whole was perfectly aware of the existence of a national political police. As early as 1884, in fact, Liberal newspapers could report matter-of-factly and approvingly on the appointment of Edward Jenkinson 'as a sort of Minister of Police'[16] and praise his work at the head of 'the new detective army, the necessity for which has been made painfully evident by recent crimes'.[17] Conservative papers too, while naturally suspicious of any Liberal schemes to reform policing, unanimously applauded the successes scored by British authorities against Fenian terrorists even in cases that were shrouded in controversy, as was, for example, the 1884 foiling of the Daly–Egan dynamite 'conspiracy'.[18]

The relationship between press and police authorities during this period, a topic that would certainly merit its own monograph, was clearly far from uncomplicated and manipulation of the former by the latter was, as we have seen, not uncommon. Scotland Yard and Home Office leadership used controlled leaks to the press during the early and mid-1880s in their battle with Jenkinson, while James Monro used the same technique in 1887 in order to defuse the politically explosive aspects of the Jubilee Plot controversy. In the 1890s William Melville also became highly adept at using the reading public's thirst for sensationalized news in order to cement his public reputation, as illustrated by the 1894 raid on the Autonomie Club and the arrest of Theodule Meunier – both performed in dramatic fashion and in full view of journalists. This prompted even Home Office bureaucrats to disapprovingly note the 'curious' amount of information that 'should get out… from what would appear to have been communicated by the Police'.[19]

There was, naturally, criticism of the political police in the newspapers, but it was almost always on grounds of not going far enough in clamping down on organized subversion and for 'knowing very little'[20] about the enemies of the British state. A case in point is provided by the many editorials criticizing the government and Scotland Yard in the wake of the 1894 Greenwich outrage. Exceptions to this rule were to be found mostly in the 'radical' press, whether Irish nationalist, anarchist or suffragist, and occasionally in the mainstream Liberal press (e.g. the *Pall Mall Gazette*'s highly partisan coverage of the 1887 Trafalgar Square riots). They do not, however, warrant a conclusion that ideological criticism of the political police was a major feature of public discourse during the three decades preceding the First World War. Describing the police precautions put in place for the queen's 1897 Diamond Jubilee celebrations, the *Daily Mail* noted how 'the route of the [Jubilee] procession [had] been laboriously examined by officers of the special branch of Scotland-yard, acting under… Melville', while *Reynolds's Newspaper* observed how 'Mr. Anderson's Political Police Agency' was keeping a close watch on the '[anarchist] clubs in

Soho and Fitzroy-square'.[21] The difference in tone is obvious and explainable by the fact that the *Daily Mail* and *Reynolds's* represented opposite ends of the political spectrum (right-wing imperialism and republican Radicalism respectively). Nevertheless, it is equally obvious that neither paper saw fit to explain to its readers the meaning of a British special branch or 'political police agency', or to comment on the legitimacy of such organizations. By the late 1900s newspapers already treated the political police, popularly embodied by Scotland Yard, as a regular and somewhat banal feature of the British state, whose existence was certainly very far from an illiberal unmentionable.

Aside from the clues provided by contemporary press accounts there is another important, if somewhat meagre, source of evidence on the British public's perceptions of political policing and that is in the number of people who actually played a constructive role in police investigations. If the 'private informer' was central to the British model of political policing, as a 1904 Home Office memorandum argued,[22] then the (anonymous) tip-off was at least as important. Indeed, it can be rightfully argued that some of the highest-profile investigations into cases of political conspiracy which occurred over the period considered here only came about as the result of intelligence contributed – whether for civic-minded or selfish reasons – by ordinary Britons. Examples can be found in the arrest of the Glasgow dynamitards and of the Gallagher gang in 1883; the arrest of Cunningham and Burton in 1885; the 1893 investigation into a presumed anarchist plot to launch attacks in London, Paris and Berlin; the conviction of Francis Polti in 1894; the arrest of George Bedborough for obscene libel in 1898; the first Scotland Yard investigation into the activities of WSPU militants in 1907; and the 1909 investigation into a possible suffragist plot to assassinate the Prime Minister.

If Britons trusted to some extent their national political police, however, the relationship between the latter and its European counterparts was an altogether different matter. Responding in 1904 to the proposal for a pan-European network of intelligence-gathering bureaux, tabled at that year's anti-anarchist conference in St Petersburg, Commissioner Henry pointed out that 'the action of English police in dealing with anarchists should not be fettered by hard and fast agreements with continental police authorities'.[23] This, in a sentence, embodied the British government's attitude to cooperation with European powers in matters of political policing – an attitude that remained constant throughout the period we have looked at.

The official explanation for this isolationism, set out by successive British administrations, was framed in ideological terms and premised on the notion that British law did not admit of the existence of a separate, political category of crime or of 'unconstitutional' arrangements with foreign governments. An early example of this strategy can be seen in the way the 1881 prosecution of Johann Most was used by William Harcourt to assuage European critics of Britain's 'open-door' immigration policy while avoiding committing the Liberal government to participation in that year's anti-Nihilist conference. Harcourt's stated justification for pursuing that course of action was a desire to neutralize continental criticism of British laws, but as subsequent developments demonstrate, the real reasons were likely more complex.

One reason was that Britain's extradition treaties with European states often excluded political crime as an extraditable offence, ironically even as such crime was deemed non-existent in Britain, leading sometimes to embarrassing standoffs between British authorities and their continental counterparts. Such standoffs could come as a consequence of European disapproval of British immigration laws, which were almost universally decried on the continent as excessively lax and protective of active revolutionaries. They could also revolve around attempts – usually successful – by European states such as France or Belgium to have their own political undesirables, particularly militant anarchists, expelled to Britain – the country that, thanks to its laws, would be least likely to send them back. Finally, they could also be engendered by European refusals to aid Britain in her pursuit of Fenian terrorists, as illustrated by the escape of Patrick J. Tynan from France to America, first in 1883 and then in 1896.

Such friction was by no means inevitable as several examples of cooperation attest, chiefly the participation of French police in the 1887 Jubilee Plot investigation, the 1894 arrest and extradition of Jean-Pierre François and Theodule Meunier (which set a precedent for politically motivated crime as an extraditable offence in Britain) and the cooperation between British, French, Dutch and Belgian police during the investigation into the 1896 Fenian dynamite conspiracy. Nevertheless, the diplomatic tension engendered by years of disputes over the legitimacy of Britain's right-of-asylum policies gradually led the British government to become more entrenched in its legal isolation, as illustrated by its refusal to participate in pan-European strategies for dealing with organized sedition.

After declining the Spanish government's invitation to take part in a proposed 1893 anti-anarchist conference, British authorities relented momentarily in 1898 (following the grisly assassination of Empress Elisabeth of Austria by an Italian anarchist), sending a delegation to that year's Anti-Anarchist Conference in Rome. Far from representing a true concession to cooperation with Europe, however, the British participation in the 1898 conference actually cemented the status quo – one aptly embodied by Sir Phillip Currie's 'we-do-not-prosecute-opinions' speech during the final plenary session, and by the fact that Britain was the only participating nation not to sign the conference's final protocol.

While it is tempting to ascribe British isolationism to a resilient liberal discourse that favoured British right over continental might, international cooperation in matters of political policing does not appear to have been a genuine party issue in Britain, even as 'cooperation with Europe' became a Liberal talking point in Parliament during the early 1890s. As we have noted, the Liberal administrations of 1881 and 1893 ultimately had the same (oppositional) view of pan-European counter-terrorist strategies as the Conservative administrations of 1898 and 1904. Whereas for Rosebery British laws were 'strong enough to deal with anarchism',[24] for Salisbury 'great objection' would have been 'felt to any attempt to meet the dangers of the anarchist conspiracy' by changing British law.[25]

If the political establishment was opposed to systematic cooperation with Europe out of a stated desire to maintain Britain's legal independence, the heads of the Metropolitan Police took the view that such cooperation would materially weaken the functioning of the national political police. We have already noted how Robert Anderson considered the 1898 plans for centralized intelligence gathering inimical to British extra-legality and it is worth recalling that earlier in the decade, the Scotland Yard chief had expressed a similar opinion by arguing against cooperation with French authorities on grounds that 'foreign governments are... very stupid in using information given them'.[26] To these misgivings we can add those of E. R. Henry who in 1901 declined an Italian offer to have 'the Metropolitan Police... work in co-operation with an [Italian] Agent' as posing the 'gravest risk' to Special Branch's operations,[27] and who in 1904 dismissed the plans laid out in St Petersburg as fettering the English police.

Was such isolationism warranted? By modern standards it certainly appears regressive and counter-productive, but given the scope of transnational political radicalism in late nineteenth- and early twentieth-century Britain, the conclusion that British authorities were right to shun European proposals for a pan-continental counter-terrorist strategy appears mostly justified. Not only were such proposals excessively punitive and centred on the policing needs of authoritarian and anti-democratic regimes like those of Germany and Russia, they also plastered over the weaknesses of continental policing systems. Such weaknesses were painfully exposed by the string of high-profile assassinations of the 1890s and particularly by the failed assassination of King Leopold II by Gennaro Rubino – an Italian double agent with a guilty conscience who had been funded by an unwitting Italian government official. More crucially, proposals for pan-European police cooperation were fundamentally at odds with the extra-legality of the British system, namely the very thing which made the policing of extremism in Britain appear unobtrusively efficient in the eyes of the public.

Whether the early British model of political policing was in fact efficient is of course debatable. On the one hand, its particular nature – hierarchical *and* fractured; institutionalized *and* beholden to individual will; non-partisan *and* subject to specific political agendas – occasionally led to inefficient or excessive responses to political threats, exposing police institutions to public criticism and ridicule (as in 1894 and 1909). On the other hand, the individuals who were most successful in shaping the structure and direction of the political police system were, by and large, competent enough (or skilled enough at hiding their incompetence) to warrant a widespread reputation for dogged energy and patient readiness (as embodied by William Melville's image in the press).

The threat posed by Fenianism was, as we have seen, a serious one to British authorities, but despite (and arguably because of) the individual efforts of William Harcourt, Edward Jenkinson, James Monro and Robert Anderson, by the mid-1880s Britain still lacked a cohesive, proactive strategy for containing it. Jenkinson's transatlantic network of informers and double agents did go a long way in sowing the seeds of self-doubt and paranoia within the Irish American Fenian milieu, but it did not entirely paralyze its militant ambitions, ultimately dissipating shortly after the controversial spymaster's fall from grace.

Arguably, if the course of Irish Nationalist politics had not changed considerably in the later 1880s, Fenian 'skirmishing' would have still been gradually abandoned given its undeniable failure in extracting any political concessions from the British government. Irish Nationalist politics did, however, undergo a dramatic, perhaps even tragic, transformation as the Parnellite decade drew to an end. The increasing opposition of the IRB to dynamite (much to the displeasure of hard-line American Clan na Gaelers), the launch of the constitutional Irish National League and the spectacular demise of the Irish Party's towering leader – all worked to fatally undermine insurgent Fenianism to a greater extent than the byzantine machinations of British spies. Britain's model of political policing may not have been wholly inefficient in its battle with Irish republican terrorism, but the demise of the latter was ultimately more fortuitous than foreseeable.

After Fenianism, there were no more significant threats to national security until the 'great labour unrest' of the immediate pre-war years and no more significant insurrectionary threats until the Easter Rising of 1916. Revolutionary anarchism, as has been shown, may have frightened many a law-abiding British subject, especially through its association with mindless violence and 'barbaric' foreignness. However, its very exoticism and ideological isolation from mainstream British socialism gradually eroded its shock value as the 1890s wore on, and by the early 1900s it was clear that 'propaganda by the deed' was a European, not a British, problem. Anarchism did make a short-lived comeback in the closing years of the Edwardian decade, but by then it had already metamorphosed into an aspect of the so-called Alien Question.

Edwardian radicalism was, despite alarmist talk of revolution in conservative circles of opinion, not quite the civilizational threat either. Militant suffragettes managed to annoy a great deal of important (and not so important) people with their campaigns of harassment, arson, window smashing and pillar box destruction, but threats of revolutionary – as opposed to symbolic – violence, such as the supposed plan to assassinate Asquith in 1909, turned out to be abortive. Non-Irish anti-colonial nationalism, though increasingly a serious threat in parts of the Empire, failed to garner momentum in the imperial metropole after the spectacular assassination of Curzon Wyllie in 1909 by an Indian Hindu radical. Even the industrial unrest of 1910–14, despite paralyzing episodes, such as the national coal strike of 1912, was ultimately divorced from any genuine potential for a revolutionary syndicalist movement. This is illustrated by the fate of the embattled South Wales miners who in 1911 lost the strike against the owners of the Cambrian Combine after being deprived of union funding and support.

In the absence of a truly destabilizing threat to national security and given the weight of contemporary public fears, being seen to be efficient becomes indistinguishable from actually being efficient. When, in other words, a great number of people fear the danger posed by lawless and foreign anarchists, being seen to be subverting the subverters in an unobtrusive and 'subterranean' manner (as the *Sunday Times* put it in 1897) becomes the mark of a ruthless and cunning performance in the service of public order. As Walter Emden, Mayor of Westminster, explained in his 1904 paean to William Melville, if preventing was better than curing, the head of Special Branch was undoubtedly 'the greatest of doctors'. 'We know not,' Emden continued 'but might in gratitude imagine now, what shocks to the civilized world, what public and private grief this one man may have saved us. If we are grateful for what has been done, we should be more grateful for what has not been done.'[28]

# Notes

## Introduction

[1] Jean-Paul Brodeur, 'High Policing and Low Policing: Remarks about the Policing of Political Activities', *Social Problems* 30 (1983), 512.

[2] Ibid., 513–14.

[3] Von Hentig, quoted in Leon Radzinowicz, *A History of English Criminal Law and Its Administration from 1750, Vol. 3: Cross-currents in the Movement for the Reform of the Police* (London: Stevens and Sons Ltd, 1948), 572.

[4] See Charles Reith, *British Police and the Democratic Ideal* (Oxford: Oxford University Press, 1943); Leon Radzinowicz, *A History of English Criminal Law and Its Administration from 1750, Vols 1–5* (London: Stevens and Sons Ltd, 1948–86); T. A. Critchley, *A History of Police in England and Wales, Second revised edition* (London: Constable, 1978); David Ascoli, *The Queen's Peace: The Origins and Development of the Metropolitan Police, 1829–1979* (London: Hamish Hamilton, 1979).

[5] See Robert D. Storch, '"The plague of blue locusts": Police Reform and Popular Resistance in Northern England, 1840–1857', *International Review of Social History* 20 (1975), 61–90; idem, 'The Policeman as Domestic Missionary: Urban Discipline and Popular Culture in Northern England, 1850–1880', *Journal of Social History* 9 (1976), 481–509; Douglas Hay and Francis Snyder, ed., *Policing and Prosecution in Britain, 1750–1850* (Oxford: Clarendon Press, 1989); V. A. C. Gatrell, 'Crime, Authority and the Policeman-State', in F. M. L. Thompson, ed., *The Cambridge Social History of Britain 1750–1950, Vol. 3: Social Agencies and Institutions* (Cambridge: Cambridge University Press, 1990), 243–310.

[6] Robert Reiner, *The Politics of the Police, Fourth edition* (Oxford: Oxford University Press, 2010), 66. See also Clive Emsley, *The English Police: A Political and Social History, Second edition* (London and New York: Longman, 1996) and for an even earlier example, Victor Bailey, ed., *Policing and Punishment in Nineteenth Century Britain* (London: Croom Helm, 1981).

[7] See Reiner, 39–78.

[8] Tony Bunyan, *The History and Practice of the Political Police in Britain* (London: Julian Friedman Publishers, 1976), 102–4.

[9] Philip Thurmond Smith, *Policing Victorian London: Political Policing, Public Order, and the London Metropolitan Police* (Westport, CT: Greenwood Press, 1985), 199.

[10] Bernard Porter, *The Origins of the Vigilant State: The London Metropolitan Police Special Branch before the First World War* (Woodbridge: The Boydell Press, 1987), 192.

[11] Ibid., 193–4.

[12] Ibid., 192.

[13] Ibid., 93.
[14] Ibid., 186.
[15] Emsley, 101.
[16] Richard Thurlow, *The Secret State: British Internal Security in the Twentieth Century* (Oxford: Blackwell Publishers, 1994), 5 ff., 38.
[17] Haia Shpayer-Makov, *The Ascent of the Detective: Police Sleuths in Victorian and Edwardian England* (Oxford: Oxford University Press, 2011), 52–3.
[18] Constance Bantman, *The French Anarchists in London, 1880–1914: Exile and Transnationalism in the First Globalisation* (Liverpool: Liverpool University Press, 2013), 149.
[19] See Tom Corfe, *The Phoenix Park Murders: Conflict, Compromise and Tragedy in Ireland, 1879–1882* (London: Hodder and Stoughton, 1968); Leon O'Broin, *The Prime Informer: A Suppressed Scandal* (London: Sidgwick & Jackson, 1971); K. R. M. Short, *The Dynamite War: Irish-American Bombers in Victorian Britain* (Atlantic Highlands, NJ: Humanities Press, 1979).
[20] See Christy Campbell, *Fenian Fire: The British Government Plot to Assassinate Queen Victoria* (London: HarperCollins, 2003); Niall Whelehan, *The Dynamiters: Irish Nationalism and Political Violence in the Wider World, 1867–1900* (Cambridge: Cambridge University Press, 2012); John Gantt, *Irish Terrorism in the Atlantic Community, 1865–1922* (Basingstoke: Palgrave Macmillan, 2010); Seán McConville, *Irish Political Prisoners, 1848–1922: Theatres of War* (London and New York: Routledge, 2003); Joseph McKenna, *The Irish-American Dynamite Campaign: A History, 1881–1896* (Jefferson, NC: McFarland & Co., 2012).
[21] See Constance Bantman, *The French Anarchists in London, 1880–1914: Exile and Transnationalism in the First Globalisation* (Liverpool: Liverpool University Press, 2013), 117–56, passim.; Paolo Di Paola, *The Knights Errant of Anarchy: London and the Italian Anarchist Diaspora, 1880–1917* (Liverpool: Liverpool University Press, 2013), 83–5, 122–56, passim; Alex Butterworth, *The World That Never Was: A True Story of Dreamers, Schemers, Anarchists and Secret Agents* (New York: Pantheon Books, 2010), 297–9, 320–1, 329–38.
[22] Bantman, 124–5, 130; Di Paola, 153–5; Butterworth, 320, 330–6.
[23] Patrick Joyce, *The State of Freedom: A Social History of the British State since 1800* (Cambridge: Cambridge University Press, 2013), 188.
[24] Memoranda by Robert Anderson, 13 December 1898 and 14 January 1899, TNA HO 45/10254/X36450.
[25] Located off Dame Street in Dublin, this medieval castle served as the seat of successive British administrations of Ireland until 1922 when it was relinquished to the new Irish government.
[26] Elun Gabriel, *Assassins and Conspirators: Anarchism, Socialism, and Political Culture in Imperial Germany* (DeKalb, IL: Northern Illinois University Press, 2014), 74.
[27] Ibid., 77.
[28] David Clay Large, *Berlin* (New York: Basic Books, 2000), chapter 1, Kindle.
[29] Daniel Beer, *The House of the Dead: Siberian Exile Under the Tsars* (London: Penguin, 2017), 291.

[30] For a full treatment of the topic, see Fredric S. Zuckerman, *The Tsarist Secret Police Abroad: Policing Europe in a Modernizing World* (Basingstoke and New York: Palgrave Macmillan, 2003).

[31] Emsley and Barbara Weinberger, ed., *Policing Western Europe: Politics, Professionalism, and Public Order, 1850–1940* (London: Greenwood Press, 1991), 37.

[32] Malcolm Anderson, *In Thrall to Political Change: Police and Gendarmerie in France* (Oxford: Oxford University Press, 2011), 270.

[33] Ibid.

[34] *Household Words*, 21 September 1850.

[35] Bernard Porter, *Plots and Paranoia: A History of Political Espionage in Britain, 1790–1988* (Boston, MA: Unwin Hyman. 1989), 81.

[36] For recent efforts in this direction, see Richard Bach Jensen, *The Battle against Anarchist Terrorism: An International History, 1878–1934* (Cambridge: Cambridge University Press, 2014), passim; and Bantman, 127–30, 149–53.

[37] Jensen, 67, 118; Bantman, 148.

[38] Memorandum by Godfrey Lushington, 7 June 1886, TNA HO 144/721/110757.

[39] *Sunday Times*, 15 August 1897.

[40] Robert Darnton, *Mesmerism and the End of the Enlightenment in France* (Cambridge, MA: Harvard University Press, 1968), viii.

## Prologue

[1] Linda Colley, *Britons: Forging the Nation, 1707–1837* (New Haven, CT: Yale University Press, 1992), 32.

[2] William Pitt the Younger, quoted in *The Parliamentary Register, vol. XXXVIII* (London: J. Debrett, 1794), 246.

[3] Glyn Williams and John Ramsden, *Ruling Britannia: A Political History of Britain, 1688–1988* (London: Longman, 1990), 151.

[4] For a brief but comprehensive account, see David Johnson, *Regency Revolution: The Case of Arthur Thistlewood* (Salisbury: Compton Russell, 1974).

[5] Johnson, 17–24.

[6] Ibid., 13, 32.

[7] Bernard Porter, *Plots and Paranoia: A History of Political Espionage in Britain, 1790–1988* (Boston, MA: Unwin Hyman. 1989), 53f.

[8] Johnson, 56.

[9] Malcolm Chase, *1820: Disorder and Stability in the United Kingdom* (Oxford: Oxford University Press, 2013), 55.

[10] Sidmouth, quoted in Williams and Ramsden, 179.

[11] Johnson, 147ff.

[12] *Chambers's Journal*, 25 September 1858. Note the early and conspicuous use of the term 'political police' to describe Home Office-sanctioned counter-subversive operations.

[13] Williams and Ramsden, 188.

[14] Porter, *Plots and Paranoia*, 66.

[15] Metropolitan Police Act 1829, 10 Geo. IV, c. 44.
[16] Tony Bunyan, *The History and Practice of the Political Police in Britain* (London: Julian Friedman Publishers, 1976), 63.
[17] Clive Emsley, *Crime and Society in England, 1750–1900*, Fourth edition (Harow: Longman, 2010), 238.
[18] Mayne, quoted in James Winter, *London's Teeming Streets, 1830–1914* (London: Routledge, 2013), 52.
[19] 'Police Committee – Report and Minutes of Evidence', quoted in *The Quarterly Review, vol. L* (London: John Murray, 1834), 265.
[20] Porter, *Plots and Paranoia*, 76.
[21] *Household Words*, 21 September 1850.
[22] *Times*, 24 August 1875.
[23] Quoted in Haia Shpayer-Makov, *The Ascent of the Detective: Police Sleuths in Victorian and Edwardian England* (Oxford: Oxford University Press, 2011), 34.
[24] Porter, *Plots and Paranoia*, 81.
[25] Brian Jenkins, *The Fenian Problem: Insurgency and Terrorism in a Liberal State 1858–1874* (Montreal and Kingston: McGill-Queen's University Press, 2008), 155.

## CHAPTER 1
## 'A spider's web of Police Communication'

[1] William Harcourt to Queen Victoria, 24 February 1881, quoted in Porter, *Origins of the Vigilant State*, 41.
[2] *Manchester Courier and Lancashire General Advertiser*, 27 January 1881.
[3] *Times*, 17 January 1881.
[4] *Belfast News-Letter*, 6 January 1881.
[5] Born in Cork in 1843, O'Donovan Rossa was arrested in Dublin in 1865 for his role in a failed Fenian uprising and subsequently jailed in England. Pardoned in 1870 along with other convicted Fenians, O'Donovan Rossa left for America where he became known as a vocal supporter of guerilla-style violence (or 'skirmishing') against mainland British authorities as a way to advance the cause of Irish independence. To this end, he established a 'skirmishing fund' which was maintained through subscriptions and sales of his *United Irishman* newspaper.
[6] In early 1871 several Fenians who had been imprisoned for treason in Ireland and Britain found their way to New York after being pardoned by Prime Minister William Ewart Gladstone. Five of the exiles in particular, including Devoy and O'Donovan Rossa, were welcomed with great acclaim by the local Irish American community and were even received at the White House by President Grant (much to the ire of British authorities).
[7] HC Deb, 22 February 1881, vol. 258, cols 1553–5.
[8] Memo by Anderson, 14 December 1870, TNA HO 144/1538/6.
[9] Jeremiah O'Donovan Rossa, *Rossa's Recollections, 1838 to 1898* (Marine's Harbor, NY: O'Donovan Rossa, 1898), 62.

[10] Founded in 1879 and presided over by Parnell himself, the Land League brought together a host of political organisations all over Ireland in the common goal of agitating for the reduction of excessive rents and the transfer of land ownership to peasants.

[11] Report by Howard Vincent, 2 January 1881, TNA HO 144/72/A19. The report was, as per Vincent's description, based on information 'from a very high & powerful element in the Irish agitation'.

[12] Harcourt to Vincent, 23 January 1881, quoted in S. H. Jeyes, *The Life of Sir Howard Vincent* (London: George Allen & Co. Ltd, 1912), 106.

[13] Harcourt to Henderson, 24 January 1881, TNA MEPO 3/3070.

[14] Gladstone, quoted in John Morley, *The Life of Gladstone* (London: Hodder and Stoughton, 1927), 390.

[15] Margaret O'Callaghan, *British High Politics and a Nationalist Ireland: Criminality, Land and the Law under Forster and Balfour* (New York: St Martin's Press, 1994), 62 ff.

[16] Childers to Harcourt, 23 January 1881, TNA HO 144/72/A19.

[17] Morley, 391.

[18] Memo by Edmund Henderson, 26 January 1881, TNA MEPO 3/3070.

[19] Police Report, 1 February 1881, TNA MEPO 3/3070.

[20] Police Report, 2 March 1881, TNA MEPO 3/3070.

[21] Police Report, 4 March 1881, TNA MEPO 3/3070.

[22] Harcourt to Queen Victoria, 24 February 1881, quoted in Porter, *The Origins of the Vigilant State*, 41.

[23] Report by Le Caron, 17 February 1881, TNA HO 144/1538/6.

[24] Niall Whelehan, *The Dynamiters: Irish Nationalism and Political Violence in the Wider World, 1867–1900* (Cambridge: Cambridge University Press, 2012), 164.

[25] Ibid.

[26] Unsigned memo, 31 March 1881, TNA MEPO 3/3070.

[27] Jeyes, 116.

[28] Quoted in *Reg.* v. *Most*, May 1881, p. 13, TNA HO 144/77/A3385.

[29] Friedrich Engels to J. P. Becker, 1 April 1880, in Karl Marx and Friedrich Engels, *Correspondence 1846–1895* (London: Martin Lawrence Ltd, 1934), 380.

[30] Bernard Porter, *The Refugee Question in Mid-Victorian Politics* (Cambridge: Cambridge University Press, 1979), 46ff.

[31] In 1858 Felice Orsini, an Italian nationalist who had momentarily taken political refuge in Britain, attempted, unsuccessfully, to assassinate Napoleon III in Paris. Tried that same year for his involvement in Orsini's conspiracy, Simon Bernard (likewise a political refugee in Britain) was acquitted by an all-English jury which, along with an overwhelming majority of the British public, had been ably persuaded by the defence counsel to regard the accused as an innocent freedom fighter hounded by a morally bankrupt Liberal government beholden to French despotism. The effect of Bernard's trial was nothing short of monumental. It neutralized Prime Minister Palmerston's attempts to strengthen the law dealing with conspiracy to murder, put the fear of populist backlash back in the hearts of government ministers and reaffirmed the sacrosanctity of political refuge on one hand, as well as the public's contempt for continental-style methods of policing dissent on the other. See Caroline Shaw, *Britannia's Embrace: Modern*

*Humanitarianism and the Imperial Origins of Refugee Relief* (Oxford: Oxford University Press, 2015), 69f.

[32] *Daily Gazette*, 19 March 1881. Although the British press' sudden interest in this obscure German-language periodical may seem strange, it is worth noting that ever since its inception in 1879 *Freiheit* had occasionally featured in the 'Foreign Intelligence' column of several British newspapers due mainly to the fact that its illegal smuggling into Germany and Austria-Hungary routinely got socialists in those countries in trouble with the law.

[33] Ponsonby to Gladstone, 20 March 1881, quoted in Bernard Porter, 'The *Freiheit* Prosecutions, 1881–1882', *The Historical Journal* 23 (1980), 842.

[34] Ibid.

[35] A. G. Gardiner, *The Life of Sir William Harcourt* (London: Constable & Co. Ltd, 1923), 404.

[36] *Reg. v. Most*, p. 16, TNA HO 144/77/A3385.

[37] Ever the politician, Harcourt conveniently brushed over the fact that having already decided in favour of prosecuting Most the day before (as he confessed to Granville), he then 'induced the Cabinet to agree with him'. Gardiner, 404.

[38] Harcourt to Liddell, 26 March 1881, TNA HO 144/77/A3385.

[39] *Standard*, 29 March 1881.

[40] *Reg. v. Most*, pp. 18f, TNA HO 144/77/A3385.

[41] Memo by A. K. Stephenson, 1 April 1881, TNA HO 144/77/A3385.

[42] Vincent to Harcourt, 31 March 1881, TNA HO 144/77/A3385.

[43] *Reg. v. Most*, pp. 22f, TNA HO 144/77/A3385.

[44] Vincent to Harcourt, 31 March 1881, TNA HO 144/77/A3385.

[45] Memo by Stephenson, 1 April 1881, TNA HO 144/77/A3385.

[46] HC Deb, 1 April 1881, vol. 260, col. 464.

[47] *Daily News*, 1 April 1881.

[48] *Times*, 1 April 1881.

[49] *Belfast News-Letter*, 11 April 1881.

[50] *Reg. v. Most*, pp. 6f, TNA HO 144/77/A3385.

[51] Reports on *Freiheit* by Inspector Charles von Tornow, 28 November 1882–24 January 1883, TNA HO 144/77/A3385.

[52] Harcourt to Queen Victoria, 9 April 1881, quoted in Porter, 'The *Freiheit* Prosecutions', 848.

[53] Ponsonby to Harcourt, 30 May 1881, quoted in ibid.

## CHAPTER 2
## 'Panic and indifference'

[1] Robert Anderson, *Sidelights on the Home Rule Movement* (New York: E. P. Dutton and Company, 1906), 91.

[2] Maurice Moser and C. F. Rideal, *Stories from Scotland Yard* (London: George Routledge and Sons, 1890), 20.

[3] Jeyes, 118.

[4] Quoted in Joseph McKenna, *The Irish-American Dynamite Campaign: A History, 1881–1896* (Jefferson, NC: McFarland & Co., 2012), 16.

[5] *Glasgow Herald*, 7 May 1881; *Daily News*, 18 May 1881.

[6] *Lloyd's Weekly Newspaper*, 12 June 1881.

[7] *Northampton Mercury*, 6 August 1881.

[8] Moser's exact role in the government's anti-Fenian operations is unclear. His 1890 *Stories from Scotland Yard* (published three years after his retirement) gives no details on the nature of his intelligence-gathering duties at Scotland Yard, concentrating instead on the entertainment value of his exploits. Tellingly, Moser refers to having been 'despatched' to Liverpool in 1881 (*Stories*, 22) while only vaguely implying that his mission had been directly sanctioned by Harcourt and Vincent (*Stories*, 26). Similarly, he describes his shadowing of Fenian exiles in Paris (during 1883–84) as in accordance with 'instructions from the Yard' without going into specifics.

[9] Moser et al., 25.

[10] Ibid., 24.

[11] Ibid., 26.

[12] James R. Lowell (1819–1891), American poet and US Minister to the Court of St James from 1880 to 1885.

[13] James G. Blaine (1830–1893), Republican statesman and US Secretary of State in 1881 and between 1889 and 1892.

[14] Harcourt to Lord Granville, 3 July 1881, quoted in Gardiner, 430.

[15] Ibid.

[16] Lowell to Blaine, 30 July 1881, quoted in Jonathan Gantt, *Irish Terrorism in the Atlantic Community, 1865–1922* (New York: Palgrave Macmillan, 2010), 143f.

[17] Gantt, 145.

[18] Clipperton to Home Office, 7–9 July 1881, TNA HO 144/72/A19.

[19] S. Stoney (JP) to Harcourt, 27 July 1881; 'Translation of a letter received at HM's Consulate at Leghorn, containing revelations [on] the fabrication of Infernal Machines in certain Ports of the U.S', 17 October 1881, TNA HO 144/84/A7266.

[20] Note by Harcourt, 6 November 1881; note by Godfrey Lushington, 4 November 1881, TNA HO 144/84/A7266.

[21] Most's ideas on the subject were published in his 1885 pamphlet *Revolutionäre Kriegswisenschaft* (lit. 'Revolutionary War Science') which shortly became the unofficial user's manual for scores of politically motivated dynamite enthusiasts.

[22] As a recent biographer has argued, Harcourt had been since his youth a proud and condescending, but also deeply insecure man prone to emotional outbursts. See Patrick Jackson, *Harcourt and Son. A Political Biography of Sir William Harcourt, 1827–1904* (Madison, NJ: Fairleigh Dickinson University Press. 2004), 19–24, 31.

[23] Gardiner, 430.

[24] Henri Le Caron, *Twenty-Five Years in The Secret Service: The Recollections of a Spy* (London: William Heinemann, 1892), 187–92.

[25] Le Caron to Robert Anderson, 12 December 1881, TNA HO 144/1538/6.

[26] Paul Bew, *Ireland: The Politics of Enmity, 1789–2006* (Oxford: Oxford University Press, 2007), 328f.

[27] Morley, 394.

[28] Bew, 332.
[29] Deposition by James Carey, 21 February 1883, TNA HO 144/98/A16380C; Tom Corfe, *The Phoenix Park Murders: Conflict, Compromise and Tragedy in Ireland, 1879–1882* (London: Hodder and Stoughton, 1968), 186–8.
[30] *Pall Mall Gazette*, 8 May 1882.
[31] Harcourt to Earl Spencer, 8 June 1882, quoted in Gardiner, 445.
[32] *Daily News*, 15 May 1882.
[33] Harcourt to Spencer, 14 May 1882, quoted in Gardiner, 442.
[34] Ibid.
[35] Frederick M. Bussy, *Irish Conspiracies: Recollections of John Mallon (The Great Irish Detective) and Other Reminiscences* (London: Everett & Co., 1910), 60, 80. Mallon, who had led the G (Detective) Division of the Dublin Metropolitan Police since 1874, was in charge of the city's anti-Nationalist operations and was a widely respected figure by everyone at Dublin Castle. As he later recalled in his memoirs (penned by Irish journalist Frederick Bussy), several members of the group responsible for the Phoenix Park murders had in fact been arrested as early as 9 May. They remained in custody until September when, due to a lack of incriminating evidence against them and the lapsing of Forster's Suspects Act, they were released.
[36] Brackenbury went on to become the first Director of Military Intelligence at the War Office in 1886, ending his career in the British Army as director-general of ordnance before his retirement in 1904. His memoirs, *Some Memories of My Spare Time*, were published in 1909. See Ian F. W. Beckett, 'Brackenbury, Sir Henry (1837–1914)', in *Oxford Dictionary of National Biography*, (Oxford: Oxford University Press, 2004), online edition [henceforth *ODNB* (online ed.)], accessed 1 March 2018.
[37] When asked on 12 May by the Assistant Chief Constable of the Lancashire Constabulary whether local police might be given across-the-board powers to open the mail of suspected local Fenians, Harcourt replied that while a one-off might be acceptable, provided 'the Post Office could arrange to have this skillfully done', it was simply impossible to 'issue a warrant giving general permission… to open all letters directed to these men' (Minute by Harcourt, 13 May 1882, TNA HO 144/98/A16380). The ghost of James Graham, the Home Secretary who had been politically destroyed after tampering with Giuseppe Mazzini's correspondence in the 1840s, evidently still haunted the halls of the Home Office.
[38] *Standard*, 22 May 1882.
[39] Spencer to Gladstone, 7 June 1882, in Peter Gordon, ed., *The Red Earl: The Papers of the Fifth Earl Spencer 1835–1910* (Northampton: Northamptonshire Record Society, 1981), 205.
[40] Harcourt to Spencer, 12 June 1882, quoted in Gardiner, 446.
[41] Pinkerton to Gladstone, 8 July 1882, TNA HO 144/1538/4.
[42] Anderson to Harcourt, 1 August 1882; Archibald to Anderson, 31 July 1882, TNA HO 144/1538/4. In 1876, Archibald had employed some of Pinkerton's detectives to monitor a group of San Francisco 'skirmishers' who were (mistakenly) thought to be planning a campaign in Britain.
[43] Harcourt to Spencer, 25 August 1882, TNA HO 144/1538/4.

44 Henry Brackenbury, *Some Memories of My Spare Time* (Edinburgh and London: William Blackwood & Sons, 1909), 312.

45 Harcourt to Gladstone, 18 June 1882, quoted in Gardiner, 448.

46 Spencer to G. O. Trevelyan, 1 August 1882, in Gordon, 217.

47 HC Deb, 3 August 1882, vol. 273, col. 685.

48 *Freeman's Journal and Daily Commercial Advertiser*, 3 August 1882.

49 Spencer to Trevelyan, 1 August 1882, in Gordon, 217.

50 Quoted in Corfe, 235.

51 Corfe, 236.

52 *Glasgow Herald*, 22 January 1883.

53 *Standard*, 22 January 1883.

54 Le Caron to Anderson, 17 June 1882, TNA HO 144/1538/6.

55 Harcourt to Spencer, 31 January 1883, quoted in Gardiner, 473.

56 Anderson, *Sidelights on the Home Rule Movement*, 91.

57 Even the queen noted how 'Mr. Gladstone [will] be dreadfully shaken by all these disclosures, as he never would believe in any connection between this Land League and the Fenians'. Ponsonby to Harcourt, 20 February 1883, quoted in Gardiner, 474.

58 Bussy, 110.

59 Order for Frank Byrne's release from police custody in Paris, 8 March 1883, *Archives de la Préfecture de Police de Paris*, Carton BA 924.

60 *Glasgow Herald*, 16 March 1883.

61 Vivian Majendie, 'Preliminary Report on the Explosions of March 15', 19 March 1883, TNA HO 144/114/A25908.

62 *Pall Mall Gazette*, 16 March 1883.

63 J. H. Codger to Harcourt, 16 March 1883, TNA HO 144/114/A25908.

64 Joining the Metropolitan Police in 1872, the Kerry-born Melville was transferred to the Scotland Yard CID in 1879 at the rank of detective-sergeant. He played an active role in Irish Branch, eventually becoming superintendent of Special Branch after its creation in 1887. For a full account of his life, see Andrew Cook, *M: MI5's First Spymaster* (Stroud: Tempus Publishing, 2006).

65 Quoted in Paul Begg and Keith Skinner, *The Scotland Yard Files: 150 Years of the C.I.D. 1842–1992* (London: Headline, 1992), 90.

CHAPTER 3

## Mr Jenkinson goes to London

1 Niall Whelehan, '"Scientific warfare or the quickest way to liberate Ireland": the Brooklyn Dynamite School', *History Ireland* 16 (2008), 42–5.

2 Whelehan, *The Dynamiters*, 159–63; John McEnnis, *The Clan-na-Gael and the Murder of Dr. Cronin* (San Francisco, CA: G. P. Woodward, 1889), 57.

3 This select group of Irish policemen had been active in England since the late 1860s, supplying information to both Dublin Castle and the Home Office on the doings of local (especially London-based) Irish republicans. Porter, *Origins of the Vigilant State*, 16f.

⁴ The Home Office Secret Service (set up during the wars with Revolutionary France to gather intelligence on domestic radicals) was, by the late nineteenth century, a 'ghost' department without any permanent staff other than its director, Robert Anderson. Its funds, amounting to £24,000 per annum in the 1870s (Porter, *Origins of the Vigilant State*, 18), were used to recruit and pay off informers and later to supplement the income of Scotland Yard's Irish and Special Branches.

⁵ John Littlechild, *The Reminiscences of Chief-Inspector Littlechild, Second edition* (London: The Leadenhall Press, 1894), 10.

⁶ Quoted in Christy Campbell, *Fenian Fire: The British Government Plot to Assassinate Queen Victoria* (London: HarperCollins, 2003), 125.

⁷ Patrick McIntyre, 'Scotland Yard', in *Reynolds's Newspaper*, 10 March 1895.

⁸ Campbell, 131f.

⁹ Ibid., 124.

¹⁰ William John Nott-Bower (Chief Constable of Liverpool City Police) to Harcourt, 29 March 1883, TNA HO 144/115/A26302; Report by Dr J. Campbell-Brown on items found in Deasey's possession, 29 March 1883, TNA HO 144/115/A26302.

¹¹ Quoted in Campbell, 127.

¹² See Chapter 2, p. 40.

¹³ Report by Chief Inspector Littlechild, 17 May 1887, TNA HO 144/116/A26493.

¹⁴ William Lane Booker to Earl Granville, 24 April 1883, TNA HO 144/116/A26493.

¹⁵ 'Information from Consul General at New York as to Gallagher, Norman, O'Connor & Lynch', 22 April 1883, TNA HO 144/116/A26493.

¹⁶ Report by William Melville, 4 April 1883, quoted in Cook, *M: MI5's First Spymaster*, 40.

¹⁷ Tasked in 1881 by Scotland Yard Superintendent Adolphus Williamson with investigating the movements of London Fenians (Littlechild, *Reminiscences*, 10), Littlechild became the Irish Branch's leading inspector in 1883 and was appointed superintendent of Special Branch (Section D) after its creation in 1887.

¹⁸ McIntyre, 'Scotland Yard', *Reynolds's Newspaper*, 24 February 1895.

¹⁹ Harcourt to Gladstone, 6 April 1883, quoted in Gardiner, 480.

²⁰ Explosives Substances Act 1883, 46 Vict., c. 3.

²¹ Gardiner, 480.

²² In the spring of 1883 Gladstone proposed a London Government Bill that would have expanded the City Corporation into an elected body responsible for the entire metropolis and in the process, wresting away control of the Metropolitan Police from the Home Secretary. Harcourt protested vociferously and threatened to resign. Gladstone's bill was shelved for two years and then permanently abandoned, marking the only occasion the Home Secretary's policing powers were seriously questioned by a serving Prime Minister until the modern era.

²³ Harcourt to Spencer, 14 June 1883, quoted in Gardiner, 481.

²⁴ Anderson to Harcourt, 20 June 1883, TNA HO 144/1537/1.

²⁵ Jenkinson to Harcourt, 11 August 1883, quoted in Porter, *Origins of the Vigilant State*, 47.

²⁶ Memorandum by Jenkinson, 10 September 1883, TNA HO 144/721/110757.

27 Note by Harcourt, 5 July 1883, TNA HO 144/115/A26302. McIntyre, 'Scotland Yard', *Reynolds's Newspaper*, 3 March 1895.

28 First established in Ireland during the early nineteenth-century, ribbon societies (so named after their distinguishing insignia) were in fact agrarian secret societies that sought to defend the rights of destitute Catholic tenant-farmers and agitate against British rule. Spreading to the British mainland by the middle of the century, ribbonism helped channel the frustrated political ambitions of many Irish immigrants who sympathized with the Nationalist cause, but was never explicitly associated with Fenianism.

29 Sean Connolly, 'Patriotism and Nationalism', in Alvin Jackson, ed., *The Oxford Handbook of Modern Irish History* (Oxford: Oxford University Press, 2014), 39.

30 Charles Tennant Couper, ed., *Report of the Trial of the Dynamitards ...* (Edinburgh: William Green, 1884), 61.

31 Testimony by William Porter, in Couper, 70.

32 Scotland Yard did not legally have a national remit, but in Fenian-related matters affecting national security authorities in London enjoyed an undisputed primacy. As the arrests of the Tradeston Gasworks bombers in late 1883 (see Chapter 3, p. 57) reveal, Glasgow CID detectives were aware and supportive of this arrangement. Occasionally, however, lack of communication between Scotland Yard and Scottish authorities in terrorism-related investigations could lead to embarrassing mishaps like the inadvertent shadowing of Irish Branch officers by Dundee police in 1884 (see Chapter 4, p. 70).

33 Porter, in Couper, 70.

34 Máirtín Ó Catháin, *Irish Republicanism in Scotland, 1858–1916* (Dublin and Portland, OR: Irish Academic Press, 2007), 133f.

35 *Glasgow Herald*, 20 December 1883; Couper, 253f.

36 Gosselin to Harcourt, 22 August 1883, quoted in Porter, *Origins of the Vigilant State*, 47.

37 Jeyes, 127; TNA HO 144/115/A27928, passim.

38 McIntyre, 'Scotland Yard', *Reynolds's Newspaper*, 17 March 1895.

39 *Times*, 31 October 1883.

40 *Birmingham Daily Post*, 1 November 1883.

41 *Morning Post*, 22 January 1884. Anderson had already warned of an impending plot against the Prince of Wales back in November 1883. Anderson to Harcourt, 11 November 1883, TNA HO 1537/1.

42 Quoted in Gardiner, 490.

43 Harcourt to Ponsonby, 21 November 1883, quoted in Gardiner, 490.

44 *Pall Mall Gazette*, 26 February 1884

45 Queen Victoria to the Home Office, 26 February 1884, TNA HO 144/133/A34707.

46 Majendie to the Home Office, 26 February 1884, TNA HO 144/133/A34707.

47 *Glasgow Herald*, 29 February 1884.

48 Ibid.

49 *Birmingham Daily Post*, 3 March 1884.

50 Metropolitan Police 'Wanted' Poster, 4 March 1884, TNA HO 144/133/A34707.

51 William Harcourt to Lewis Harcourt, 29 February 1884, quoted in Gardiner, 503.

52 Harcourt to Queen Victoria, 29 February 1884, quoted in Gardiner, 503.

[53] In February 1884 it was finally agreed to increase the pay of Irish Branch constables to match that of their other colleagues in the CID. Harcourt noted that while 'the payment [had to] be sanctioned... some limit ought to be placed on the number of add[itiona]l constables employed in future'. Note by Harcourt, 5 February 1884, TNA HO 144/130/A34371.

[54] Anderson to Harcourt, 29 January, 15 February 1884, TNA HO 144/1537/1.

[55] There were other instances of juvenile labour being used by Scotland Yard authorities. In late 1883, for example, Thomas Carter, a 'destitute British boy' of sixteen whose apparent familiarity with several languages brought him to the attention of Howard Vincent, was taken out of the workhouse and 'temporarily maintained' until he was eventually found a position in the duke of Montrose's household. Memo by Godfrey Lushington, 11 January 1884, TNA HO 144/130/A34328.

[56] Gosselin to Harcourt, 29 January 1884, quoted in Porter, *Origins of the Vigilant State*, 48.

[57] Harcourt to Spencer, 4 March 1884, quoted in Gordon, 266.

[58] Harcourt to Spencer, 4 March 1884, quoted in Porter, *Origins of the Vigilant State*, 49.

[59] Bew, 337.

[60] Spencer to Trevelyan, 7 March 1884, in Gordon, 266.

[61] Memorandum by Jenkinson, 6 March 1884, TNA HO 144/721/110757.

[62] Memorandum by Harcourt, 10 March 1884, TNA HO 144/721/110757.

[63] Ibid.

## CHAPTER 4

## 'The new detective army'

[1] *Glasgow Herald*, 14 April 1884.

[2] *Freeman's Journal and Daily Commercial Advertiser*, 19 March 1884.

[3] *Lloyd's Weekly Newspaper*, 23 March 1884.

[4] *Standard*, 11 April 1884.

[5] Jenkinson to Spencer, 12 April 1884, quoted in Porter, *Origins of the Vigilant State*, 51f.

[6] Liddell to the Chancellor of the Exchequer, 7 March 1884, TNA HO 144/133/A34848B.

[7] The scheme presupposed the passengers' right of free landing at any British port given that, as H. Murray, Secretary of the Board of Customs, explained in a memorandum to the Home Office, 'fresh legislation would appear to be necessary [to render] it penal for any person to land from any... ship except at a place approved [by authorities]'. Murray to Home Office, 8 May 1884, TNA HO 144/133/A34848B/18.

[8] Memorandum by Jenkinson, 11 March 1884, TNA HO 144/133/A34848B. Established in 1881 with a small group of detectives posted at northern European ports like Le Havre, Calais and Boulogne in order to keep watch over the movements of Fenians and socialists (Cook, *M*, 50), the British foreign port police was reconstituted after 1883 as Section C of Scotland Yard.

[9] Frederic Bernal to Jenkinson, 16 December 1884, TNA HO 144/133/A34848B/42.

[10] Jenkinson to Liddell, 18 December 1884, TNA HO 144/133/A34848B/42.
[11] Charles Du Cane (Chairman of the Board of Customs) to Harcourt, 14 March 1884, TNA HO 144/133/A34848B/4.
[12] Jenkinson to Harcourt, 11 March 1884, TNA HO 144/133/A34848B.
[13] Memorandum by Jenkinson, 24 March 1884, TNA HO 144/133/A34848B/6.
[14] Circular by Henderson, 12 March 1884, TNA HO 144/133/A34848B/a.
[15] Charles Du Cane to Harcourt, 28 June 1884, TNA HO 144/133/A34848B/34.
[16] 'Estimate...', 9 April 1884, TNA HO 144/133/A34848B/9a.
[17] Years later, Inspector John Sweeney of Irish and Special Branches recalled how 'I saw [the passengers'] baggage examined by the Customs officials, but the examination was done very cursorily.' John Sweeney, *At Scotland Yard* (London: Grant Richards, 1904), 52.
[18] Memo by J. Blair, 28 April 1884, TNA HO 144/133/A34848B/40. H. Muray (Secretary of the Board of Customs) to Liddell, 8 May 1884, TNA HO 144/133/A34848B/18.
[19] K. R. M. Short, *The Dynamite War: Irish-American Bombers in Victorian Britain* (Atlantic Highlands, NJ: Humanities Press, 1979), 174 ff.
[20] *Birmingham Daily Post*, 12 April 1884.
[21] *Glasgow Herald*, 12 May 1884; *Reynolds's Newspaper*, 18 May 1884.
[22] Jenkinson to Spencer, 3 April 1884, quoted in Campbell, 144.
[23] Short, 181; Campbell, 139.
[24] *Freeman's Journal and Daily Commercial Advertiser*, 3 May 1884.
[25] Jenkinson to Lushington, 28 August 1885, TNA HO 144/136/A35496E; note by Charles Troup, 7 October 1887, TNA HO 144/136/A35496. See also Porter, *Origins of the Vigilant State*, 74.
[26] *Glasgow Herald*, 14 April 1884.
[27] Jenkinson to Spencer, 18 April 1884, in Stephen Ball, ed., *Dublin Castle and the First Home Rule Crisis: The Political Journal of Sir George Fottrell, 1884–1887* (Cambridge: Cambridge University Press, 2008), 199. Although not reflected in its title, this volume contains several of the memoranda and letters written by Jenkinson in the early 1880s as well as a short biographical sketch of the man (see pp. 328–31).
[28] Report by Inspector C. Mailer, 30 May 1884; H. Murray (Secretary of the Board of Customs) to Liddell, 20 May 1884, TNA HO 144/133/A34848B.
[29] Vivian D. Majendie and A. Ford, "Report to the... Secretary of State...", p. 8, TNA EF 5/10.
[30] Sweeney, 22. Report by Edmund Henderson, 31 May 1884, TNA MEPO 3/3070.
[31] Receiver of Police to the Home Office, 2 June 1884, TNA HO 144/137/A35842.
[32] Majendie and Ford, 'Report', p. 10, TNA EF 5/10.
[33] Jenkinson to Spencer, 31 May and 2 June 1884, quoted in Porter, *Origins of the Vigilant State*, 52.
[34] Sweeney, 22.
[35] Report by Littlechild, 24 April 1884; Report by Smith, 25 June 1884, TNA HO 144/137/A35842.
[36] *Dundee Courier & Argus and Northern Warder*, 1 July 1884.
[37] Jeyes, 144; *Birmingham Daily Post*, 4 July 1884.

38 Born in 1838 in Edinburgh, Monro joined the Indian Civil Service in 1857, becoming District Judge and Inspector General of Police in Bengal in 1877. Following his appointment as Assistant Commissioner at Scotland Yard, Monro went on to briefly serve as Chief Commissioner between 1888 and 1890. See M. C. Curthoys, 'Monro, James (1838–1920)', in *ODNB* (online ed.), accessed 1 March 2018.

39 *P. I. P.: Penny Illustrated Paper and Illustrated Times*, 8 December 1888.

40 Jenkinson to Spencer, 3 June 1884; Gosselin to Harcourt, 7 August 1883; Jenkinson to Harcourt, 12 July 1883; Jenkinson to Spencer, 2 June 1884. Quoted in Porter, *Origins of the Vigilant State*, 54.

41 HC Deb, 21 February 1884, vol. 284, col. 1610; 7 February 1884, vol. 284 cols 177–8; HC Deb, 4 April 1884, vol. 286, cols 1654–5.

42 Harcourt to Queen Victoria, 7 June 1884, quoted in Porter, *Origins of the Vigilant State*, 63.

43 Porter, *Origins of the Vigilant State*, 63.

44 *Dundee Courier & Argus and Northern Warder*, 18 April 1884. See also *Manchester Courier and Lancashire General Advertiser*, 15 April 1884; *Cheshire Observer*, 19 April 1884; *Times*, 14 April 1884.

45 HC Deb, 4 July 1861, vol. 164, cols 368–9.

46 Michael Bentley, *Lord Salisbury's World: Conservative Environments in Late Victorian Britain* (Cambridge: Cambridge University Press, 2001), 177.

47 Gardiner, 504.

48 'Memorandum on the Condition of the Metropolitan Police Fund as regards the current and ensuing financial years (1883–4 + 1884–5)', 10 September 1883, TNA HO 144/115/A25928/30.

49 Memo by Jenkinson, 3 September 1884; Memo by Monro, 9 September 1884, TNA MEPO 3/3070.

50 Jenkinson to Spencer, 14 September 1884, in Ball, 207.

51 Ibid.

52 Spencer to Jenkinson, 28 September 1884, in Ball, 215.

53 Jenkinson, 'Memorandum on the organization of the United Brotherhood, or Clan-na-Gael in the United States', 22 January 1885, in Ball, 232.

54 Jenkinson to Anderson, 2 October 1884, TNA HO 144/1538/5.

55 *Bristol Mercury and Daily Post*, 29 November 1884; *Morning Post*, 6 December 1884.

56 Lomasney to John Devoy, 31 March 1881, quoted in Whelehan, *The Dynamiters*, 95.

57 *Glasgow Herald*, 15 December 1884; *Belfast News-Letter*, 17 December 1884.

58 *Glasgow Herald*, 15 December 1884.

59 *Birmingham Daily Post*, 19 December 1884.

60 Jenkinson to Spencer, 12 December 1884, quoted in Porter, *Origins of the Vigilant State*, 52.

61 Jenkinson to Monro, 26 December 1884, TNA MEPO 3/3070.

62 Jenkinson to Spencer, 15 December 1884, quoted in Porter, *Origins of the Vigilant State*, 52.

63 Jenkinson to Monro, 26 December 1884, TNA MEPO 3/3070.

64 Unsigned Home Office Memorandum, 20 December 1884, TNA HO 144/145/A38008.
65 Ibid.
66 *Pall Mall Gazette*, 3 January 1885.
67 *Pall Mall Gazette*, 26 January 1885; *Daily News*, 26 January 1885; *Freeman's Journal and Daily Commercial Advertiser*, 26 January 1885; *Glasgow Herald*, 26 January 1885; *Daily News*, 27 January 1885.
68 *Standard*, 26 January 1884.
69 Gardiner, 522.
70 Memorandum by Jenkinson, 28 January 1885, TNA MEPO 3/3070.
71 Harcourt to Spencer, 25 January 1885, quoted in Gardiner, 521.
72 Jenkinson to Spencer, 25 January and 14 February 1885; Jenkinson to Harcourt, 18 December 1884. Quoted in Porter, *Origins of the Vigilant State*, 55.
73 Memorandum by Jenkinson, 9 March 1886, TNA HO 144/721/110757.
74 Henderson to Jenkinson, 10 January 1885, TNA MEPO 3/3070.
75 *Daily News*, 27 January 1885; Report by Hamilton Cuffe (Assistant Solicitor to the Treasury), 18 June 1885, TNA HO 144/133/A34707/36; *Evening News*, 5 February 1885.
76 *Evening News*, 5 February 1885.
77 *Pall Mall Gazette*, 9 February 1885.
78 *Reynolds's Newspaper*, 8 February 1885.
79 *Daily News*, 17 February 1885.
80 *Belfast News-Letter*, 19 May 1885.
81 *Lloyd's Weekly Newspaper*, 15 February 1885; *Times*, 24 April 1886.
82 Memo by Henderson, 8 June 1885, TNA HO 144/147/A38369C.
83 Quoted in *The Times*, 17 March 1885.
84 Jenkinson to Spencer, 11 March 1885, in Ball, 23.
85 Jenkinson to Spencer, 21 May and 17 June 1885, quoted in Porter, *Origins of the Vigilant State*, 56.
86 Jenkinson to Spencer, 17 June 1885, quoted in ibid.
87 Harcourt to Jenkinson, 9 June 1885, quoted in Lindsay Clutterbuck, 'An Accident of History? The Evolution of Counter Terrorism Methodology in the Metropolitan Police from 1829 to 1901, with Particular Reference to the Influence of Extreme Irish Nationalist Activity' (unpublished PhD dissertation, University of Portsmouth, 2002), 210.
88 Monro, quoted in Clutterbuck, 200.

CHAPTER 5

## 'Waiting games'

1 Gladstone to Jenkinson, 12 December 1885, in Ball, 285.
2 Harcourt to Spencer, 19 May 1885, quoted in Gordon, 285.
3 Given Liberal fatigue and the fact that a general election could not be held (the new electoral rolls were not yet compiled following the 1884 extension of the franchise), Salisbury courted the support of Parnell by promising a scheme of land purchase for Irish tenants and the suspension of Coercion in Ireland. Deciding nevertheless to turn

against Home Rule and Parnell, Salisbury continued in office until 27 January 1886 when the Irish Nationalists voted against the government. Salisbury then resigned.

[4] Memorandum by Cross, 7 July 1885, TNA HO 144/721/110757.

[5] Cross to Lushington, 15 August 1885, TNA HO 144/147/A38369C.

[6] Ibid.

[7] Of the thirteen all but three were Englishmen, something which Chief Commissioner Henderson believed hampered their ability to make 'enquiries amongst their countrymen in various parts of London'. Memo by Henderson, 22 April 1884, TNA HO 144/133/A34848B.

[8] Cross to Carnarvon, 11 July 1885, TNA PRO 30/6/62.

[9] Ibid.

[10] Memorandum by Jenkinson, 5 August 1885, TNA PRO 30/6/62.

[11] Memoranda by Jenkinson, 24 July and 5 August 1885, TNA PRO 30/6/62.

[12] Jenkinson to Carnarvon, 8 August 1885; Carnarvon to Cross, 31 August 1885, TNA PRO 30/6/62.

[13] Memorandum by Jenkinson, 2 September 1885, TNA PRO 30/6/62.

[14] Ibid.

[15] Campbell, 176.

[16] Jenkinson, 'Memorandum on the present situation in Ireland', 2 November 1885, TNA CAB 37/16/52.

[17] Jenkinson to Carnarvon, 6 November 1885, in Ball, 273f.

[18] Spencer to Trevelyan, 21 July 1882, quoted in Gordon, 218.

[19] Jenkinson to Gladstone, 14 December 1885, in Ball, 286.

[20] As outlined in the Liberal Government of Ireland Bill, introduced in 1886, Gladstone's version of 'self-government' for Ireland was premised principally on three aspects: a separate Irish parliament in Dublin to deal with internal affairs, continued British control over Irish defence, trade and foreign affairs, and an end to Irish representation in the Westminster Parliament.

[21] Gladstone to Jenkinson, 12 December 1885, in Ball, 285.

[22] Gardiner, 409.

[23] A former journalist of conservative sympathies, Hyndman converted to socialism in 1880 and helped found the Social Democratic Federation (SDF) a year later as a broad-church socialist party. Gradually alienating many within the party with his authoritarian and fractious leadership, Hyndman also controversially expressed support for antisemitism and jingoistic patriotism.

[24] A socialist since his youth, the London-born Burns joined the SDF in 1881 and worked closely with Henry Hyndman, becoming in the later 1880s a prominent trade union organizer. Elected Liberal MP for Battersea in 1892, he later served in the Liberal cabinets of Henry Campbell-Bannerman and H. H. Asquith.

[25] Donald C. Richter, *Riotous Victorians* (Athens, OH: Ohio University Press, 1981), 118.

[26] *Aberdeen Weekly Journal*, 11 February 1886; *Standard*, 10 February 1886.

[27] *Pall Mall Gazette*, 20 February 1886.

[28] Ibid.

[29] *Pall Mall Gazette*, 17 February 1886. Beginning his journalistic career with the Liberal *Northern Echo* in 1870, William Thomas Stead rapidly became one of the most influential columnists and editors of the late-Victorian period, gaining praise from Liberal leaders like William Gladstone and John Morley. As editor of the *Pall Mall Gazette* (1883–89) Stead was known for his tireless crusading against a variety of social evils, from child prostitution to police corruption. In April 1912 he became one of over 1,500 people to perish on the RMS Titanic. See Joseph O. Baylen, 'Stead, William Thomas (1849–1912)', *ODNB* (online ed.), accessed 1 March 2018.

[30] *Freeman's Journal and Daily Commercial Advertiser*, 11 February 1886.

[31] *Aberdeen Weekly Journal*, 11 February 1886; *Leeds Mercury*, 23 February 1886; *Freeman's Journal and Daily Commercial Advertiser*, 23 February 1886.

[32] *Freeman's Journal and Daily Commercial Advertiser*, 23 February 1886.

[33] *Pall Mall Gazette*, 25 February 1886.

[34] Memorandum by Jenkinson, 9 March 1886, TNA HO 144/721/110757.

[35] Ibid.

[36] Ibid.

[37] *Pall Mall Gazette*, 27 February 1886.

[38] *Pall Mall Gazette*, 13 March 1886.

[39] Memorandum by Jenkinson, 31 May 1886, TNA HO 144/721/110757.

[40] Warren to Evelyn Ruggles-Brise (Private Secretary to the Home Secretary), 16 May 1888, TNA MEPO 1/48.

[41] Ibid.

[42] See TNA HO 144/721/110757.

[43] Memorandum by Monro, 1 June 1886, TNA HO 144/721/110757.

[44] Memoranda by Warren, 2 June 1886, TNA HO 144/721/110757.

[45] The son of a Whig MP, the London-born Lushington had been in his youth a member of the liberal-aligned Jamaica Committee, a teacher at the Working Men's College in London and an advocate of trade union rights. He joined the Home Office in 1869 and was appointed Permanent Under-Secretary in 1885.

[46] Memorandum by Lushington, 31 May 1886, TNA HO 144/721/110757.

[47] Memorandum by Lushington, 7 June 1886, TNA HO 144/721/110757.

[48] Memorandum by Childers, 9 June 1886; Jenkinson to Childers, 13 June 1886; Monro to Warren, 13 June 1886, TNA HO 144/721/110757.

[49] A barrister by training, Matthews was elected Conservative MP for Birmingham East at the 1886 general election, being subsequently appointed Home Secretary by Lord Salisbury. A devout Roman Catholic, Matthews became the first non-Protestant cabinet member since the reign of James II. See A. Lentin, 'Matthews, Henry, Viscount Llandaff (1826–1913)', *ODNB* (online ed.), accessed 1 March 2018.

[50] Salisbury to Carnarvon, 6 January 1886, TNA PRO 30/6/62.

[51] Memorandum by Lushington, 3 August 1886, TNA HO 144/721/110757.

[52] *Saturday Review*, 13 June 1896.

[53] Memorandum by Monro, 12 October 1886, TNA 144/721/110757.

[54] Ibid.

[55] Matthews to Lushington, 15 October 1886, TNA 144/721/110757.

56 Matthews to Jenkinson, 11 December 1886; Jenkinson to Spencer, 12 December 1886. Quoted in Campbell, 203.

57 *Freeman's Journal and Daily Commercial Advertiser*, 20 December 1886; Mrs Annabella Jenkinson to Spencer, 7 January 1887, quoted in Campbell, 204.

58 K. R. M. Short suggests that Jenkinson in fact wilfully burned all of his documents immediately before leaving the Home Office 'probably in protest over the government's running down of [the] Secret Service [sic]' (*The Dynamite War*, 266). Whatever the truth of this claim, the conspicuous scarcity of documents authored by Jenkinson, especially those dealing with his work in Ireland, is certainly highly unusual.

59 *Pall Mall Gazette*, 10 January 1887.

## CHAPTER 6
## 'A long and complicated inquiry'

[1] Memorandum by Anderson [signed by Monro], 4 November 1887, TNA HO 144/1537/2.

[2] Memorandum by Monro, 17 March 1886, TNA MEPO 3/3070.

[3] 'Return, showing Total Numbers...', TNA MEPO 4/487; Memorandum by Monro, 11 November 1887, TNA HO 45/10002/A49463.

[4] Irish Branch numbered two inspectors, four sergeants and twenty constables.

[5] Memorandum by Warren, 2 December 1886, TNA HO 144/133/A34848B.

[6] Ibid.

[7] Charles Murdoch (Home Office clerk) to Lushington, 8 November 1888, TNA HO 144/189/A46281; 'Return showing Pay and Allowances...', 21 December 1887, TNA MEPO 5/65.

[8] Warren to Charles Stuart-Wortley, 8 November 1888; Monro to the Home Office, 20 September 1887; Note by Charles Troup, 10 October 1887, Note by Warren, 19 October 1887, TNA HO 144/189/A46281/3.

[9] 'Return showing Pay and Allowances of each officer employed on special duty in connection with Fenian matters in the Criminal Investigation Department', 21 December 1887, TNA MEPO 5/65.

[10] 'Special Confidential Section of the C.I.D.', 28 July 1888, TNA HO 144/208/A48000M.

[11] Warren to Charles Stuart-Wortley, 12 October 1887, TNA HO 144/189/A46281/3.

[12] Monro to the Home Office, 20 September 1887, TNA HO 144/189/A46281/3.

[13] Sweeney, 49. In late 1886, DS Sweeney of Irish (and subsequently Special) Branch had been sent to infiltrate a 'secret' Clan na Gael meeting in London which turned out to be an innocuous evening of Gaelic *seanchas*.

[14] Robert Anderson, *The Lighter Side of My Official Life* (London: Hodder and Stoughton, 1909), 123f.

[15] Curthoys, 'Monro, James (1838–1920)', in *ODNB* (online ed.)

[16] Vivian Majendie, 'Greek (or Fenian) Fire – Confidential'; Memo by Majendie, 21 April 1887, TNA HO 144/196/A46866B.

[17] Ibid.

[18] *Evening Telegraph*, 4 May 1887.

[19] *Shields Daily News*, 3 May 1887; *Carlisle Patriot*, 3 June 1887.

[20] *Evening Telegraph*, 4 May 1887.

[21] For a patchy but thrilling account of Millen's fascinating life, see Christy Campbell's *Fenian Fire*, passim.

[22] See Campbell, 210f; 357–60 for examples.

[23] Anderson, *Lighter Side of My Official Life*, 112.

[24] Ibid., 113.

[25] The theory that Jenkinson actively encouraged Millen to organize (and then betray) an assassination plot against the queen on the day of her Golden Jubilee as a way to promote Home Rule (as proposed by Christy Campbell in *Fenian Fire*) is, all things considered, not entirely credible. Jenkinson had clearly used agents provocateurs on several occasions, but as his 1884 Home Rule 'manifesto' demonstrates, his understanding of the Irish situation was sophisticated enough to preclude belief in the constructive value of any 'false flag' scheme. An illustration of Jenkinson's genuine belief in the constitutional road to a pacified Ireland is afforded by the fact that in 1892 the ex-spymaster ran, unsuccessfully, as a Gladstonian Liberal in the parliamentary seat of East Grinstead. Following this attempt, Jenkinson retired permanently from politics and government work, becoming, in the latter stage of his professional life, the chairman of the Daimler Motor Company.

[26] Memorandum by Anderson [signed by Monro], 4 November 1887, TNA HO 144/1537/2. The report bears Monro's oversized signature on the last page but the handwriting is unmistakably Anderson's – something which further cements the notion that the latter was the only one, other than possibly Jenkinson, with any real knowledge of the facts behind the so-called Jubilee Plot.

[27] Anderson, *Lighter Side of My Official Life*, 117f.

[28] In the original, serialized version of his memoirs, the name does appear as 'Jenks'.

[29] For an account of the celebrations, see Julia Baird, *Victoria the Queen: An Intimate Biography of the Woman Who Ruled an Empire* (New York: Random House, 2016), 433–7.

[30] Report by Monro, 14 June 1887, TNA HO 144/275/A60551.

[31] Anderson, *Lighter Side of My Official Life*, 119.

[32] Philip Currie (Assistant Permanent Under-Secretary of State for Foreign Affairs) to Matthews, 14 June 1887; Monro to Matthews, 17 June 1887, TNA HO 144/275/A60551.

[33] 'Decypher of despatch sent by Lord Lyons (HM's ambassador in Paris) to Foreign Office', 15 June 1887, TNA HO 144/275/A60551.

[34] 'Renseignement transmis á Monsieur le Consul d'Angleterre á Boulogne', 16 June 1887, TNA HO 144/275/A60551.

[35] Cook, 66f.

[36] Monro to Matthews, 14 June 1887, TNA HO 144/275/A60551.

[37] Memorandum by Anderson [signed by Monro], 4 November 1887, TNA HO 144/1537/2.

[38] Unsigned Home Office memorandum, 1 December 1890, TNA MEPO 2/210.

[39] Anderson, *Lighter Side of My Official Life*, 118. It is unclear who Thomson (retired since the early 1880s) worked for, but Monro later claimed the ex-detective was there at his behest.

40 Ibid., 119.
41 Memorandum by Anderson [signed by Monro], 4 November 1887, TNA HO 144/1537/2.
42 Ibid.
43 'Il ne sort pas de son hôtel et c'est sa dame qui va à la poste pour lui ... Il a annoncé hier á son hotel qu'il partirait sans doute demain ... et qu'il veut se rendre en Amérique. Je surveillerai son depart et j'en aviserai l'agent anglais en temps utile.' Untitled report by L. Tournon, 23 June 1887, TNA HO 144/275/A60551.
44 Memorandum by Anderson [signed by Monro], 4 November 1887, TNA HO 144/1537/2.
45 Ibid.
46 Ibid.
47 'Proposed Distribution of [reward] amount [in the case of Harkins and Callan]', 10 February 1888, TNA HO 144/211/A48482.
48 Memorandum by Anderson [signed by Monro], 4 November 1887, TNA HO 144/1537/2.
49 Ibid.
50 Nancy Ellenberger, *Balfour's World: Aristocracy and Political Culture at the Fin de Siècle* (Woodbridge: Boydell and Brewer, 2015), 161.
51 Ibid.
52 Ibid.
53 *Pall Mall Gazette*, 27 October 1887.
54 Monro, quoted in Clutterbuck, 261.
55 *Birmingham Daily Post*, 28 October 1887.

## CHAPTER 7
## The battle of Trafalgar Square

1 Memorandum by Anderson [signed by Monro], 4 November 1887, TNA HO 144/1537/2.
2 *Times*, 29 November 1887; *Sheffield Evening Telegraph*, 3 February 1888. Both were granted an early release (Harkins in 1891 and Callan in 1893, respectively).
3 On 28 June 1887 Elizabeth Cass, who had recently moved to London to work as a seamstress, was arrested by a uniformed constable in Regent Street for suspected solicitation. She was found not guilty, but the perjury committed by the constable who arrested her and the incompetence of the presiding magistrate triggered a minor political crisis, forcing Matthews to order an inquiry into the affair. This exonerated both the policeman and the magistrate, giving the Liberal press, especially the *Pall Mall Gazette*, a cause célèbre to pummel a supposedly corrupt, venal and Conservative-controlled police force.
4 This was Israel Lipski who was arrested the same day as Elizabeth Cass for murdering his young neighbour Miriam Angel in the heat of passion before attempting suicide. The evidence in his case was notoriously patchy and circumstantial, and Queen Victoria probably spoke for a significant portion of the public when she privately expressed doubts regarding Lipski's guilt, while the *Pall Mall Gazette* took up the case as

further proof of police incompetence. Lipski was nonetheless found guilty after a jury deliberation which lasted only eight minutes, prompting accusations of xenophobia and institutionalized antisemitism (Lipski, like his believed victim, was a Jew and a recent immigrant). Swayed by the controversy, Matthews postponed the execution for a week while reconsidering the verdict, but to everyone's surprise, on 21 August Lipski, who had always professed his innocence, made a full confession of guilt and was executed the following morning. Doubts about the verdict lingered on, however, with the *Pall Mall Gazette* of 24 August 1887 insisted that 'the Whitechapel mystery will remain a mystery'.

[5] *Lloyd's Weekly Newspaper*, 10 July 1887.

[6] See Jane Martin, *Women and the Politics of Schooling in Victorian and Edwardian England* (London: Bloomsbury, 2010), 33f.

[7] *Justice*, 2 October 1887.

[8] Richter, *Riotous Victorians*, 135f. See also Paul Avrich, *The Haymarket Tragedy* (Princeton, NJ: Princeton University Press, 1986).

[9] Unsigned note re socialist meetings, 17 February 1886, TNA MEPO 2/182.

[10] Note by Monro, 19 February 1886, TNA MEPO 2/182.

[11] Monro to Lushington, 26 June 1886, TNA HO 144/172/A3793.

[12] Memorandum by Childers, 1 July 1886, TNA HO 144/172/A3793.

[13] E. H. Kossman, *The Low Countries, 1780–1940* (Oxford: Clarendon Press, 1978), 316.

[14] *Times*, 30 July 1886.

[15] *Justice*, 2 October 1886.

[16] Report by Monro, 21 September 1886, TNA HO 144/183/A45225.

[17] Unsigned police report, 24 September 1886, TNA HO 144/183/A45225/2.

[18] Monro to Warren, 4 October 1886, TNA HO 144/183/A45225/4.

[19] Note by Matthews, 12 October 1886, TNA HO 144/183/A45225/6.

[20] Memorandum by Lushington, 12 October 1886, TNA HO 144/183/A45225/6.

[21] Monro to Warren, 19 October 1886, TNA HO 144/183/A45225.

[22] Note by Lushington, 27 October 1886, TNA HO 144/183/A45225.

[23] Sweeney, 70; 'Proposed Distribution of [reward] Amount [in the Harkins and Callan case]', March 1888, TNA HO 144/211/A48482.

[24] Sweeney, 71f.

[25] Report by Inspector J. Allison, 19 October 1887, TNA MEPO 2/182.

[26] Cuffe to Monro, 27 October 1887, TNA MEPO 2/182.

[27] Report by Inspector John Pope, 28 October 1887, TNA MEPO 2/182.

[28] Porter, *Origins of the Vigilant State*, 93.

[29] Warren to Matthews, 25 October 1887, TNA HO 144/204/A47976-1to20.

[30] Surveillance of known brothels as well as arrests of suspected prostitutes were temporarily suspended by direct orders from Warren. Matthews to Warren, 30 October 1887, TNA HO 144/208/A48043.

[31] Matthews to Warren, 30 October 1887, TNA HO 144/208/A48043. Warren had previously complained that magistrates were in the habit of making biased and detrimental remarks about the Force in court. Police Orders, 19 July 1887, TNA HO 144/208/A48000M.

[32] Police Orders, 19 July 1887, TNA HO 144/208/A48000M.
[33] Warren to Matthews, 1 November 1887, TNA HO 144/208/A48043.
[34] Matthews to Warren, 3 November 1887, TNA HO 144/208/A48043.
[35] Lushington to Warren, 7 November 1887, TNA HO MEPO 2/182.
[36] *Pall Mall Gazette*, 9 November 1887.
[37] *Pall Mall Gazette*, 10 November 1887.
[38] Ellenberger, *Balfour's World*, 162.
[39] *Derby Daily Telegraph*, 10 September 1887.
[40] Ellenberger, 168.
[41] *Glasgow Herald*, 19 November 1887.
[42] *Pall Mall Gazette*, 14 November 1887.
[43] Ibid.
[44] Ibid.; Richter, 145ff.
[45] Stead to Gladstone, 14 November 1887, quoted in Richter, 148.
[46] Quoted in Richter, 150.
[47] *Daily News*, 14 November 1887.
[48] *Pall Mall Gazette*, 14 November 1887.
[49] Unsigned note, 18 November 1887, TNA MEPO 2/182.
[50] *Pall Mall Gazette*, 9 October 1888.
[51] Monro to Warren, 10 February 1888.
[52] Note by Lushington, 12 April 1888, TNA HO 144/211/A48482.
[53] Note by H. B. Simpson, 1 March 1888, TNA HO 144/211/A48482.
[54] Memorandum by Monro, 11 November 1887, TNA HO 144/190/A46472B.
[55] Note by Dr Bond, 7 February 1888; Monro to Warren, 7 February 1888, TNA HO 144/190/A46472B.
[56] Warren to Evelyn Ruggles-Brise (Private Secretary to the Home Secretary), 16 May 1888, TNA MEPO 1/48.
[57] Monro to Warren, 19 March 1888, TNA HO 144/190/A46472B.
[58] Memorandum by Warren, 27 March 1888; Warren to Monro, 26 March 1888, TNA HO 144/190/A46472B.
[59] Warren to Matthews, 31 March and 11 April 1888, TNA HO 144/190/A46472B.
[60] Monro to Warren, 31 March 1888, TNA HO 144/190/A46472B.
[61] *Pall Mall Gazette*, 9 October 1888; Warren to Matthews, 7 May 1888, TNA HO 144/190/A46472B.
[62] Note by Edward Leigh Pemberton (Legal Assistant Under-Secretary at the Home Office), 23 April 1888, TNA HO 144/212/A48606/3.
[63] Warren to Matthews, 21 April 1888, TNA HO 144/212/A48606/3.
[64] Home Office to Warren, 2 April 1888, TNA MEPO 4/487.
[65] Memorandum by Lushington, 18 April 1887, TNA HO 144/208/A48043; Notes by Charles Murdoch and E. L. Pemberton, 23 April 1888, TNA HO 144/212/A48606/3.
[66] HC Deb, 13 February 1888, vol. 322, col. 264.
[67] Ibid., col. 294.
[68] Ibid., col. 286.
[69] Home Office memorandum, 28 March 1891, TNA MEPO 2/186.
[70] Ibid.

[71] Ibid.

[72] Monro, quoted in Martin Howells and Keith Skinner, *The Ripper Legacy: The Life and Death of Jack the Ripper* (London: Sidgwick & Jackson, 1991), 93.

[73] Memorandum by Monro, 11 June 1888, TNA HO 144/190/A46472B.

[74] Memorandum by Matthews, 17 August 1888, TNA HO 144/190/A46472C.

[75] Matthews, speech in the House of Commons, quoted in *The Standard*, 7 November 1888.

[76] Note by GHT (?), 24 November 1888, TNA HO 144/222/A49500M; Murdoch to Lushington, 7 November 1888, TNA HO 144/189/A46281.

[77] Monro, quoted in Howells and Skinner, 94.

[78] *Manchester Courier and Lancashire General Advertiser*, 4 September 1888.

[79] *Pall Mall Gazette*, 9 October 1888. An excerpt of the article is included in the file dealing with the conflict between Monro and Warren in early 1888 (TNA HO 144/190/A46472B).

CHAPTER 8

## Scandal averted

[1] Warren to Ruggles-Brise, 4 October 1888, TNA MEPO 1/48.

[2] *Leicester Chronicle and the Leicestershire Mercury*, 17 November 1888.

[3] Warren, 'The Police of the Metropolis', *Murray's Magazine*, November 1888, 578, 587.

[4] Memorandum by Lushington, 7 November 1888, TNA HO 144/208/A48043.

[5] *Times*, 9 November 1888; *Pall Mall Gazette*, 9 November 1888; Warren to Matthews, 8 November 1888, TNA HO 144/208/A48043.

[6] Warren to Matthews, 8 November 1888, TNA HO 144/208/A48043.

[7] Monro to Lushington, 10 January 1889, TNA MEPO 1/48. It is also worth noting that in December 1888 no fewer than 253 police officers were still 'specially employed [in London] for the inside and outside protection of Public Buildings and the residences of H. M. Ministers'. TNA HO 144/222/A49500M/7.

[8] Report by Majendie, 25 November 1889, TNA HO 144/230/A51038.

[9] Quoted in F. S. L. Lyons, *Charles Stewart Parnell* (Oxford: Oxford University Press, 1971), 388.

[10] See John MacDonald, *Diary of the Parnell Commission: Revised from "The Daily News"* (London: T. Fisher Unwin, 1890).

[11] Disgraced by an adulterous relationship and abandoned by virtually all of his political allies as a result, Parnell quickly succumbed to a pernicious type of kidney disease in October 1891.

[12] Robert Anderson, 'The Lighter Side of My Official Life', in *Blackwood's Edinburgh Magazine, vol. CLXXXVII, January–June 1910* (New York: The Leonard Scott Publication Co., 1910), 364. This serialized version of Anderson's memoir, published in 1910 by *Blackwood's Magazine*, was reprinted in book form that same year by Hodder and Stoughton, but did not include some of the more controversial passages in the original (such as that dealing with Anderson's work for *The Times*).

[13] Ibid.

14 Campbell, 313.
15 Thomas J. Clarke, *Glimpses of an Irish Felon's Prison Life* (Dublin and London: Maunsel & Roberts Ltd, 1922), 28f.
16 Denis Grube, *At the Margins of Victorian Britain: Politics, Immorality and Britishness in the Nineteenth Century* (London: I. B. Tauris, 2013), 43.
17 Anderson, 'The Lighter Side of My Official Life', *Blackwood's*, 366.
18 Andrew Dunlop, *Fifty Years of Irish Journalism* (Dublin: Hanna & Neale, 1911), 246.
19 HC Deb, 20 March 1889, vol. 334, col. 300.
20 HC Deb, 20 March 1889, vol. 334, col. 276.
21 HC Deb, 20 March 1889, vol. 334, col. 277.
22 *Daily News*, 2 March 1889; *Glasgow Herald*, 6 March 1889; *Morning Post*, 20 March 1889; *Birmingham Daily Post*, 21 March 1889.
23 Ellenberger, 169.
24 Ibid.
25 Joan Ballhatchet, 'The Police and the London Dock Strike of 1889', *History Workshop* 32 (1991), 55–60.
26 Note by Matthews, 30 April 1890; Monro to Lushington, 30 April 1890, TNA MEPO 2/226.
27 Monro to Matthews, 28 November 1889, TNA MEPO 1/48.
28 Clive Emsley, *The English Police: A Political and Social History*, Second edition (London and New York: Longman, 1996), 98.
29 *Daily News*, 21 June 1890.
30 Quoted in Howells and Skinner, 92.
31 Appointed Superintendent of the Thuggee and Dacoity Department (which had been set up to combat agrarian crime in India) in 1874, Bradford became Chief Commissioner of Ajmir province only four years later. Starting in 1887 he briefly served as Secretary of the Political and Secret Department at the India Office in London before taking up the Commisionership of the Metropolitan Police. See Henry Wells, 'Bradford, Sir Edward Ridley Colborne (1836–1911)', *ODNB* (online ed.), accessed 1 March 2018.
32 Evelyn Ruggles-Brise recalled that Matthews 'quarreled with Bradford, and if you couldn't get on with Bradford you could get on with nobody'. Quoted in Begg and Skinner, 117.
33 Note by GHT (?), 24 November 1888, TNA HO 144/222/A49500M.
34 Nunzio Pernicone, *Italian Anarchism, 1864–1892* (Oakland, CA, Edinburgh, Baltimore, MD: AK Press, 2009), 264.
35 Report by Melville, 27 April 1891, TNA FO 45/677. Alterations almost certainly made by E. Leigh Pemberton, Legal Assistant Under-Secretary at the Home Office.
36 Report by Giuseppe Tomielli, 29 April 1891, quoted in Pernicone, 264, n27.
37 Gardiner, 479.
38 A memorandum drafted in 1889 or 1890 for the benefit of then Chief Secretary for Ireland Arthur Balfour referred to the system of '"shadowing", or constant supervision of suspects in Ireland by the police [a] system [which] was practically initiated and established by Sir E. Jenkinson when Assist[ant] Under Secretary for Crime to Lord Spencer in 1883'. Memo by Mr Waters, 1889/90, TNA PRO 30/60//7.

[39] Anderson, *Sidelights on Home Rule*, 89.
[40] Ellenberger, 168.

CHAPTER 9

## 'A bomb has burst'

[1] *Commonweal*, 25 November 1893.

[2] An Oxford-educated barrister, Asquith was elected Liberal MP for East Fife in 1886 and acted as counsel to John Burns during the latter's trial for involvement in the Bloody Sunday riots. A junior counsel to Charles Stewart Parnell during the 1888–89 special commission into 'Parnellism and crime', Asquith was appointed Home Secretary after the Liberals returned to power in 1892, becoming Prime Minister in 1908. See H. C. G. Matthew, 'Asquith, Herbert Henry, first earl of Oxford and Asquith (1852–1928)', *ODNB* (online ed.), accessed 1 March 2018.

[3] *Daily Telegraph*, 5 June 1893.

[4] Graham Robb, *Rimbaud* (Basingstoke and Oxford: Picador, 2000), 189.

[5] For a full account of the influence of Ravachol and the importance of martyrdom in the self-mythology of nineteenth-century French anarchism, see Jean Maitron, *Ravachol et les anarchistes* (Paris: René Juillard, 1964).

[6] *Reg. v. Charles and others*, March 1892, p. 1, TNA ASSI 6/27/9.

[7] *Sheffield Daily Telegraph*, 8 January 1883; *Standard*, 16 January 1885; *Morning Post*, 30 April 1890.

[8] *Times*, 7 April 1892.

[9] Ibid.

[10] Deakin to Charles Taylor (Chief Constable of Walsall Police), 15 January 1892, TNA ASSI 6/27/9.

[11] Confidential Report by Anderson, 19 May 1892, TNA HO 144/242/A53582/15; Anderson to Lushington, 25 March 1892, TNA MEPO 1/54.

[12] *Reg. v. Charles and others*, p. 84, TNA ASSI 6/27/9.

[13] Sweeney, 216.

[14] *Times*, 19 February 1892.

[15] *Commonweal*, 9 April 1892.

[16] Trial of David John Nicoll, Charles Wilfred Mowbray, May 1892 (t18920502-493), *Old Bailey Proceedings Online*, accessed 1 March 2018.

[17] *Freedom*, May 1892.

[18] Bradford to Matthews, 1 July 1892, TNA HO 144/242/A53582/21.

[19] Matthews to the Chairman of the Watch Committee (Walsall), April 1892, TNA HO 144/242/A53582/15.

[20] 'The Walsall Anarchists: Precis of the Case...', p. 4, September 1895, TNA HO 144/242/A53582/28.

[21] Ibid.

[22] McIntyre blamed his dismissal on a heavy-handed official reaction following his affair with the widow of a known northern Irish anarchist around the time of the Nicoll trial. *Reynolds's Newspaper*, 19 May 1895.

[23] *Reynolds's Newspaper*, 21 April 1905.

[24] Ibid.
[25] Clutterbuck, 317ff, 424.
[26] Sweeney, 223.
[27] Anderson to Lushington, 28 April 1892, TNA HO 144/242/A53582/15.
[28] Ibid.
[29] Although Chief Constable Taylor had been involved in the surveillance and arrest of the Walsall anarchists, there is no evidence to indicate that he knew Coulon in any capacity; it is therefore likely the telegram was sent at Melville's behest.
[30] Cook, *M*, 98.
[31] Porter, *Origins of the Vigilant State*, 141.
[32] Bradford to Lushington, 24 December 1891, TNA MEPO 1/54.
[33] Ibid.
[34] Peter Latouche, *Anarchy: An Authentic Exposition of the Methods of Anarchists and the Aims of Anarchism* (London, 1908), 63; Andrew R. Carlson, *Anarchism in Germany, vol. I: The Early Movement* (Metuchen, NJ, 1972), 336.
[35] Report by Melville, 24 May 1893, TNA HO 45/9739/A54881/2.
[36] *Le Petit Journal*, 27 April 1892. The French anarchist Ravachol, whose terror campaign against prominent Parisian judges and lawyers had scandalized public opinion earlier that year, had been arrested there on 30 March 1892 after an employee had tipped off local police.
[37] *Le Petit Journal*, 28 April 1892.
[38] *Le Petit Journal*, 11 April 1892.
[39] McIntyre, 'Scotland Yard', in *Reynolds's Newspaper*, 21 April 1895.
[40] 'The Examination of Gaston Fedée [*sic*] and Jules Pierre Marie Jolwell', 18 November 1892, TNA HO/144/485/X37842A/.
[41] Les Archives de la Préfecture de Police, BA/139, pièce 162; *Le Petit Journal*, 10 April 1893.
[42] *Le Petit Journal*, 12 April 1893; 'An Appeal on Behalf of the "Right of Asylum" in England', p. 2, 26 November 1892, TNA HO 144/485/X37842A/8.
[43] *Times*, 2 December 1892; Cook, 106.
[44] Report by French spy 'agent Zéro', one of several *mouchards* employed by the Sûreté to spy on the French anarchists in London. Quoted in Cook, 105.
[45] McIntyre, 'Scotland Yard', in *Reynolds's Newspaper*, 21 April 1895.
[46] Constance Bantman has identified 'three or four regular [French] agents at a time from the end of 1892 to the end of 1894'. One French prefect called them 'the dregs of society [who do not] speak English and [who use] the trip as an opportunity for making merry'. See Bantman, *The French Anarchists in London, 1880–1914: Exile and Transnationalism in the First Globalisation* (Liverpool: Liverpool University Press, 2013), 117–20.
[47] McIntyre, 'Scotland Yard', in *Reynolds's Newspaper*, 21 April 1895.
[48] Cook, 106.
[49] McIntyre, 'Scotland Yard', in *Reynolds's Newspaper*, 21 April 1895.
[50] Ibid.
[51] Ibid.
[52] *Times*, 15 October 1892.

53 *Times*, 17 November 1892.

54 John Bridge (Chief Magistrate for London) to Asquith, 14 December 1892, TNA HO 144/485/X37842A/12.

55 Report by Inspector Roberts, 1 March 1892, TNA MEPO 2/260/122801/2.

56 *Evening News*, 24 November 1892.

57 The son of Prime Minister Gladstone, Herbert followed his father into politics, being elected Liberal MP for Leeds West at the 1885 general election. Appointed Under-Secretary of State at the Home Office in 1892, he later went on to become Home Secretary (1905) and Governor-General of the Union of South Africa (1910). See H. C. G. Matthew, 'Gladstone, Herbert John, Viscount Gladstone (1854–1930)', in *ODNB* (online ed.), accessed 1 March 2018.

58 Anderson to the Home Office, 24 November 1892, TNA MEPO 1/54.

59 Ibid.

60 *Reynolds's Newspaper*, 4 December 1892.

61 Ibid.

62 *Standard*, 2 December 1892.

63 Ibid.

64 Anderson to Lushington, 29 November 1892, TNA MEPO 1/54.

65 Ibid.

66 Rudolf Rocker, *The London Years* (Edinburgh, Oakland, CA, Baltimore, MD: AK Press, 2005), 14–16.

67 Pietro Di Paola, *The Knights Errant of Anarchy: London and the Italian Anarchist Diaspora, 1880–1917* (Liverpool: Liverpool University Press, 2013), 63ff. In contrast to the communist anarchists, the individualists scorned all forms of organization, including trade unions, emphasizing the primacy of the 'individual act' of violence as the harbinger of an anti-capitalist revolution.

68 Sweeney, 221.

69 S. Reuschel to Asquith, 11 and 12 January 1893, TNA HO/144/485/X37842/3-4.

70 Anderson to Murdoch, 13 January 1892, TNA HO/144/485/X37842/5.

71 Ibid.

72 Probably Parmeggiani's *Libera Iniziativa*.

73 On 9 December 1893 Auguste Vaillant, another would-be avenger of Ravachol, exploded a bomb in the French Chamber of Deputies.

74 *El Dia*, 9 November 1893.

75 Ibid.

76 Wolff to Asquith, 22 November 1893, TNA HO 45/10254/X36450/8.

77 Ibid.

78 Foreign Office reply to Cipriano del Mazo (Spanish ambassador to the Court of St James), December 1893, TNA HO 45/10254/X36450/8.

79 *Evening Telegraph and Star and Sheffield Daily Times*, 14 April 1893; *Glasgow Herald*, 28 January 1893; *Manchester Courier and Lancashire General*, 3 October 1893.

80 *Commonweal*, 25 November 1893.

81 HC Deb, 30 November 1893, vol. 19, cols 103–4.

82 'Anarchists & Trafalgar Square', 5 December 1893, TNA HO 144/545/A55176/9.

83 Anderson to Lushington, 2 January 1894, TNA HO 144/587/B2840C/3214/393.

[84] *Daily News*, 7 July 1894.
[85] *Times*, 20 February 1894.
[86] Sweeney, 229.

**CHAPTER 10**

## 'Men of bad character'

[1] *Glasgow Herald*, 7 July 1894.
[2] See John Merriman, *The Dynamite Club: How a Bombing in Fin-de-Siècle Paris Ignited the Age of Modern Terror* (Boston, MA: Houghton Mifflin, 2009).
[3] *Times*, 16 February 1894.
[4] Anderson, *The Lighter Side of My Official Life*, 176.
[5] *Times*, 27 February 1894.
[6] *Times*, 16 and 27 February 1894.
[7] Joseph Conrad's *The Secret Agent*, published in 1907.
[8] *Times*, 16–27 February 1894; *St. James's Gazette*, 16 February 1894; *Weekly Times & Echo*, 18 February 1894; *Tit-Bits*, 14 March 1894.
[9] *Times*, 22 February 1894.
[10] Anderson, *The Lighter Side of My Official Life*, 176.
[11] Ibid.
[12] *Times*, 16 February 1894.
[13] Melville was not officially promoted to Superintendent until 1899 (Bradford to Home Office, 19 December 1899, TNA MEPO 1/54). Littlechild had resigned in 1893, ostensibly for reasons of ill health, though he continued working as a private investigator, resurfacing on the side of the prosecution during the Oscar Wilde trials.
[14] *Graphic*, 24 February 1894.
[15] *Pall Mall Gazette*, 17 February 1894.
[16] *Pall Mall Gazette*, 17 February 1894.
[17] *Graphic*, 24 February 1894; *Pall Mall Gazette*, 17 February 1894; *Times*, 27 February 1894.
[18] *La Lanterne*, 29 June 1894.
[19] *Times*, 23 February 1894.
[20] TNA HO 144/257/A55660.
[21] *Times*, 20 February 1894.
[22] *Times*, 22 February 1894.
[23] *St James's Gazette*, 16 February 1894.
[24] *Times*, 17 February 1894.
[25] Asquith to Bradford, 22 February 1894, TNA HO 144/257/A55660/5.
[26] *Times*, 23 February 1894.
[27] *Daily News*, 24 February 1894.
[28] *Times*, 24 February 1894.
[29] Ibid.
[30] *Daily News*, 24 February 1894.
[31] *Morning Leader*, 26 February 1894.
[32] Supplement to *Freedom*, March 1894, p. 12.

[33] *Times*, 27 February 1894.

[34] Anderson, *The Lighter Side of My Official Life*, 176.

[35] Haia Shpayer-Makov, 'Anarchism in British Public Opinion 1880–1914', *Victorian Studies* 31 (1988), 500.

[36] Alex Butterworth, *The World That Never Was: A True Story of Dreamers, Schemers, Anarchists and Secret Agents* (New York: Pantheon Books, 2010), 331.

[37] Porter, *Origins of the Vigilant State*, 131; Butterworth, 331.

[38] See Isabel Meredith, *A Girl Among the Anarchists* (London: Duckworth, 1903); Michael Newton, 'Four Notes on "The Secret Agent": Sir William Harcourt, Ford and Helen Rossetti, Bourdin's Relations, and a Warning Against Δ', *The Conradian* 32 (2007), 129–46.

[39] McIntyre, 'Scotland Yard', in *Reynolds's Newspaper*, 28 April 1895. McIntyre was no longer with Special Branch by the time the Greenwich Park explosion took place.

[40] Majendie to Asquith, 1 March 1894, TNA HO 45/9741/A55680/1.

[41] Ibid.

[42] Majendie to Asquith, 12 April 1894, TNA HO 45/9741/A55680/4.

[43] Ibid.

[44] Ralph Thompson (Under-Secretary of State for the War Office) to Lushington, 2 November 1894, TNA HO 45/9741/A55680/16.

[45] *Illustrated Police News*, 14 April 1894.

[46] Note by Murdoch, 23 April 1894, TNA HO 144/259/A55860/1.

[47] Sweeney, 235.

[48] McIntyre, 'Scotland Yard', in *Reynolds's Newspaper*, 28 April 1895.

[49] Sweeney, 236.

[50] Ibid., 239–42.

[51] Ibid.

[52] Bradford to Lushington, 17 May 1894, TNA HO 144/259/A55860C/2.

[53] Ibid.

[54] Sweeney, 243.

[55] Ibid., 251.

[56] Di Paola, 133f.

[57] Report by Swanson, 27 June 1893, TNA HO 144/249/A54906.

[58] Sweeney, 250–7.

[59] 'Transfer of anarchist Farnara from Parkhurst to Broadmoor on expiry of sentence', TNA HO 144/1711/A55860D/14.

[60] *Daily Graphic*, 17 February 1894.

[61] *Commonweal*, 28 April 1894.

[62] Cook, 112.

[63] H. W. Primrose to Murdoch, 23 April 1894, TNA HO 144/545/A55176/26.

[64] Anderson to Lushington, 23 April 1894, TNA HO 144/259/A55860/1; H. W. Primrose to Murdoch, 23 April 1894, TNA HO 144/545/A55176/26.

[65] *Lancaster Gazette and General Advertiser for Lancashire, Westmorland, and Yorkshire*, 2 May 1894.

[66] *Aberdeen Weekly Journal*, 2 May 1894.

[67] Sweeney, 267.

[68] Sweeney, 269–72.

[69] Trial of Fritz Brall, June 1894 (t18940625-580), *Old Bailey Proceedings Online*, www.oldbaileyonline.org, version 7.0, accessed 1 March 2018.

[70] Sweeney, 277.

[71] *La Lanterne*, 29 June 1894.

[72] Bentley, *Lord Salisbury's World*, 72.

[73] *Glasgow Herald*, 7 July 1894.

[74] Ibid.

[75] Ibid.

[76] HL Deb, 17 July 1894, vol. 27, col. 127.

[77] *Morning Post*, 1 August 1894.

[78] *Reynolds's Newspaper*, 5 August 1894.

[79] Occasionally, information on the anarchists could come from unexpected sources. On 27 July 1894, for example, the South Kensington – later Victoria and Albert – Museum received two anarchist pamphlets, one in French, the other one in Italian, which were then forwarded to the Home Office. Harry B. Simpson, a Home Office clerk, noted that 'they must have been sent by a fool or a lunatic', but it is just as likely the sender was a concerned, if somewhat confused, citizen. Note by Simpson, 28 July 1894, TNA HO 144/258/A55684/3.

[80] Report by John Maguire, 14 August 1894, TNA HO 144/587/B2840C/40a.

[81] Thomas Sanderson (Permanent Under-Secretary at the Foreign Office) to Lushington, 13 August 1894, TNA HO 144/587/B2840C/42a.

[82] Report by Anderson, 25 August 1894, TNA HO 144/587/B2840C/42a.

[83] Bantman, 120.

[84] *Evening Telegraph and Star and Sheffield Daily Times*, 11 August 1894.

[85] *Manchester Courier and Lancashire General Advertiser*, 15 August 1894; *Evening Telegraph and Star and Sheffield Daily Times*, 15 August 1894.

[86] *Glasgow Herald*, 17 August 1894.

[87] Anderson to Lushington, 24 September 1894; H. Percy Anderson (Foreign Office) to Lushington, 24 September 1894, TNA HO 144/587/B2840C/47-48.

[88] *Illustrated Police News*, 29 September, 6 October 1894.

[89] Report by Anderson, 19 September 1894, TNA HO 144/587/B2840C/52a.

[90] By contrast, there was also an increasing public fascination with anarchist villainy, as evidenced by the several 'anarchxploitation' potboilers published in the early 1890s: *Hartmann the Anarchist* (1892) by Edward Douglas Fawcett, *Strange Tales of a Nihilist* (1892) by William Le Queux (1892), *The Angel of the Revolution* (1893) by George Griffith and *Olga Romanoff* (1894), also by Griffith.

[91] In January 1894 a revolt by anarchist quarrymen in the Lunigiana region of north-central Italy forced the government in Rome to intervene militarily in order to restore order. In July of the same year the Spanish government passed special legislation significantly increasing police powers to prosecute anarchist agitators.

[92] *Standard*, 9 November 1894.

[93] *Star*, 1 December 1894.

[94] Sweeney, 281.

## CHAPTER 11
## 'Surtout pas trop de zèle'

[1] Melville Macnaghten to Charles Murdoch, 30 July 1897, TNA HO 144/587/B2840C/83.

[2] Pyotr Kropotkin, quoted in Michael Schmidt and Lucien van der Walt, *Black Flame: The Revolutionary Class Politics of Anarchism and Syndicalism* (Edinburgh, Oakland, CA, Baltimore, MD: AK Press, 2009), 133f.

[3] See Rudolf Rocker, *The London Years*, especially the chapter entitled 'The Campaign against the Sweating System'.

[4] John Quail, *The Slow Burning Fuse* (St Albans and London: Paladin, 1978), 203.

[5] Anderson to Lushington, 29 November 1894, TNA MEPO 1/54.

[6] Note by H. B. Simpson, 14 August 1897, TNA HO 144/587/B2840C/92.

[7] Report by Sweeney, 23 January 1895, TNA HO 144/587/B2840C/54a.

[8] *Manchester Courier and Lancashire General Advertiser*, 24 January 1895.

[9] *Essex Newsman*, 6 July 1895.

[10] McIntyre, 'Scotland Yard', in *Reynolds's Newspaper*, 3 March 1895.

[11] Hardie to Asquith, 21 May 1895, TNA HO 144/242/A53582.

[12] 'The Walsall Anarchists: Precis of the Case for the Convicts...', September 1895, TNA HO 144/242/A53582/28. The committee behind the report included several familiar names of British socialism: G. B. Shaw, William Morris, Michael Davitt and Walter Crane. David Nicoll was also a member.

[13] Note by Ridley, 18 September 1895, TNA HO 144/242/A53582/28.

[14] *Daily News*, 10 January 1895.

[15] *Aberdeen Weekly Journal*, 21 August 1895.

[16] *Devon and Exeter Gazette*, 16 February 1895.

[17] *Evening News*, 7 September 1895; *Standard*, 6 September 1895.

[18] Porter, *Origins of the Vigilant State*, 118.

[19] David Fitzpatrick, *Henry Boland's Irish Revolution* (Cork: Cork University Press, 2003), 339, n85.

[20] Owen McGee, *The IRB: the Irish Republican Brotherhood, from the Land League to Sinn Féin* (Dublin: Four Courts Press, 2005), 219.

[21] All of the released were described as being in various states of physical debilitation. *Evening Telegraph and Star and Sheffield Daily Times*, 18 and 28 August 1896.

[22] HC Deb, 22 January 1897, vol. 45, col. 359.

[23] Patrick Tynan, *The Irish National Invincibles and their Times* (London: Chatham and Co., 1894), passim.

[24] 'Intelligence Methods' (1909), p. 32, TNA KV 1/4.

[25] *New York Times*, 15 September 1896.

[26] Trial of Edward Bell, alias Edward J. Ivory, January 1897 (t18970111-146), *Old Bailey Proceedings Online*, www.oldbaileyonline.org, version 7.0, accessed 1 March 2018.

[27] Ibid.

[28] *Times*, 19 January 1897.

[29] The RIC had kept a permanent post in Glasgow since the beginning of 1896 in order to keep a watch on local Fenian clubs. *Daily News*, 16 September 1896.

30 *Glasgow Herald*, 15 September 1896.
31 Ibid.
32 *Standard*, 21 September 1896.
33 *Daily News*, 16 September 1896.
34 *Standard*, 26 September 1896.
35 *Pall Mall Gazette*, 14 October 1896.
36 *Lloyd's Weekly Newspaper*, 20 September 1896.
37 Anderson, *Sidelights on Home Rule*, 131.
38 *Standard*, 14 November 1896.
39 *Morning Post*, 14 November 1896; *Standard*, 14 November 1896.
40 *Morning Post*, 14 November 1896.
41 *Standard*, 14 November 1896.
42 Anderson, *Sidelights on Home Rule*, 128f.
43 Trial of Edward Bell, alias Edward J. Ivory, January 1897 (t18970111-146), *Old Bailey Proceedings Online*, www.oldbaileyonline.org, version 7.0, accessed 1 March 2018.
44 *New York Times*, 24 January 1897.
45 Anderson, *Sidelights on Home Rule*, 127f.
46 HC Deb, 26 March 1897, vol. 47, col. 1487.
47 Trial of Edward Bell, alias Edward J. Ivory, January 1897 (t18970111-146), *Old Bailey Proceedings Online*, www.oldbaileyonline.org, version 7.0, accessed 1 March 2018.
48 Gosselin, quoted in Owen McGee, 'Keeping the Lid on an Irish Revolution: The Gosselin–Balfour Correspondence', *History Ireland* 15 (2007), 38.
49 'T D Farrall's purchase of P J P Tynan's book: correspondence from Nicholas Gosselin to J S Sandars', April 1905, PRO 30/60/13/2; 'Secret Service Papers: Claims by T D Farrall for money owed to him by the Conservative and Unionist Party for arranging publication of P J P Tynan's account of the Phoenix Park murders in America', 1904–7, PRO 30/60/13/3.
50 The only reported name was that of Paul Rabinovitz, a Chicago Nihilist who had allegedly funded Tynan's passage to Europe. Whatever the truth of that claim, it appears Rabinovitz disappeared shortly after Tynan's arrest and was never heard from again. *Chicago Daily Tribune*, 16 September 1896.
51 John Mallon, the Dublin detective who had brought the Phoenix Park murderers to justice, surmised in his ghostwritten memoirs that the 1896 dynamite plot had in fact been 'a gosling plot that failed', Gosselin's nickname at the Home Office. See Bussy, *Irish Conspiracies*, 161.
52 *Reynolds's Newspaper*, 2 May 1897. By contrast the *Times*' correspondent in Spain argued that 'seldom... a more healthy prison and more happy-looking prisoners' were to be found than at Montjuich. *Times*, 26 July 1897.
53 HC Deb, 22 February 1897, vol. 46, cols 868-9.
54 'Revival of the Inquisition' (1897), TNA HO 45/9743/A56151C.
55 'Spanish Atrocities Committee', June 1897, TNA HO 45/9743/A56151C/3.
56 Ibid.
57 *Pall Mall Gazette*, 10 April 1897.
58 Report by Majendie, 25 May 1897, TNA EF 5/10.
59 *Daily Mail*, 21 June 1897.

60 *Reynolds's Newspaper*, 13 June 1897.

61 One anonymous letter received by Scotland Yard in April declared that 'the Anarchist Committee [sic] ... will blow up some of the royal persons that are coming in June' (TNA MEPO 3/2767), while another, more cryptic missive addressed directly to Melville simply contained 'the design of the Royal Standard, [an] ace of diamonds, an ivy leaf, and an Egyptian gold ring'. *Daily Mail*, 19 July 1897.

62 *Reynolds's Newspaper*, 20 June 1897.

63 *Evening Telegraph and Star and Sheffield Daily Times*, 29 July 1897.

64 Sweeney, 279.

65 *Daily Mail*, 3 August 1897; Latouche, *Anarchy*, 150.

66 Note by Macnaghten, 30 July 1897, TNA HO 144/587/B2840C/82; Macnaghten to Murdoch, 30 July 1897, TNA HO 144/587/B2840C/83.

67 Minute by Charles Murdoch, 20 July 1897, TNA HO 144/587/B2840C/70.

68 'Decypher from Mr Barclay [British chargé d'affaires in] San Sebastian', 22 July 1897, TNA HO 144/587/B2840C/72.

69 Note by Charles Murdoch, 30 July 1897, TNA HO 144/587/B2840C/83.

70 *El Dia*, 9 August 1897.

71 Juan Avilés Farré, *Francisco Ferrer y Guardia: Pedagogo, Anarquista y Mártir* (Madrid: Marcial Pons, Ediciones de Historia, 2006), 81.

72 *Daily News*, 12 August 1897.

73 *Daily Mail*, 10 August 1897.

74 Report by Commissioner E. R. Henry on Italian proposals for closer police cooperation, March 1903, TNA HO 144/545/A55176/51.

75 Angiollilo's trial statement, quoted in Pier Carlo Masini, *Storia degli Anarchici Italiani nell'Epoca degli Attentati* (Milano: Rizzoli Editore, 1981), 115.

76 Nunzio Pernicone, 'The Case of Pietro Acciarito: Accomplices, Psychological Torture, and Raison d'État', *Journal for the Study of Radicalism* 5 (2011), 67–104.

77 *Times*, 18 August 1897.

78 *Glasgow Herald*, 20 August 1897.

79 *Sunday Times*, 15 August 1897.

80 *Daily News*, 12 August 1897.

81 *Sunday Times*, 15 August 1897.

82 *Daily News*, 12 August 1897.

83 Note by H. B. Simpson, 25 June 1897, TNA HO 144/545/A55176/31.

84 Trial of Vladimir Bourtzeff, Klement Wierzbicki, February 1898 (t18980207-174), *Old Bailey Proceedings Online*, www.oldbaileyonline.org, version 7.0, accessed 1 March 2018.

85 Ibid.

86 Robert Henderson, *Vladimir Burtsev and the Struggle for a Free Russia: A Revolutionary in the Time of Tsarism and Bolshevism* (London: Bloomsbury, 2017), 88.

87 Born in 1853 into an aristocratic family, Rachkovsky started his career as a secret agent in his early twenties and by the mid-1880s was directing the Okhrana's operations in Western Europe out of the Russian embassy in Paris. His reputation stretched well beyond the seedy world of espionage, into the upper echelons of French political life and journalism. Under Rachkovsky's influence, right-wing newspapers like *Le Figaro*

and *Le Petit Parisien* came to espouse increasingly pro-Russian views and on at least one occasion Rachkovsky even moonlighted as Émile Loubet's chief of security, during the latter's term as president. See Jonathan Daly, *Autocracy under Siege: Security Police and Opposition in Russia, 1866–1905* (DeKalb, IL: Northern Illinois University Press, 1998), 45f.

[88] Quoted in Henderson, 61.
[89] Melville to Rachkovsky, quoted in Cook, 136f.
[90] Melville to Rachkovsky, quoted in Cook, 136f.
[91] 'Proceedings against publisher of Russian periodical "Narodovoletz" L.O.O.1029', 1897–98, TNA HO 144/272/A59222/4.
[92] Trial of Vladimir Bourtzeff, Klement Wierzbicki, February 1898 (t18980207-174), *Old Bailey Proceedings Online*, www.oldbaileyonline.org, version 7.0, accessed 1 March 2018.
[93] Rachkovsky to Melville, quoted in Cook, 138.
[94] A reference to Grant Allen's 1895 *The Woman Who Did*, a controversial feminist novel that focused on the social obstacles faced by unmarried mothers.
[95] Sweeney, 184.
[96] *Daily Mail*, 16 April 1898.
[97] Sweeney, 178f.
[98] Ibid., 178.
[99] Ibid., 181.
[100] Edward Royle, *Radicals Secularists and Republicans: Popular Freethought in Britain, 1866–1915* (Manchester: Manchester University Press, 1980), 276.
[101] Sweeney, 186.
[102] Ibid., 186f.
[103] Trial of George Bedborough, October 1898 (t18981024-715), *Old Bailey Proceedings Online*, www.oldbaileyonline.org, version 7.0, accessed 1 March 2018.
[104] Royle, 277.
[105] *Reynolds's Newspaper*, 12 June 1898.
[106] Sweeney, 189.

## CHAPTER 12

### 'We do not prosecute opinions'

[1] Sir Philip Currie to Lord Salisbury, 3 December 1898, TNA HO 45/10254/X36450/79.
[2] Edward Morgan Alborough De Burgh, *Elizabeth, Empress of Austria: a Memoir* (Philadelphia, PA: J. B. Lippencott Co., 1899), 323.
[3] *L'Aurore*, 11 September 1898.
[4] Masini, 118.
[5] In a letter to the president of the Swiss Confederation, Lucheni asked to be tried in the Canton of Lucerne, 'knowing that in that territory, [the death] penalty is still in place'. Quoted in Masini, 118.
[6] Alessandro Guiccioli, *Diario di un conservatore* (Rome: Edizioni di Borghese, 1973), 239f.

[7] *Standard*, 26 September 1898.

[8] Richard Bach Jensen, 'The International Anti-Anarchist Conference of 1898 and the Origins of the Interpol', *Journal of Contemporary History* 16 (1981), 326f.

[9] Salisbury to the Foreign Office, 12 October 1898, TNA HO 45/10254/X36450/31.

[10] Currie to Salisbury, 30 November 1898, TNA HO 45/10254/X36450/73.

[11] Report by Currie, 1 December 1898, TNA HO 45/10254/X36450/68.

[12] Currie to Salisbury, 3 December 1898, TNA HO 45/10254/X36450/79.

[13] Ibid.

[14] Jensen, 332.

[15] Currie to Salisbury, 20 December 1898, TNA FO 881/7179/30.

[16] 'Rapport présenté au nom de la commission chargée de l'étude des mesures administratives', p. 115, TNA HO 45/10254/X36450.

[17] Ibid., pp. 122ff.

[18] 'Commission chargée de l'étude des mesures legislatives', p. 128; 'Sixieme Séance, Mardi, 20 décembre 1898', p. 49, TNA HO 45/10254/X36450.

[19] 'Quatrième Séance, 7 décembre 1898', p. 150, TNA HO 45/10254/X36450.

[20] 'Rapport présenté au nom de la commission chargée de l'étude des mesures administrative', p. 118, TNA HO 45/10254/X36450.

[21] Ibid.

[22] As early as 1893 the Home Office had expressed a keen interest in adopting Francis Galton's new fingerprinting method of identification as the new modus operandi at Scotland Yard, but by the late 1890s Galton's work was still in progress and the Yard had to settle for a hybrid of abridged Bertillonage and fingerprinting. Melville Macnaghten, *Days of My Years* (London: Edward Arnold, 1914), pp. 146f. See also Francis Galton, *Fingerprint Directories* (London: Macmillan and Co., 1895).

[23] 'Cinquième Séance, Lundi, 19 décembre 1898', p. 40, TNA HO 45/10254/X36450.

[24] Ibid., p. 41.

[25] Note by Majendie, 28 August 1892, TNA HO 45/10254/X36450/1.

[26] Memorandum by Anderson, 13 December 1898, TNA HO 45/10254/X36450/77.

[27] Memorandum by Anderson, 14 January 1899, TNA HO 45/10254/X36450/92.

[28] Note by Digby, 15 December 1898, TNA HO 45/10254/X36450/77.

[29] Anderson's claim of having recently broken up a London-based conspiracy to assassinate the king of Italy was mocked as 'far-fetched' by Commissioner Bradford. Memorandum by Anderson [annotated by Bradford], 14 January 1899, TNA HO 45/10254/X36450/92.

[30] 'Extradition: Memorandum of Points still remaining for Consideration and Settlement', 1898–99, TNA HO 45/10254/X36450/72.

[31] The Germans had already been slighted in August 1900 after a proposal to send several German detectives over 'to study the English police system' was deemed 'objectionable' by British authorities. Bradford to Kenelm Digby, 2 August 1900, TNA MEPO 1/54.

[32] *Daily News*, 7 April 1900.

[33] Ibid.

[34] Ibid.

35 TNA HO 144/566/A61909/18. Having 'renounced his anarchist ways', the adult Sipido professed his 'veneration' for King Edward VII, whose portraits he avidly collected. *Le Nouveau Precurseur* (Antwerp), 9 March 1909.

36 Martin Clark, *Modern Italy, 1871 to the Present*, Third edition (New York: Pearson Longman, 2008), 127.

37 Quail, 217f. The *Liverpool Mercury* of 4 August 1900 noted how 'clubs which were rampant in the East End five years ago are now loyal institutions; houses in the vicinity of Fitzroy-square which harboured the associates of Bourdin are now tenanted by innocent folk, and all traces is lost of former underground rendezvous'.

38 *Daily Mail*, 5 May 1900; *Sheffield Daily Telegraph*, 3 August 1900.

39 Herbert to Digby, 27 April 1900, TNA HO 144/545/A55176/32A; Bailey to Pauncefote, 7 August 1900, TNA HO 144/545/A55176/33; Boothby to Lansdowne, 31 December 1900, TNA HO 144/545/A55176/36B.

40 *Sunday Times*, 16 November 1902.

41 Bradford to Murdoch, 21 November 1902, TNA HO 144/668/X84164.

42 Ibid.

43 Report by Melville, 3 December 1902, TNA HO 144/683/102620/2a.

44 Note by H. B. Simpson, 8 December 1902, TNA HO 144/683/102620/2.

45 'Deportation of Jaffei, an Anarchist from Belgium', TNA HO 144/668/X84164.

46 Memo by Henry, 16 March 1903, TNA HO 144/545/A55176/51.

47 Ibid.

48 See Colin Beavan, *Fingerprints: The Origins of Crime Detection and the Murder Case that Launched Forensic Science* (New York: Hyperion, 2001), 116–22, 145–55.

49 See F. E. C. Gregory, 'Henry, Sir Edward Richard (1850–1931)', *ODNB* (online ed.), accessed 1 March 2018.

50 Named after its chairman, the ninth earl of Elgin, the Commission was tasked with investigating the administrative and intelligence failings revealed during the Second Boer War, a project which the Committee for Imperial Defence sought to expand by centralizing and streamlining the channels linking the War Office, the Admiralty and the Foreign Office.

51 Christopher Andrew, *The Defence of the Realm: The Authorized History of MI5* (London: Penguin Books, 2010), 5.

52 *Times*, 1 January 1904.

53 The committee included several Conservative MPs and Church of England figures, as well as the German ambassador, the duke of Marlborough, Alfred de Rothschild and Sir Arthur Conan Doyle, whose Lestrade arguably bears more than a passing resemblance to Melville.

54 Henry to Sanderson, 28 September 1903, quoted in Cook, 163f.

55 William Melville, 'Memoir', p. 3, TNA KV 1/8. This twenty-six-page autobiographical valediction, submitted by Melville on his actual retirement from public service in 1917, deals only with the years after 1904 and only in the most cursory fashion.

56 Melville, 'Memoir', pp. 3f.

57 By the mid-1890s Asquith had already run the gamut from Radical populist to Liberal Imperialist ready to sanction the use of troops against striking workers, as he

did in 1893 when two coalminers were fatally shot at Featherstone in Yorkshire during a dispute over wages.

[58] Porter, *Origins of the Vigilant State*, 193f.

[59] D. P. [sic], 'A Policeman to Remember: Sir Patrick Quinn, M.V.O.', *The Police Journal* 38 (1965), 472.

[60] Cook, 15–32.

[61] Mark Bevir, *The Making of British Socialism* (Princeton, NJ: Princeton University Press, 2011), 82.

[62] Ben B. Fischer, *Okhrana: The Paris Operations of the Russian Imperial Police* (Collingdale, PA: Diane Publishing, 1999), 61.

[63] Currie to Salisbury, 3 December 1898, TNA HO 45/10254/X36450/79.

[64] Foreign Office to Cipriano del Mazo, December 1893, TNA HO 45/10254/X36450/8.

## CHAPTER 13

## Dangerous aliens

[1] On 13 June 1901 President William McKinley was fatally shot during a visit in Buffalo, New York by a twenty-eight-year-old Polish-American named Leon Czolgosz, a self-confessed follower of Emma Goldman and other American anarchists.

[2] Theodore Roosevelt, 'First Annual Message', 3 December 1901, *The American Presidency Project*, accessed 1 March 2018, www.presidency.ucsb.edu/ws/?pid=29542.

[3] In January 1902, the US signed a Treaty for the Extradition of Criminals and for Protection against Anarchism with sixteen Latin American countries. This was immediately followed by the New York Criminal Anarchy Act (which outlawed all anarchist propaganda in the state of New York) as well as a new Immigration Act barring entry into the US to anarchists and other revolutionaries.

[4] Marquess of Lansdowne to Count Benckendorff, 17 June 1904, TNA HO 144/757/118516/3.

[5] By 1903 the sense that the German Empire was Britain's new arch-rival had already seeped into British popular culture thanks to Erskine Childers' hugely popular *Riddle of the Sands: A Record of Secret Service*, which told the tale of a sinister German plot to invade the British Isles and its subsequent foiling by a couple of dutiful and daring Oxford old boys.

[6] Melville, 'Memoir', pp. 8f, TNA KV 1/8.

[7] 'Memorandum as to the Protocol of 1904 respecting Anarchist Crimes', 13 July 1906, TNA HO 144/757/118516/15.

[8] Ibid.

[9] Home Office memorandum, 21 June 1904, TNA HO 144/757/118516/3.

[10] Home Office memorandum, 13 July 1906, TNA HO 144/757/118516/15.

[11] Ibid.

[12] Report by Henry, May 1904, TNA HO 144/757/118516/2.

[13] Note by Henry, 7 December 1904, TNA MEPO 2/260.

[14] Report by Mulvany, 6 December 1904, TNA MEPO 2/260.

[15] See David Glover, *Literature, Immigration and Diaspora in Fin-de-Siècle England: A Cultural History of the 1905 Aliens Act* (Cambridge: Cambridge University Press, 2012).

[16] *Times*, 12 August 1903.

[17] 'Direction as to custody of alien when certificate with view to expulsion has been given by a court', December 1905, TNA HO 45/10330/134961.

[18] Rudolf Rocker, *The London Years*, 96–100.

[19] A mix of bellicose xenophobia and authoritarian populism advocated by the French general and politician Georges Boulanger (1837–91) and his supporters.

[20] Paul Knepper, 'The Other Invisible Hand: Jews and Anarchists in London before the First World War', *Jewish History* 22 (2008), 310.

[21] Report by Supt W. Jenkins, 7 February 1909, TNA MEPO 3/194. It is not clear whether the rest of the money was ever successfully recovered.

[22] Although the press occasionally gave Jacob's last name as Lapidus, Special Branch detectives were 'quite convinced that the man's name [was] not Lapidus'. *Times*, 27 January 1909.

[23] Herbert T. Fitch, *Traitors Within: The Adventures of Detective Inspector Herbert T. Fitch* (London: Hurst & Blackett, 1933), 37; Harold Brust, *I Guarded Kings: The Memoirs of a Political Police Officer* (New York: Hillman-Curl, 1936), 97.

[24] Nancy Green, *The Pletzl of Paris: Jewish Immigrant Workers in the Belle Epoque* (New York and London: Holmes & Meier Publishers, 1986), 98.

[25] Macnaghten, *Days of My Years*, 269.

[26] Melville, 'Memoir', p. 24, TNA KV 1/8. The Home Office rejected the proposal as incompatible with the Metropolitan Police's mandate and capabilities.

[27] *Daily Mail*, 19 February and 30 May 1908; *Sunday Times*, 9 February and 22 March 1908; *Times*, 7 March 1908; *Manchester Courier and Lancashire General Advertiser*, 23 January 1908.

[28] Glover, 183.

[29] Citing the example of a Belgian recidivist, a Scotland Yard inspector explained how 'the prisoner... easily managed to evade the Home Office order [barring his entry into Britain] by [journeying] from Ostend to the London Docks [under an assumed name] with £5 in his pocket [which] enabled him to pass without any trouble'. *Daily Mail*, 2 February 1909.

[30] The *Daily Mail* noted how the Act defined an 'immigrant ship' as one which 'carries more than twenty alien... passengers [and] Mr [Herbert] Gladstone... could... reduce it to any figure he pleased. He did as a fact reduce it to two in the case of the port of Leith to deal with the case of the German gipsies [sic]'. *Daily Mail*, 3 February 1909.

[31] *P.I.P.: Penny Illustrated Paper and Illustrated Times*, 6 February 1909.

[32] *Times*, 27 January 1909.

[33] With the irrevocable decline of 'individualist' terrorism, certain strands of communist anarchism were finding an outlet on the continent in the newly emerging revolutionary unionism known in France as *syndicalisme*. In 1906, for example, the *Confédération Générale du Travail*, the largest trade union in France at the time, adopted its so-called Amiens Charter, a document co-authored by the anarchist Émile Pouget, a onetime frequenter of the Autonomie Club, which consistently argued for

trade unions as the principal organ of class struggle against the capitalist state. A year later, at the 1907 International Anarchist Congress in Amsterdam, syndicalism once again headed the agenda and by 1910 it was becoming clear that whatever was going to survive of organized anarchism would have to adopt syndicalism as its modus operandi. This was confirmed by the formation of the syndicalist *Confederación Nacional del Trabajo* in Barcelona that same year and the *Unione Sindacale Italiana* in 1912, both of which declared anarchist communism as their ultimate goal. See Vadim Damier, *Anarcho-Syndicalism in the 20th Century* (Edmonton, AB: Black Cat Press, 2009).

[34] David Cannadine, *Ornamentalism: How the British Saw Their Empire* (Oxford: Oxford University Press, 2002), 90.

[35] F. H. Brown, 'Wyllie, Sir (William Hutt) Curzon (1848–1909)', *ODNB* (online ed.), accessed 1 March 2018.

[36] A classic example was the Mitra Mela, a secret society founded in Pune around the turn of the twentieth century, which evolved into the Abhinav Bharat [Young India] Society – a deliberate reference to Mazzini's Young Italy – under the guidance of pro-independence luminary and Hindu nationalist Vinayak Damodar Savarkar, who by 1906 was a law student in London. See Prabhu Bapu, *Hindu Mahasabha in Colonial North India, 1915–1930: Constructing Nation and History* (London and New York: Routledge, 2013), 95f.

[37] *Times*, 5 July 1909.

[38] True to its orientalist narrative, the dress code specified that 'visitors were expected to wear either evening dress or native costume'. *Times*, 3 July 1909.

[39] Trial of Madar Lal Dhingra, July 1909 (t19090719-55), *Old Bailey Proceedings Online*, www.oldbaileyonline.org, version 7.0, accessed 1 March 2018.

[40] Ibid.

[41] *Times*, 8 July 1909.

[42] *Times*, 3 July 1909.

[43] Trial of Madar Lal Dhingra, July 1909 (t19090719-55), *Old Bailey Proceedings Online*. Dhingra was sentenced to death and executed at Pentonville prison on 17 August 1909.

[44] Brust, *I Guarded Kings*, 103.

[45] Richard J. Popplewell, *Intelligence and Imperial Defence: British Intelligence and the Defence of the Indian Empire, 1904–1924* (London: Frank Cass, 1995), 128ff.

[46] Ibid.

[47] Brust, 103.

[48] Fitch, *Traitors Within*, 41.

[49] Police Orders, 24 December 1907, TNA MEPO 3/1760.

[50] In early 1909 Section B numbered one chief inspector, eleven sergeants and sixteen constables, while Section D included only one superintendent and five inspectors. Section C was by then only a remnant of its former self with '9 vacancies… and… no intention… of filling [them] up'. Quinn to Henry, 7 July 1902, TNA MEPO 2/1297.

[51] Ibid.

[52] Over the next five years Quinn submitted at least four requests to have this augmentation extended permanently, his wish being granted only on 27 July 1914. TNA MEPO 2/1297.

53 Popplewell, 132.

54 *Times*, 15 July 1909.

55 Trial of Arthur Fletcher Horsley, July 1909 (t19090719-54), *Old Bailey Proceedings Online*, www.oldbaileyonline.org, version 7.0, accessed 1 March 2018.

56 Ibid.

57 Home Office file on Guy Alfred Aldred, TNA HO/144/22508.

58 Trial of Guy Alfred Aldred, September 1909 (t19090907-44), *Old Bailey Proceedings Online*, www.oldbaileyonline.org, version 7.0, accessed 1 March 2018.

59 *The Indian Sociologist*, August 1909, in TNA HO/144/22508.

60 Ibid.

61 Quoted in James W. Douglass, *Gandhi and the Unspeakable: His Final Experiment with Truth* (Maryknoll, NY: Orbis Books, 2012), 31.

62 *P.I.P.: Penny Illustrated Paper*, 20 August 1910.

63 Paul Avrich, *Russian Anarchists* (Princeton, NJ: Princeton University Press, 1971), 54.

64 Maris Goldmanis, 'Latvian Anarchism – The Story of Peter the Painter', *Latvian History*, http://archive.is/2AnRK, accessed 1 March 2018.

65 *Times*, 17 December 1910.

66 Report by John Stark (Chief Superintendent of the City Police), 23 December 1910, TNA HO 144/19780/3.

67 Ibid.

68 As recent research by Philip Ruff in the declassified Soviet archives in Riga suggests, Jānis Žāklis was an ex-member of the Latvian Social Democratic Party and an ardent supporter of revolutionary 'expropriation'. It is unclear how Peter the Painter – so nicknamed on account of his artistic inclinations – managed, unlike Svaars and Sokolov, to evade police capture or where he eventually ended up. See Goldmanis, 'Latvian Anarchism – The Story of Peter the Painter'. For Ruff's Latvian-language monograph, see *Pa Stāvu Liesmu Debesīs: Nenotveramā latviešu anarhista Pētera Māldera laiks un dzīve* (Riga: Dienas Grāmata, 2012).

69 Report by Supt J. Mulvany, 7 January 1911, TNA HO 144/19780/25.

70 Ibid.

71 Testimony by Churchill, 18 January 1911, TNA HO 144/19780.

72 Ibid.

73 The video can be streamed from the British Pathé website at www.britishpathe.com/video/london-sidney-street-siege. Accessed 1 March 2018.

74 *Daily Mail*, 4 January 1911.

75 Testimony by Albert Edward Edmonds (Bethnal Green Fire Station), 9 January 1911, TNA HO 144/19780.

76 Ibid.

77 Testimony by Charles Graham Grant, Police Surgeon (H Division), 6 January 1911, TNA HO 144/19780.

78 F. A. Campbell (Foreign Office) to Troup, 9 January 1911; Note by Henry, 10 January 1911, TNA HO 144/19780.

79 Ramsay Macdonald, speech in the House of Commons, HC Deb, 22 August 1911, vol. 29, col. 2298.

[80] *Times*, 5 January 1911.

[81] In the wake of the 'siege', *The Standard* – previously famous for its moderate conservatism and exemplary war journalism – began publishing a series of exposés on 'the inhabitants of the Ghetto' couched in a virulently, and erstwhile completely atypical, antisemitic language. See 'Problem of the Alien I-III', *Standard*, 25–30 January 1911.

[82] *Lieutenant Rose and the Royal Visit*, directed by Percy Stow (London: Clarendon, 1911); *The Aerial Anarchists*, directed by Walter R. Booth (London: Kineto Films, 1911).

[83] 'Alleged Anarchist plot against King George V', 1911, TNA HO 144/1112/202225.

## CHAPTER 14

## 'A doctrine of lawlessness'

[1] Report by Captain Lionel Lindsay, 5 November 1910, TNA HO 144/1551/199768

[2] David Lloyd George, speech in the House of Commons, HC Deb, 29 April 1909, vol. 4, col. 548.

[3] *Times*, 25 January 1910.

[4] George Dangerfield, *The Strange Death of Liberal England* (New York: Capricorn Books, 1961), 241f; *Financial Times*, 2 November 1910.

[5] Report by Lindsay, 5 November 1910, TNA HO 144/1551/199768.

[6] Among the labour groups the SWMF supported financially were the London-based Central Labour College and the Rhondda-based Plebs League, both run by a small but committed group of socialist dissenters dedicated to the dissemination of Marxist and syndicalist ideas. See G. D. H. Cole and Raymond Postgate, *The British Common People, 1746–1946* (Methuen: London, 1961), 483f.

[7] William Abraham, the Lib-Lab MP for Rhondda, opposed industrial militancy on principle despite his trade unionist past, while the leadership of the SWMF sought unsuccessfully to convince the striking miners to accept the owners' offer of a largely symbolic wage increase. The widening chasm between the Rhondda miners and their official leadership was so obvious that as early as 3 November 1909 the *Daily Mail* warned of a 'revolt of workers against [their] formerly trusted leaders'. See also Robert Moore, *Pitmen, Preachers and Politics* (Cambridge: Cambridge University Press, 1979), 37; Dangerfield, 241.

[8] After inter-party negotiations failed to end the constitutional deadlock elicited by the House of Lords' opposition to the controversial Liberal budget, the government sought a new popular mandate for its far-reaching reforms. In late November 1910 a new general election was scheduled to take place the following month.

[9] The son of a prominent Victorian actor, Macready saw active service in the Second Boer War before being appointed Assistant Adjutant-General at the War Office in 1907 and tasked with helping to organize the Territorial Army. Briefly replacing E. R. Henry as Commissioner of the Metropolitan Police after the former's retirement in 1918, Macready was given command over the troops in Ireland the following year. Known for taking a hard line against republican insurgents, Macready nevertheless met in person with Sinn Fein and IRA leaders in order to facilitate dialogue, ensuring the peaceful withdrawal of British troops from southern Ireland in 1923. See Keith Jeffery, 'Macready, Sir (Cecil Frederick) Nevil, (1862–1946)', *ODNB* (online ed.), accessed 1 March 2018.

[10] Churchill to Lindsay, 8 November 1910, TNA HO 144/1551/199768/6. In total, Macready was given command over two hundred cavalry troops and five hundred infantry troops stationed in Cardiff, Swindon and Newport, as well as the contingents of Metropolitan Police.
[11] Ibid.
[12] *Daily Mail* (Hull), 8 November 1910.
[13] 'Statement of W. M. Wilkins', 9 December 1910, TNA MEPO 3/200.
[14] 'Report on the Disturbance at Aberaman on 8 November 1910', TNA MEPO 3/200.
[15] 'Memorandum by General Macready on Certain Points Connected with the Strike in South Wales', TNA MEPO 3/200.
[16] Churchill to Macready, 9 November 1910, TNA HO 144/1551/199768/10.
[17] Unsigned report based on information supplied by J. F. Moylan addressed to Troup [undated], TNA HO 144/1551/199768/50. Moylan had been dispatched to South Wales by Churchill as a secret Home Office observer. See Roger Geary, *Policing Industrial Disputes: 1893 to 1985* (Cambridge: Cambridge University Press, 2011), 28ff.
[18] 'Memorandum by General Macready on Certain Points...', TNA MEPO 3/200.
[19] Macready to Churchill, 19 November 1910, TNA HO 144/1551/199768/96.
[20] Macready to Churchill, 16 November 1910, TNA HO 144/1551/199768/51.
[21] Note by Troup, 19 November 1910, TNA HO 144/1551/199768/80.
[22] 'Memorandum by General Macready on Certain Points...' TNA MEPO 3/200.
[23] Dangerfield, 246.
[24] 'Memorandum by General Macready on Certain Points...' TNA MEPO 3/200; Lindsay to Churchill, 14 November 1910, TNA HO 144/1551/199768.
[25] Roy Church, *Strikes and Solidarity: Coalfield Conflict in Britain, 1889–1966* (Cambridge: Cambridge University Press, 2002), 61.
[26] Churchill, quoted in Barbara Weinberger, 'Keeping the Peace? Policing Strikes 1906–26', *History Today* 37 (1987), 32.
[27] Church, *Strikes and Solidarity*, 114f.
[28] Macnaghten to Troup, 15 January 1912, TNA HO 144/7062.
[29] An engineer by training, Mann joined the SDF in 1884 and began agitating for the eight-hour workday before becoming involved in the 1889 London dock strike as a socialist organizer. Thereafter Mann became increasingly active in trade union politics, outlining, along with Ben Tillet, the guidelines for a 'new unionism' that aimed at being more inclusive (as opposed to craft-based) and openly socialist. After a decade spent organizing trade unions and socialist parties in Australia, Mann returned to Britain in 1910 and helped establish the Industrial Syndicalist Education League as a vehicle for propagating French-style syndicalism (which favoured revolution and industrial militancy over conciliation with employers). In 1920 Mann became a founding member of the Communist Party of Great Britain. See Chris Wrigley, 'Mann, Thomas (1856–1941)', *ODNB* (online ed.), accessed 1 March 2018.
[30] The Home Office had already received copies of Mann's previous publication, *The Syndicalist Railwayman*, back in October 1911 and on 13 January 1912 Special Branch DS Fitch was sent to attend a meeting of the Industrial Syndicalist Education League in Battersea.

[31] Note by Troup, 17 January 1912, TNA HO 144/7062.
[32] Tom Mann, *Memoirs* (London: The Labour Publishing Company Ltd, 1923), 289.
[33] Note by Troup, 17 January 1912, TNA HO 144/7062.
[34] *Times*, 19 June 19, 1912.
[35] Incitement to Mutiny Act 1797. 37 Geo. III, c. 70.
[36] Keith Ewing and Conor Anthony Gearty, *The Struggle for Civil Liberties: Political Freedom and the Rule of Law in Britain, 1914–1945* (Oxford: Oxford University Press, 2011), 119.
[37] In a report from 25 March 1912, Special Branch DI George Riley noted with surprise that notwithstanding their political radicalism 'both these men are married and have families who appear very respectable, and the children are being well brought up'. TNA HO 144/7062.
[38] Bowman had already come to the attention of the Home Office six years earlier, after being expelled from Spain for anarchist agitation. TNA HO 144/757118516/46.
[39] *Times*, 11 March 1912.
[40] 'Rex v Tom Mann – Evidence and Summing Up', 9 April 1912, TNA HO 144/7062.
[41] Trial of Guy Bowman, Charles Ernest Buck, Benjamin Edward Buck, March 1912 (t19120319-45), *Old Bailey Proceedings Online*, www.oldbaileyonline.org, version 7.0, accessed 1 March 2018. It is worth noting that one of the defendants' counsel was a young James B. Melville, son of William, who very unlike his father was known to be a vocal and active socialist (having worked for the defence team during the trial of Gardstein's acolytes in connection with the Houndsditch murders). He later rose to the post of Solicitor General during the second Labour government (1929–31).
[42] Minute by H. B. Simpson, 7 May 1912, TNA HO 144/7062.
[43] In a letter to the Home Secretary, Judge Bankes argued that if Mann 'had been properly defended… [and] a less prominent person… I should certainly have bound him over'. Bankes to McKenna, 18 May 1912, TNA HO 144/7062.
[44] 'Rex v Tom Mann – Evidence and Summing Up', 9 April 1912, TNA HO 144/7062.
[45] *Times*, 19 June 1912.
[46] HC Deb, 28 February 1912, vol. 34, col. 1372.
[47] Transcript of Victor Grayson' speech at Market Square, Wigan, 31 March 1912, TNA HO 144/7062.
[48] 'Labour Day – Hyde Park Demonstration' [excerpt from unnamed newspaper], TNA HO 144/7062.
[49] Memo by McKenna, 1 April 1912, TNA HO 144/7062.
[50] HC Deb, 30 May 1912 vol. 38, col. 1567.
[51] Memo by Troup, 18 June 1912, TNA HO 144/7062.
[52] 'Report of Meeting addressed by Mr. Tom Mann at the Selly Oak Institute on Monday, November 4th [1914]', TNA HO 144/7062.
[53] Ewing and Gearty, 120.

## CHAPTER 15
## 'Suffrage forces in the field'

[1] Emmeline Pankhurst, *My Own Story*, (London: Eveleigh Nash, 1914), 86.

[2] Inspector Neville, Telegram to Cannon Row Police Station; Report by Chief Inspector Scantlebury, 23 October 1906, TNA MEPO 2/1016.

[3] Following her 1879 marriage to the Manchester-based barrister Richard Pankhurst, Emmeline (who at the time shared her husband's left-wing convictions) became acquainted with a host of influential British socialists, including Keir Hardie and G. B. Shaw. After becoming involved with the Women's Franchise League, which in 1894 helped secure the right to vote in local (but not national) elections for married women, Emmeline became exclusively devoted to advancing the cause of female enfranchisement on the same legal terms as men. Increasingly disillusioned with male politicians who paid lip service to 'votes for women' while doing little to promote the issue in Parliament, Mrs Pankhurst (as Emmeline widely became known) founded the WSPU in 1903 along with her daughters Christabel, Sylvia and Adele as an explicitly militant organization. See June Purvis, 'Pankhurst [née Goulden], Emmeline (1858–1928)', *ODNB* (online ed.), accessed 1 March 2018.

[4] Emmeline Pankhurst, *My Own Story*, 74.

[5] Ibid., 75.

[6] Report by Scantlebury, 23 October 1906, TNA MEPO 2/1016.

[7] *Daily Chronicle*, 24 October 1906.

[8] By contrast the 'able bodies... working quietly and unostentatiously for universal women's suffrage', were still referred to as 'suffragists' (*Daily Mail*, 4 March 1907) although in other publications, *The Times* most notably, the two terms continued to be used interchangeably.

[9] A Yorkshire-born millworker's daughter, Kenney gravitated towards socialist and trade union politics from a very early age. After hearing Christabel Pankhurst give a public speech in support of votes for women in 1905, Kenney dedicated herself completely to the WSPU, subsequently becoming a full-time organizer for the militant group's London branch. As Christabel's right-hand woman, Kenney went on to play a prominent role in the WSPU's militant campaign of the early 1910s. See Brian Harrison, 'Kenney, Annie (1879–1953)', *ODNB* (online ed.), accessed 1 March 2018.

[10] Report by Inspector James Jarvis, 24 October 1906, TNA MEPO 2/1016.

[11] Ibid.

[12] A founding member of the WSPU, Christabel was an early proponent of an aggressive, unrelenting militancy as the only means of significantly advancing the suffragette cause in the national political discourse. Gradually coming to reject the socialist politics of her Manchester upbringing, Christabel focused instead on securing the financial and moral support of middle- and upper-class women, becoming openly hostile to the Labour Party (as well as all other male-dominated organizations) by the early 1910s. See June Purvis, 'Pankhurst, Dame Christabel Harriette (1880–1958)', *ODNB* (online ed.), accessed 1 March 2018.

[13] Andrew Rosen, *Rise Up, Women! The Militant Campaign of the Women's Social and Political Union, 1903–1914* (London and Boston, MA: Routledge & Kegan Paul, 1974), 50, 64f.

[14] *Times*, 27 October 1906.

[15] *Times*, 24 October 1906; *Daily Chronicle*, 24 October 1906.

[16] HC Deb, 26 October 1906, vol. 163, cols 518–19.

[17] *Times*, 26 November, 12 December 1906.

[18] Pankhurst, 76; Martin Pugh, *The Pankhursts: The History of One Radical Family* (London: Vintage Books, 2008), 147.

[19] *Manchester Courier and Lancashire General Advertiser*, 18 December 1906.

[20] Report by Supt Wells, 19 February 1907, TNA MEPO 2/1016.

[21] Note by Henry, 19 February 1907, TNA MEPO 2/1016.

[22] Pankhurst, 84.

[23] Report by Supt Wells, 5 March 1907, TNA MEPO 2/1016.

[24] Despite the new sense of purpose she had brought to the Union, Christabel's overbearing, iron-fisted approach as lead strategist made her a controversial figure within the organization, contributing to more than one irreconcilable rift after 1907.

[25] Pankhurst, 83.

[26] HC Deb, 15 February 1907, vol. 169, col. 416.

[27] Campbell-Bannerman, quoted in Sylvia Pankhurst, *The Suffragette: The History of the Women's Militant Suffrage Movement, 1905–1910* (New York: Sturgis & Walton Co., 1911), 150.

[28] A Women's Anti-Suffrage Society had come into existence specifically to rally support against the proposed Bill, laying the groundwork for the future Women's National Anti-Suffrage League.

[29] Report by Supt Wells, 5 March 1907, TNA MEPO 2/1016.

[30] Report by Supt Wells, 3 April 1907, TNA MEPO 2/1016; *Daily Mail*, 21 March 1907.

[31] *Manchester Courier and Lancashire General Advertiser*, 21 March 1907; Rosen, 82.

[32] *Daily Mail*, 21 March 1907.

[33] *Western Times*, 21 March 1907.

[34] Sylvia Pankhurst, *The Suffragette*, 154f.

[35] Report by Dew, 11 April 1907, TNA MEPO 2/1016.

[36] Partly due to their wealth and status, but also because of their initially unquestioning devotion to the Pankhursts, Emmeline Pethick-Lawrence and her husband – the only male member of the WSPU – quickly rose through the ranks to become part of the inner circle which practically directed the course of the organization. The rooms at 4 Clement's Inn remained the unofficial WSPU headquarters until 1912, when the Pethick-Lawrences irrevocably fell out with the Pankhursts.

[37] Report by Dew, 11 April 1907, TNA MEPO 2/1016.

[38] Ibid.

[39] Emmeline Pankhurst, *My Own Story*, 86.

[40] Chris Cook and John Stevenson, *A History of British Elections since 1689* (Abingdon and New York: Routledge, 2014), 288.

[41] Pankhurst, *My Own Story*, 91ff.

[42] Ibid.

[43] Worried that Emmeline and Christabel's increasingly authoritarian stances were eroding any semblance of democratic control within the organisation, a group of about seventy WSPU members decided to break away in early September 1907 to form a rival organization under the name of the Women's Freedom League.

[44] *Times*, 20 and 22 June 1908; *Daily Mail*, 22 June 1908.

[45] Helen Fraser, quoted in Rosen, 105.

[46] HC Deb, 27 April 1892, vol. 3, col. 1510.

[47] *Times*, 22 June 1908.

[48] Ibid.

[49] *Western Times*, 24 June 1908.

[50] *Cornishman*, 9 July 1908; *Sunday Times*, 23 August 1908.

[51] *Manchester Courier and Lancashire General Advertiser*, 30 June 1909.

[52] Emmeline Pankhurst, *My Own Story*, 140f.

[53] *Daily Mail*, 30 June 1909.

[54] Emmeline Pankhurst, *My Own Story*, 142.

[55] *Daily Mail*, 30 June 1909; *Manchester Courier and Lancashire General Advertiser*, 30 June 1909.

[56] *Manchester Courier and Lancashire General Advertiser*, 28 July 1909.

[57] Christabel Pankhurst to Balfour, 22 July 1909, quoted in Rosen, 121.

[58] Rosen, 121.

[59] H. H. Asquith, *Memoirs and Reflections, 1852–1927, vol. 1* (Toronto: McClelland and Stewart, 1928), 308.

[60] *Daily Mail*, 7 September 1909.

[61] Scottish-born and Oxford-educated, Troup joined the Home Office as a junior clerk in 1880. Becoming senior clerk in 1886, he subsequently served as Permanent Under-Secretary between 1908 and 1922. See P. W. J. Bartrip, 'Troup, Sir Charles Edward (1857–1941)', *ODNB* (online ed.), accessed 1 March 2018.

[62] Memo by Gladstone, 9 September 1909, TNA HO 144/1043/183461.

[63] Memo by Henry, 11 September 1909, TNA HO 144/1043/183461.

[64] Note by Assistant Under-Secretary W. P. Byrne, 17 September 1909, TNA HO 144/1043/183461. Using the Metropolitan Police fund was one option, but as Troup was quick to point out, 'it would be impossible… to charge to the London ratepayer the cost of protecting Cabinet ministers all over the country'. The augmentation was eventually paid for with moneys from the Imperial Funds which already covered the costs of Section D of CID, C and B being in the charge of the English and Welsh Police Fund and the Home Office, respectively. Memo by Troup, 18 September 1909, TNA HO 144/1043/183461/1.

[65] *Daily Mail*, 18 September 1909.

[66] Memo by Gladstone, 14 September 1909, TNA HO 144/1043/183461/1. On 4 September five suffragettes had been arrested in Manchester for interrupting a pro-budget meeting headlined by Augustine Birrell, Chief Secretary for Ireland, by throwing 'iron balls' onto the venue's glass-panelled roof. *Western Times*, 7 September 1909.

[67] The exception to this rule were the 150 female members of local Liberal associations and the wives of attending MPs. *Western Times*, 18 September 1909.

[68] *Western Times*, 18 September 1909.

[69] *Daily Mail*, 18 September 1909.

[70] Asquith, *Memoirs, vol. 1*, 261.

[71] *Times*, 21 September 1909.

[72] As with the previous expansion, the Home Office initially envisioned it as a temporary one, '[until] the present troubles [have ceased]', only relenting after Henry insisted that 'in view of the obviously non-deterrent nature of the punishments practically enforceable against these women, there seems no reason to anticipate any reduction in their activity in the immediate future'. The augmentation of one first-class inspector, nine detective-sergeants and ten detective-constables was finalized on 2 October 1909. Troup to Henry, 22 September 1909; Henry to Troup, 27 September 1909; Police Orders, 2 October 1909, TNA MEPO 2/1310.

[73] Report by Riley, 27 September 1909, TNA HO 144/1709/425859.

[74] Gladstone to Edward Grey, 10 October 1909, quoted in Rosen, 127.

[75] Memo by Troup, 27 September 1909, TNA HO 144/1709/425859.

[76] Ibid.

[77] Introduced in August 1909 in response to the successful hunger strike campaign, forced feeding became standard practice by the end of the year. Laura Ainsworth, one of the women arrested for involvement in the Birmingham protest, described the experience after her release from Winson Green prison in the following terms: 'I was raised into a sitting position, and a tube about two feet long was produced. My mouth was prised open with what felt like a steel instrument and then I felt them feeling for the proper passage... I experienced great sickness, especially when the tube was being withdrawn. Twice a day morning and evening, I was fed in this way'. Despite pressure from Labour MPs and independent Liberals, the government defended the practice as necessary to 'prevent [the suffragettes] from committing the felony of suicide'. *Daily Mail* (Hull), 5 October 1909; *Daily Mail* (London), 28 September 1909.

[78] *Manchester Courier and Lancashire General Advertiser*, 31 December 1909; *Sunday Times*, 14 November 1909. Churchill had, on occasion, paid lip service to female enfranchisement following his 1904 defection to the Liberal Party, but was by 1909 an ardent opponent (and target) of militant suffragettes.

[79] Rosen, 134.

[80] *Manchester Courier and Lancashire General Advertiser*, 16 February 1910.

[81] Rosen, 139. Sir Edward Grey (a suffrage reform sympathizer) was put in the awkward position of having to officially announce the Bill's demise on 12 November 1910.

[82] Memorandum by Henry, 11 July 1910, TNA MEPO 2/1308.

[83] *Times*, 19 November 1910.

[84] 'A letter including a Statement re Nov. 18th, 1910', 17 December 1910, TNA HO 144/1106/200455/17.

[85] Elizabeth Crawford, *The Women's Suffrage Movement: A Reference Guide, 1866–1928* (London: Routledge, 2003), 759.

[86] Crawford, 451.

[87] Minute by Churchill, 23 November 1910, TNA HO 144/1106/200455/3.

[88] Memo by Henry, 29 November 1910, TNA HO 144/1106/200455/3.
[89] Memo by Henry, 25 March 1911, TNA HO 144/1106/200455/42; 'Memorandum by Commissioner of Police on Allegations contained in Mr. Brailsford's Memorial of the 18th February, 1911', TNA HO 144/1106/200455/22.
[90] C. Mansell-Moulin in *The Daily Telegraph*, 23 November 1910.
[91] Brailsford, 'Treatment of the Women's Deputations by the Police', TNA HO 144/1106/200455/19.
[92] *Times*, 11 March 1911.
[93] Minute by Troup, 19 November 1910, TNA HO 144/1106/200455/4.
[94] Antonia Raeburn, *The Militant Suffragettes* (London: Michael Joseph, 1973), 157.
[95] Henry to the Home Office, 18 November 1910, TNA MEPO 2/1408.
[96] Henry to the Home Office, 26 January 1911, TNA MEPO 2/1438.
[97] Ibid.
[98] 'Memorandum re suffragettes', 20 February 1911, TNA MEPO 2/1438.
[99] Henry to the Home Office, 4 February 1911, TNA HO 144/1119/203651/2.
[100] Minute by Troup, 4 February 1911, TNA HO 144/1119/203651/2.
[101] TNA HO 144/1119/203651.
[102] Report by Sergeant Arthur Randall, 10 November 1911, TNA HO 144/1119/203651/6.
[103] Kate Parry Frye, *Campaigning for the Vote: Kate Parry Frye's Suffrage Diary*, ed. Elizabeth Crawford (London: Francis Boutle Publishers, 2013), 79.
[104] Emmeline Pankhurst, quoted in Rosen, 157.

CHAPTER 16

## The waning of militancy and the rise of counter-espionage

[1] 'Report to the... Secretary of State... [on] the disturbances at Rotherhithe on the 11th June, 1912', TNA MEPO 3/217.
[2] Rosen, 156–66.
[3] *Times*, 15 July 1912.
[4] Ibid.
[5] Quoted in Rosen, 169. Although sentenced to nine months' imprisonment, Craggs successfully staged a hunger strike for eleven days and was subsequently released.
[6] *Daily Mail*, 19 July 1912.
[7] Crawford, 339.
[8] HC Deb, 29 July 1912, vol. 41, col. 1656W.
[9] Frederick Pethick-Lawrence, *Fate Has Been Kind* (London: Hutchinson & Company Limited, 1943), 98f.
[10] Emmeline Pankhurst, quoted in Rosen, 176.
[11] Ibid.
[12] Millicent Garrett Fawcett, 'Constitutional Suffragists and Sentences on Militants', *Times*, 8 June 1912.
[13] *Illustrated London News*, 28 September 1912.

14 Ian Christopher Fletcher, '"Women of the Nations, Unite!": Transnational Suffragism in the United Kingdom, 1912–1914', in Fletcher et al., ed., *Women's Suffrage in the British Empire: Citizenship, Nation and Race* (London: Routledge, 2012), 103–21.

15 Ibid. The WSPU had already declared war on Irish Nationalists earlier that year for their refusal to support the Conciliation Bill.

16 *Western Times*, 27 November 1912.

17 *Evening Post* (Wellington, NZ), 16 January 1913.

18 *Times*, 29 November 1912.

19 *The Suffragette*, 13 December 1912.

20 Note by Troup, 4 December 1912, TNA HO 45/10695/231366/2.

21 Troup and McKenna agreed that 'it would be undesirable to prosecute, even if there were a reasonable prospect of success [as this] would give the remarks… which come very near an incitement to murder… a wider currency and might lead some half-mad woman to act on them'. Note by Troup, 11 December 1912, TNA HO 45/10695/231366/3.

22 Mary Blathwayt, quoted in Crawford, 442.

23 Report by DS Thomas McGrath, 20 December 1912, TNA HO 45/10695/231366/6.

24 'Copy of circular from the [WSPU] forwarded anonymously to Scotland Yard..', January 1913, TNA HO 45/10695/231366/11.

25 Minute by H. B. Simpson, 14 January 1913, TNA HO 45/10695/231366/10.

26 *Times*, 31 January and 1 February 1913; Rosen, 189.

27 The Lloyd George Papers (Parliamentary Archives), LG/C/10/2/25.

28 *Morning Post*, 20 February 1913.

29 Minute by Troup, 8 February 1913, TNA HO 45/10695/231366/22.

30 Samuel to McKenna, 1 March 1913, TNA HO 45/10695/231366/31.

31 W. H. Stoakley (editor of *Wimbledon Boro News*) to McKenna, 6 March 1913, TNA HO 45/10695/231366/35.

32 Troup to Sir Alexander King (General Post Office), 16 April 1913, TNA HO 45/10700/236973/1.

33 Henry to WSPU Secretary, 16 April 1913, TNA HO 45/10700/236973/2.

34 Memo by Troup, 3 May 1913, TNA HO 45/10700/236973/2.

35 'Explosive found in lavatory of Piccadilly Tube Station', TNA HO 45/10700/236973/36.

36 Memo by Troup, 3 May 1913, TNA HO 45/10700/236973/2.

37 *Times*, 1 May 1913.

38 *The Suffragette*, 2 May 1913.

39 Ibid.

40 *Times*, 3 May 1913.

41 Ibid.

42 *Morning Post*, 5 May 1913; Minute by Henry, 19 May 1913, TNA MEPO 2/1556.

43 As Andrew Rosen has pointed out, 'the destruction attributed to suffragettes in May 1913 was more than double that of April, reaching a total of £36,475' and an impressive £54,000 in June. Rosen, 197–201.

44 Troup to the Treasury, 8 May 1913, TNA HO 45/10700/236973/33.

45 Minutes by Ernley Blackwell and McKenna, 13 May 1913, TNA HO 45/10700/236973/33.
46 Ibid.
47 Rosen, 203.
48 Report by Supt Edward Selwood, 15 August 1913, TNA HO 45/10700/236973/116.
49 *Morning Post*, 8 May 1913.
50 Constituted in late 1912 in the wake of George Lansbury's electoral defeat, the East End WSPU was from the very start imbued with Sylvia's socialist ethos, embracing a democratic structure and non-sectarian stance.
51 Sylvia Pankhurst, quoted in police report, 30 June 1913, TNA HO 144/1558/234191/42.
52 Rosen, 201f.
53 *Western Times*, 30 July 1913; *Cornishman*, 17 July 1913.
54 Rosen, 212f.
55 Prior to the formation of its Mobile Patrol Experiment in 1919, which evolved into the Flying Squad during the 1920s, the Metropolitan Police made little if any use of motorized vehicles in the course of everyday police work.
56 An ex-colonial administrator, Thomson served as governor of several British prisons in the 1890s before being appointed Secretary of the Prisons Commission in 1908. As head of Scotland Yard (1913–21) and Director of Intelligence (1919–21), Thomson played an active and prominent role in suppressing political subversion, being tasked by Lloyd George's War Cabinet in 1917 with investigating and reporting on the activities of British pacifists and socialists. See Noel Rutherford, 'Thomson, Sir Basil (1861–1939)', *ODNB* (online ed.), accessed 1 March 2018.
57 Thomson to Henry, 1 and 13 October 1913, TNA MEPO 2/1566.
58 Report by Quinn, 6 January 1914, TNA MEPO 2/1566.
59 Report by DS John Bannon, 6 November 1913, TNA HO 45/10701/236973/139.
60 'Report of proceedings at a meeting of Bow Branch of WSPU', 13 November 1913, TNA HO 45/10701/236973/140.
61 Christabel Pankhurst to Sylvia Pankhurst, 27 November 1913, quoted in Rosen, 219.
62 June Purvis, *Emmeline Pankhurst: A Biography* (London: Routledge, 2004), 250.
63 Report by Major H. Coningham (Inspector of Explosives), 2 March 1914, TNA EF 5/10.
64 *Daily Telegraph*, 3 and 6 April 1914.
65 'Actionable Passages in The Suffragette', 23 April 1914, TNA HO 45/10701/236973/160.
66 *Standard*, 14 May 1914.
67 *Manchester Courier and Lancashire General Advertiser*, 22 May 1914.
68 *Times*, 27 May 1914; *Morning Post*, 3 June 1914.
69 *Times*, 25 May 1914.
70 *Times*, 10 June 1914.
71 Henry to the Home Office, 10 June 1914, TNA HO 144/1318/252288/2.
72 Memo by Ernley Blackwell, 11 June 1914, TNA HO 144/1318/252288/2.

[73] McKenna, quoted in Jane Marcus, *Suffrage and the Pankhursts* (New York: Routledge, 2010), 315.
[74] *Daily Telegraph*, 12, 13 and 16 June 1914; *Times*, 4 June 1914.
[75] Quoted in Popplewell, 139.
[76] McKenna, quoted in Rosen, 237.
[77] Christabel Pankhurst, quoted in Rosen, 247.
[78] Rosen, 247.
[79] Quoted in Raeburn, 238.
[80] Basil Thomson, *My Experiences at Scotland Yard* (Garden City, NY: Doubleday, Page & Co., 1923), 298.
[81] See Christopher Andrew, *The Defence of the Realm: The Authorized History of MI5*.
[82] Not to be confused with the earlier Home Office Secret Service which by the early 1900s (following the retirement of Robert Anderson and Nicholas Gosselin) existed only as a funding mechanism for the Scotland Yard's 'political department'. Memo by Troup, 22 September 1909, TNA HO 144/1043/183461.
[83] 'Memorandum re Formation of a SS Bureau', 27 August 1909, TNA KV 1/3.
[84] Ibid.
[85] Kell, Six-monthly report, May 1911, TNA KV 1/9; Kell, Diary, 3 March 1911, TNA KV 1/10.
[86] Note by J. S. Ewart (Director of Military Operations), 2 December 1908, TNA KV 1/2.
[87] 'Memorandum', 27 August 1909, TNA KV 1/3.
[88] 'Espionage in time of peace' (January 1909), p. 26, TNA KV 1/2.
[89] Andrew, 82.
[90] Report by J. S. Ewart (War Office), 31 December 1908, TNA KV 1/2.
[91] Kell, Diary, 11 July 1910, TNA KV 1/10.
[92] Kell, Diary, 22 August 1910, 6 and 20 January 1911, TNA KV 1/10.
[93] Kell, Six-monthly report, May 1911, TNA KV 1/9.
[94] Kell, Diary, 6 March 1911, TNA KV 1/10.
[95] 'Intelligence Methods' (1909), p. 42, TNA KV 1/4.
[96] For a highly colourful autobiographical account, see Basil Thomson, *The Scene Changes* (Garden City, NY: Doubleday, 1937).
[97] Andrew, 106–9.
[98] *Time*, 28 December 1925.
[99] Andrew, 82.
[100] Ibid., 37.
[101] Melville, 'Memoir', p. 23, TNA KV 1/8.
[102] Report by J. S. Ewart (War Office), 31 December 1908, TNA KV 1/2.
[103] Kell, Six-monthly report, October 1913, TNA KV 1/9.
[104] Melville, 'Memoir', pp. 4, 18, TNA KV 1/8.
[105] Kell, Six-monthly report, October 1912, TNA KV 1/9.
[106] 'Bureau Organization, April 1914', TNA KV 1/9.
[107] For terms of the Act, see www.legislation.gov.uk/ukpga/Geo5/1-2/28/contents. Accessed 1 March 2018.

[108] 'Details of cases tried', July 1912, TNA KV 1/9.
[109] Andrew, 55, 84.
[110] Ibid., 96.
[111] Andrew Staniforth, *The Routledge Companion to UK Counter Terrorism* (London: Routledge, 2013), 28.

## Conclusion

[1] See p. 184.
[2] Memo by A. K. Stephenson, 1 April 1881, TNA HO 144/77/A3385.
[3] Warren to Ruggles-Brise, 4 October 1888, TNA MEPO 1/48.
[4] Cook, 112.
[5] Porter, *The Origins of the Vigilant State*, 144.
[6] Memo by Ernley Blackwell, 11 June 1914, TNA HO 144/1318/252288/2.
[7] Porter, *The Origins of the Vigilant State*, 193f; Emsley, *The English Police*, 106.
[8] Jackson, *Harcourt and Son*, 19ff.
[9] Memo by Edward Jenkinson 4 January 1883, TNA HO 144/72/A19.
[10] Cook, 136f.
[11] Porter, *The Origins of the Vigilant State*, 96.
[12] Anthony Howe, *Free Trade and Liberal England, 1846–1946* (Oxford: Clarendon Press, 1998), 123.
[13] William Harcourt to Lewis Harcourt, 29 February 1884, quoted in Gardiner, 503.
[14] Constance Bantman, *The French Anarchists in London, 1880–1914: Exile and Transnationalism in the First Globalisation* (Liverpool: Liverpool University Press, 2013), 129.
[15] J. H. Codger (a 'Liberal and workingman') to William Harcourt, 16 March 1883, TNA HO 144/114/A25908.
[16] *Lloyd's Weekly Newspaper*, 23 March 1884.
[17] *Glasgow Herald*, 14 April 14 1884.
[18] *Dundee Courier & Argus and Northern Warder*, 18 April 1884; *Manchester Courier and Lancashire General Advertiser*, 15 April 1884.
[19] Note by Charles Murdoch, April 1894, TNA HO 144/259/A55860/1.
[20] *Times*, 20 February 1894.
[21] *Daily Mail*, 21 June 1897; *Reynolds's Newspaper*, 13 June 1897.
[22] 'Memorandum as to the Protocol of 1904 respecting Anarchist Crimes', p. 3, TNA HO 144/757/118516/15.
[23] Report by E. R. Henry, May 1904, TNA HO 144/757/118516/2.
[24] Foreign Office reply to Cipriano del Mazo (Spanish ambassador to the Court of St James), December 1893, TNA HO 45/10254/X36450/8.
[25] Salisbury to the Foreign Office, 12 October 1898, TNA HO 45/10254/X36450/31.
[26] Robert Anderson to Charles Murdoch, January 1893, TNA HO/144/485/X37842/5.
[27] Memo by E. R. Henry, 16 March 1903, TNA HO 144/545/A55176/51.
[28] *Times*, 1 January 1904.

# Bibliography

## Primary sources

*Documents in the British National Archives at Kew*

Cabinet Papers: CAB 37.
Domestic Records of the Public Record Office: PRO 30.
Home Office Papers: EF 5/10; HO 45, 144.
Foreign Office Papers: FO 45, 881.
Metropolitan Police Papers: MEPO 1–5.
Records of Justices of Assize, Gaol Delivery, Oyer and Terminer and Nisi Prius: ASSI 6.
Records of the Security Service: KV 1.

*Documents in the Parliamentary Archives (UK)*

The Lloyd George Papers – LG/C/10/2/25.

*Documents in the Archives de la Préfecture de Police de Paris*

Carton BA 139.
Carton BA 924.

*Contemporary periodicals*

*Aberdeen Weekly Journal*
*Belfast News-Letter*
*Birmingham Daily Post*
*Blackwood's Edinburgh Magazine*
*Bristol Mercury and Daily Post (Bristol)*
*Cheshire Observer (Chester)*
*Commonweal (London)*
*Cornishman (Penzance)*
*Daily Chronicle (London)*
*Daily Gazette (Middlesbrough)*
*Daily Graphic (London)*
*Daily Mail (Hull)*
*Daily Mail (London)*
*Daily News (London)*
*Daily Telegraph (London)*

*Derby Daily Telegraph*
*Devon and Exeter Gazette (Exeter)*
*Dundee Courier & Argus and Northern Warder*
*El Día (Zaragoza)*
*Essex Newsman (Chelmsford)*
*Evening News (Portsmouth)*
*Evening Post (Wellington, NZ)*
*Evening Telegraph (Dundee)*
*Evening Telegraph and Star and Sheffield Daily Times*
*Financial Times (London)*
*Freedom (London)*
*Freeman's Journal and Daily Commercial Advertiser (Dublin)*
*Gazette des Tribunaux (Paris)*
*Glasgow Herald*
*Graphic (London)*
*Household Words (London)*
*Huddersfield Daily Chronicle*
*Illustrated London News (London)*
*Illustrated Police News (London)*
*Indian Sociologist (London)*
*Justice (London)*
*L'Aurore (Paris)*
*La Justice (Paris)*
*La Lanterne (Paris)*
*Lancaster Gazette and General Advertiser for Lancashire, Westmorland, and Yorkshire*
*Le Nouveau Precurseur (Antwerp)*
*Le Petit Journal (Paris)*
*Leicester Chronicle and the Leicestershire Mercury*
*Liverpool Mercury*
*Lloyd's Weekly Newspaper (London)*
*Manchester Courier and Lancashire General Advertiser*
*Morning Leader (London)*
*Morning Post (London)*
*Murray's Magazine (London)*
*Northampton Mercury*
*Northern Echo (Darlington)*
*P. I. P.: Penny Illustrated Paper and Illustrated Times (London)*
*Pall Mall Gazette (London)*
*Penny Illustrated Paper and Illustrated Times (London)*
*Punch (London)*
*Reynolds's Newspaper (London)*
*Sheffield Daily Telegraph*
*Sheffield Evening Telegraph*
*St James's Gazette (London)*
*Standard (London)*
*Star (Saint Peter Port)*
*Suffragette (London)*
*Sunday Times (London)*
*Times (London)*

*Weekly Times & Echo (London)*
*Western Times (Exeter)*

## Parliamentary Acts

Incitement to Mutiny Act 1797. 37 Geo. III, c. 70. London: HMSO.
Metropolitan Police Act 1829. 10 Geo. IV, c. 44. London: HMSO.
Extradition Act 1870. 33 & 34 Vict., c. 52. London: HMSO.
Explosives Act 1875. 38 Vict., c. 17. London: HMSO.
Explosives Substances Act 1883. 46 Vict., c. 3. London: HMSO.

## Parliamentary debates (Hansard)

HC Deb, 22 February 1881, vol. 258, cols 1553–5.
HC Deb, 1 April 1881, vol. 260, col. 464.
HC Deb, 3 August 1882, vol. 273, col. 685.
HC Deb, 21 February 1884, vol. 284, col. 1610.
HC Deb, 7 February 1884, vol. 284, cols 177–8.
HC Deb, 4 April 1884, vol. 286, cols 1654–5.
HC Deb, 4 July 1861, vol. 164, cols 368–9.
HC Deb, 13 February 1888, vol. 322, col. 264.
HC Deb, 20 March 1889, vol. 334, col. 300.
HC Deb, 20 March 1889, vol. 334, col. 276.
HC Deb, 20 March 1889, vol. 334, col. 277.
HC Deb, 27 April 1892, vol. 3, col. 1510.
HC Deb, 30 November 1893, vol. 19, cols 103–4.
HC Deb, 22 January 1897, vol. 45, col. 359.
HC Deb, 26 March 1897, vol. 47, col. 1487.
HC Deb, 22 February 1897, vol. 46, cols 868–9.
HC Deb, 26 October 1906, vol. 163, cols 518–19.
HC Deb, 15 February 1907, vol. 169, col. 416.
HC Deb, 29 April 1909, vol. 4, col. 548.
HC Deb, 22 August 1911, vol. 29, col. 2298.
HC Deb, 28 February 1912, vol. 34, col. 1372.
HC Deb, 30 May 1912 vol. 38, col. 1567.
HC Deb, 29 July 1912, vol. 41, col. 1656W.
HL Deb, 17 July 1894, vol. 27, col. 127.

## Old Bailey trial proceedings

Trial of David John Nicoll, Charles Wilfred Mowbray, May 1892 (t18920502-493). *Old Bailey Proceedings Online*. www.oldbaileyonline.org, version 7.0. Accessed 1 March 2018.

Trial of Fritz Brall, June 1894 (t18940625-580). *Old Bailey Proceedings Online*. www.oldbaileyonline.org, version 7.0. Accessed 1 March 2018.

Trial of Edward Bell, alias Edward J. Ivory, January 1897 (t18970111-146). *Old Bailey Proceedings Online*. www.oldbaileyonline.org, version 7.0. Accessed 1 March 2018.

Trial of Vladimir Bourtzeff, Klement Wierzbicki, February 1898 (t18980207-174). *Old Bailey Proceedings Online*. www.oldbaileyonline.org, version 7.0. Accessed 1 March 2018.

Trial of George Bedborough, October 1898 (t18981024-715). *Old Bailey Proceedings Online*. www.oldbaileyonline.org, version 7.0. Accessed 1 March 2018.

Trial of Madar Lal Dhingra, July 1909 (t19090719-55). *Old Bailey Proceedings Online*. www.oldbaileyonline.org, version 7.0. Accessed 1 March 2018.

Trial of Arthur Fletcher Horsley, July 1909 (t19090719-54). *Old Bailey Proceedings Online*. www.oldbaileyonline.org, version 7.0. Accessed 1 March 2018.

Trial of Guy Alfred Aldred, September 1909 (t19090907-44). *Old Bailey Proceedings Online*. www.oldbaileyonline.org, version 7.0. Accessed 1 March 2018.

Trial of Guy Bowman, Charles Ernest Buck, Benjamin Edward Buck, March 1912 (t19120319-45). *Old Bailey Proceedings Online*. www.oldbaileyonline.org, version 7.0. Accessed 1 March 2018.

## Correspondence, memoirs and diaries

Anderson, Robert. *Sidelights on the Home Rule Movement*. New York: E. P. Dutton and Company, 1906.

——. *The Lighter Side of My Official Life*. London: Hodder and Stoughton, 1909.

Asquith, Herbert Henry. *Memoirs and Reflections, 1852–1927*, 2 vols. Toronto: McClelland and Stewart, 1928.

Ball, Stephen, ed. *Dublin Castle and the First Home Rule Crisis: The Political Journal of Sir George Fottrell, 1884–1887*. Cambridge: Cambridge University Press, 2008.

Brackenbury, Henry. *Some Memories of My Spare Time*. Edinburgh and London: William Blackwood & Sons, 1909.

Brust, Harold. *I Guarded Kings: The Memoirs of a Political Police Officer*. New York: Hillman-Curl, 1936.

Bussy, Frederick M. *Irish Conspiracies: Recollections of John Mallon (The Great Irish Detective) and Other Reminiscences*. London: Everett & Co., 1910.

Clarke, Thomas J. *Glimpses of an Irish Felon's Prison Life*. Dublin and London: Maunsel & Roberts Ltd., 1922.

Dunlop, Andrew. *Fifty Years of Irish Journalism*. Dublin: Hanna & Neale, 1911.

Fitch, Herbert T. *Traitors Within: The Adventures of Detective Inspector Herbert T. Fitch*. London: Hurst & Blackett, 1933.

Gordon, Peter, ed. *The Red Earl: The Papers of the Fifth Earl Spencer 1835–1910*. Northampton: Northamptonshire Record Society, 1981.

Guiccioli, Alessandro. *Diario di un Conservatore*. Rome: Edizioni di Borghese, 1973.

Le Caron, Henri (Thomas Beach). *Twenty-Five Years in The Secret Service: The Recollections of a Spy*. London: William Heinemann, 1892.

Littlechild, John. *The Reminiscences of Chief-Inspector Littlechild, Second edition*. London: The Leadenhall Press, 1894.

McIntyre, Patrick. 'Scotland Yard: Its Mysteries and Memoirs'. *Reynolds's Newspaper*. London, February–May 1895.

Macnaghten, Melville. *Days of My Years*. London: Edward Arnold, 1914.

Mann, Tom. *Memoirs*. London: The Labour Publishing Co. Ltd, 1923.

Marx, Karl and Friedrich Engels. *Correspondence 1846–1895*. London: Martin Lawrence Ltd, 1934.

Moser, Maurice and Charles F. Rideal. *Stories from Scotland Yard*. London: George Routledge and Sons, 1890.
Pankhurst, Emmeline. *My Own Story*. London: Eveleigh Nash, 1914.
Pankhurst, Sylvia. *The Suffragette: The History of the Women's Militant Suffrage Movement, 1905–1910*. New York: Sturgis & Walton Co., 1911.
Parry Frye, Kate. *Campaigning for the Vote: Kate Parry Frye's Suffrage Diary*. Edited by Elizabeth Crawford. London: Francis Boutle Publishers, 2013.
Pethick-Lawrence, Frederick. *Fate Has Been Kind*. London: Hutchinson & Co. Ltd, 1943.
Rocker, Rudolf. *The London Years*. Edinburgh, Oakland, CA, Baltimore, MD: AK Press, 2005.
Rossa, Jeremiah O'Donovan. *Rossa's Recollections, 1838 to 1898*. Marine's Harbor, NY: O'Donovan Rossa, 1898.
Sweeney, John. *At Scotland Yard*. London: Grant Richards, 1904.
Thomson, Basil. *My Experiences at Scotland Yard*. Garden City, NY: Doubleday, Page & Co., 1923.
Tynan, Patrick J. *The Irish National Invincibles and their Times*. London: Chatham and Co., 1894.

## Works of fiction

Childers, Erskine. *Riddle of the Sands: A Record of Secret Service*. New York: Dodd, Mead and Co., 1915.
Conrad, Joseph. *The Secret Agent: A Simple Tale*. London: Methuen & Co., 1907.
Fawcett, Douglas E. *Hartmann the Anarchist: or, The Doom of the Great City*. London: Edward Arnold, 1893.
Griffith, George. *The Angel of the Revolution: A Tale of the Coming Terror*. London: Tower Publishing Co., Ltd, 1893.
––. *Olga Romanoff: or, the Syren of the Skies*. London: Tower Publishing Co., Ltd, 1894.

## Miscellaneous

*London – Sidney Street Siege*. London, UK: British Pathé, 1911. Newsreel. Available at: www.britishpathe.com/video/london-sidney-street-siege. Accessed 1 March 2018.
Ablett, Noah et al. 'The Miner's Next Step'. Tonypandy: Robert Davies & Company, 1912.
Churchill, Winston. 'The Approaching Conflict (The Coming Election)', 29 January 1909. *The International Churchill Society*. Available at: www.winstonchurchill.org/resources/speeches/1901-1914-rising-star/the-approaching-conflict-the-coming-election/. Accessed 1 March 2018.
Couper, Charles Tennant. *Report of the Trial of the Dynamitards*. Edinburgh: William Green, 1884.
Galton, Francis. *Fingerprint Directories*. London: Macmillan and Co., 1895.
MacDonald, John. *Diary of the Parnell Commission: Revised from "The Daily News"*. London: T. Fisher Unwin, 1890.
McEnnis, John. *The Clan-na-Gael and the Murder of Dr. Cronin*. San Francisco, CA: G. P. Woodward, 1889.
Roosevelt, Theodore. 'First Annual Message', 3 December 1901. *The American Presidency Project*. Available at: www.presidency.ucsb.edu/ws/?pid=29542. Accessed 1 March 2018

## Secondary sources

### Books

Anderson, Malcolm. *In Thrall to Political Change: Police and Gendarmerie in France*. Oxford: Oxford University Press, 2011.
Andrew, Christopher. *The Defence of the Realm: The Authorized History of MI5*. London: Penguin Books, 2010.
Avrich, Paul. *The Russian Anarchists*. Princeton, NJ: Princeton University Press, 1971.
––. *The Haymarket Tragedy*. Princeton, NJ: Princeton University Press, 1986.
Bailey, Victor, ed. *Policing and Punishment in Nineteenth Century Britain*. London: Croom Helm, 1981.
Bantman, Constance. *The French Anarchists in London, 1880–1914: Exile and Transnationalism in the First Globalisation*. Liverpool: Liverpool University Press, 2013.
Bapu, Prabhu. *Hindu Mahasabha in Colonial North India, 1915–1930: Constructing Nation and History*. London and New York: Routledge, 2013.
Beavan, Colin. *Fingerprints: The Origins of Crime Detection and the Murder Case that Launched Forensic Science*. New York: Hyperion, 2001.
Beer, Daniel. *The House of the Dead: Siberian Exile Under the Tsars*. London: Penguin, 2017.
Begg, Paul and Keith Skinner. *The Scotland Yard Files: 150 Years of the C.I.D. 1842–1992*. London: Headline, 1992.
Bentley, Michael. *Lord Salisbury's World: Conservative Environments in Late Victorian Britain*. Cambridge: Cambridge University Press, 2001.
Bevir, Mark. *The Making of British Socialism*. Princeton, NJ: Princeton University Press, 2011.
Bew, Paul. *Ireland: The Politics of Enmity, 1789–2006*. Oxford: Oxford University Press, 2007.
Bunyan, Tony. *The History and Practice of the Political Police in Britain*. London: Julian Friedman Publishers, 1976.
Butterworth, Alex. *The World That Never Was: A True Story of Dreamers, Schemers, Anarchists and Secret Agents*. New York: Pantheon Books, 2010.
Campbell, Christy. *Fenian Fire: The British Government Plot to Assassinate Queen Victoria*. London: HarperCollins, 2003.
Cannadine, David. *Ornamentalism: How the British Saw Their Empire*. Oxford: Oxford University Press, 2002.
Chase, Malcolm. *1820: Disorder and Stability in the United Kingdom*. Oxford: Oxford University Press, 2013.
Church, Roy. *Strikes and Solidarity: Coalfield Conflict in Britain, 1889–1966*. Cambridge: Cambridge University Press, 2002.
Clark, Martin. *Modern Italy, 1871 to the Present, Third edition*. New York: Pearson Longman, 2008.
Cole, G. D. H. and Raymond Postgate. *The British Common People, 1746–1946*. London: Methuen, 1961.
Colley, Linda. *Britons: Forging the Nation, 1707–1837*. New Haven, CT: Yale University Press, 1992.
Cook, Andrew. *M: MI5's First Spymaster*. Stroud: Tempus Publishing, 2006.
Cook, Chris and John Stevenson. *A History of British Elections since 1689*. New York: Routledge, 2014.

Corfe, Tom. *The Phoenix Park Murders: Conflict, Compromise and Tragedy in Ireland, 1879–1882*. London: Hodder and Stoughton, 1968.
Crawford, Elizabeth. *The Women's Suffrage Movement: A Reference Guide, 1866–1928*. London: Routledge, 2003.
Daly, Jonathan. *Autocracy under Siege: Security Police and Opposition in Russia, 1866–1905*. DeKalb, IL: Northern Illinois University Press, 1998.
Damier, Vadim. *Anarcho-syndicalism in the 20th Century*. Edmonton, AB: Black Cat Press, 2009.
Dangerfield, George. *The Strange Death of Liberal England*. New York: Capricorn Books, 1961.
Di Paola, Paolo. *The Knights Errant of Anarchy: London and the Italian Anarchist Diaspora, 1880–1917*. Liverpool: Liverpool University Press, 2013.
Douglass, James W. *Gandhi and the Unspeakable: His Final Experiment with Truth*. Maryknoll, NY: Orbis Books, 2012.
Ellenberger, Nancy. *Balfour's World: Aristocracy and Political Culture at the Fin de Siècle*. Woodbridge: Boydell and Brewer, 2015.
Emsley, Clive. *The English Police: A Political and Social History, Second edition*. Harlow: Longman, 1996.
– –. *Crime and Society in England, 1750–1900, Fourth edition*. Harlow: Longman, 2010.
– – and Barbara Weinberger, eds. *Policing Western Europe: Politics, Professionalism, and Public Order, 1850–1940*. London: Greenwood Press, 1991.
Ewing, Keith and Conor Anthony Gearty. *The Struggle for Civil Liberties: Political Freedom and the Rule of Law in Britain, 1914–1945*. Oxford: Oxford University Press, 2011.
Farré, Juan Avilés. *Francisco Ferrer y Guardia: Pedagogo, Anarquista y Mártir*. Madrid: Marcial Pons, Ediciones de Historia, 2006.
Fischer, Ben B. *Okhrana: The Paris Operations of the Russian Imperial Police*. Collingdale, PA: Diane Publishing, 1999.
Fitzpatrick, David. *Henry Boland's Irish Revolution*. Cork: Cork University Press, 2003.
Gabriel, Elun. *Assassins and Conspirators: Anarchism, Socialism, and Political Culture in Imperial Germany*. DeKalb, IL: Northern Illinois University Press, 2014.
Gantt, John. *Irish Terrorism in the Atlantic Community, 1865–1922*. Basingstoke: Palgrave Macmillan, 2010.
Gardiner, A. G. *The Life of Sir William Harcourt*, 2 vols. London: Constable & Co. Ltd, 1923.
Geary, Roger. *Policing Industrial Disputes: 1893 to 1985*. Cambridge: Cambridge University Press, 2011.
Glover, David. *Literature, Immigration and Diaspora in Fin-de-Siecle England: A Cultural History of the 1905 Aliens Act*. Cambridge: Cambridge University Press, 2012.
Grube, Denis. *At the Margins of Victorian Britain: Politics, Immorality and Britishness in the Nineteenth Century*. London: I. B. Tauris, 2013.
Henderson, Robert. *Vladimir Burtsev and the Struggle for a Free Russia: A Revolutionary in the Time of Tsarism and Bolshevism*. London: Bloomsbury, 2017.
Howells, Martin and Keith Skinner. *The Ripper Legacy: The Life and Death of Jack the Ripper*. London: Sidgwick & Jackson, 1991.
Jenkins, Brian. *The Fenian Problem: Insurgency and Terrorism in a Liberal State 1858–1874*. Montreal and Kingston: McGill-Queen's University Press, 2008.
Jensen, Richard Bach. *The Battle against Anarchist Terrorism: An International History, 1878–1934*. Cambridge: Cambridge University Press, 2014.

Jeyes, S. H. *The Life of Sir Howard Vincent*. London: George Allen & Co. Ltd, 1912.
Johnson, David. *Regency Revolution: The Case of Arthur Thistlewood*. Salisbury: Compton Russell, 1974.
Joyce, Patrick. *The State of Freedom: A Social History of the British State since 1800*. Cambridge: Cambridge University Press, 2013.
Kossman, E. H. *The Low Countries, 1780–1940*. Oxford: Clarendon Press, 1978.
Latouche, Peter. *Anarchy, An Authentic Exposition of the Methods of Anarchists and the Aims of Anarchism*. London: Everett & Co., 1908.
Lyons, F. S. L. *Charles Stewart Parnell*. Oxford: Oxford University Press, 1971.
Maitron, Jean. *Ravachol et les Anarchistes*. Paris: René Juillard, 1964.
Marcus, Jane. *Suffrage and the Pankhursts*. New York: Routledge, 2010.
Martin, Jane. *Women and the Politics of Schooling in Victorian and Edwardian England*. London: Bloomsbury, 2010.
Masini, Pier Carlo. *Storia degli Anarchici Italiani nell'Epoca degli Attentati*. Milan: Rizzoli Editore, 1981.
McGee, Owen. *The IRB: The Irish Republican Brotherhood, from the Land League to Sinn Féin*. Dublin: Four Courts Press, 2005.
McKenna, Joseph. *The Irish-American Dynamite Campaign: A History, 1881–1896*. Jefferson, NC: McFarland & Co., 2012.
Merriman, John. *The Dynamite Club: How a Bombing in Fin-de-Siècle Paris Ignited the Age of Modern Terror*. Boston, MA: Houghton Mifflin, 2009.
Moore, Robert. *Pitmen, Preachers and Politics*. Cambridge: Cambridge University Press, 1979.
Morley, John. *The Life of Gladstone*. London: Hodder and Stoughton, 1927.
Ó Catháin, Máirtín. *Irish Republicanism in Scotland, 1858–1916*. Dublin and Portland, OR: Irish Academic Press, 2007.
O'Callaghan, Margaret. *British High Politics and a Nationalist Ireland: Criminality, Land and the Law under Forster and Balfour*. New York: St Martin's Press, 1994.
Pernicone, Nunzio. *Italian Anarchism, 1864–1892*. Edinburgh, Oakland, CA, Baltimore, MD: AK Press, 2009.
Popplewell, Richard J. *Intelligence and Imperial Defence: British Intelligence and the Defence of the Indian Empire, 1904–1924*. London: Frank Cass, 1995.
Porter, Bernard. *Plots and Paranoia: A History of Political Espionage in Britain, 1790–1988*. Boston, MA: Unwin Hyman, 1989.
––. *The Origins of the Vigilant State: The London Metropolitan Police Special Branch before the First World War*. London: Weidenfeld and Nicolson, 1987.
––. *The Refugee Question in Mid-Victorian Politics*. Cambridge: Cambridge University Press, 1979.
Pugh, Martin. *The Pankhursts: The History of One Radical Family*. London: Vintage Books, 2008.
Purvis, June. *Emmeline Pankhurst: A Biography*. London: Routledge, 2004.
Quail, John. *The Slow Burning Fuse: The Lost History of the British Anarchists*. St Albans and London: Paladin, 1978.
Raeburn, Antonia. *The Militant Suffragettes*. London: Michael Joseph, 1973.
Reiner, Robert. *The Politics of the Police, Fourth edition*. Oxford: Oxford University Press, 2010.
Reith, Charles. *British Police and the Democratic Ideal*. Oxford: Oxford University Press, 1943.
Richter, Donald C. *Riotous Victorians*. Athens, OH: Ohio University Press, 1981.

Robb, Graham. *Rimbaud*. Basingstoke and Oxford: Picador, 2000.
Rosen, Andrew. *Rise Up, Women! The Militant Campaign of the Women's Social and Political Union, 1903–1914*. London and Boston: Routledge & Kegan Paul, 1974.
Royle, Edward. *Radicals Secularists and Republicans: Popular Freethought in Britain, 1866–1915*. Manchester: Manchester University Press, 1980.
Schmidt, Michael and Lucien van der Walt. *Black Flame: The Revolutionary Class Politics of Anarchism and Syndicalism*. Edinburgh, Oakland, CA, Baltimore, MD: AK Press, 2009.
Shaw, Caroline. *Britannia's Embrace: Modern Humanitarianism and the Imperial Origins of Refugee Relief*. Oxford: Oxford University Press, 2015.
Short, K. R. M. *The Dynamite War: Irish-American Bombers in Victorian Britain*. Atlantic Highlands, NJ: Humanities Press, 1979.
Shpayer-Makov, Haia. *The Ascent of the Detective: Police Sleuths in Victorian and Edwardian England*. Oxford: Oxford University Press, 2011.
—— and Clive Emsley, eds. *Police Detectives in History, 1750–1950*. Aldershot: Ashgate, 2006.
Smith, Philip Thurmond. *Policing Victorian London: Political Policing, Public Order, and the London Metropolitan Police*. Westport, CT: Greenwood Press, 1985.
Staniforth, Andrew. *The Routledge Companion to UK Counter Terrorism*. London: Routledge, 2013.
Thurlow, Richard. *The Secret State: British Internal Security in the Twentieth Century*. Oxford: Blackwell Publishers, 1994.
Whelehan, Niall. *The Dynamiters: Irish Nationalism and Political Violence in the Wider World, 1867–1900*. Cambridge: Cambridge University Press, 2012.
Williams, Glyn and John Ramsden. *Ruling Britannia: A Political History of Britain, 1688–1988*. London: Longman, 1990.
Winter, James. *London's Teeming Streets, 1830–1914*. London: Routledge, 2013.
Zuckerman, Fredric S. *The Tsarist Secret Police Abroad: Policing Europe in a Modernizing World*. Basingstoke and New York: Palgrave Macmillan, 2003.

## Articles and anthology chapters

Ballhatchet, Joan. 'The Police and the London Dock Strike of 1889'. *History Workshop* 32 (1991), 54–68.
Brodeur, Jean-Paul. 'High Policing and Low Policing: Remarks about the Policing of Political Activities'. *Social Problems* 30 (1983), 507–20.
Connolly, Sean. 'Patriotism and Nationalism'. In *The Oxford Handbook of Modern Irish History*. Ed. Alvin Jackson, pp. 27–45. Oxford: Oxford University Press, 2014.
D. P. 'A Policeman to Remember: Sir Patrick Quinn, M.V.O.'. *The Police Journal* 38 (1965), 472–6.
Fletcher, Ian Christopher. '"Women of the Nations, Unite!": Transnational Suffragism in the United Kingdom, 1912–1914'. In *Women's Suffrage in the British Empire: Citizenship, Nation and Race*. Ed. Ian Christopher Fletcher, Philippa Levine and Laura E. Nym Mayhall, pp. 103–21. London: Routledge, 2012.
Goldmanis, Maris. 'Latvian Anarchism – The Story of Peter the Painter'. *Latvian History*. http://archive.is/2AnRK. Accessed 1 March 2018.
Jensen, Richard Bach. 'The International Anti-Anarchist Conference of 1898 and the Origins of the Interpol'. *Journal of Contemporary History* 16 (1981), 323–47.

Knepper, Paul. 'The Other Invisible Hand: Jews and Anarchists in London before the First World War'. *Jewish History* 22 (2008), 295–315.

McGee, Owen. 'Keeping the Lid on an Irish Revolution: The Gosselin–Balfour Correspondence'. *History Ireland* 15 (2007), 36–41.

Newton, Michael. 'Four Notes on "The Secret Agent": Sir William Harcourt, Ford and Helen Rossetti, Bourdin's Relations, and a Warning Against Δ'. *The Conradian* 32 (2007), 129–46.

Pernicone, Nunzio. 'The Case of Pietro Acciarito: Accomplices, Psychological Torture, and Raison d'État'. *Journal for the Study of Radicalism* 5 (2011), 67–104.

Porter, Bernard. 'The Freiheit Prosecutions, 1881–1882'. *The Historical Journal* 23 (1980), 833–56.

Shpayer-Makov, Haia. 'Anarchism in British Public Opinion 1880–1914'. *Victorian Studies* 31 (1988), 487–516.

Weinberger, Barbara. 'Keeping the Peace? Policing Strikes 1906–26'. *History Today* 37 (1987), 29–35.

## Unpublished thesis

Clutterbuck, Lindsay. 'An Accident of History? The Evolution of Counter Terrorism Methodology in the Metropolitan Police from 1829 to 1901, with Particular Reference to the Influence of Extreme Irish Nationalist Activity'. PhD dissertation, University of Portsmouth, 2002.

# Index

Admiralty  78, 229, 254
*Adult, The*  177–8
  *see also* Legitimation League
agents provocateurs  8, 10, 20, 67, 121, 132,
    191, 257–8
Aldred, Guy Alfred  206–7
Alexander II, Czar of Russia  9, 31
aliens
  Act (1905)  199, 201, 210
  and government policy  158, 195, 197, 198,
    203, 255
  and political radicalism  183, 199, 205,
    207–8, 209, 269
  bill (1894)  157, 173
  in the press  183–4, 201, 210
  *see also* asylum, immigration, xenophobia
America: *see* United States of America
Amsterdam  100, 166
anarchism  3, 5, 6, 101, 127, 138, 150–1, 156,
    160, 164, 168, 171, 177, 178, 179, 184, 185,
    186, 189, 195, 212, 258
  and syndicalism  161, 216, 259
  communist  161
  coverage of in the British press  15, 129,
    132, 133, 154, 169, 172, 201, 269
  debates on in the British Parliament  132,
    143–4, 151, 157–8, 267
  debates on at the 1898 Rome
    Conference  180–3, 262
    *see also* Rome Anti-Anarchist
      Conference
  hostility to in Britain  15, 35, 135, 149, 155,
    201
  impact on British foreign policy  141–2,
    170, 173, 182, 183, 187, 191, 196–7, 254,
    266
  in London  5, 14, 34, 100, 104, 105, 119, 130,
    131, 132, 134, 135–7, 138, 140, 143, 145–7,
    148–9, 152–3, 154–5, 156, 158, 161, 163,
    171–2, 173, 185, 186, 199–201, 207–10
  in provincial British cities  128–30, 132,
    159, 170–1
  individualist  140
  Jewish  199, 209, 252
  Latvian  208–10

laws against on the continent  10, 34, 101,
    127–8, 142, 157, 168–9, 172
  native British  128, 143, 145, 162, 170,
    206–7, 214
  propaganda by the deed  32, 128, 151, 155
  views of at Scotland Yard  102, 120, 131,
    133, 137, 140, 147–8, 152, 153, 159, 197–8,
    204, 205, 252, 265
Anderson, Robert  7, 8, 13, 38, 44, 62, 99, 111,
    127, 133, 142, 143, 146, 151, 152, 162, 165,
    166, 170, 176, 187, 190, 191, 252, 262, 263,
    264, 267, 268
  activities prior to 1881  28
  involvement in Jubilee Plot (1887)  93–6, 97
  involvement in 'Parnellism and crime'
    special commission (1888-89)  114,
    115, 118
  relationship with Edward Jenkinson  51,
    63, 72–3
  relationship with William Harcourt  50,
    61, 117, 121
  relationship with Henri Le Caron (Thomas
    Beach)  30, 40, 47, 55, 72, 92, 116, 263
  relationship with William Melville  134,
    153, 155
  religious beliefs of  91
  views on anarchism in Britain  131, 201
  views of British political police system  47,
    167, 183–4, 257
  views of continental policing  141, 147, 159
  views of Social Democratic
    Federation  139–40
Antwerp  64, 159, 164, 165, 167–8, 187
anti-anarchist conference
  1893 (proposed)  142, 180, 191, 266
  1898 (Rome): *see* Rome Anti-Anarchist
    Conference
antisemitism  198, 199, 210, 310 n.81
  *see also* Jews
Anti-Socialist Laws, German (1878)  31, 34,
    101, 143
Angiolillo, Michele  172–3
Archibald, Edward M.  44, 51
Asquith, Herbert Henry  127, 140, 143, 146,
    148–9, 153, 162, 189, 228, 234

as target of suffragettes   229, 230, 231–3, 238–9, 269
lack of intelligence on anarchist activity   151, 155, 253, 261
political evolution of   139, 220, 305 n.57
views on British laws dealing with anarchism   142, 158
Assistant Under-Secretary for Police and Crime (Ireland): see Brackenbury, Jenkinson
asylum, political (British policy)   22, 32, 138
anarchist views of   154–5
official views of in Europe   32, 37, 183, 266
in the British press   129, 201, 146
political opposition to in Britain   144, 157–8, 183
Austria-Hungary   158, 162, 180, 182, 196, 275 n.32
Autonomie Club   135–6, 140, 146–7, 149, 157, 158, 199, 264

Balfour, Arthur James   97, 104–5, 118, 168, 229, 293 n.38
Balmoral Castle   58–9, 164, 166
Barcelona   142–3, 168,
Beach, Thomas: see Le Caron
Bedborough, George   177–8, 265
Belgium   101, 180, 266
Bengal   70, 107, 108, 110, 187
see also India
Bernard, Simon   32, 274 n.31
Bertillon, Alphonse   182–3, 187
Besant, Annie   100, 102
Birmingham   52–3, 59, 66, 67, 71, 221
anarchist presence in   143, 159
arrests of Fenians in   65–6, 71
Chief Constable of: see Farndale
suffragette activities in   231–2, 240
'Black Friday' (1910)   235–6, 237, 252, 259
see also suffragettes
Blackwell, Ernley   246, 250
'Bloody Sunday' (1887): see Trafalgar Square riots
Boer War (1899–1902)   185, 188, 199
bombs: see Explosives Act, dynamite
Bourdin, Martial   145–51, 153, 160
Bow Street Police   19, 20, 77, 78, 136, 138, 152, 166, 245
Brackenbury, Henry   43–4, 45
Brailsford, Henry Noel   233, 236
Bradford, Edward   127, 148, 152, 159, 187, 188
relationship with the Home Office   119
views on informers   133, 153
Bresci, Gaetano   185, 187

British Empire   43, 70, 119, 202, 203, 269
see also India, Ireland
Brodeur, Jean-Paul   1–2
Brooklyn, New York   50, 52
Brussels   159, 167, 184, 186
Burke, Thomas Henry   41–2, 46, 114
see also Phoenix Park murders
Burns, John   83, 99, 118, 139, 285
Burton, Harry   77–8, 79, 265
Burtsev, Vladimir   174–7, 191, 207, 258
see also Nihilists
Byrne, Frank   47, 48, 93

Café Terminus outrage (1894)   145, 150
see also anarchism, France
Café Very outrage (1894)   152, 135, 136, 138
see also anarchism, France
Cails, Victor   129–30, 132
see also anarchism, Walsall anarchist conspiracy
Callan, Thomas   99, 107
Campbell-Bannerman, Henry   222, 228
Carey, James   47–8
Carnarvon, fourth earl of (Henry Herbert)   80–1, 82, 84
Carnot, Nicolas Léonard Sadi   147, 156–7, 158, 161
Carpenter, Edward   169, 178
Carson, Edward   220, 249
'Cat and Mouse' (Temporary Discharge for Ill-health) Act (1913)   242, 245, 247, 248
Cato Street conspiracy (1820)   19–21
see also Thistlewood
Cavendish, Frederick Charles   41–2, 46
see also Phoenix Park murders
Caxton Hall   223, 226, 229, 234
censorship
in Britain   235, 245, 246, 250, 259
in continental Europe   162, 182, 275 n.32
Charing Cross Station   43, 58, 59, 69, 78, 237
Charles, Frederick   129, 131
Chartism   3, 4, 11, 21–2, 157
Chatham Prison   116, 117, 168
Chicago   166, 212, 301 n.50
Chief Inspector of Explosives: see Majendie
Childers, Hugh Culling Eardley   29, 83, 84, 86, 87, 100, 122, 127
child labour, use of by British police   61, 138, 281 n.55
Churchill, Winston   234, 253, 260, 262
cooperation with MO5   255
involvement in Sidney Street 'siege' (1911)   209–10

role in quelling industrial unrest
(1909–12)   214, 215, 216, 217, 259
role in the policing of suffragette
demonstrations   235–6, 237
suffragette attacks on   233
views on women's suffrage   234
City of London Police   30–1, 77, 99
role in maintaining public order   139
role in the Houndsditch affair
(1910)   208–9
Clan na Gael   27, 40, 61, 67, 73, 79, 91, 163, 257, 268
involvement in the Jubilee Plot (1887)   92–3, 94, 95, 96, 97
rapprochement with the Russian government   164
role in the dynamite campaign of 1881–85   52, 55, 68, 72
see also Fenian
Clement's Inn   226, 227, 238
Clerkenwell   45, 101, 153, 154, 189
1867 explosion   23, 48, 73, 241
Clipperton, Robert   38, 39, 40
Coercion (policy): see Ireland
Commons, House of: see Parliament
*Commonweal*   132, 133, 143, 145, 150, 155, 158, 160
see also *Freedom*, *Liberty*
Conservative Party   12, 13, 29, 71, 80, 82, 83, 87, 93, 117, 143, 157, 198, 233, 262, 263
Cork   51, 52, 54, 56, 57, 105, 109, 117, 122
see also Ireland
corruption, police   23, 67, 186, 190
Coulon, Auguste   130–1, 133–4, 135, 150, 162, 189–90
counter-espionage   2, 188, 253–4, 255–6
see also MI5, MO5
Criminal Investigation Department (London):
see Scotland Yard
Cross, Richard Assheton   80, 81–2, 84, 121
Cuffe, Hamilton   102–3, 176
Cunningham, James   77–8, 79, 265
Currie, Phillip   180–1, 182, 183, 184, 266

*Daily Mail* (London)   170, 191, 201, 230
see also press
Dalton, Henry   53, 54, 56
Daly, John   65–6, 67, 68, 71, 85, 116, 117, 163, 257, 264
Deakin, Joseph   129, 130–1, 134, 135
see also Walsall anarchist conspiracy
Deasy, Denis   51–2, 56
detection, crime   22, 44, 54, 57, 64, 65, 69–70, 76, 85, 137–8, 159, 190, 205, 252

British attitudes to   2, 11, 20, 23, 67–8, 71, 79, 113
see also Irish Branch, Scotland Yard, Special Branch
Detective Branch, London Metropolitan Police: see *under* Metropolitan Police (London)
Devoy, John   28, 73
Dew, Walter   226–7
Dhingra, Madan Lal   202–4, 206, 232
see also Krishnavarma, India
Dickens, Charles   11, 22
Dilke, Charles   49, 120, 169
Dover   141, 159, 173, 187, 254
Dublin   41, 42, 43, 47, 53, 55, 61, 87, 88, 93, 122, 127, 220, 239, 277 n.35
see also Ireland, Phoenix Park murders
Dublin Castle   8, 44, 45, 56, 62, 64, 89, 92, 105
Duck Island (London)   152, 244
see also Majendie
dynamite   32, 40, 50, 55, 61, 67, 69, 75, 76, 77, 78, 79, 81, 89, 92, 93, 94, 96, 100, 107, 129, 162, 163–5, 166–8, 174, 183, 258, 261, 268
campaign in Britain (1881–85)   11, 38–9, 40, 43, 45, 47, 51–2, 53, 54, 56–7, 58, 59–60, 65–6, 68–9, 73–4, 75–6, 114
see also Fenian
outrages in Ireland   73, 127
use of by anarchists   128–9, 133, 136, 145, 149, 159, 160, 189

East End (London): see *under* London
Edward VII, King   185, 205, 252, 305 n.35
Egan, James Francis   66, 67, 116, 257, 264
Elisabeth, Empress of Austria   180, 266
espionage   15, 23, 71, 92, 95, 116, 133, 146, 149, 162, 173–4, 255
official attitudes in Britain to   11, 21, 71, 113, 256
political uses of in Britain before 1880   11, 19–20, 23
political uses of by European states   154, 172, 175
use of by Germany in Britain   253–4
see also counter-espionage, Le Caron, MI5, MO5
Explosives Act
1875 version   55
1883 version   55, 66, 128, 154, 156, 165, 174, 183, 184
expulsion (legal punishment)   137, 143, 183
extradition   31, 48, 136, 138, 140, 141, 142, 152, 165–6, 168, 181, 182, 183, 184, 199, 207, 266

Farnara, Giuseppe   153–5, 160, 174, 201
Farndale, Joseph   66, 67, 257
Featherstone riots (1893)   218, 259, 305 n.57
Featherstone, Timothy   51–2, 53, 54, 55, 56–7, 122, 164
Fenian   3, 4, 5–6, 8, 10, 23, 28–9, 30, 32, 33, 38, 40, 42, 44, 50, 55, 57–8, 61, 66, 70, 72, 77, 81, 85, 87, 108, 114
   1887 conspiracy: *see* Jubilee Plot
   1896 conspiracy   163–8, 183, 266
   Brotherhood   23, 27, 95
   declining activities in Britain   15, 119, 127, 151, 258
   dynamite campaign in Britain (1881–85): *see under* dynamite
   'fire' (explosive)   69, 91
   Rising (1867)   73, 92
   support for Charles Stewart Parnell: *see under* Parnell
   *see also* Clan na Gael, Irish Republican Brotherhood
fingerprinting   187, 304 n.22
First World War   2, 9, 10, 15, 195, 205, 252, 253, 261, 264
   *see also* counter-espionage, MI5, MO5
Fitch, Herbert   200, 262, 311 n.30
Fitzrovia: *see* London
Foreign Office   16, 64–5, 82, 88, 94, 119, 120, 176, 180, 182
Forster, William Edward   29, 41, 42
Fouché, Joseph   89, 120
France   10, 15, 18, 19, 21, 22, 32, 92, 151, 162, 171, 180, 182, 192, 244, 255
   anarchist movement in   5, 14, 127, 128, 129, 135–6, 138, 140–1, 143, 145, 147, 152, 154, 156, 159, 160, 200
   Fenians in   47–8, 92, 93, 164–5
   *see also under* Fenian
   views of British laws in   16, 94, 137, 138, 141, 156–7, 266
   *see also* Préfecture de police de Paris, Sûreté
François, Jean-Pierre   135–8, 140, 152, 183, 266
*Freedom*   105, 133, 149, 171
   *see also Commonweal, Liberty*
free speech   35, 105, 122, 177, 178, 207, 245, 257
*Freiheit*   31–3, 34, 35, 37, 135, 275 n.32
   *see also* Most
French Revolution   18–19, 22, 23

Gallagher, Thomas   40, 52–3, 54–5, 56, 69, 107, 116, 163, 265
Gardstein, George   208–9, 210
Geneva   141, 179

Germany   9, 10, 31, 33, 101, 135, 143, 159, 180, 182, 196, 267
   cooperation with Britain in policing matters   32, 34, 184
   rivalry with Britain before the First World War   85, 189, 204, 252, 253–4, 256
   *see also* Anti-Socialist Laws, espionage
Gladstone, Herbert   233, 234, 253, 261
   as Home Office Under-Secretary   139, 141
   as Home Secretary   223, 229, 235, 262
   attacks by suffragettes on   230
   views on suffragettes   230, 232
Gladstone, William Ewart   29, 32, 42, 43, 44, 55, 72, 106, 110, 157, 227, 262, 279 n.22
   relationship with Charles Stewart Parnell   41, 114
   support for Coercion in Ireland   29, 41
   support for Home Rule   41, 83, 87, 285 n.20
Glamorgan   213, 214, 260
   *see also* Tonypandy riot
Glasgow   128, 164, 167
   Fenian activity in   47, 48, 50, 51, 54, 55, 56, 122, 265
   police   56–7, 165, 280 n.32
*Glasgow Herald*   67, 70
   *see also* press
Gosselin, Nicholas   55, 58, 61, 64, 66, 67, 70, 88, 163, 168
Graham, Cunninghame   132, 169
Greenwich Park outrage (1894)   15, 145–6, 147–8, 149–50, 151, 153, 155, 158, 191, 261, 264
   *see also* anarchism, Bourdin

Hamilton, Robert   81, 88
Harcourt, William Vernon   34, 35, 39, 40, 43, 47, 55, 63, 67, 76, 96, 120, 190, 255, 259, 260, 263, 266, 268
   as Home Secretary   27–8, 31, 35, 50, 58, 60, 62, 74–5, 76, 80
   creation of Irish Branch (Section B)   10–11, 49, 120
   liberal convictions of   4, 32, 72, 117, 122, 262
   on secret policing   29, 30, 32, 33, 44, 70–1, 121
   on duties of English police   78–9
   relationship with Edward Jenkinson   51, 52, 62, 64, 65, 66, 74, 79
   relationship with James Monro   70, 79
   relationship with Robert Anderson   50, 61, 73, 117
   support for Coercion in Ireland   29, 42
Hardie, Kier   155, 162, 220, 223

Harkins, Michael   96–7, 99, 107
Hawkins, Henry   78, 132, 133, 156, 160
Healy, Timothy   28, 40–1, 117
Henderson, Edmund   29, 65, 75, 77, 78, 80, 84, 85, 100, 119
Henry, Edward Richard   204, 205, 206, 247, 253
   colonial background   187
   cooperation with Vernon Kell and MO5   253–4, 255
   opposition to cooperation with continental police   197–8, 210, 265, 267
   role in policing suffragette militants   226, 230, 231, 234, 235, 236–7, 244, 250
   views on William Melville   188–9
   *see also* Melville
Holloway Prison   223, 224, 229, 242, 251
Home Office: *see* Secret Service (Home Office)
Home Rule: *see* Ireland
Houndsditch affair (1910)   208–9
Hull   57, 216
Hyde Park   100, 102, 103, 105, 132, 155, 221, 228, 249, 255
Hyndman, Henry Mayers   83, 99, 155, 199, 202
   *see also* Social Democratic Federation, socialists

immigration   4, 35, 146, 154, 173, 195, 208, 210, 252, 266
   Jewish   139, 198–9, 200, 209, 289 n.4
   political opposition to in Britain   157–8, 172, 201
Imperial Institute   202–3, 205
imperialism: *see* British Empire
India   45, 203, 204, 205
   agrarian violence in   108
   Hindu nationalism in   202, 207
   policing in   187, 204, 250
   *see also* Bengal, Dhingra
India House   202–3, 204, 206, 207
   *see also* Krishnavarma
India Office   203, 204, 206,
individualism: *see* anarchism
informers, use of by British authorities   2, 9, 18, 20, 40, 43–4, 50, 52, 55, 56, 82, 90, 92, 115, 133–4, 140–1, 154, 167, 173, 189, 197, 205, 248, 265
   *see also* espionage
Ireland   15, 17, 18–19, 30, 43, 45, 61, 81, 86, 96, 97, 118, 164, 166, 260
   agrarian unrest in   29, 80
   British policing methods in   8, 10, 43–4, 50, 52, 62, 63, 121, 256

   British support for Home Rule in   82, 105, 262
   Fenian activity in   51, 55, 56, 73, 114
   policy of Coercion in   39, 41, 42, 71, 83, 122
   Irish Branch (Section B of Scotland Yard)   10, 29, 49, 50, 53, 54, 57, 60, 62, 64, 69–70, 90–1, 107, 109, 120, 122, 127, 168, 252, 262
   *see also* Melville, Quinn, Scotland Yard, Special Branch
Irish National Brotherhood   163, 166, 168
Irish National Invincibles   46, 47–8, 56, 116, 168
Irish Republican Brotherhood   27, 30, 66, 67, 73, 79, 268
   *see also* Fenian
isolationism (British policy)   13, 14, 196, 265, 266–8
Italy   119, 154, 159, 179, 180, 217
   counter-subversion laws in   119–20, 172, 182, 186–7
   social unrest in   160, 185

Jack the Ripper   77, 112
Jacobins   18–19, 20
   *see also* Cato Street Conspiracy, Thistlewood
Jenkinson, Edward George   110, 111, 120, 121, 122, 163, 168, 189, 257, 258, 259, 260, 264, 268
   activities in Ireland   8, 10, 45, 61, 71, 81
   at the Home Office   50–1, 61–2, 64–5, 69, 70, 80–1, 87, 89
   cooperation with provincial British police   55, 67
   in the British and Irish press   63, 67–8, 70, 84, 88–9, 123
   involvement in the Jubilee Plot (1887)   92–4, 95
   liberal views of   82, 88, 260, 262
   relationship with William Harcourt: *see under* Harcourt
   relationship with John Poyntz Spencer, fifth earl Spencer   45, 51, 55, 63, 66, 69, 72, 76, 79, 81, 88
   relationship with Robert Anderson: *see under* Anderson
   relationship with James Monro   72, 74, 76, 79, 84–5, 86, 87–8, 90–1, 93
   relationship with Henry Matthews   87–9
   relationship with Charles Warren   86, 87, 88
   resignation of   11, 88
   support for Home Rule   81, 82–3

# Index   337

use of informers and agents provocateurs   51–2, 57, 66–7, 91, 92, 268
Jews   139, 157, 161, 198–9, 209, 252, 255
  see also anarchism, antisemitism, immigration, Houndsditch affair, Sidney Street 'siege'
Jubilee Plot (1887)   90–6
*Justice*   101, 207
  see also Social Democratic Federation

Kearney, John Francis   57, 71, 164–6, 167, 168
Kell Vernon   254–6
Kenney, Annie   222, 223, 244, 247
Kerry, county   73, 190, 278 n.64
  see also Ireland
Kilmainham   41, 42, 46, 116
Krishnavarma, Shyamji   202, 204, 206, 207
  see also India House
Kropotkin, Pyotr   100, 128

Labour Party   214, 227, 233, 245
Lancashire   226, 277 n.37
Land League   28, 29, 41, 47, 93, 108
  see also National League
Lansbury, George   220, 240, 248
Latvia: see Houndsditch affair, Sidney Street 'siege'
Le Caron, Henri (Thomas Beach)   51, 72–3, 263
  as subject of debate in Parliament   117
  involvement in special commission on 'Parnellism and crime' (1888-89)   95, 116
  relationship with Robert Anderson   28, 30, 40, 47, 55, 91, 92
  see also espionage, informers
Legitimation League   177–8, 191, 258
Leigh, Mary   228, 231, 239–40
Leopold II, King of the Belgians   186, 267
liberalism (British)   4, 10, 11, 21, 80, 81, 82, 98, 169, 210, 214, 215, 220, 222, 231
  and Ireland   29, 41, 42, 59, 72, 87, 88, 105, 109, 260
  and political policing   22–3, 43, 87, 121–2, 132, 148, 151, 158, 170, 180, 191, 192, 261–2
  and popular attitudes to Fenianism   48–9
  and the press   35, 42, 63, 99, 104, 106, 111, 223, 264
  and women's suffrage   224, 227, 230, 233, 234, 236, 237, 241, 242
  fluid nature of   6–7, 12
  impact on legal definitions of political crime   142, 143–4
  impact on official views of policing   12, 13, 72, 110, 157, 260, 263, 267

Liberal Party   12, 41, 80, 98, 105, 108, 127, 132, 139, 160, 162–3, 169, 213, 224, 233, 248, 261, 266
  break with Liberal Unionists   87
  see also liberalism
*Liberty*   150, 155
  see also *Commonweal*, *Freedom*
Liddell, Adolphus   33, 65
Lindsay, Lionel   213–14, 215, 216
Littlechild, John   53, 54, 69, 90–1, 103, 107, 116, 119, 127, 139, 146
Liverpool   27, 51, 66, 71, 128, 171
  Fenian activity in   38–9, 40, 47, 51–2, 54, 56
  industrial unrest in (1911)   216–17, 260
Lloyd George, David   234, 240, 241
Lomasney, William Mackey   73, 78
London   14, 17, 23, 31, 39, 43, 44, 48, 55, 57, 59, 60, 64, 68, 75, 88, 90, 91, 95, 96, 101, 106, 108, 112, 139, 152, 164, 174, 175–6, 187, 202, 207–8, 212, 221, 254, 256
  anarchist presence in: see *under* anarchism
  as the birthplace of political policing in Britain   21, 33, 51, 67, 190, 255
  City Police: see City of London Police
  early nineteenth-century radicalism in   18–19, 20
  East End of   137, 157, 208, 248
  Fenian outrages in: see *under* dynamite, Fenian
  immigration to: see immigration
  republican conspiracies in: see Cato Street conspiracy
  Royal Irish Constabulary presence in   80
  socialist militancy in: see *under* socialists
  suffragette activities in: see *under* suffragettes
  see also Metropolitan Police, Scotland Yard, socialists, Trafalgar Square riots
London Bridge   73–4
London Metropolitan Police: see Metropolitan Police
Lords, House of: see Parliament
Lushington, Godfrey   86, 91, 127, 143, 161
  liberal views of   122, 262, 286 n.45
  participation in the Rome Anti-Anarchist Conference (1898)   180, 182
  relationship with Charles Warren   109, 113
  relationship with Edward Jenkinson   87, 89
  views on continental policing   87, 122
  views on socialism   101–2

MI5   188, 253, 255
  see also counter-espionage, MO5
MO5   253–4, 255–6

### 338　Index

mail, interception of　10, 54, 66, 250, 255, 277 n.37
　see also Post Office
Macnaghten, Melville　111, 118, 217, 254
　as Assistant Commissioner　201
　colonial past　107–8
　views on policing anarchism　171
Macready, Nevil　17, 214–16, 217, 260
Madrid　142, 171
Maguire, John　153, 158
Majendie, Vivian Dering　39, 48, 59, 60, 69, 75, 91, 147, 150, 154, 160, 170, 191
　views on French policing　151–2
　views on policing anarchism　142, 151, 183
Malatesta, Errico　119–20, 128, 161
Mallon, John　43, 45, 277 n.35
Manchester　27, 143, 218, 221, 223, 231, 240
　Fenian activity in: see Salford explosion (1881)
Mann, Tom　217–20, 221
　see also syndicalism
Mansion House　30, 31, 43, 50, 100
martial law　101, 142, 215, 217, 260
Marx, Karl　22, 127
Matthews, Henry　11, 67, 94, 105, 127, 133, 135, 189
　knowledge of Walsall anarchist conspiracy (1892)　132
　relationship with Edward Jenkinson: see under Jenkinson
　relationship with James Monro　108–9, 110–11, 118–19
　relationship with Charles Warren　99, 103–4, 107, 113
　views on policing socialist militancy in London (1886-87)　101–2
May Day　200, 220
McDermott, James 'Red Jim'　51, 56, 71, 257
McIntyre, Patrick　49, 53, 69, 107, 109, 137, 138, 151, 262
　allegations about police use of agents provocateurs　133–4, 162, 189, 260
McKenna, Reginald　220, 221, 262
　cooperation with Vernon Kell　255
　views on suffragette militancy　239, 241, 245–6, 249, 250, 251
Melville, William　8, 90, 133, 141, 159, 258, 259, 260, 262, 269
　activities with Irish Branch　49, 53, 64
　activities with Special Branch　94, 95, 96, 107, 119, 135, 136, 138, 146–7, 152, 155, 156, 157, 161, 170, 171, 173, 174, 178, 186–7
　collusion with Pyotr Rachkovsky　175–7
　see also Okhrana

counter-espionage work　188–9, 201, 254
early background　190
involvement in the Walsall anarchist conspiracy (1892)　129–32, 134, 135, 189
popular perception of　153, 252, 264, 268
use of informers after 1892　150, 154, 196
　see also Walsall anarchist conspiracy
views of British police　255, 256
Metropolitan Police (London)　7, 29, 30, 49, 62, 63, 83, 87–8, 103, 107, 110, 112, 117–18, 120, 187, 190, 201, 204, 267
　criticism of in the press　76, 84–5, 99, 104–5, 111, 113, 123, 236
　Detective Branch of　22, 23, 190
　early use of political policing　3–4, 22–3, 35
　reforms to　55, 72, 80, 187, 247
　role in enforcing public order　84, 105–6
　　see also Trafalgar Square riots
　role in quelling industrial unrest　214–15, 216, 238
　　see also Tonypandy riot
　see also City of London Police, Irish Branch, Scotland Yard, Special Branch
Meunier, Théodule　136–7, 145, 152, 183, 264, 266
Mexico　92, 241
Michel, Louise　128, 161
military　19, 44, 55, 58, 83, 85, 101, 113, 119, 127, 166, 188, 248, 253, 254, 260, 262
　involvement in Sidney Street 'siege' (1911)　209–10
　use of in quelling industrial unrest　213, 214, 215, 216, 217–18
　　see also Tonypandy riot
　see also counter-espionage, MI5, MO5
Millen, Francis Frederick　92–6, 97, 104
　see also Fenian, informers, Jubilee Plot (1887)
Monro James　8, 72, 78, 84, 90, 91, 94, 95, 96, 100, 101, 102, 112, 118–19, 121, 189, 264, 268
　and the British press　70, 97–8, 108–9, 111
　assumes title of 'Secret Agent'　91, 114
　background　70, 107
　political and religious views of　91, 118, 262
　relationship with Charles Warren　107–9, 110, 111
　relationship with Edward Jenkinson: see under Jenkinson
　relationship with Robert Anderson: see under Anderson
　relationship with William Harcourt: see under Harcourt

views on arrest procedure   109–10
Montjuich (prison)   169, 171–2
　see also Barcelona, Spain
Mooney, Thomas   30, 31, 50, 56, 57
Morley, John   86, 87
Moroney, John   96–7, 108
Morris, William   100, 132, 155
Moser, Maurice   39, 48, 276 n.8
Most, Johann   31–5, 38, 40, 133, 143, 175, 266
　see also Freiheit
Mowbray, Charles   132–3
Murdoch, Charles   109, 141, 153, 155, 169, 171

National League, Irish   47, 80, 268
　see also Land League
National Union of Women's Suffrage Societies   223, 246
Netherlands   100, 101, 165, 166, 180, 266
New York   31, 44, 51, 54, 72, 92, 94, 96, 163, 164, 165, 166, 167
Nicholas II, Czar of Russia   164, 166, 175
Nicoll, David   132–3, 134, 150
Nihilists   28, 32, 37, 164, 168, 266
　1881 assassination of Czar Alexander II of Russia by   9, 31
　and William Melville   196
　presence in London   102, 129, 141, 174, 175, 208
　see also Burtsev
Norman, William   52, 53–4, 56

O'Brien, William   96, 104
O'Neill, Daniel 'Big Dan'   66, 257
obscenity   178, 265
　see also Bedborough, Legitimation League
Okhrana   175, 208, 258
　activities in France   10
　activities in Germany and Eastern Europe   9–10
　and William Melville   175–7
　see also Rachkovsky
Old Bailey   21, 35, 156, 206

*Pall Mall Gazette*   105, 264
　criticisms of the Metropolitan Police   84–5, 104, 106, 111
　views on Edward Jenkinson   89, 123
　see also press, Stead
Pankhurst, Christabel   223, 224, 227, 228, 229, 232, 237, 238, 239, 240, 245, 246, 247, 248, 251
Pankhurst, Emmeline   222, 224, 227, 229, 234, 238, 239–40, 241–2, 247, 249, 251
Pankhurst, Sylvia   246, 247–8

Paris: see France, *Préfecture de police de Paris*, *Sûreté*
Parliament (Palace of Westminster)   18, 48, 52, 53, 66, 67, 74, 77, 80, 96, 108, 109, 113, 114, 183, 222, 224, 226, 228, 229, 232, 234, 237
　bomb outrage (1885)   75–7
　debates on anarchism in   35, 132, 142–3, 151, 158, 169
　debates on Fenianism in   28, 29, 41, 55, 115, 167–8
　debates on immigration in   157, 199
　debates on political policing in   13, 132, 220
　debates on women's suffrage in   223, 224, 234, 236, 250
Parnell, Charles Stewart   1, 28, 29, 71, 81, 82, 109, 164, 268
　and special commission on 'Parnellism and crime' (1888–89)   93, 114–15, 116, 117–18, 119, 261, 263
　relationship with William Gladstone   41, 83
　ties to Fenianism   31, 41, 96, 116
Peel, Robert   21, 83
Pethick-Lawrence, Emmeline and Frederick   226, 228, 238–9, 248, 314 n.36
Phoenix Park murders (1882)   41–3, 45–6, 47, 48, 81, 93, 114, 116, 164, 165
　see also Burke, Cavendish, Fenian, Irish National Invincibles
Pigott, Richard   115, 116–17
Pinkerton's National Detective Agency   44, 212
police cooperation
　as focus of political debate in Britain   13, 173–4, 191
　between Britain and continental Europe   14, 16, 37, 94, 120, 137, 147, 165, 175–7, 181–2, 183–4, 186, 197, 265, 266–8
　between Britain and Ireland   29, 52, 64, 65–6, 80, 91
　between London and provincial forces   53–4, 57, 64, 66, 67, 165, 255, 257, 277 n.37, 300 n.29
　see also Metropolitan Police, Rome Anti-Anarchist Conference, Royal Irish Constabulary
'political police', historical uses of the phrase   21, 170
Polti, Francesco (Francis)   153–5, 160, 201, 265
Pope, John   49, 90, 103
port police: see Section C
port protection scheme (British)   64–5
　ineffectiveness of   66, 68, 72

Porter, Bernard   4–5, 11, 12, 16, 22, 135
Post Office   170, 242, 277 n.37
*Préfecture de police de Paris*   10, 94, 137, 152, 159
   *see also* France, *Sûreté*
press (British)   70, 77, 89, 111, 190, 199, 203, 263, 265
   official 'leaks' of information to the   63, 89, 111, 154, 264
   on anarchism   32, 35, 128–9, 149, 151, 152–3, 159, 168, 171, 172, 201
   on Fenianism   30, 42, 48, 78, 92, 94, 97–8, 118
   on police incompetence   83, 99, 148, 191
      *see also Pall Mall Gazette*
   on police violence   105–6
   on political policing   17, 63, 67–8, 70, 122, 153, 170, 191, 264–5, 268
   on suffragettes   222, 230, 233, 240, 247, 248, 259
prostitution   99, 290 n.30
protection
   of British and foreign royalty   58, 59, 164, 185, 205, 212
   of British government officials   72, 205–6, 231
   of public buildings   58, 76, 90, 237, 292 n.7
public assistance to police   13, 52–3, 56–7, 69, 77–8, 138, 141, 153, 156, 178, 226, 232, 241, 252, 256, 265, 299 n.79
public order: *see under* Metropolitan Police

Quinn, Patrick   90, 107, 190, 205, 206–7, 230, 237, 244, 252, 254
   *see also* Irish Branch, Melville, Special Branch

Rachkovsky, Pyotr   175–6, 191, 258
   *see also* Burtsev, Melville, Okhrana, Russian Empire
racism   198, 204, 210, 252,
   *see also* antisemitism, xenophobia
Radicals (British)   32, 35, 85, 98, 103, 105, 110, 115, 220, 245, 262, 265
raids, police   18, 34, 46, 52, 73, 133, 134, 137, 147, 148, 154, 157, 158, 165, 184, 190, 224, 226, 238, 244, 249, 250
Ravachol (François Claudius Koenigstein)   128, 136, 143
refugees, political   48, 116, 128, 142, 146, 152, 154, 159, 165, 173, 181, 208
   *see also* asylum, immigration
revolution, fears of in Britain   15, 18–9, 83, 101, 102, 146, 216–17, 252, 269

rewards, police   54, 67, 75, 80, 107, 138, 153
*Reynolds's Newspaper*   105, 133–4, 158, 162, 169, 170, 191, 264–5
   *see also* press
ribbon societies   56, 122, 280 n. 28
   *see also* Fenian
Ridley, Matthew White   7, 162–3, 167, 171
Romania   180, 182, 196, 198
Rome Anti-Anarchist Conference (1898)   13, 142, 180–4, 191, 196, 262, 266
Roosevelt, Theodore   195, 196
Rosebery, fifth earl of (Archibald Philip Primrose)   82, 142, 157, 267
Rossa, Jeremiah O'Donovan   28, 30, 31, 38, 39, 40, 42, 43, 47, 50, 51, 52, 57, 73, 78, 92
Rossetti, Helen   150–1
   *see also* Greenwich Park outrage
Rotterdam   64, 164, 165
Rowan, Charles   22, 23
Royal Irish Constabulary   50, 52, 53, 64, 65, 73, 81, 91, 256, 257
   presence in Glasgow   165
   presence in London   54, 80, 117
Royal Observatory, Greenwich: *see* Greenwich Park outrage
Rubino, Gennaro   186–7
Russian Empire   9–10, 31, 32, 128, 130, 164, 166, 174–6, 180, 181, 182, 188, 196, 198, 201, 208, 267
   *see also* Burtsev, Nihilists, Okhrana, St Petersburg

St Petersburg   31, 175, 196, 197, 265, 267
   *see also* Russian Empire
Salford explosion (1881)   27–8, 30, 122
   *see also* dynamite, Fenian, Manchester
Salisbury, third marquess of (Robert Gascoyne-Cecil)   80, 83, 87, 142, 173, 181, 182, 263, 267
   critic of British immigration laws   157, 158, 159, 171
   critic of increased police powers   12, 71, 180
   involvement in political policing   82, 94, 115, 118, 167, 262
   on anarchism   143, 199
Samuels, Henry   143, 145, 150–1, 158, 175
   *see also* Commonweal, Greenwich Park outrage
Savarkar, Vinayak Damodar   206, 207
   *see also* Dhingra, Krishnavarma
Scantlebury, Charles   222, 229
Scotland   57, 64, 69, 122, 175, 256
   *see also* Glasgow

Scotland Yard (Criminal Investigation Department, London)   4, 7, 13, 22, 23, 50, 52, 53, 54, 63–4, 70, 74, 75, 79, 84, 85, 87, 88, 91, 95, 97, 102, 110, 116, 117, 118, 119, 121, 143, 147, 152, 162, 185, 187, 189, 195, 247, 250, 253, 259
  cooperation with foreign police forces: *see under* police cooperation
  efforts to police subversive activity prior to 1883   28–9, 32, 34, 38, 39, 40, 43, 48, 262
  explosion (1884)   68–9, 70
  popular perceptions of   84–5, 97, 104, 111, 146, 148, 252, 264–5
    *see also under* press
  relationship with MO5   253–4, 255
    *see also* MI5, MO5
  relationship with provincial police forces: *see under* police cooperation
  role in policing anarchism: *see under* Special Branch
  role in policing Fenianism after 1883: *see under* Irish Branch
  role in policing Indian nationalism: *see under* Special Branch
  role in policing socialist militancy: *see under* Social Democratic Federation
  role in policing suffragette militancy: *see under* Special Branch
  *see also* Metropolitan Police (London)
'Secret Agent' (official title)   91, 108, 109, 114
  *see also* Monro
Secret Service (Home Office)   23, 62, 87, 88, 92, 93, 115, 122, 163
Secret Service (counter-espionage): *see* MI5, MO5
Section C (Scotland Yard)   64, 205, 308 n.50
'shadowing' (police practice)   8, 12, 70, 71, 86, 138, 153, 161–2, 190, 252, 254, 258, 293 n.38
Shaw, George Bernard   100, 177, 178
Siberia   9, 128, 174
  *see also* Okhrana, Russian Empire
Sidney Street 'siege' (1911)   209–12, 252, 260
  *see also* anarchism, Houndsditch affair
Sipido, Jean-Baptiste   184–5
Social Democratic Federation   12, 101, 199, 122, 129, 140, 161, 263
  involvement in public demonstrations   100, 112, 139
  under surveillance by Special Branch   17, 102–3, 263
  use of drilling exercises   101–2
socialists   15, 17, 31, 35, 102, 104, 129, 132, 161, 179, 191, 214, 216, 217, 221, 247, 248, 252

  activity in continental Europe   34, 101, 143, 169, 186, 195
  involvement in public disturbances   83, 99–100, 112, 119, 245
    *see also* Trafalgar Square riots
  police surveillance of foreign   100
  police surveillance of native British: *see under* Social Democratic Federation
South Africa   184, 233
  *see also* Boer War
South Wales Miners' Federation   214, 216
  *see also* syndicalism, Tonypandy riot
Spain   116, 127, 142, 144, 160, 161, 168, 171–2, 180, 185
  *see also* Barcelona
Spanish Atrocities Committee   169–70, 173
  *see also* anarchism
Special Branch (Section D of Scotland Yard)   4–5, 8, 10, 15, 96, 106, 111, 116, 127, 144, 155, 165, 174, 175, 178, 187, 188, 189, 190, 196, 204, 252, 256, 258–9, 261, 262, 263, 267
  formation and early structure   90–1, 94, 135
  in the press   152–3, 170, 173, 264–5
  increase in staff   161, 205–6, 231–2, 253
  official funding for   91, 315 n.64
  relations with MO5   254–5
    *see also* MO5, MI5
  role in policing anarchism   119–20, 132–3, 134, 135, 137–8, 145–7, 154, 156, 158, 160, 177, 186, 200–1, 206–7, 208
  role in policing Indian nationalism   204, 205–6
  role in policing socialist militancy: *see under* Social Democratic Federation
  role in policing suffragette militancy   226, 227, 229, 230–1, 236, 240–1, 244, 247, 249–50, 251
    *see also* anarchism, Melville, McIntyre, Quinn, Sweeney
Special Irish Branch: *see* Irish Branch
Spencer, fifth earl (John Poyntz Spencer)   41, 50, 72, 82, 122
  relationship with Edward Jenkinson: *see under* Jenkinson
  relationship with William Harcourt   43, 52, 61, 62, 76
spies: *see* agents provocateurs, counter-espionage, espionage, informers
*Standard, The*   31, 43, 63, 76
  *see also* press
Stead, William Thomas   84, 104, 106
  *see also* *Pall Mall Gazette*, press

strikes   118, 127, 185, 213–17, 218, 220, 229, 238, 239, 242, 260, 269
  *see also* syndicalism, Tonypandy riot
*Suffragette, The*   239, 240, 242, 244, 245–6, 249, 251, 259
suffragettes   6, 195, 202, 206, 224
  activities in London   222, 227, 228, 237, 245
  confrontations with police   223–4, 226, 228, 229
  factional splits   232, 239, 248
  forced feeding of   233, 239, 242, 252, 316 n.77
  left-wing   246, 247–8
  militant tactics   8, 223–4, 228, 231, 232, 233–4, 246
  physical violence against   234–5, 242, 246
  support from political establishment   224, 233, 245
  upper-class   233
  use of hunger strikes by   229–30
  use of vandalism by   237, 238–9, 240, 241, 244–5, 246, 249, 269
  working-class   222, 226–7
  *see also* Women's Social and Political Union, Women's Freedom League
Sullivan, Alexander (Fenian)   40, 52
*Sunday Times*   15, 173, 191, 269
  *see also* press
Sûreté (French police force)   10, 135, 136, 137, 138, 147, 159
Sweeney, John   69, 102, 133, 134, 144, 153, 156, 160, 162, 177, 178, 201, 262
Switzerland   159, 180
syndicalism   161, 214, 215, 216, 217–18, 220, 245, 259, 261, 269
  *see also* Mann

Thistlewood, Arthur   19, 20–1
  *see also* Cato Street Conspiracy
Thomson, Basil   247, 249, 255
*Times, The*   17, 48, 56, 71, 101, 108, 147, 188, 201, 216, 223, 228, 232
  accusations against Charles Stewart Parnell   93, 114–16, 117, 118, 263
  criticism of political policing   23, 146, 148
  on anarchism in Britain   35, 129, 172, 201, 208
  *see also* press
Tonypandy riot (1910)   17, 214–15, 216, 252
Tottenham outrage (1909)   199–201
Tower of London explosion (1885)   76–7, 78
trade unions   19, 161, 199, 214, 252
  *see also* South Wales Miners' Federation, syndicalism, Tonypandy riot

Trafalgar Square riots (1887)   99, 103–4, 105–7, 113, 264
treason: *see* espionage, counter-espionage, MI5, MO5
Treasury   91, 168, 229, 245
Trevelyan, George Otto   42, 45, 61, 82
Troup, Charles Edward   230, 231, 245, 253, 254, 255
  liberal convictions of   262
  views on suffragettes   232–3, 234, 237, 261
  views on syndicalist agitation   217–18
Tynan, Patrick Joseph Percy   47, 48, 93, 164–5, 166, 167, 168, 266
  *see also* Irish National Invincibles, Phoenix Park murders

Ulster   39, 55, 239,
  Volunteers   220, 248, 249
  *see also* Ireland
Umberto I, King   172, 185, 195
unemployed   99, 149
  marches   83, 100, 103, 139, 140, 198
  *see also* Social Democratic Federation, socialists, Trafalgar Square riots
United States of America   35, 44, 48, 52, 56, 57, 60, 67, 73, 93, 95, 96, 97, 101, 116, 156, 157, 185, 195, 196, 266
  criticism of in Britain   32, 39, 40, 55, 60
  reports on Fenian activity from   27–8, 30, 32, 38, 43, 58, 68, 78, 82, 91, 92, 163, 166
Uruguay   173, 191

Vaillant, Auguste   128, 145, 147,
Victoria, Queen   32, 33, 83, 106, 169, 180, 264
  Golden Jubilee of (1887)   91–2, 94
  *see also* Jubilee Plot
  official protection for   58–9
  relationship with William Harcourt   30, 37, 60, 71
  threats to   164, 166, 170
  views on Fenian terrorism   59, 76
Vincent, Howard   43, 50, 68, 121, 122, 262
  as Scotland Yard Director   28–9, 34, 38, 40, 70
  criticism of asylum and immigration policies   172, 181
  involvement in surveillance of Fenians   29, 31
  participation in the Rome Anti-Anarchist Conference (1898)   180–2

Wales   72, 213–14, 216, 256, 260, 269
  *see also* Glamorgan, South Wales Miners' Federation, Tonypandy riot

Walsall anarchist conspiracy (1892)   15, 128–35, 150, 154, 155, 160, 162–3, 189–90, 258
  *see also* anarchism, Melville, Special Branch
War Office   27, 188, 201, 215, 253, 254, 255
  *see also* espionage, counter-espionage, MO5
Warren Charles   85, 90, 91, 99, 101, 105–6, 113, 119, 257
  and extra-legal actions by police   112, 121
  conflict with the Home Office   104, 109
  in the press   104, 106, 262
  liberal convictions   103, 122
  relationship with Edward Jenkinson: *see under* Jenkinson
  relationship with James Monro: *see under* Monro
Wedgwood, Josiah   220, 245
Westminster, Palace of: *see* Parliament
Westminster Abbey   100, 250
Whigs   21, 22, 45, 67
  *see also* liberalism
Whitehall   8, 13, 14, 29, 47, 51, 61, 63, 71, 81, 92, 93, 94, 104, 107, 113, 114, 118, 151, 153, 157, 196, 215, 230, 253, 256, 260, 263
  *see also* Parliament
Whitehead, Albert   52–3, 54, 67, 163

Williamson, Adolphus   49, 50, 53, 54, 59, 64, 74, 75, 77, 95, 107, 118
Wilson, Henry   53, 54, 116
Women's Freedom League   202, 232, 233, 236
Women's Social and Political Union
  government efforts to suppress   230–1, 232–3, 235, 236–7, 240–1, 242, 244, 245–6, 247, 249–51, 259, 261
  leadership of: *see* Pankhurst, Christabel; Pankhurst, Emmeline
  militant tactics of   223–4, 228–9, 230, 231–2, 238, 239–40
  opposition to Liberal Party   223, 227, 231, 232, 241
  police raids on   244, 250
  police reports on   226–7
  political demands of   195, 222, 233, 251
  use of hunger strikes by: *see under* suffragettes
  use of motor vehicles by   247
  waning support for   247, 248, 251
  *see also* suffragettes, Women's Freedom League
Wyllie, William Hutt Curzon   202–3

xenophobia   198–9, 210